BATTLEGROUND
BUSINESS

BATTLEGROUND

BUSINESS

VOLUME 1 (A–N)

Edited by Michael Walden and Peg Thoms

GREENWOOD PRESS
Westport, Connecticut • London

Library of Congress Cataloging-in-Publication Data

Battleground : business / edited by Michael Walden and Peg Thoms.
   p. cm.
   Includes bibliographical references and index.
   ISBN-13: 978–0–313–34065–9 (set : alk. paper)
   ISBN-13: 978–0–313–34066–6 (v. 1 : alk. paper)
   ISBN-13: 978–0–313–34067–3 (v. 2 : alk. paper)
   1. Business.   2. Commerce.   I. Walden, M. L. (Michael Leonard), 1951–   II. Thoms, Peg, 1948–
   HF1008.B38   2007
   658—dc22   2007021681

British Library Cataloguing in Publication Data is available.

Library of Congress Catalog Card Number: 2007021681
ISBN-13: 978–0–313–34065–9 (set)
978–0–313–34066–6 (vol. 1)
978–0–313–34067–3 (vol. 2)

First published in 2007

Greenwood Press, 88 Post Road West, Westport, CT 06881
An imprint of Greenwood Publishing Group, Inc.
www.greenwood.com

Printed in the United States of America

The paper used in this book complies with the
Permanent Paper Standard issued by the National
Information Standards Organization (Z39.48–1984).

10 9 8 7 6 5 4 3 2 1

CONTENTS

GUIDE TO RELATED TOPICS

Following are the entries in this book arranged by broad topics:

ETHICAL ISSUES
Corporate Social Responsibility
Environmental Degradation
Ethics in Business at the Individual Level
Media Coverage of Business
Personal Success without Selling Your Soul
Price Gouging
Shareholder Activism and the Battle for Corporate Control
Whistle-Blowers

ECONOMIC ISSUES, INTERNATIONAL
Chinese Currency
The Dollar
Dumping
Foreign Direct Investment
Free Trade
Outsourcing and Offshoring
Rich Country/Poor Country
Trade Surpluses and Deficits

ECONOMIC ISSUES, UNITED STATES
Booms and Busts
Deficits

Supply Chain Security and Terrorism
Team-Based Cultures and Individual Rewards
Technological Connectivity
Wholesale Buying by Big-Box Retailers

MARKETING ISSUES
Advertising and the Invasion of Privacy
Blogs
Credit Card Marketing to College Students
Marketing of Alcohol and Tobacco
Marketing to Baby Boomers
Marketing to Children
Marketing to Women and Girls
Online Auctions
Sex and Advertising

SALARY AND WELL-BEING ISSUES
CEO Compensation
Education and Economic Competitiveness
Glass Ceiling
Minimum Wage
Pensions
Poverty and Race
Salary Disparity
Same-Sex Partner Benefits

PREFACE

Many of the most important and controversial issues in the United States today relate to business. Even wars have economic causes and implications. For better or worse, if there is a debatable issue, it usually has to do with money, how it is earned, who is earning it, and how it should be managed. In *Battleground: Business,* we have identified the most important issues related to business and economics by speaking with some of the leading experts, carefully reviewing the current business literature, listening to the news and political candidates, and discussing concerns of Americans with a wide range of people.

Battleground: Business is designed to provide information about the most controversial issues in modern business to a wide audience, including high school and college students, concerned citizens, and generally curious people. The two volumes cover a wide range of topics currently under discussion, including health care, immigration, CEO compensation, and taxes. Answers are provided to commonly asked questions about business such as how WalMart keeps prices low, why advertisers use sex to sell products, whether lotteries are the answer for state finances, and whether Social Security will be around for future retirees. Readers are given not just basic facts about the controversies, but also references, suggestions for further reading, and opinions from experts on each topic.

This reference set is meant to be an introduction to each of the issues that will spur readers to explore the questions further using the bibliographies included in each chapter. The book was written by leaders in their fields, who have summarized concisely the most important points—not providing all the answers, but giving a means for readers to find them.

The book contains 77 entries, conveniently arranged alphabetically by topic. The alphabetical listing provides a quick resource for the reader. The guide to related topics helps readers readily identify entries likely to interest them. Each entry contains a concise overview and explanation of the topic itself. Then the authors describe why the issue is controversial and give both sides. Sometimes the authors have strong opinions on the issue, which they share with readers, and in other cases, the authors are still making up their own minds. All the entries provide readers with additional resources so that they can further explore the topic.

The reference book ends with a selected general bibliography, which provides readers with some of the most important sources of information on current business issues. Our intention is to give readers valuable information that will assist them in research on the topics of importance in business.

ADVERTISING AND THE INVASION OF PRIVACY

ADVERTISING IN THE MOVIES

In the 2006 movie *Talladega Nights: The Ballad of Ricky Bobby,* viewers probably were not too surprised to see the obvious pitches for NASCAR, Sprint, Wonder Bread, and Power Ade as the story unfolded. In fact, the advertising connection between the movie and products continued into the retail environment, as grocery stores began to sell NASCAR-branded hotdogs and other Talladega-branded merchandise. Sports events, particularly auto racing, have long been associated with corporate sponsorships, which have grown to be an acceptable part of the experience. However, is the blitz of products as props, or part of the story line in a movie, an invasion of the customer's privacy? Consumers pay to be entertained by a movie, not to be exposed to a two-hour-long commercial.

Corporate sponsorship through product placements in movies, TV shows, and video games has become an ever-increasing method of promotion. Global spending on paid product placement promotion increased by 42 percent in 2005 and by another 39 percent in 2006. The United States is the world's fastest-growing market in the phenomenon, generating $1.5 billion in 2006. Companies have found that this method of promotion is more precise in reaching their targeted audiences than regular television advertising since technology has allowed customers to skip over commercials or record their TV programs on TiVo.

Movie executives have embraced the use of product placement as a means to bolster their movie budgets and offset costs before the film is ever introduced to the public. One of the most profitable product placement agreements was in the 2002 movie *Minority Report,* starring Tom Cruise. Corporate sponsors paid close to $25 million in product placement fees for their products, representing one-fourth of the movie's total budget. Even the plot itself deals with the business of advertising. In the film, Tom Cruise walks through a shopping mall bombarded by holograph advertising messages as he passes each store. While, in the movie, this was a scene from the future year 2054, today's technology has increased the many ways that marketers are getting to their prospective customers. The future is already here in the world of advertising.

AD SPENDING BY MEDIA

Media	Expenditure
Newspapers	$25.2 billion
Consumer magazines	$21.7 billion
Internet	$8.3 billion*
Network TV	$22.4 billion
Cable TV	$15.9 billion
Outdoor	$3.5 billion
Network radio	$1.0 billion
Local radio	$7.4 billion
Product placements	$3.5 billion

*Does not include paid search advertising.
Source: AdAge, February 28, 2006

SEARCHING FOR THE CUSTOMER

Advertisers have used many forms of media to get their messages to potential customers over the years. Spending on advertising through radio, magazines, newspapers, and outdoor media (billboards) all peaked in the mid-1940s with the advent of television. Until 1994, newspapers were the largest ad medium. In 2006, television was the largest medium, with newspapers a distant second. While marketers are looking to other technologies to communicate to their customers, for example, the Internet, the majority of media buys are still for the older types of media. One reason for this may be that costs to place ads on radio, on TV, in the newspapers, or on billboards are higher than those for the Internet or other forms of direct marketing.

The cost issue may also be the reason the companies are looking for other ways to reach their target audiences. One of these ways is for advertisers to show regular 30- and 60-second commercials in movie theaters before the featured movie begins. Advertisers look to this venue for two primary reasons: (1) they are able to reach a specific target segment with their ads and (2) they have a captive audience. It is easier for a company to determine who is watching a certain genre movie than it is to target who is watching a television program, and it is likely that the viewer is not going to be able to TiVo the ad or switch to another station on the remote. An additional benefit to the advertiser is the effectiveness of this medium. Research shows that the audience retains the information in an ad shown in a movie theater better than in one provided by television or other media.

Cinema advertising has grown almost 40 percent in the last five years and is expected to double to $1 billion by 2008.

TRACKING THE CUSTOMER

Another fast-growing method for targeting specific audiences and delivering advertising is through radio signal tracking. When radios are tuned in, they not only receive signals, they also transmit them as well. Technology allows companies to pick up radio signals from passing cars, determining what station the occupants are listening to at the time. While the technology was first used by companies to measure consumers' actual listening habits of the various radio stations, it is now being used for a more interactive purpose. MobilTrak, a company specializing in this technology, can pick up radio signals and give retail businesses specific data about the type of radio stations that the passing traffic is listening to. While a radio station can claim that it is the number one station in the market, it may be number one on the east side of town, but not on the west. *MobilTrak* can help retailers target their advertising buys more specifically, so that they can place their commercials on the specific stations that are most popular in their geographical area. This type of technology is also being used in outdoor advertising, where radio signals from passing traffic help to determine the specific ads that are on billboards. With the advent of multiple-ad billboards, where the ads change frequently through computer panels, several companies can share the cost of the single location. These electronic billboards can be set to change every few seconds, showing a new commercial ad. However, with the radio signal tracking, the ads change depending on the average demographic driving by at the time, determined by which radio stations they have tuned in. If the majority of the drivers are listening to a country station, the ad might be for a local truck dealer; however, if the majority of the drivers are listening to a public radio station, the ad might be for the local symphony.

REACHING THE CUSTOMER BY PHONE

The idea of tracking specific customers as they pass by is not limited to radio signal technology. Marketers realize that people are spending more time on the Web, PDAs, and cell phones than watching television, and so they are finding ways to develop commercials that get to the customer on these types of devices. According to an article in *Adweek,* over 200 million consumers in the United States own cell phones, providing a viable format for reaching large numbers of potential customers. In the film *Minority Report,* Tom Cruise is bombarded by holographic messages as he walks by the stores. Today, the technology is here that allows retailers to text message commercial ads as customers walk through the mall. They can identify specific customers and send a message about new items that are in the store or about specific items that are on special that day. Marketers can also send commercials to the cell phone screen. Many companies are revising the usual television ads and formatting them for the smaller screen. For now, it does not appear that consumers are offended by the ads; however, as more companies engage in this type of promotion, the public's attitude may change. The trend for mobile marketing is expected to grow significantly in the next few years.

TECHNOLOGY ENABLES NEW METHODS

Technology has also enabled marketers to target their customers more specifically. For several years, personalized ads have run in magazines that are targeted to specific subscribers. Ads are included in magazines with the individual's name imprinted on the page, making the ad not only more personal, but also more recognizable, therefore increasing the likelihood that the individual actually reads the message. This same type of technology is now being used to print special commercial messages on bank statements. Companies like Wachovia, Chase, and Wells Fargo have been foregoing the usual mail inserts and instead have been imprinting personalized messages in the statements themselves, through print or online. Currently the messages are for other products that the companies offer or related products in which consumers may have an interest, like a financial planning seminar. However, in the future, these specialized ads could be for other companies' products and services.

SOME ALTERNATIVE FORMS OF ADVERTISING

Whether enabled by technology, a spark from a creative advertiser's mind, or just plain common sense, there are many new, alternative means for the world of advertising to reach the potential customer.

The company marketing the hand sanitizer Purell invented a new campaign that would reach potential customers in doctors' offices ("Purell" 2006). The company placed bright yellow, two- by three-inch stickers on the top right corners of the magazines in a doctor's office waiting room. The stickers read "Caution" in large type: "How many patients have coughed on this . . ." or "gently sneezed on this . . ." or "Exposing patients to more than germs . . . ," all pointing to the need for Purell hand sanitizer. The ads further suggested that hand washing was not enough—that a hand sanitizer was necessary to kill the germs.

A related sickness ad reported by a National Public Radio program was that U.S. Airways was planning to begin placing advertising for other companies on its air sickness bags. Seeing the blank space on the bags, a clever marketer felt that it would be able to bring some needed cash to the airline's bottom line.

CUSTOMER PREFERENCES IN ADVERTISING

Prefer marketing that

is short and to the point.	43%
I can choose to see when it is convenient for me.	33%
provides information about price discounts or special deals.	29%
is customized to fit my specific needs and interests.	29%

Source: "2005 Marketing Receptivity Study by Yankelovich Partners, Inc." Chapel Hill, NC: American Association of Advertising Agencies, April 2005.

Other companies have found blank space on city sidewalks, street posts, and even trees. Called *wild posting,* companies spray paint ads on the sidewalks and street posts. While illegal, the fines they must pay are a fraction of what legitimate advertising would cost. In 2006, Reebok painted over 200 of these mini billboards on the sidewalks of Manhattan. Their fine was $11,000 in cleanup costs; however, if they had placed the same ads on 200 phone booths during the same period, it would have cost them over $400,000. Old Navy found blank space on the trees along one Manhattan street and tied Old Navy logos on them (McLaren 2007).

On the golf course, many of the conveniences offered to golfers are also media for advertising messages. GPS screens, mounted on the golf carts, offer several services: golfers can place orders at the clubhouse restaurant so that they can be ready when the game is over or keep electronic scores and compare themselves to other golfers. The screens also provide space for advertising, which can be tailored to the specific hole the cart is approaching. Additionally, ads have been placed in the bottom of each hole on the golf course so that when the player picks up the ball, the ad is seen. The golf course is an attractive medium to marketers due to the demographics of the players. It is estimated that there are 27 million golfers in the United States, a number that continues to grow—perhaps at a more exaggerated rate, with the number of baby boomers who will be retiring in the next decade. The players tend to be male (85%), own their own homes (80%), well educated (47% are college graduates), and have an average household income of over $100,000 (Prentice 2006).

Perhaps the most invasive form of alternative advertising is following us into the public bathroom. Initially, the ads were in the form of posters, primarily on the back of the stall doors and above the urinals. However, they have gone to new locations to reach the captive customer. Companies are placing their ads on urinal mats in men's rooms, and while not every company savors the idea of men urinating on their logo, there are many that do. In fact, urinal mats are big business in bar bathrooms, and bathroom advertising is currently the fastest-growing form of indoor advertising. In addition to the urinal mat, there are also audio ads, delivered via talking toilet paper dispensers, interactive poster ads that will emit a fragrance sample when pressed, and digital screens placed in the floor right in front of the toilet. All of these media are designed to reach a captive audience and can be tailored to fit the demographic of the audience. Ads can be placed in the men's or women's rooms and can be targeted to the age group likely to be customers. Most interactive bathroom advertising is in the restrooms of nightclubs, bars, or restaurant-bar combinations.

WHEN IS IT TOO MUCH?

While consumers have grown to expect advertising messages to appear through various forms of media, the proliferation of ads and the means by which marketers reach us could have negative consequences. At some point, consumers may say enough. Consider a couple who have traveled out of town to attend a friend's wedding. After checking in, they retire to their hotel room and see the message light blinking on the phone. Expecting to retrieve their messages, they first hear a 30-second commercial for the restaurant down the street. Later, they go to dinner, maybe in that same restaurant, and have a meal. The gentleman excuses himself to go to the restroom and, while relieving himself, reads an advertisement printed on a urinal mat. But our couple's exposure to commercial messaging does not stop here. When they get to their friend's wedding, they find that corporate sponsors have been invited to the wedding. The food is sponsored by a local restaurant, which has imprinted its logo and ad on the wedding tableware. The florist has a mobile billboard located just inside the reception hall, and the photographer's business cards are located at each table setting. The wedding has become a promotional event.

FROM THE MARKETER'S POINT OF VIEW

While there are many critics of advertising, the fact that our culture is exposed to advertising is a sign of an open society. Additionally, research suggests that the public actually *likes* advertising—but prefers that it be less obtrusive and on a time schedule that they select (see sidebar on Customer Preferences in Advertising). Marketers consider advertising to be a form of free speech and a part of doing business in a capitalistic society. Additionally, advertising is necessary for informing the public about the many products that are offered for sale. Gone are the days when Henry Ford offered his car only in black. Today, improvements in industrialization processes and technology have made it possible to offer a proliferation of products that can be tailored to every need. No longer does a customer go to the store to simply buy toothpaste; he is now met with a number of choices that even a decade ago was not thought to be possible. One can buy toothpaste made by Aim, Aquafresh, Colgate, or Crest, in paste or gel, and in flavors of mint, cinnamon, or orange. Add to that the many benefit configurations, and one has choices for sensitive teeth, tartar control, whitening, cavity prevention, and on and on. The average supermarket in the United States offers the customer approximately 33,000 products to choose from. It is estimated that every year, there are an additional 25,000 new consumer products offered for sale; some are truly new products, and some are modifications of existing ones. However, the majority of these new products fail—as many as 90 percent of them in some industries—which keeps down the total number in stores at any time. To cut through the product offering clutter, marketers feel the need to get the word out to their customers and inform them of the product's benefits, both tangible and intangible.

CUSTOMER ATTITUDES TOWARD ADVERTISING

I am constantly bombarded with too much advertising.	65%
Advertising exposure is out of control.	61%
Advertising is much more negative than just a few years ago.	60%
I avoid buying products that overwhelm me with advertising and marketing.	54%
I am interested in products and services that would help skip or block marketing.	69%

Source: "2005 Marketing Receptivity Study by Yankelovich Partners, Inc." Chapel Hill, NC: American Association of Advertising Agencies, April 2005.

However, marketers also know that there is a saturation point for advertising, a point at which any additional expenditures are wasted on the customer. This saturation point differs by industry, type of product, content of the ad, and other variables, but it can be calculated for the specific ad and product. The question is, At what point does the customer become saturated by advertising in general? It may be very difficult for marketers to calculate this saturation point due to the number of products, ads, and media by which we are exposed to advertising every day. There are estimates of the number of messages each of us is exposed to every day: 3,500 is the reported high number. However, it is suggested that we can only process and recall about 1 percent of them (Kitcatt 2006).

Will marketers continue to search for new methods to reach their targeted audiences? Will consumers grow weary of the onslaught of advertising, or worse, grow indifferent? At what point does it all become overkill?

See also: Drug Testing in the Workplace; Marketing to Baby Boomers; Marketing to Children; Marketing to Women and Girls; Sex and Advertising

References

Kitcatt, Paul. 2006. "Be Heard—Speak Softly." *Marketing* (July 12): 24.

McLaren, Carrie. 2007. *As Advertisers Race to Cover Every Available Surface, Are They Driving Us Insane?* Available at: http://www.stayfreemagazine.org/archives/18/adcreep.html. Accessed January 26, 2007.

Prentice, Kathy. 2006. *Fore! The Latest on Golf Course Ads.* Available at: http://www.medialifemagazine.com/news2003/jan03/jan06/1_mon/news5monday.html. Accessed January 3, 2006.

Purell: Guerilla Marketing in the Doctor's Office. 2006. Available at: http://www.caffeine marketing.com/guerilla-marketing/purell-guerilla-marketing-in-the-doctors-office.

Further Reading: Berger, Arthur. 2007. *Ads, Fads, and Consumer Culture.* 3rd ed. Lanham, MD: Rowman and Littlefield; Kirkpatrick, Jerry. 2007. *In Defense of Advertising: Arguments from Reason, Ethical Egoism, and Laissez-Faire Capitalism.* Claremont, CA: TLJ Books; Ries, Al, and Laura Ries. 2002. *The Rise of PR and the Fall of Advertising.* New York: Collins; Schwartz, Barry. 2004. *The Paradox of Choice: Why More Is Less.* New York: HarperCollins; Stanford, Eleanor. 2007. *Advertising: Introducing Issues with Opposing Viewpoints.* San Diego: Greenhaven Press.

Phylis M. Mansfield

AFFIRMATIVE ACTION

Affirmative action is the practice of preferential hiring for minorities to ensure that employees in businesses represent population demographics. In the American business world, there is a growing debate about whether or not affirmative action is effective, or even necessary. This chapter will concentrate on the history of the affirmative action concept in the United States and illustrate the arguments on each side of the affirmative action debate.

FIVE MYTHS OF AFFIRMATIVE ACTION

1. *Affirmative action only benefits African Americans.* Affirmative action is designed for, and applied to, all minority groups, including white women.
2. *Over the last 30 years, affirmative action has clearly leveled the playing field for minority groups.* According to a recent study, although blacks represent approximately 12 percent of the U.S. population, they make up less than 5 percent of the management ranks and considerably less than 1 percent of senior executives (Morrison 1992). The disparity is prevalent among gender, too. Another study shows that women who are working full-time throughout the year are earning approximately 76 percent as much as men (Feminist Majority Foundation 2001).
3. *Affirmative action costs a lot of white workers their jobs.* According to the U.S. government, there are fewer than 2 million unemployed African Americans and more than 100 million employed whites. Considering that affirmative action policies extend to only qualified job applicants, if every unemployed, and qualified, African American took the place of a white worker, less than 1 percent of whites would be affected (Office of Affirmative Action 2007).
4. *Affirmative action gives preference to women and people of color based only on their race.* No one is ever hired or accepted strictly based on skin color. This practice is prohibited by law.
5. *Once one hires an affirmative action candidate, he has a job for life, no matter how poor his performance.* The terms of performance in the workplace are the same for minorities as they are for white males. Often, minorities are expected to contribute more to the workplace than white males due to stereotypes that all minorities in business are hired due to affirmative action.

Other myths surrounding affirmative action are that it was developed as a means to end poverty within certain social groups or that it was designed to make amends for slavery or similar economic hardships placed on various minority groups throughout the history of the United States. It was designed to open the door to a certain minority group's ability to obtain a foothold in workplaces from which they had consistently been excluded.

HOW AND WHY DID AFFIRMATIVE ACTION BEGIN?

Affirmative action began largely as a result of the African American civil rights movement of the 1950s and 1960s. The first person to use the term *affirmative action* was President John F. Kennedy. His goal was to use affirmative action to ensure that the demographics of federally funded positions represented the nation's racial demographics more proportionately. With the passage of the 1964 Civil Rights Act, eight months after Kennedy was assassinated, affirmative action began to spread to realms outside of government. Title VI of the act stated that "no person . . . shall, on the ground of race, color, or national origin, be excluded from participation in, be denied the benefits of, or be subjected to discrimination under any program or activity receiving Federal financial assistance." Title VII laid out exemptions to this law, stating that under special circumstances, gender, religion, or national origin could be used as a basis for employee selection. This was the beginning of the type of preferential hiring that we now refer to as affirmative action.

Kennedy's successor, Lyndon B. Johnson, was the first to use the term *affirmative action* in legislation. In Executive Order No. 11,246 (1965), Johnson required federal contractors to use affirmative action to ensure that applicants are employed, and that employees are treated during employment, without regard to race, creed, color, or national origin. Johnson also wanted to extend Title VII into realms outside government-financed jobs.

Johnson's affirmative action was designed to implement institutional change so that American organizations could comply with the Civil Rights Act. The need for this change was based on the following assumptions: (1) white males comprise the overwhelming majority of the mainstream business workforce. Providing moral and legislative assistance to underrepresented minorities is the only way to create a more equal space in the business place. (2) The United States, as the so-called land of opportunity, has enough economic space for all its citizens. (3) Especially after the Civil Rights Act, the government assured itself, and the citizens of the United States, that public policy was the proper mechanism to bring about equality of opportunity. (4) Racial prejudice exists in the workplace, and it adversely affects the business and academic worlds' hiring of minorities. (5) Social and legal coercion is necessary to bring about desired change.

One of the most common misconceptions of affirmative action is that it sanctions quotas based on race or some other essential group category such as gender. It does not. This was affirmed in 1978 when the U.S. Supreme Court, in *Regents of the University of California v. Bakke,* ruled that racial quotas for college admissions violated the 14th Amendment's equal protection clause, unless they were used to remedy discriminatory practices by the institution in the past. In *Bakke,* white applicant Allan P. Bakke argued that his application to the University of California–Davis's Medical School was denied due to the university's use of quotas to admit a specific number of minority students to the medical school each year. In its highly fractious decision, the Supreme Court ruled that Bakke's application was rejected because of the quota and ruled quotas unlawful. Muddying the waters, however, was Justice Powell's *diversity rationale* in the majority decision. The diversity rationale posited that ethnic and racial diversity can be one of many factors for attaining a heterogeneous student body in places of higher education. Thus, while *Bakke* struck down sharp quotas, the case created a compelling government interest in diversity.

LEGAL HISTORY OF DIVERSITY IN THE AMERICAN PUBLIC SPHERE

Equal Pay Act of 1963

- Requires that male and female workers receive equal pay for work requiring equal skill, effort, and responsibility, and performed under similar working conditions.

Civil Rights Act of 1964

- Title VI states that "no person . . . shall, on the ground of race, color, or national origin, be excluded from participation in, be denied the benefits of, or be subjected to discrimination under any program or activity receiving Federal financial assistance."
- Title VII laid out exemptions to this law, stating that under special circumstances, gender, religion, or national origin could be used as basis for employee selection.
- Executive Order No. 11,246 (1965) stated that "the head of each executive department and agency shall establish and maintain a positive program of equal employment opportunity for all civilian employees and applicants for employment within his jurisdiction in accordance with the policy set forth in Section 101."

1978, Regents of the University of California v. Bakke

- The U.S. Supreme Court decided that any strictly racial quota system supported by the government violated the 14th Amendment and the Civil Rights Act of 1964.

2003, Gratz and Hamacher/Grutter v. The Regents of the University of Michigan

- The Supreme Court upheld the University of Michigan's law school admissions policy, which considered race as a factor.

HOW IS AFFIRMATIVE ACTION IMPLEMENTED?

Affirmative action requires companies to perform an analysis of minority employment, establish goals to create a more demographically representative workforce, and finally, develop plans to recruit and employ minority employees. For most companies that have effective programs, affirmative action extends beyond hiring practices to include maintaining a diverse workforce, periodic evaluations of the affirmative action program, educating and sensitizing employees concerning affirmative action policies, and providing a work environment and management practices that support equal opportunity in all terms and conditions of employment. Many of the biggest companies in America today have departments and legal staffs dedicated entirely to ensuring diversity in the workplace.

There are a multitude of problems that inhibit or complicate the enforcement of affirmative action. The bulk of these problems include issues surrounding practices common to the modern business world, stereotypes, and employee preferences. Most of these problems are extremely hard to investigate, and oftentimes, they involve serious issues, such as personal relationships or job loss, that make the problem even more complicated.

One of the biggest problems facing American companies today is how to handle affirmative action when downsizing. What role should affirmative action play when deciding who is expendable during downsizing? Rarely do companies plan downsizing strategies that include consideration of workforce diversity. When deciding who to downsize, employers have a great number of factors to consider. These factors include race, gender, seniority, tenure with the company, rank, and personal relationships. There is no standard way of dealing with downsizing because each situation, and each employer, is different. Juggling the aforementioned factors, while paying attention to the levels of merit between employees, now competing for jobs, can become incredibly complicated and pressured.

Perhaps the most widespread problem facing effective affirmative action practices today is also the hardest to identify and fix, and is the most complicated. This problem is commonly referred to as the *good old boy factor*. The good old boy factor involves nepotism, the employment of friends and family over those who may be more qualified for certain positions. The basic problem behind this type of employment is that the employer's family and close personal friends most often share the same ethnic background as the employer, thus limiting diversity in certain realms of employment. Ironically, although not termed this, the good old boy factor is, for all effective purposes, a form of affirmative action. However, this type of affirmative action does not require any amount of education, experience, competence, or overall job qualifications for employment. The way to handle this problem is to change the employment practices and values of the highest ranking executives in a company. However, because they are the highest ranking executives, they may not have anyone to whom they answer, and their immediate subordinates are often people hired due to their relationships as well. In reality, white males have been hired for years, and continue to be hired, due to racial and personal preferences.

THE GOOD OLD BOY FACTOR

The career of former Federal Emergency Management Agency (FEMA) director Michael Brown is an example of the good old boy factor at work. Before taking over FEMA, Brown was the judges and stewards commissioner for the International Arabian Horse Association (IAHA), from 1989 to 2001. Brown resigned his $100,000 a year post in 2001 amid scandal. Brown left the IAHA so financially depleted that the organization was forced to merge with the Arabian Horse Registry of America and has since ceased to exist.

Shortly after his dismissal, Brown joined FEMA as general council, under the guidance of then FEMA director Joe Allbaugh, who ran President Bush's 2000 election campaign. When Allbaugh resigned in 2003, Brown, with Allbaugh's recommendation, became the new head of FEMA, with a $148,000 annual salary.

When Hurricane Katrina hit the city of New Orleans on August 29, 2005, it quickly became one of the most horrific natural disasters to ever affect the United States. The storm killed more than 400 people, displaced approximately one million Gulf Coast residents, cost nearly 400,000 jobs, and caused as much as $200 billion in damage ("Katrina" 2005). While the storm was obviously beyond human control, the U.S. government, specifically FEMA and Brown, received criticism from across the globe pertaining to its slow response to the storm. Democratic and Republican politicians criticized FEMA and called for Brown's immediate dismissal. Brown was forced to resign on September 12, 2005, after a significant tragedy in American history.

On September 9, 2005, *Time* magazine reported that it had found false claims in Brown's biography on the FEMA Web site. The biography exaggerated previous emergency experience, lied about a teaching award and job status at Central State University, and fabricated a role with the organization known as the Oklahoma Christian Home. Another member of the press, Michelle Malkin (2005), stated that Brown was a "worthless sack of bones. . . . And I don't care if he has 'Bush appointee' stamped on his forehead or a GOP elephant tattooed to his backside. Brown's clueless public comments after landfall are reason enough to give him the boot . . . and he should never have been there in the first place." Columnist Russ Baker (2006) wrote that "Michael Brown will forever remain the poster child for federal incompetence" and "it makes absolutely no sense that Michael Brown should have been holding any major government post." So why did this happen?

The answer is the good old boy factor. Mike Brown and Joe Allbaugh were college roommates and had been friends for decades. Allbaugh served on George Bush's administration while Bush was the governor of Texas and ran his 2000 presidential campaign. Allbaugh appointed Brown director of FEMA after his resignation from the post, despite Brown reportedly having few supporters within the organization. Instead of relying on credentials, President Bush, and long-time political ally Joe Allbaugh, hired one of Allbaugh's old friends, who, despite a misleading résumé and an apparent display of incompetence at his last job, had similar political interests. This is an example of good old boy affirmative action. Mike Brown received his job because of his long-time friendship with the administration, while other potential FEMA administrators were passed over. Good old boy hiring occurs in the business world all the time, and many believe that it is a key factor in inhibiting the objectives of affirmative action.

THE ARGUMENT AGAINST AFFIRMATIVE ACTION

Since its inception, affirmative action has constantly faced harsh critics who would like to see the process changed, altered, or disbanded altogether. The critics of affirmative action claim that the practice actually creates unequal hiring practices; is impractical; is unfair to those who, they claim, lose jobs due to the practice; and is even unfair to those who gain employment because they may not be able to do the work. One of the most common misconceptions about those who are against affirmative action is that they are all white conservative males. However, many minorities, even liberal ones, are also opposed to affirmative action, if not as a concept, then to the way it is implemented in the American system. This section will outline some of the major arguments against affirmative action as it is used in America today.

The most prevalent argument against affirmative action is that the practice creates reverse discrimination. Those who argue this stance most often point to Title VI of the 1964 Civil Rights Act, which was designed to prevent exclusion of minority groups based on race, religion, sex, or national origin. Those who claim reverse discrimination when arguing against affirmative action claim that white males are now victims of discrimination due to their race and sex.

One of the biggest changes in American society over the past 40 years has been the cultural and judicial insistence on civil rights for every American citizen. The most famous impetus for this sociological development was the civil rights movement of the 1950s and 1960s, which produced wide gains in the public sphere for African Americans. Included in these gains was the Civil Rights Act of 1964, which outlawed discrimination in public realms such as education, housing, and hiring practices. To many Americans, the treatment that African Americans experienced in this nation until this act was passed was unacceptable and unfair. By enacting the Civil Rights Act of 1964, President Lyndon B. Johnson created, in many citizens' eyes, an equal playing ground for African Americans. To them, affirmative action went beyond the means and goals of the Civil Rights Act of 1964 and was excessive because discrimination was now outlawed by the federal government, and African Americans would be on equal footing with whites.

Furthermore, many argue that affirmative action is unfair because those who lose, supposedly the white majority, and those who gain, supposedly all minority groups, are not all victims of the historical process that created past inequalities. They ask, why should contemporary whites have to pay for the inequalities created by past generations before they were born? At the same time, they ask, why should minorities, specifically African Americans, benefit from the socio-economically subordinate positions their ancestors held in society? In essence, why should whites pay for discrimination that took place before they were born, and why should contemporary African Americans benefit from the suffering of their ancestors, which they have never experienced?

One of the most common arguments against affirmative action that comes from minority leaders is that affirmative action turns people into victims. When expecting the government to take care of minorities and give them preferential treatment, individuals tend to act as if the government owes them something. Some do not consider this progress because it tends to alienate historically underprivileged minority groups from mainstream society.

Another part of this argument is that affirmative action taints minorities in the workplace. When minorities are hired for high-level positions, it is automatically assumed that they received their jobs due to affirmative action. This argument basically claims that individual accomplishments by people from minority groups are virtually impossible because of the cloud created by affirmative action. That cloud, they argue, often leads to assumptions that every minority person in the workplace is there because he or she is a minority and that this person took the job of a white male. This creates stereotypes and ineffective working environments because many minority employees may not be taken seriously.

There are many arguments against affirmative action as we know it today. The arguments are made from various viewpoints and from various political, racial, and economic groups. The opponents of affirmative action are many, and their arguments are multifaceted, with conflicting views prevalent even among would-be allies against this practice.

The arguments for affirmative action are somewhat different and have changed over the course of this practice. As a new type of anti–affirmative action ideology has developed, affirmative action advocates have answered the challenge.

THE ARGUMENT FOR AFFIRMATIVE ACTION

The historical origins of the argument for affirmative action are obvious. Throughout America's history, white males have dominated nearly every aspect of the social landscape. Affirmative action was developed in tandem with civil rights advancements to open more fully opportunities for minority citizens. The arguments supporting affirmative action have now taken the form of debunking myths and exposing truths that indicate problems and misconceptions in the arguments opposing affirmative action.

The biggest and most obvious argument in support of affirmative action challenges the notion of reverse discrimination and beliefs that job markets are closed to whites when competing with minorities. Proponents of affirmative action are quick to point out that even though minority groups have achieved great gains, they are still underrepresented in the workforce, specifically in white-collar jobs. For example, African Americans and Latinos make up approximately 22 percent of the U.S. labor force. In comparison, they make up only 9 percent of U.S. doctors, 6 percent of lawyers, 7 percent of college professors, and less than 4 percent of scientists (Jackson 1996). Proponents of affirmative action are quick to point out that the labor force does not mirror an equal employment system. The number of age-eligible employees does not correlate to the percentage employed. If the system was equal, than employment figures should not be as lopsided as they are.

This argument also suggests that the Civil Rights Act of 1964 did not solve America's racial issues. It simply hid them. After the Civil Rights Act of 1964, and even today, African American and Latin American U.S. citizens are proportionately poorer than their white counterparts. The Civil Rights Act of 1964 opened spaces in the public sphere, but it did not provide concrete economic or financial means for success among minority groups.

Affirmative action backers also argue that diversity is good for society as a whole. Owing to the hiring, promotion, and economic advancement of minorities, diversity has started to seep into more realms of American life. In essence, diversity is becoming more mainstream than it was in the past. Because of this increased diversity, prejudices held about various minority groups have become less prevalent. Partially due to mainstream diversity, America is becoming more culturally affluent and accepting. Prejudice is no longer acceptable in most realms of American society, and affirmative action offices and practices create environments in which diversity is accepted, learned, and experienced.

Pro–affirmative action advocates also argue that affirmative action has helped foster the development of minority role models as more and more minorities enter professional and political positions. Furthermore, their entry has led to the development of a raised consciousness among the American citizenry about issues such as racism, rape, immigration, and poverty that before were invisible to mainstream American society.

Affirmative action advocates argue that contrary to popular opinion, affirmative action is still necessary. The research being done by advocates shows very clearly that there is still a major discrepancy between America's population demographics and its social and economic characteristics. This discrepancy is most prevalent in the workplace and education, where affirmative action has been used the most. Not only do the advocates back their claims of inequality, they show how, in many ways, minorities in this country are hardly better off than they were when affirmative action was first implemented in American society. They argue that affirmative action measures should be increased because of a lack of effectiveness and because of the token affirmative action that many firms use today. For all effective purposes, token affirmative action is affirmative action with quotas. In token affirmative action, the quota usually equals one. Companies will hire a token minority and appoint him or her to a public position to eliminate any doubts concerning the organization's diversity. It is often the case that beyond these token appointments, minority groups are underrepresented in all other sectors of the organization.

Affirmative action advocates have also argued that affirmative action is good for all people involved because it increases workplace diversity and expands traditional ideas. It not only helps individuals obtain positions previously unavailable to them, but it also helps create a broader sense of the world within individuals and within organizations. In essence, it forces people to broaden their horizons.

CONCLUSION: THE FUTURE OF AFFIRMATIVE ACTION

Affirmative action has become a very controversial topic. Opponents suggest that affirmative action causes reverse discrimination that hurts white males and, in fact, is detrimental to minorities who are placed because of it. Furthermore, they believe that the practice of affirmative action contradicts the basic civil rights guaranteed by the Constitution. Advocates believe that discrimination still exists and that affirmative action gives minorities a chance to work, which affects every aspect of their lives. The debate will continue until minorities are represented in every job class and type.

See also: Drug Testing in the Workplace; Glass Ceiling; Immigrant Workers in the United States

References

Baker, Russ. 2006. *Unholy Trinity: Katrina, Allbaugh and Brown.* Available at: http://www.russ baker.com/The%20Real%20News%20Project%20-%20Unholy%20Trinity%20Katrina, %20Allbaugh%20and%20Brown.htm.

Civil Rights Act of 1964. U.S. Code 20, §1681.

Executive Order No. 11,246. 1965. *Code of Federal Regulations,* title 30, sec. 12319.

Feminist Majority Foundation. 2001, August. "Highlights of Women's Earnings in 2000." Report 252. U.S. Department of Labor, Bureau of Labor Statistics.

Jackson, J. L. 1996. "People of Color Need Affirmative Action." In *Affirmative Action,* ed. A. E. Sadler, 8–13. San Diego, CA: Greenhaven Press.

Katrina Numbers Illustrate Storm's Toll. 2005. Available at: http://www.planetark.com/ dailynewsstory.cfm/newsid/32446/story.htm.

Malkin, Michelle. 2005. *Not Another Damned Commission.* Available at: http://michellemalkin. com/archives/003492.htm.

Morrison, A. M. 1992. *The New Leaders.* San Francisco: Jossey-Bass.

Office of Affirmative Action. 2007. "Information." Oshkosh: University of Wisconsin.

Further Reading: Anderson, Terry H. 2004. *The Pursuit of Fairness: A History of Affirmative Action.* New York: Oxford University Press; Beckwith, F., and T. Jones, eds. 1997. *Affirmative Action: Social Justice or Reverse Discrimination?* Amherst, NY: Prometheus Books; Curry, G., and C. West, eds. 1996. *The Affirmative Action Debate.* New York: Perseus Books; Katznelson, Ira. 2005. *When Affirmative Action Was White: An Untold History of Racial Inequality in Twentieth-Century America.* New York: W. W. Norton.

William M. Sturkey

B

BLOGS

The evolution of the social network has progressed from physical interaction into a virtual community, which children and adults are beginning to recognize as a culture they want to fully experience. The blogosphere is an interconnected community of blogs. *Blog* is the short form universally used for the term *weblog*, a type of Web site where entries, similar to those in a journal or diary, are constructed and usually displayed in reverse chronological order. Bloggers are those who create and maintain their own blogs and use them not only as a way to journal, but as a way to express their opinion to the world, to present current information, or to allow others to express themselves collaboratively.

Simply put, a blog is an online diary for a person or even a business or any kind of organization. It can be very similar to a standard news page, or it can be personalized. Long before blogs, there were newsgroups and online message boards, with the blog becoming the latest and greatest successor. Most of today's blogs allow visitors to offer feedback for other readers and the author. The Internet has opened the door to immediate information, providing the world with the ability to offer opinions and thoughts instantly, and for others to provide feedback. The notion of blogging, which began as journaling, is now a forum for open communication, with many providing an immediate audience for any agenda.

Jorn Barger, a software programmer, created the term *weblog* in 1997. The short form, *blog*, was created by Peter Merholz, a well-known information architect, who jokingly broke the word *weblog* into the phrase *we blog*. The term *blog* was quickly adopted as a noun and verb, with the term *blog* meaning the existence of a weblog as well as the process of posting to one's weblog or online journal.

Blogs traditionally are a way for individuals to journal in an online forum. They allow others to view their journal entries, link to them, reference them in their own journaling, and even post comments. However, the blog has grown from personal to business use quite rapidly and is widely used by organizations all over the world to enhance their ability to reach their target market, provide customer service, or simply put a human face to the online world of business.

Blogs that provide commentary or news on a particular subject, such as food, politics, or local news, rather than strictly functioning as personal online diaries are rapidly growing. A typical blog combines text, images, and links to other blogs, Web pages, and other media related to its topic. Most blogs are primarily textual, although some focus on sharing photographs, as with a photoblog; sharing videos using a vlog; or audio and video combinations such as podcasting. All are part of a wide network of social media used personally and professionally. Podcasting, for example, is becoming quite popular in academia. A podcast is a media file that is distributed over the Internet for playback on iPods, cell phones, PDAs, or computers. Many faculty use the podcast for a lecture, an explanation of a concept, a test review, or anything else that can enhance the course presentation and student learning experience.

Early weblogs were manually updated components of static Web sites. However, the evolution of software and server-side scripting languages like ASP and PHP provided new blog tools and make the publishing process possible to a much larger, less technical population. This resulted in a significant surge of online publishing, with individuals and organizations publishing information for the world to view.

Two well-known blog sites or social networking sites for young people are MySpace and FaceBook. Both allow members to share journals, pictures, links, and comments with each other. Both present a focused blogosphere for a targeted group and use a browser-based software to create, maintain, and present the blog page. MySpace and FaceBook provide free hosting for the member blogs and have a content management approach for the blogger to add and edit his information. Blogs are also run using blog software, such as Blogger or LiveJournal, which provide a self-contained online community where individual users can keep a blog or where organizations or individuals can use the software on their own servers to set up their own virtual communities.

There are various blog classifications. Each classification relates to how the content is presented or written. As mentioned, a vlog is a blog that uses video as its principal presentation format. It is usually a combination of video, text, and graphics, as opposed to a linklog, which shares links. The device used to create a blog can also define the type or classification. A moblog is a blog written by a mobile device like a mobile phone or PDA. More commonly today, blogs focus on a particular subject, such as political blogs or travel blogs. With the upcoming elections, most candidates utilize blogging to share their platforms with a broader audience. This has proven successful in many forums.

Barack Obama used a vlog to announce his candidacy for president and to provide more information about himself. On his official Senate site, Obama uses podcasts to provide audio reports on issues affecting his home state of Illinois and the country in general. During those podcasts, Obama discusses the issues coming before the Senate each week, his position on those issues, and how he plans to vote.

A blog can be private or personal, as in most cases, or it can be for business purposes. Corporate blogs are used internally to enhance the communication and culture in a corporation or externally for marketing, branding, or public relations purposes. The use of corporate blogs to communicate with customers, employees, and shareholders is quickly growing. Blogs can be located as part of organizational sites or may be located with a blog search engine. Several blog search engines are used to search blog content (also known as the blogosphere), such as Blogdigger, Feedster, and Technorati, where you can search for blogs by topic and sort by relevance or date. Blogdigger, for example, is a blog search engine owned by Google. It provides current information on blog sites based on the topic entered. It shows the number of blog sites for that particular topic in the same manner you would see sites listed on Google.

WHO IS BLOGGING?

Traditionally, blogging has been an individual phenomenon, with young people using social networking communities like Xanga, MySpace, and FaceBook to share journals, pictures, links, and comments with each other. Such a focused community has provided an online social networking opportunity for primarily teens and adults in their early twenties, a targeted group with specific intent: to socialize. Often called the MySpace generation, a large percentage of their time is spent online. The online activities of the MySpace generation encompass purchasing and playing games, socializing, and listening to music, all of which make this generation influential as they grow in their purchasing power. Patricia was surprised by the online music her 16-year-old son Ron was listening to. She never heard the bands Brand New or Snow Patrol on the radio. How did he know about them? Before they gained fame, the bands established a presence on MySpace. With so many young people accessing their space and listening to their music, they grew in popularity and fame, which propelled them to recording contracts. Many schools are using blogs to communicate with students and parents. Instead of sending the flyer home in the backpack, schools are providing information online. Principals and counselors are blogging to present an approachable image to both students and parents as well. As this generation moves into the workforce, they will expect to continue to communicate in the same manner; thus the corporate world must adjust its approach to accommodate the MySpace generation as employees and consumers.

Will they resist? According to Business Week Online, the demographics are already beginning to change, with around 78 percent of the MySpace members being over the age of 18 and under the age of 40. The rate of growth in membership on MySpace is approximately 150,000 new users a day, bringing the number of unique accounts to 24.2 million as of October 2006. During that month, there were 11.6 billion page views alone (Baker 2006). Many companies have established MySpace profiles to reach that demographic through online ads and research.

Additionally, many companies are establishing social networks for employees to share information with other employees, conduct online meetings, or simply allow for socialization. Microsoft has gone as far as allowing employee blogs for the outside world to view. It feels that this will put a human face on the company, providing a look into the culture of the company and creating a greater sense of customer loyalty. Some of the other companies that encourage blogging activity include General Motors, Sun Microsystems, Boeing, Google, Hewlett-Packard, IBM, and Yahoo!.

Many conservative executives worry that employees expressing their thoughts without corporate review could actually hurt the organization. This was the case initially at Microsoft as well. When one employee began to blog about his experiences as a Microsoft employee, providing technical tips and support to the outside world, the conservatives in upper management wanted him fired. They did not want the world to misunderstand the company as Microsoft was already seen as a cold, uncaring corporate monopoly willing to chew up and spit out anyone offering competition. However, his boss had faith in him and allowed him to continue to blog. Others in the company began to blog as well, with Microsoft supporting the blogging as long as the employees adhered to the confidentiality guidelines set forth by the company. There are hundreds, if not thousands, of company employees now blogging on their MSDN blog site. Robert Scoble, also an employee of Microsoft, decided to develop a video blog where he would go to various departments in the company and videotape the employees in their work environment. He provided conversations with the developers of Microsoft products about how they came up with the idea and suggestions or tips about the product. He called it his "anti-Marketing Marketing," where rather than have a group of marketing executives plan how they will push the information to the public, there is a natural unedited conversation with the product developer. Yahoo! has addressed the concern of employees sharing confidential information or presenting the company in a negative way by creating personal blog guidelines for employees. While encouraging employees to express themselves freely, the guidelines emphasize the need to think before they speak, considering how their loved ones, coworkers, and company management would accept any testimonial. They emphasize that the employee is legally responsible for statements made on his blog.

CORPORATE BENEFITS OF BLOGGING

While many companies still view blogging as a personal social network, there are many who have embraced it as a tool to cultivate trust and build relationships with the customer. People still need personal contact, and a blog provides a way for the organization to speak directly with the customer. Blogs enable the organization to articulate its perspective, knowledge, and expertise with a larger audience. In addition, they allow the customer to provide feedback about the organization, services, and products. They provide a forum for communicating with media, stockholders, or potential investors as well. Additionally, blogs allow the organization to tell its story many times over, setting it apart from the competition. They add a dynamic component to a potentially static Web site and provide a reason for users to return to the site on a regular basis, enhancing the potential for growth and profitability. Once people are attracted to the site, a blog will keep them coming back to check up on what is being said, potentially subscribing to the site.

Blogging is of great benefit to organizational marketing. It provides companies with an opportunity for increased knowledge of a specific market and allows them to keep up with what the competitors are doing. If well written, blogs provide an increased presence on major search engines. A well-written, routinely updated blog that contains numerous keywords that relate to the topic and has many links to and from relevant sites or other blogs will eventually produce free traffic to the Web site.

Blogging is an inexpensive, simple Web publishing solution. Many small businesses do not have the time to learn Web design or the money to hire a Web developer. Blogging offers an inexpensive method to get the company name out on the Internet with easy-to-use, low-cost blogging software. Even Bill Gates agrees that Web sites are static beasts that do not change much. Blogging provides an ongoing dynamic presentation of information that raises the curiosity of a visitor and turns him into a regular user. It provides for better communication with the media, the customer, and the potential customer and helps the organization fill an industry niche.

Retailers who sell their products online are jumping into the blogosphere as well. Consumers are used to shopping in a brick-and-mortar store with continuous human interaction. For those who sell online as well, or who only sell online, a blog is a way to put a human face to the online purchasing experience. Blogs provide the online shopper comfort in knowing that he will get immediate feedback, and it gives the retailer more personality. Burger King has joined the blogging revolution by establishing a MySpace site where their exposure to their primary target market—teens—will be the greatest. It provides coupons and gifts, in addition to having online conversations with other MySpacers.

The media has also joined the blogosphere as they feel that bloggers are leading conversations about subjects like politics. CNN agrees. It incorporated bloggers into its coverage of the midterm elections by holding an "e-lection nite blog party," which brought together some top online opinion makers. This event allowed for instant reaction as the results came in.

LIMITATIONS OF BLOGGING

Although the blog revolution has presented many benefits to society and the corporate world through real conversation and a continuous river of information, there are also limitations to this new and exciting model of communication. For the young, there are risks Youth who reveal too much information in their profiles are at risk of becoming crime victims, as the statistics on pedophiles connecting with children demonstrate. Additionally, provocative photos or comments children post might come back to haunt them later. Employers have actually begun to use these types of Web sites to do background checks on their future employees before hiring them. Joe was graduating from college last May. In February, he was offered a nice job in accounting with a sizeable firm. He was very excited about his future, but failed to think about his past and the information he posted on the Web. The company, after offering the position, withdrew the offer when it came on Joe's postings, seeing him drunk and in questionable situations. A number of school administrators are using the same technique to see if students are posting pictures at parties drinking alcohol and doing drugs.

The amount of time spent in virtual communities poses a problem for young adults. Constantly checking the site to see who has posted and spending a great deal of time reading the postings demonstrate how virtual social networks may encourage addictive behavior among these users. This addictive behavior affects the MySpace generation in that they have difficulty managing their time in addition to their academic and work responsibilities.

A number of the MySpace generation have difficulty with other forms of communication. They are so used to having the computer to help them that they are not at all comfortable with personal contact. When speaking to someone in person, that person will be able to get a much better idea of who someone is by observing things like posture, body movement, facial expressions, gestures, and tone. Some individuals of this generation may not have as much exposure to physical interaction as previous generations. This can lead to greater desensitization. Some young adults may not have the same empathy for others due to their inability to read body language. Many argue that the online social networking boom has weakened our social and communication skills and made us lazier as a society.

In the corporate world, there are many issues to consider. First, if the company is to allow employees to blog and become part of the online social network, it must consider the amount of time put into blogging. The time employees spend blogging and not performing their regular job duties might not produce the needed return on investment. Additionally, if the company wants blogging to occur, it must motivate employees to do so. Just asking someone to create a blog will not lead to much interesting use if the employee is not comfortable or does not have experience in the language or style of exchange required. An effective blog requires time, discipline, and experience. Thus the company may have to invest in training along with scheduled time allocation.

Establishing a blogging environment opens the door to both positive and negative comments. If the company feels the need to market itself via the blog, it must be prepared to experience negative comments from foes. Proponents of blogging state that there are going to be negative comments about any organization. Blogging provides the opportunity to find out firsthand about the negative comments and respond to them in an open forum. Most likely, supporters of the organization will jump in with a defense before the organization does. Additionally, if all information about the organization is glowing, others will begin to suspect that the blog is completely controlled by the company and may not be valid. This can, in turn, work against the organization. Furman University was one of the first to provide student blogging opportunities through freshman journals. The student bloggers are preselected by the university, thus allowing for some degree of a controlled blogging environment. Although students are preselected, they do seem to be honest in their journaling, and they have the opportunity to post their journal entries and photos. Students express frustration with school and show what fun they have as well. Furman University is sending the message that it is on top of technology as well as the needs of its target audience: students and prospective students.

Many organizations are concerned that blogging will open the door for employees to disclose confidential information, whether intentional or not. This is a limitation in many forums, including e-mail and the good, old-fashioned phone. Organizations had nondisclosure guidelines before blogging, so those should apply to this new phenomenon as well. If an employee becomes dissatisfied with the organization and chooses to use the blogosphere to vent his anger or provide confidential information, he is at risk of losing his job and being sued. Thus most should think about what they say in the blogosphere. This also includes what an organization says about other organizations. Many companies choose to speak highly of the competition and their products. Microsoft found that this approach gave them a competitive advantage as readers of the blogs found them to be more credible.

One of the most significant limitations of blogging is maintenance and follow-up. If an organization allows for blogging, it must provide time for the bloggers each day to maintain their blogs. Though blog design allows for the collection of comments and stimulated discussion, some styles of blogging can quickly move from one topic to the next posting without proper follow-up. It is important that a blog author edit the original posting to summarize what has been learned from the posted comments. If legitimate complaints are posted, they should not be ignored as such behavior can damage the credibility of the organization.

SUMMARY

Although blogging provides advantages and disadvantages to any organization, it is one more way that many people are choosing to communicate. Thus organizations must embrace this technology to maintain and expand their customer base. Blogging is inexpensive, instantaneous, and quite easy to implement. It encourages conversations and allows for targeted communications. Blogging also provides a dynamic component to static Web sites, allowing the organization to provide a human side to its Web presence. In contrast, blogging is time consuming, requiring a significant commitment by the organization and potential expense relative to training and time taken away from other employee responsibilities. Blogging is yet another communication tool added to the large bucket of tools, potentially diluting the significance of each and causing confusion to those who use the tools. Blogging presents more risks to the organization, but also opens the door to a broader audience. The youth of today view blogging as a natural approach to communication. As they become productive adults with purchasing power, their expectations will set the tone for how organizations will implement blogging as part of their marketing strategies. Today's youth have strong ideas about the ease of publishing and the risks of public revelation. It is hoped that they will take this technology and find a way to overcome the limitations and use it as a tool for successful communication within their organizations and the community in general.

See also: Corporate Social Responsibility; Ethics in Business at the Individual Level; Marketing to Children

Reference

Baker, Stephen. 2006. *The Inside Story on Company Blogs.* Available at http://www.businessweek.com/technology/content/feb2006/tc20060214_402499.htm.
Further Reading: Byron, D. L., and S. Broback. 2006. *Publish and Prosper: Blogging for Your Business.* Berkeley, CA: New Riders; Holtz, S., and T. Demopoulos. 2006. *Blogging for Business: Everything You Need to Know and Why You Should Care.* New York: Kaplan Business; Scoble, R., and S. Israel. 2003. *Naked Conversations.* Hoboken, NJ: John Wiley; Stone, B. 2003. *Blogging: Genius Strategies for Instant Web Content.* Berkeley, CA: New Riders.

Kathleen J. Noce and James A. Stanford

BLUE-COLLAR AND WHITE-COLLAR JOBS

Much of a person's personal identity is related to the job he has. Often, one of the first questions one is asked by a new acquaintance is, What do you do for a living? Feelings of self-worth, salary earned, and the respect one receives from others is, to some degree, tied to one's job.

A tremendous amount of change in the types of jobs available in our economy has occurred over the last half century. Three generations ago, factory jobs, construction jobs, and other occupations where workers made, built, and maintained the machines, structures, and other products that propel the economy were plentiful. These so-called blue-collar jobs—after the collars on the blue denim shirts often worn by factory workers—were respected and sought-after positions. Most blue-collar jobs required only a high school degree, if that, and paid well enough to support a family. My father, a blue-collar worker from the 1940s to 1980s, earned enough to provide his family with a decent, if inextravagant, standard of living.

The job picture has changed over the last 50 years for America's working class. The percentage of factory jobs in the overall economy has declined significantly, dropping from almost 30 percent in 1959 to barely 10 percent in 2005 (Figure B.1). Between 1979 and 2005, over five million factory jobs were cut. Factory jobs are now the exception, rather than the rule.

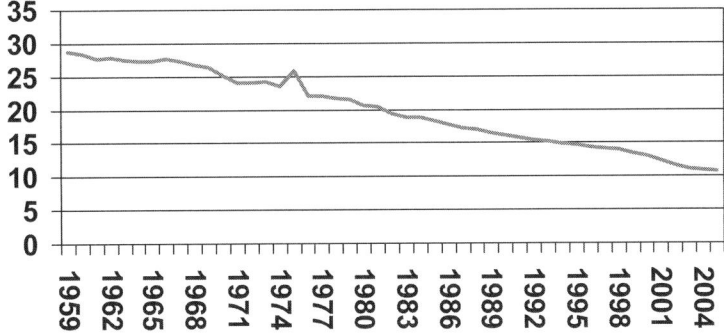

Figure B.1 Percentage of jobs in manufacturing.

Source: Economic Report of the President. Washington, DC: U.S. Government Printing Office, 2006.

REASONS

Why has this happened, and is it good or bad? Let me answer the why part first. Technology has certainly had an impact on the job shift. Factories today are crammed full of time-saving machinery, computers, and other high-tech equipment. These modern marvels are more efficient than humans and do a better job producing manufactured goods. While there are fewer workers on the factory floors, this equipment and technology allow each worker to produce more. Between 1959 and 2005, the output per factory worker per year increased an incredible 350 percent.

A second reason comes from how people spend additional money they earn. Studies show that as consumer income has increased over the past 50 years, people have spent more of it on services such as health care, dining out, house cleaning and lawn maintenance services, and gyms and personal trainers. Consumers buy more manufactured goods, too, but at a rate slower than they purchase service goods. Job creation usually follows consumer consumption patterns. The correlation in the rise in service jobs with the rise of consumer spending on services has been inversely paralleled by the decline in manufacturing jobs with the (relative) decline in consumer spending on manufactured goods.

International trade is a third reason for the relative decline in factory jobs. Barriers to international trade have dropped in recent decades, making trade between countries easier. Where production costs are lowest often determines where a company is likely locate its factories, rather than geography or attachment to place. Current reality is that for many labor-intensive manufactured products, such as clothing, furniture, appliances, and audio-visual equipment, production costs are lowest in countries outside the United States. Thus, as factories making these products have moved overseas, so, too, have their jobs.

WHAT ARE SERVICE JOBS?

Service jobs have a bad reputation. Mention them, and people think of fast food workers, checkout clerks, and janitors—all honorable positions, but certainly low paying. My first job was flipping hamburgers at a fast food restaurant. I earned $1.00 an hour (although this was in 1967). I was elated when I moved on to a furniture warehouse and was paid $1.65 an hour!

So when people hear news reports that most of the employment gains in a given month were in the service sector, they shake their heads because they think of lowly paychecks. But service jobs include much more than fast food workers, checkout clerks, and janitors. Service jobs include all occupations outside of farming, manufacturing, and construction. Doctors, lawyers, architects, engineers, scientists, and teachers are all classified as service occupations. Service jobs now comprise 83 percent of all jobs, and the range in their average salary is from $15,000 to near $200,000.

Below is a sample list of service occupations, along with their average salaries in 2005. Without a doubt, you can live very well, or only very modestly, with a service job:

Surgeon	$177,690
Chief executive	$139,810
Financial manager	$96,620
Pharmacist	$88,650
Veterinarian	$77,710
Civil engineer	$69,480
Architect	$68,560
Computer programmer	$67,400
Fashion designer	$67,370
Chemist	$63,470
Microbiologist	$63,360
Accountant	$58,020
Nurse	$56,880
Historian	$49,620
Librarian	$49,110
Insurance appraiser	$48,740
Police officer	$47,270
Elementary school teacher	$46,990
Paralegal	$43,510
Firefighter	$40,420
Social worker	$38,780
Radio or TV announcer	$35,600
Ambulance dispatcher	$33,590
Surveyor	$33,390
Tax preparer	$31,000
Bill collector	$29,860
Barber	$24,700

Security guard	$22,690
Bank teller	$22,020
Janitor	$21,120
Home health aide	$19,420
Bartender	$17,640
Cashier	$17,300
Waiter/waitress	$16,310
Fast food cook	$15,500

Source: U.S. Bureau of Labor Statistics. 2006. Available at www.bls.gov.

GOOD OR BAD?

Now on to perhaps the most important question: is the shift from blue-collar jobs to white-collar jobs good or bad? As with most questions in economics and business, the answer is not crystal clear, but fuzzy.

Certainly if white-collar, or service, jobs have increased partly in response to what people want and how they spend their money, then this is a good thing. If more people are willing to pay someone else to mow their lawn or are willing to spend money on a personal trainer, then we would expect and applaud the increase in jobs in these occupations. Also, there is little doubt that the relative increase in service jobs has helped more women get paid positions in the workforce (Table B.1).

The biggest concern about these service jobs is their salary. The popular image is of well-paying factory jobs, with wages of $20 or $25 an hour, being replaced by service jobs barely paying the minimum wage.

How accurate is this picture? Look at Table B.1 which shows the occupations losing jobs and those gaining jobs between 1990 and 2005. Over two million blue-collar jobs were lost, paying an average salary in 2005 of a little over $31,000. About three million farm jobs were lost, as were 150,000 jobs in marketing and sales. Even though we have more food available than ever before, machinery, modern planting techniques, and technology have significantly increased the amount of food each farmer can produce, so fewer farmers are needed. Like-wise, modern techniques of marketing and selling, again using technology like computers and cell phones, have replaced some jobs in these areas.

The lower part of the table lists the occupations gaining in jobs over the 15-year period. All but construction workers would be considered service positions, and most would also be thought of as white-collar jobs. Notice the range of salaries. In the top four categories—each adding over two million jobs—are professional workers earning about $54,000 and restaurant workers making under $20,000. In between are teachers and construction workers, with moderate salaries of near $40,000.

The table reveals one other interesting fact. The average salary of the jobs added exceeds the average salary of the jobs lost by a fairly wide margin: $33,496 to $25,510.

Table B.1 Changes in Occupations (1990–2005).

Occupations losing	Number lost	Salary
Farmers	3,062,930	$21,010
Blue-collar workers[a]	2,219,600	$31,203
Marketing and sales workers	157,680	$32,800
Total	5,440,210	
Weighted average salary[b]		$25,510

Occupations gaining	Number gained	Salary
Restaurant workers	3,092,700	$17,840
Teachers	2,391,500	$43,450
Construction workers	2,370,400	$38,260
Professional workers[c]	2,034,270	$53,882
Health care support workers	1,391,800	$23,850
Cleaning service workers	907,550	$21,930
Administrative support and clerical workers	833,330	$29,210
Protective service workers	790,660	$35,750
Personal care service workers	214,850	$22,180
Total	14,027,060	
Weighted average salary[d]		$33,496

Source: Author's calculations from Bureau of Labor Statistics data.

[a] Includes occupations in factory production, transportation and material moving, and installation, maintenance, and repair.

[b] Weighted by proportion of total jobs lost in each category.

[c] Includes occupations in management, medicine, finance, architecture, engineering, science, and law.

[d] Weighted by proportion of total jobs gained in each category.

Beyond the numbers, this information reveals a few trends in the job market. The movement out of blue-collar and related jobs into white-collar and service jobs is changing the entire complexion of the workforce. It also refutes the claim that we are trading in high-pay factory jobs for low-pay service jobs. It is true that many low-paying service jobs, like those in restaurants, cleaning services, and personal care, have been created. But even more moderate- and high-paying jobs have been created—enough to cause average salaries to rise, in fact.

ANY WORRIES?

So is the ongoing shift from blue- to white-collar occupations making everyone better off? Certainly not. Although the average salary of jobs created beats the average salary of jobs lost, this is not necessarily the situation in all individual cases. Not every laid-off blue-collar factory worker was fortunate enough to move into a higher-paying professional or teaching job. Many moved to a lower-paying restaurant, health-care support, cleaning service, clerical, or personal care job, or maybe took two such jobs to equal the salary of their former factory job.

The problem, then, is not that the economy is destroying good-paying jobs and replacing them with bad-paying ones. A mix of both good- and bad-paying jobs is being created and destroyed, and actually, the result has been a net plus for earnings.

HIGH PAY WITH LITTLE SCHOOLING: WHY PROFESSIONAL ATHLETES ARE PAID SO MUCH

In the modern economy, there is a strong relationship between education and salary. Those with more education and training earn higher salaries. This is especially true for white-collar, or service, jobs.

An exception is professional athletes. Many professional athletes have only a high school education, or if they earned a college diploma, it was on the way to perfecting their athletic skills. For professional football and basketball, especially, colleges serve as the minor leagues for these sports.

Two questions therefore arise. First, why are professional athletes paid so much for essentially playing a game? Second, is becoming a professional athlete a reasonable career goal?

Simple economics can explain why professional athletes are paid such handsome salaries. On one hand, professional athletes earn large amounts of money for their teams. Fans directly or indirectly spend billions each year on tickets, media contracts, and team merchandise, all related to watching or rooting for the players and team. It is these revenues that form the basis for the large player salaries.

At the same time, very few individuals have the skills to be a successful professional athlete. Although millions of young boys dream of being the next Michael Jordan, Roger Clemens, or Peyton Manning, few have the ability to hit three-point shots consistently, pitch a 90-mile-an-hour fastball, or accurately throw a football downfield in heavy coverage.

It is this combination—of a relatively few number of people who can generate very large amounts of money for their employers (the professional teams)—that results in stratospheric salaries. In addition, players benefit from competition for their services. Unlike decades ago, when many teams could effectively control their players for life, today, players can shop themselves among many teams at particular points in time. In baseball, this is called *free agency.* Players can consider offers from many teams and choose the highest contract if they like. In baseball, player salaries have skyrocketed since the advent of free agency in the 1970s.

Of course, both players and teams can make mistakes. Players can make mistakes by signing with a team that does not do well and that therefore makes the player, and his revenue earning ability, look bad. Or teams can make mistakes by signing a player to a big contract and then seeing the player not perform as expected.

Now, what about the second question, of whether becoming a professional athlete is a reasonable career plan for a young person? I certainly want everyone to have dreams. But when you consider that only 1 in every 22,000 workers currently plays for one of the four major professional leagues (Major League Baseball, the National Football League, the National Basketball Association, and the National Hockey League), the best advice is to have a dream, but also have a backup plan!

The problem is that not everyone fits the average result. A significant number of workers who have lost jobs are unable to find new ones that pay just as much because they do not have the skills needed for the better-paying occupations. These workers need training and further education, and both the desire and money to do this are often absent.

Expect the trends outlined in this chapter to continue. Forecasts show that the biggest future job gains will be in the high-paying professional, managerial, and technical occupations as well as in the low-paying restaurant, health-care support, and clerical fields. The jobs will be there. What happens to a person's American dream will crucially depend on the individual's education and skills.

See also: Downsizing; Labor Shortages; Outsourcing and Offshoring

Further Reading: "Employment Industry Output and Projections to 2014." 2005. *Monthly Labor Review* (November): 45–69.

Michael L. Walden

BOOMS AND BUSTS

The economy can be a roller coaster. One year, everything can appear fine: the stock market is rising, jobs are being added, and families and households are getting ahead. Another year, the pendulum can swing the other way, with plunging investments, rising unemployment, and people who are falling further behind in their payments and debts.

So if there is an economic roller coaster, what causes it? Are the ups longer and stronger than the downs? How do they affect businesses, investments, and our everyday lives? What can be done, if anything, to tame the gyrations and smooth out the bumps? And to protect ourselves, what signs can we look for to tell when the next curve in the economic road will occur? These are some of the important questions addressed in the essay.

PATTERNS IN ECONOMIC UPS AND DOWNS

The technical term for the economic roller coaster is the *business cycle*. The business cycle is the irregular ups and downs in the economy. There are four parts to the business cycle. *Expansion* occurs when the economy is growing, which usually implies increasing jobs, rising incomes, and an improving standard of living. The *peak* is when the expansion tops out and the economy has hit its maximum, at least for the time being. The next phase is *recession*, when the economy nosedives, jobs are lost, and incomes drop. The economy bottoms out in the fourth phase—the *trough*—after which the whole process is repeated.

Each combination of expansion-peak-recession-trough is one complete business cycle. Since World War II, there have been 10 complete business cycles. Table B.2 shows the dates and lengths of the four components of each cycle. A

Table B.2 Business Cycles Since World War II.

Expansion date	Expansion length (months)	Recession date	Recession length (months)
October 1945–November 1948	37	November 1948–October 1949	11
October 1949–July 1953	45	July 1953–May 1954	10
May 1954–August 1957	39	August 1957–April 1958	8
April 1958–April 1960	24	April 1960–February 1961	10
February 1961–December 1969	106	December 1969–November 1970	11
November 1970–November 1973	36	November 1973–March 1975	16
March 1975–January 1980	58	January 1980–July 1980	6
July 1980–July 1981	12	July 1981–November 1982	16
November 1982–July 1990	92	July 1990–March 1991	8
March 1991–March 2001	120	March 2001–November 2001	8

couple of conclusions can be drawn from the table. First—fortunately—expansions tend to be much longer than recessions. Since World War II, the average expansion has lasted 57 months, compared to 10 months for the average recession. Second, recent recessions have gotten even shorter. For example, the recessions of 1990–1991 and 2001 each lasted only eight months, while their preceding expansion averaged 106 months.

Another way to measure the business cycle is by the severity of the drop from peak to trough. Figure B.2 gives this information for the post–World War II business cycles using the change in production of goods and services as the measure. The recessions of 1957–1958 and 1981–1982 were the most severe, and the recessions of 1969–1970 and 2001 were the least severe.

It is important to remember that this discussion of the business cycle is from the perspective of the entire economy, and not from the viewpoint of any individual sector or component. Not all parts of the economy move at the same

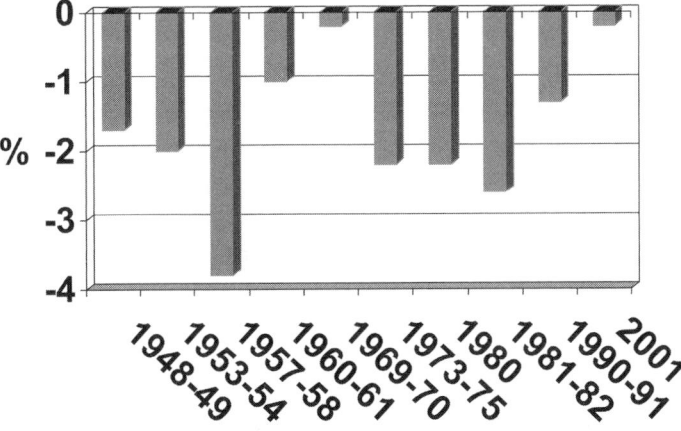

Figure B.2 Reduction in economic output during post–World War II recessions.
Source: U.S. Department of Commerce, Bureau of Economic Analysis, www.bea.gov.

pace. For instance, the entire economy can be in an expansion, and yet some individual sectors are not doing well—the U.S. auto and textile sectors are good examples today—or the entire economy can be in a recession and some parts are booming. During the 2001 recession, the housing and construction industries continued to grow.

BEHIND THE BUMPS: REASONS FOR THE BUSINESS CYCLE

Why business cycles occur has been one of the most studied questions by economists. If the causes of the economic ups and downs can be identified, then maybe the economic roller coaster can be tamed and the economic train put on the permanent track to prosperity.

Unfortunately, economists have discovered that there are many possible causes of the business cycle, and further, they are not that easy to perceive; that is, they are better noticed with the aid of hindsight! Still, knowing the causes can give us insights into changes in the economy that might make for smoother sailing.

One of the most direct causes of the business cycle is changes in the price of a key product in the economy. The best example is oil. Oil, along with its key derivative, gasoline, is a major energy source in the modern economy. Homes are heated and factories are run on oil. Plus, of course, workers are moved and products are delivered in cars and trucks powered by gas.

So when oil and gas prices drop, the energy of today's economy becomes cheaper. Factory costs go down so products can be made more cheaply. Consumers spend less filling their gas tanks, leaving them more to spend on other goods and services. The result is an increase in producing, selling, and buying—in short, a booming economy.

The reverse happens when oil prices jump. Now it becomes more expensive to run factories, so product prices rise. Consumers also pay more for gas and therefore have less to spend on other goods and services. Here all the characteristics of a recession are present. The recessions of 1973–1975 and 1980 were brought about by spiraling oil prices. The recessions ended after oil prices fell, and new expansions began.

Another reason for business cycles is the inability of businesses to predict the future accurately. Say that the economy is expanding and consumers are buying. In this situation, no business wants to be left behind, so bosses will hire more workers and increase production. But if all businesses do this, the growth in production will likely overwhelm the ability of consumers to purchase it. In economics lingo, there will be more supply than demand, meaning a glut of output. Unsold products will cause businesses to cut production—perhaps dramatically—and lay off workers. This, in turn, leads to less worker income and a drop in consumer buying. The economy tumbles downward into a recession.

The recession of 2001 is an example of this kind of recession, and it also illustrates a factor that often accompanies such a business cycle: a stock market crash. When the economy is doing well and businesses are profitable, the stock market rises. As optimism spreads about the economy and company profits, the market rise can be extraordinary. However, when overproduction becomes apparent and businesses ultimately cut back—meaning profits are also cut back—investors' attitudes can quickly switch from joy to concern, causing stocks to be sold and values to plunge. The fall in the stock market reduces the wealth of consumers and deepens the recession.

The economy revives when two things happen. First, businesses sell out their inventories and so need to restart factory assembly lines. Second, stocks will drop to such a level that they appear cheap, and so investors begin buying again, and wealth is rejuvenated.

The 2001 recession was ignited by the tremendous expansion in the technology industry in the 1990s. With the advantage of hindsight, we can see that technology firms expanded too rapidly and drove up stock prices too far and too fast. But this was difficult to see at the time.

Changes in consumer attitudes can also be a factor behind business cycles. When consumers are optimistic about the future, they buy, and their buying fuels factory production and employment. If something happens to change consumer optimism to pessimism, the opposite chain reaction occurs—buying drops, factory production falls, and unemployment rises. Consumer pessimism was a reason behind the big drop in consumer spending during the 1930s, creating an economic downturn called the Great Depression.

The last force behind the business cycle is changes in laws that affect the economy. Historically, two types of changes have been important. One is changes in tax laws. Laws that increase taxes, whether economy-wide or for a particular

RECESSIONS VERSUS DEPRESSIONS

Although people often use the terms *recession* and *depression* interchangeably, economists actually have special meanings for the two words. While recessions occur with some frequency, there has only been one official depression in the country in the last 100 years.

Recessions are that part of the business cycle where the economy stops growing and, in fact, gets smaller. For an official recession to occur, the economy must move in reverse (become smaller) for a period of at least six months. Economic declines over a shorter period of time are not considered severe enough to warrant the term *recession*.

A depression can be thought of as a severe recession. By definition, a depression only occurs if the drop in economic production exceeds 10 percent.

This definition has only been met one time in the twentieth century—in the 1930s—in what is now called the Great Depression. Between 1929 and 1933, the nation's output of goods and services plunged by 33 percent! In 1933, one-fourth (25%) of workers did not have a job. Today, if output declines by 2 percent and unemployment rises above 5 percent, commentators talk of an economic crisis. But today's recessions pale in comparison to the desperation people felt about the economy in the 1930s.

So clearly, there has been no economic downturn like the Great Depression, and it is hoped that there never will be!

sector, can send the economy into a tailspin. The increase in taxes on real estate in the 1980s helped bring about the recession of 1990–1991. After the economy adjusts to the tax increases—in the case of real estate, by lower real estate prices—the economy will revive.

The second legislative change that can spark a business cycle is changes in international trade laws. Trade is an essential part of any economy. Trade allows people and countries to specialize in those activities they do best and most inexpensively. With trade, people get products and services at the lowest cost. If laws are passed that restrict trade, then costs can rise, consumers will buy less, and the economy can contract into a recession. Conversely, if laws are passed that make trade easier between countries, costs can fall, consumers will buy more, and the economy will improve.

Laws were passed in the United States in the 1930s that made international trade more expensive, and many economists think those laws contributed to the Great Depression of that decade. On the opposite side, laws were enacted in the early 1990s that promoted more international trade and fostered the rapid economic growth later in the decade.

There is another possible cause of the business cycle that is ironic because it is supposed to actually control the economic roller coaster. This factor is government economic policy, the subject of the next section.

CORRALLING THE CYCLE

The federal government has tools it can use to smooth out the business cycle, that is, to shave off some of the tops of the expansions and cut back the depths of recessions. These tools are called *monetary policy* and *fiscal policy.*

Monetary policy is operated by the central bank of the country—the Federal Reserve—and it involves changing interest rates and the availability of credit. To restrain an expansion, the Federal Reserve (often referred to as the Fed) will increase interest rates and reduce credit availability. By doing so, consumers will spend less, and some of the steam will be taken out of the economy. In contrast, to soften a recession, the Fed will decrease interest rates and increase credit availability.

HOUSING MARKET CYCLES

It is often said that a home is a person's castle. It is where one lives, raises a family, creates livelong memories, and dies.

But homes are also investments. For most families, a home is their biggest investment, exceeding money they have in the stock market and other investment holdings. So homeowners are right to be concerned about whether house prices go through cycles of ups and downs.

The answer depends, in part, on who you ask, or, in this case, what measure of house prices you track. Figure B.3 shows the average price of homes sold and the average price of homes sold with the same characteristics. Both series are adjusted for inflation, meaning that the purchasing power, or value, of the dollars is the same in all years.

It should be clear from the figure that home prices do go through cycles. Looking at actual prices, there are periods when housing prices fall. Usually, these declines coincide with recessions in the economy. The 2001 recession was an exception, when housing prices

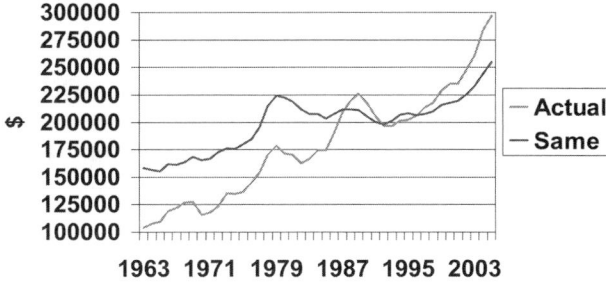

Figure B.3 Actual prices of homes sold versus prices of homes sold with same characteristics, in 2005 dollars.
Source: U.S. Census Bureau, 2006, www.census.gov.

did not decline. Yet over the entire time period (1963–2005), actual prices of new homes sold rose 185 percent, even after taking out inflation.

However, one problem in comparing home prices over time is that the characteristics of homes built and sold can change. For example, if new homes built today are larger, with more rooms and features, than new homes built in the past, then certainly their price will be higher. Yet comparing the price of bigger homes to smaller homes and drawing conclusions about the trend in home prices is an apples-and-oranges comparison.

The blue line in the figure addresses this issue by only comparing the prices of homes with the same characteristics. As might be expected, here the price increase has been much smaller, 54 percent, from 1963 to 2005. This implies that much of the increase in new home prices over time has been due to homes being built with more square footage and more features like central air-conditioning, hardwood floors, and upscaled kitchens.

So when hearing or reading about changes in home prices, be careful to know exactly what is being compared.

Fiscal policy is handled jointly by the president and Congress through the federal budget. To moderate an expansion, taxes are increased and federal spending is decreased. This takes spending power away from consumers. Then, to rein in a recession, taxes are cut and federal spending is increased. This puts more spending power in the hands of consumers.

These ideas of using government policies to control the business cycle have been around for 70 years, and as might be expected, they have attracted considerable criticism. There are three potential problems. One is timing. It is difficult for government officials always to determine accurately the phase of the economy. This means that at any point in time, they do not know for sure if the economy is expanding or in a recession. Therefore government policy makers may not know whether to apply the brakes or the gas to the economy.

The second potential problem is force. In their eagerness to moderate an expansion or prevent a recession, government officials may apply too much of the brake during an expansion and too much of the gas during a recession. Although their efforts may have the desired immediate effects, they may have adverse longer-term consequences. Too much brake during an expansion could ultimately lead to a recession, while too much gas during a recession can result in a future out-of-control expansion that brings with it rapid inflation.

The third problem is speed. Developing government policies takes time. Even if the condition of the economy is known with certainty, politicians can argue about what to do for a long time. By the time a decision is reached, the condition of the economy may have changed and the wrong policy medicine been applied.

For these reasons, some economists—the late Nobel Prize–winning economist Milton Friedman being perhaps the most prominent—think that government economic policy can actually contribute to a more volatile business cycle, instead of a tamer one. These critics think that a government hands-off policy may really be the best approach.

RIDING THE ECONOMIC WAVES

So what can you do about the business cycle to prevent it from becoming a personal tsunami? Although you certainly cannot prevent the business cycle from happening, you can learn to live with it in a way that minimizes its adverse personal effects.

Step one in riding the economic wave is predicting when it is going to rise and when it is going to fall. Of course, you can pay attention to the media to inform you, but it is best to try to be ahead of the curve. Waiting until the media tells you that the economy is up or down can be too late.

Instead, pay attention to two key indicators: interest rates and the stock market. For interest rates, watch the level of rates on short-term loans and investments compared to the level of rates on long-term loans and investments. When the economy is expanding, and is expected to continue to expand, long-term interest rates are higher than short-term interest rates. But when the economy is expected to slow down, and perhaps go into a recession, typically, short-term interest rates are higher than long-term interest rates. In fact, this situation has been one of the best—although not infallible—predictors we have ever had of an upcoming recession. Several financial newspapers, such as the *Wall Street Journal,* print a picture of the relationship between short-term and long-term interest rates on a daily basis.

The stock market is also a good predictor of the economic future. This is because the financial fortunes of investors depend largely on where the economy is headed. So if investors are optimistic about where the economy is headed, that optimism is usually reflected in a rising value of stocks. Conversely, if investors are worried about the economic future and perhaps expect a recession, their pessimism should cause the stock market to tumble. Most recessions have been preceded by a decline in stocks six months to a year in advance. So even if you do not have money in the stock market, watch its movement for a hint of where we are on the business cycle.

Now, if you know what part of the business cycle we are on, what should you do? Well, if the economy is in an expansion, and the growth is thought to continue, that means good economic times are ahead. Opening a new business, looking for a different job, and approaching the boss for a pay raise would all make sense in this economic environment.

But if the economy is headed for, or actually is in, a recession, be glad you have a job, and do everything you can to keep it. Do not expect big pay raises. You might even have to work more hours for the same pay! Do not try to open a business. If you lose your job, consider going back to school to upgrade your skills. If you have loans, try to refinance them because interest rates will usually be lowest during a recession.

THE GOOD AND THE BAD

The good news is that the business cycle has become more favorable. Expansions are longer and higher, and recessions are shorter and shallower. We have been able partially to tame the economic roller coaster.

The bad news is that the business cycle exists and likely will always exist. Plus, the deep part of the cycle—recessions—can still wash away livelihoods. So beware: do not get caught up in the economic good times and expect them to last forever. Likewise, recognize that economic bad times do come to an end. Always try to look around the corner for the next big economic wave.

See also: Chinese Currency; The Dollar; Foreign Direct Investment; Free Trade; Stock Market Predictions; War and the Economy

Michael L. Walden

C

CEO COMPENSATION

The popular press has made much out of CEO pay recently. As stock prices are falling in some companies, CEO compensation is increasing. Is it fair that CEO pay packages continue to increase, while employees in some industries are asked to make billions of dollars in wage concessions ("Fat Cats" 2006)? Can a connection be made between CEO pay and company profitability? Or maybe more importantly, can a connection be made between CEO pay and company stock price? When stock price fell at Home Depot and CEO pay increased, the company spokesperson made the argument that the best measure of CEO performance may be company earnings, even though the corporate proxy states that stock price is the intended measure (Nocera 2006a, 2006b). Many have tried to find explanations for CEO pay and have found little evidence to support its increases. This argument got the attention of lawmakers when the Revenue Reconciliation Act of 1993 was passed. This law set a tax deduction limit of $1,000,000 on CEO and other executive pay, unless the pay was tied directly to performance (Villasana 1995).

A BRIEF SUMMARY OF THE BASIC ISSUES INVOLVED

There are two clearly distinct sides to this issue. One side asserts that the CEO and the stockholders share a common goal: to increase wealth. If the CEOs are enriched by enriching the shareholders, then there are no victims. In that regard, no agency problem exists, and the system is working well. This side further argues that if the press makes note of CEO pay abuses, those instances are isolated, and market forces will correct abuses. This argument is clearly illustrated in the case of Richard Grasso, former chairman of the New York Stock Exchange, who was forced to resign when it was revealed that he would be awarded $140 million in accumulated benefits in one year (Landon 2006).

The other side of the argument is that CEOs are paid far beyond their worth. Their pay is based on factors other than performance, and certainly not on long-term performance. People on this side of the argument assert that boards (typically made up of CEOs) and the compensation committees of these boards pay higher salaries to CEOs who have more power than they have or to influence the market value of CEO pay for selfish reasons.

A board of directors has many committees reporting to it. One example is the audit committee. This committee is charged with ensuring that the company's accounting controls are functioning properly and hold up to the scrutiny of an audit. Another example is the compensation committee. The compensation committee is charged with creating a compensation structure for the executives that is fair and beneficial to all parties concerned. Specifically, the compensation committee recommends to the board of directors the pay package for the CEO. This is especially important during the CEO recruitment phase. Furthermore, these committees and boards disguise these high salaries with complicated features and explanations. These complicated features and explanations are created by compensation consultants, hired by CEOs, who propose handsome pay packages for the CEO to present to the compensation committee. The compensation consultant can base the package on any number of factors, so he chooses those factors that benefit the CEO.

HIGHEST PAID CEOS

The 10 highest paid CEOs in 2005 were as follows (Decarlo 2005):

Rank	Name	Company	Total compensation (thousands of dollars)	Age
1	Terry S. Semel	Yahoo!	230,554	62
2	Barry Diller	IAC/InterActiveCorp	156,168	63
3	William W. McGuire	UnitedHealth Group	124,774	57
4	Howard Solomon	Forest Labs	92,116	77
5	George David	United Technologies	88,712	63
6	Lew Frankfort	Coach	86,481	59
7	Edwin M. Crawford	Caremark Rx	77,864	56
8	Ray R. Irani	Occidental Petroleum	64,136	70
9	Angelo R. Mozilo	Countrywide Financial	56,956	66
10	Richard D. Fairbank	Capital One Financial	56,660	54

CEOS ARE NOT OVERPAID

This side of the argument is based on the premise that CEOs are paid well, but not overpaid. Many people see CEOs' pay packages and do not look further to see that a CEO's pay is not the whole story. What are the factors that might support a CEO compensation package?

Only Extreme Cases of Overpay Hit the Press

Proponents of the argument that CEOs are not overpaid state that this argument seems to center around extreme cases of overpay, and that blinds us to the fact that the majority of CEOs are paid fairly. A prime example of this is the case of Richard Grasso. Grasso was the CEO of the New York Stock Exchange. Grasso's pay was not an issue in the press until he requested the board of directors to cash out (i.e., withdraw) $140 million from his retirement package (Landon 2006). This requested withdrawal was not a recurring item, nor was it a part of his annual compensation package. He simply wanted a one-time withdrawal from his retirement account. This large dollar request hit the news and put pressure on the board of directors of the New York Stock Exchange (at that time, a not-for-profit entity) to deny his request because of appearances. How could a not-for-profit organization allow such a large payout? Nobody was denying that Grasso was entitled to the money or that he had not earned it. The only issues were whether the board of directors should allow the withdrawal in one lump sum and prior to Grasso's retirement. As a result of the negative press over this subject, the board of directors approved the withdrawal and then asked for Grasso's resignation. Grasso took the money and resigned. At the time of Grasso's resignation, no charges of unlawful conduct were considered to be a part of this issue. However, Elliot Spitzer, the attorney general for New York State, filed suit against Grasso, subsequent to his resignation, contending that his compensation was unreasonable and a violation of New York's not-for-profit laws.

In concluding this segment, was Grasso overpaid? Overpaid compared to what? No mention was made in the press over concern about the quality of Grasso's work. In fact, Grasso is lauded due to his fine response to the September 11, 2001, attacks on New York City's financial district. This issue is focused solely on the $140 million retirement withdrawal, which blinds critics to his work and the work of other CEOs that are not considered to be overpaid.

Good CEOs Cost More Than Average CEOs

We must now examine a basic theory of economics: you get what you pay for. If a CEO commands a handsome pay package, then she must have proven to the board of directors that she is worth it.

The board of directors represents the shareholders of the company. The CEO reports to and works for the board of directors. It is through the board that the shareholders can voice their opinions and make their desires known. It is the board's responsibility to act on behalf of the shareholders in carrying out their wishes to management. Management starts with the CEO, who is then responsible for hiring managers to act as agents for the owners (i.e., the shareholders). It is in the best interest of each board member to represent the shareholders to the best of his ability. Board members are elected by the shareholders. If a board member falls out of favor with the shareholders, then he stands the chance of losing his seat on the board. Therefore, if members of the board make a mistake in hiring a CEO, those members cannot make too many more mistakes, or they will lose their seats on the board.

A basic theory of finance is that the goal of a firm (or company) is to maximize shareholder wealth. Therefore shareholders look to the board of directors to maximize their wealth. One of the best ways to maximize shareholder wealth is to hire good people, and the most important person to hire is the CEO. Since we expect that good CEOs cost more than average CEOs, the board is certainly working in the shareholders' interest by hiring the most qualified CEO, and that will cost more money. But all interests are served because it is the job of the CEO to see that shareholder wealth is maximized.

CEOs Are Paid to Participate in the Risk with Shareholders

Another tenet of economic theory is as follows: high risk relates to high reward. In a nutshell, this means that to return high rewards to yourself or those to whom you report, you will have to take risks.

As mentioned earlier, CEOs are paid to maximize shareholder wealth. This does not mean simply increasing shareholder wealth during the CEO's time in office. Shareholders' investment in the company is not permanent. Shareholders can sell their shares and invest in another company with relative ease. In fact, it is in the shareholders' interest to invest their money in the best investment they can find. It is not in the company's best interest to have shareholders that want to sell their shares because that will decrease the share price. A CEO must not only try to increase the company's share price and stock dividends (i.e., maximizing shareholder wealth), but he must do so relative to investments competing for the shareholders' capital.

To maximize shareholder wealth, a CEO must take risks. The CEO is not only putting the shareholders at risk; she is also putting her job and her private fortune at risk. Her private fortune is at risk because she most likely has a large investment in company stock or has the right to buy a large block of company stock (i.e., employee stock options), and she is definitely putting her salary at risk. She is therefore participating in risk with the shareholders, and that is what she is paid to do. If the risks that the CEO take fail, no one suffers more than the CEO. In conclusion, by acting in her own best interest, she is also acting in the best interest of the shareholders.

CEO Pay and Its Relationship with the Pay of Other Employees

If CEO pay is increasing as corporate profits and stock prices are also increasing, why would anyone be concerned? The answer is that few of the gains have trickled down to hourly wage earners, supervisors, and middle managers. The CEO, other executives, and shareholders may not be sharing the wealth with the rest of the organization. In 1992, CEOs were paid 82 times the average of blue-collar workers; in 2004, they were paid more than 400 times those salaries

(Chang 2005). Statistics like this enable critics to change the focus of the debate to equity issues. This is not relevant to the debate.

CEOS ARE OVERPAID

Proponents of this side of the argument assert that CEO pay packages are not only excessive, they are justified by arguments that are not related to performance. Proponents on this side also assert that CEOs may be paid well even if a company's performance is declining.

Compensation Committees Do Not Want Their CEOs to Get Below Average Pay Packages

As mentioned earlier, good CEOs cost more than average CEOs. When the board is considering an offer of employment to a prospective CEO, the board relies on recommendations from the compensation committee. In turn, the compensation committee may hire a compensation consultant to put together a compensation package. This package will be submitted to the board to accompany their offer of employment to the prospective CEO. Additional compensation may also be negotiated with the candidate. The better the candidate, the more negotiating room is available. Compensation consultants are also hired to review existing compensation packages for CEOs.

The process described above can have inherent problems. In the case of making an offer to a CEO candidate, compensation committees often have biases toward a CEO candidate because the board has already expressed its interest in hiring that candidate. Additionally, the board has gone to great expense to find a CEO candidate that it feels is suitable for the job. Good CEO candidates are very difficult to find. As a result, the committee would be at fault if the candidate rejected the offer because the compensation committee's pay package was not satisfactory to the candidate. Sometimes the compensation committee wants to offer an above average package for the future CEO of its company. This issue tends to increase the committee's pay recommendation. If every CEO is paid above average, then the pay packages are ever increasing. In the case of a compensation consultant reviewing the existing pay package of a CEO, the CEO usually hires the consultant. The CEO then reviews the recommendation. If it is satisfactory to her, she presents it to the board of directors. As a consequence, the CEO will only hire a compensation consultant that will create a very handsome package for her to use as support for an increase in her pay.

The result of this is that CEOs can easily be paid far beyond their worth simply because of the conflicts of interest discussed above.

Overpaying a CEO May Indicate Bigger Problems

Many problems in business can be solved with money. Many problems seem to disappear with money. The problem is that if the money dries up, the

problems may reappear twofold. Some have argued that the overcompensation of CEOs is a byproduct of bigger problems (Chang 2005). The company
can defer the need to address concerns with employees by simply increasing
their pay. This is especially true with the highest-ranking employee, the CEO.
Overpayment may be indicative of a badly functioning company, a changing product market, lack of resources, or poor corporate governance (Annett
2006).

The issue of paying CEOs and other executives for reasons other than performance has been such a problem that the federal government stepped into
the fray with the enactment of the Revenue Reconciliation Act of 1993 (Landon
2006). This law includes a provision that eliminates the corporate tax deduction
for publicly traded companies for senior executive pay in excess of $1 million
annually if the pay package is not performance based. The definition of performance in this law is broad and could be achieved even by a poorly performing
company and CEO. Although companies must pay attention to compensation
packages, if for no other reason than to comply with this law, such a loosely
worded regulation is unlikely to create a roadblock to excessive CEO pay.

Power Drives Pay and Tenure Equals Power

Many employees have been at their present employer for many years. Those
years of experience enable employees to know how things work and who to go
to, to get things done. This is especially true for high-ranking employees. Longevity at one employer, also known as tenure, is therefore very beneficial to senior executives.

Companies tend to pay CEOs with long tenure more than CEOs with less
tenure. This holds true even if the less tenured CEO has more relevant experience. This also holds true regardless of performance. How can this be explained?
Some conclude that pay is driven by power, and power is determined by tenure.
Seniority is considered a useful variable when determining pay across levels in
most organizations. We tend to believe that those with experience perform better. In some cases, this could be true, but tenure does not necessarily correlate
with company performance.

Concentration of Stock Ownership

In large companies, CEOs tend not to be paid above average if there is an individual stockholder with a significant number of shares. This is because stock-
voting power is concentrated in that one stockholder. That one stockholder can
effect change and control situations without having to form a consensus with
other shareholders. Forming a consensus is time consuming and replete with
compromise, both of which do not lend themselves to swift and targeted corporate governance. Therefore this inability to control CEO pay through stock
concentration gives compensation committees and boards of directors more
freedom to approve above average CEO pay packages.

In small companies, a lack of stock concentration does not lead to the overpayment of CEOs.

SUMMARY

In summation, one could find enough information in this controversy to support either view. Many people are trying to understand why CEOs are paid so much, and others are trying to understand what all the fuss is about. Much research has been done to find a link between pay and performance, but only a limited connection has been made between compensation packages and performance. One could see how quickly CEO pay could get out of hand, especially in a cash-rich company, if corporate governance is lacking. A quality CEO compensation package would be only one result of good corporate governance. In conclusion, are CEOs overpaid? Many examples of pay for factors other than performance have been explored here. In those cases, one would have to conclude that yes, many CEOs are overpaid.

See also: Corporate Tax Shelters; Personal Success without Selling Your Soul; Salary Disparity; Shareholder Activism and the Battle for Corporate Control

References

Annett, Tim. 2006. "Great Divide: CEO and Worker Pay." *Wall Street Journal* (May 12). Available at: http://online.wsj.com/public/article/sb114719841354447998-CKSOvdXu2 TSMc6ZVSwNaA3zCMtw_20060611.html. Accessed May 18, 2006.

Chang, Helen K. 2005. *CEO Skill and Excessive Pay: A Breakdown in Corporate Governance?* Available at: http://www.gsb.stanford.edu/news/research/compensation_daines_ceopay. shtml. Accessed May 18, 2006.

Decarlo, Scott. 2005. "Special Report: CEO Compensation." *Forbes* (April 21). Available at: http://www.forbes.com/2005/04/20/05ceoland.html.

"Fat Cats Feeding." 2006. *Economist* (October 9). Available at: http://www.economist.com/ printerfriendly.cfm?story_id=2119378. Accessed May 18, 2006.

Nocera, Joe. 2006a. "The Board Wore Chicken Suits." *New York Times* (May 27, national edition). Available at http://select.nytimes.com/2006/05/27/business/27nocera.html. Accessed May 25, 2007.

Nocera, Joe. 2006b. "A Column That Needs No Introduction." *New York Times* (June 3, national edition): C1.

Thomas, Landon, Jr. 2006. "The Winding Road to That Huge Payday." *New York Times* (June 25, national edition). Available at http://www.nytimes.com/2006/06/25/business/ yourmoney/25grasso.html. Accessed June 25, 2006.

Villasana, George A. 1995. "Executive Compensation and RRA '93. (Revenue Reconciliation Act of 1993)." *CPA Journal Online* (February). Available at: http://www.nysscpa.org/ cpajournal/old/16641858.htm.

Further Reading: Balsam, S. 2002. *An Introduction to Executive Compensation.* Burlington, MA: Academic Press; Crystal, Graef S. 1991. *In Search of Excess: The Overcompensation of American Executives.* New York: W. W. Norton; Ellig, Bruce R. 2002. *The Complete Guide to Executive Compensation.* New York: McGraw-Hill.

Carl R. Anderson

CHARISMATIC LEADERSHIP

Every culture around the world has its heroes. Many of the heroes we celebrate are great leaders who have inspired others to follow them, men and women whose accomplishments make them seem larger than life. What makes a leader great? Some academic researchers and practicing managers believe that the magical quality of charisma is what separates ordinary leaders from extraordinary leaders. Throughout history, the accomplishments of charismatic leaders have been impressive: they have mobilized nations, established political or social movements, won wars, and inspired religious devotion. Within the business world, charismatic leaders have been credited with starting successful companies, turning around poorly performing organizations, and motivating employees to perform beyond expectations.

It might sound like charismatic leaders can do no wrong, but not everyone agrees with this assessment. Some critics note that the power of charismatic leadership can be used for nefarious purposes. Throughout history, there have been many charismatic leaders who have manipulated followers into accomplishing extraordinarily *bad* results (e.g., Adolph Hitler). In other words, charismatic leaders are just as likely to be villains as heroes.

There is a third perspective in this debate. Some argue that the importance attached to charisma is overblown. From this point of view, charisma is not a prerequisite of greatness. There have been many great leaders who have lacked charisma. Charisma is just one of many attributes that leaders might possess to be effective. In fact, a slavish devotion to charisma can be dangerous. Overemphasizing charisma obscures the fact that leaders need many qualities and skills to perform effectively.

So which perspective is correct? Is charismatic leadership the secret to great leadership—leadership that builds nations, mobilizes people, and drives successful companies? Does charismatic leadership have a dark side—a type of leadership that leaves behind a trail of destruction? Or is the emphasis on charismatic leadership much ado about nothing? We will explore all sides of this controversy. But first, we will clarify what the concept of charismatic leadership entails in more detail. We begin by considering two basic questions: What is charismatic leadership? and Why do people follow charismatic leaders?

WHAT IS CHARISMATIC LEADERSHIP?

According to leadership experts, charismatic leadership describes a style of leadership that is inspiring and stimulating. Charismatic leaders set forth an appealing vision of the future—oftentimes a vision that radically departs from the status quo. They are likable individuals who possess a magnetism that mobilizes others to follow them and become devoted to their vision. Among nonexperts, conventional use of the term *charismatic* is often applied to someone who has an engaging personality and excellent public speaking skills.

Interest in charismatic leadership took off in the 1970s and 1980s, but the concept of charisma goes back many centuries. Early Christians spoke of charisma as a gift from God. In the early 1900s, German sociologist Max Weber noted that charismatic leadership was rare and was attributed only to leaders with extraordinary talents and gifts. Contemporary conceptions of charismatic leadership downplay its mystical origins and do not attach super-human qualities to the men and women who demonstrate this style of leadership. Nevertheless, within contemporary management thought, charismatic leadership is thought to be one of the most powerful and effective styles of leadership.

CHARISMATIC LEADERSHIP: AN EVOLUTION OF THE CONCEPT

- In Christianity, a *charism* is a special gift from God. Although some of these gifts are routine, St. Paul's letter to the Corinthians describes some of the more extraordinary gifts of the Holy Spirit such as the ability to heal the sick, work miracles, and speak in tongues. Modern day charismatic leaders are not credited with possessing magical gifts. Nevertheless, the term *charismatic* continues to connote something special.

- In the early 1900s, German sociologist Max Weber described charisma as a personality characteristic that sets someone apart from ordinary people. According to Weber, charismatic leaders are treated as having superhuman powers. These magical powers allow charismatic leaders to attract followers. Weber considered charismatic leadership as a temporary phenomenon—something that could not be sustained over time, especially since it is difficult for successors to fill the void left by a charismatic leader. Over time, he argued that charismatic leadership gravitates back toward a more ordinary type of leadership. Finally, Weber wrote that charismatic leadership was incompatible with the modern bureaucratic business organization in which followers are directed by formal systems of accountability and authority and not by devotion to a leader with superhuman qualities.

- In the 1970s and 1980s, management experts became dissatisfied with traditional ways of thinking about leadership. Abraham Zaleznik made a distinction between management and leadership. According to Zaleznik, many business organizations focused on management and not enough on leadership. Managers desire to preserve the status quo, are task oriented, unemotional, and focus on short-term goals. Leaders are agents of change who arouse strong emotions and set long-term visions of the future. Zaleznik's work encouraged a new emphasis on inspiring leadership. Other leadership experts, such as Robert House, Jay Conger and Rabindra Kanungo, and Bernard Bass, developed theories of charismatic leadership that are relevant to modern business organizations. Their theories form the basis for contemporary management thought on charismatic leadership. These authors have published many articles and books written for students and mangers interested in learning more about modern day charismatic leadership.

So if charismatic leadership is no longer considered a divine gift, where does it come from? Is it something that leaders are born with, or is it something they can develop? Research suggests that charismatic leaders are in part born that way and in part made. To the degree that charisma is a personality trait, and personality is partially heritable, then charismatic leadership is something that leaders are born with. On the other hand, charismatic behaviors, such as setting an inspiring vision and making dynamic public speeches, may be acquired over time. Charismatic leadership might come naturally to some people, but almost everyone can develop skills that are associated with this style of leadership.

It is important to remember that charisma, like all styles of leadership, rests in the eye of the beholder. Even though we speak of charisma as a set of objective characteristics and behaviors of a leader, ultimately, charisma is a perception or judgment call. Not all followers will agree that a given leader is truly charismatic. For example, look at the case of two famous U.S. presidents. Was Ronald Reagan a charismatic leader? How about Bill Clinton? Depending on whether you ask a liberal Democrat or a conservative Republican, you are likely to get very different answers. Nevertheless, there are many individuals whose names appear frequently on lists of famous charismatic leaders.

NOTABLE CHARISMATIC LEADERS

To some degree, charismatic leadership is in the eye of the beholder. Nevertheless, here is a list of leaders who commonly appear on lists of charismatic leaders:

Mary Kay Ash	Herb Kelleher
Charlotte Beers	John F. Kennedy
Winston Churchill	Martin Luther King Jr.
Gandhi	Charles Manson
Bernie Ebbers	Mother Teresa
Adolph Hitler	Lech Walesa
John Paul II	Jack Welch
Jim Jones	

WHY DO PEOPLE FOLLOW CHARISMATIC LEADERS?

In the past, charismatic leaders attracted followers because it was believed that these individuals possessed divine gifts and extraordinary powers. But why do people follow charismatic leaders today? Two key processes make charismatic leadership so powerful. The first is called *identification*. To identify with someone means that we find that person likable and attractive. We want to be like him and are eager to please him. Charismatic leaders have a magnetic personality that attracts and inspires others. Followers come to identify personally with a charismatic leader. The other process that makes charismatic leadership so powerful is called *internalization.* To internalize means to share the same values and beliefs. The charismatic leader promotes a vision that points out the shortcomings with the status quo and offers followers the hope of a better future. Followers internalize the charismatic leader's vision and will work very hard to make this dream become a reality. Combine an attractive personality with an appealing vision, and you can see why many people argue that charismatic leadership is the most powerful style of leadership for influencing others (for better or for worse).

Research on human motivation by psychologist David McClelland has shed some light on the differences between leaders who use this power in beneficial

KEY TERMS

- *Socialized charismatic leadership* refers to a leader who desires to use his power to serve others. Self-sacrifice and altruism are the heart of socialized charismatic leadership. Martin Luther King Jr. and Mother Teresa are prime examples of socialized charismatic leaders. Each dedicated his or her life in the service of a higher noble cause. King risked and ultimately lost his life to promote the common good and a better society based on racial equality and civil rights for Americans of color. Mother Teresa gave up a life of comfort to live in poverty, caring for the poorest of the poor in the streets of Calcutta, India.

- *Personalized charismatic leadership* refers to a leader who uses power to promote his own agenda and self-benefit. Recent corporate ethics scandals have shed light on a number of personalized charismatic leaders. One of the most notable is Bernie Ebbers, former founder of WorldCom. Ebbers built Worldcom into a telecommunications giant. Unfortunately, much of Worldcom's success was an illusion that resulted from cooked books. Worldcom's collapse resulted in the largest corporate bankruptcy in U.S. history (surpassing Enron). Ebbers was convicted of securities fraud, conspiracy, and filing false documents with regulators and is currently serving a 25-year prison sentence.

- *Transformational leadership* is closely related to charismatic leadership. Transformational leaders are charismatic, intellectually challenging, and consider the individual needs of their followers. Many leadership scholars mention charismatic and transformational leadership in the same breadth.

- *Transactional leadership* is a style of leadership that is based on an exchange between leaders and followers. Transactional leaders rely on rewards and punishments to motivate follower behavior. Research suggests that effective leaders utilize both transformational and transactional styles of leadership.

and harmful ways. Leaders with a *socialized* power motive desire to use their power to serve others and benefit the common good. Leaders that have a *personalized* power use power in a self-serving way to benefit themselves ahead of others. One of the best ways to distinguish between socialized and personalized charismatic leaders is to examine how they treat people. Socialized charismatic leaders are altruistic and considerate of others. They not only influence their followers, but are willing to be influenced by them because their ultimate goal is to promote and protect their followers' welfare. Personalized charismatic leaders are more likely to use and abuse others to accomplish their goals. Therefore, as we consider the various sides of the controversy, it is important to distinguish between socialized and personalized charismatic leaders.

ARGUMENTS IN SUPPORT OF CHARISMATIC LEADERSHIP

Socialized charismatic leadership has been the most studied style of leadership in the past 30 years. Decades of research by leadership scholars has shown quite clearly that socialized charismatic leadership is an effective and powerful style of leadership. In the workplace, individuals who are led by charismatic leaders are more motivated, satisfied, and committed to their jobs. Socialized charismatic leadership has been shown to increase cooperative behavior in work groups and improve organizational profitability. Socialized charismatic leadership has also been related to low levels of employee deviant behavior in the workplace. Socialized charismatic leaders have more sophisticated moral reasoning skills, and they are perceived by their employees as being ethical leaders.

Overall, the research on socialized charismatic leadership has been carried out in many different settings such as public, private, military, and educational organizations around the world. The results speak for themselves. Socialized charismatic leadership is associated with many positive outcomes.

ARGUMENTS AGAINST CHARISMATIC LEADERSHIP

Compared to socialized charismatic leadership, the research on personalized charismatic leadership is paltry. Nevertheless, many concerns have been raised about the dangers of charismatic leadership. One of the most serious objections has to do with the ethics of the charismatic influence process. Many business ethicists are concerned that the power of charisma can be too easily used for the wrong purposes. They warn that followers of charismatic leaders can easily fall under the spell of charismatic leaders and become too dependent on them. Although there has been little social scientific research, throughout history, there have been many examples of personalized charismatic leaders who have established a cult of personality. One of the most famous examples was the cult leader Reverend Jim Jones. Jones built a cult in the United States and moved to Jonestown, Guyana, after allegations from ex–cult members of financial irregularities and physical abuse began to surface. In 1978, Jones, a drug addict who considered himself to be god, directed his followers to participate in a mass suicide. Almost 1,000 people died in this tragedy. Critics contend that charismatic leaders like Jones encourage follower dependence and demand blind obedience, which can lead to tragic results.

ARGUMENTS THAT CHARISMATIC LEADERSHIP IS OVERBLOWN

The final perspective, that too much emphasis is placed on charismatic leadership, is neither a direct support nor a criticism of the concept. Many advocates of this point of view acknowledge that charismatic leadership is a powerful and effective style of leadership. However, some critics contend that contemporary treatments of charismatic leadership are watered down compared to the heroic and mystical qualities ascribed to these leaders in the past. They also argue that research has shown that charismatic leadership is quite commonplace and ordinary, which contradicts the definition of a charismatic leader as someone who is extra-ordinary.

Finally, the most important argument to support this position is based on many decades of research. This research has shown that charisma is just one of many factors that positively influence employee and organizational outcomes. For example, management expert Abraham Zaleznik pointed out that organizations need both ordinary managers and inspiring leaders to function effectively (Zaleznik 2004). An organization with too many inspiring visionaries and too few administrators to implement the plans will not succeed. Similarly, research shows that there are many nonleadership factors (such as hiring practices, job design, and compensation systems) that influence employee satisfaction and commitment as much as or more than any style of leadership. Critics are worried that by focusing so much attention on charismatic leadership, many organizations are overlooking other styles of leadership and nonleadership factors that are necessary for the effective management of individuals and organizations.

RECONCILING THE PERSPECTIVES

Can we reconcile these different perspectives? If so, how can they be reconciled? Can this controversy be resolved? Each of the perspectives we have discussed has good reasoning or evidence to support it. Proponents of charismatic leaders have solid research to support their position extolling the benefits of socialized charismatic leadership. There has been less research on the dark side of charisma, but there are many historical examples that illustrate the terrible consequences that can result from personalized charismatic leadership. Finally, there is ample research to support the idea that many other styles of leadership and nonleadership factors that contribute to individual and organizational effectiveness are being overlooked because of our zeal for charismatic leadership.

Ultimately, a resolution to this controversy is not possible, nor is it desirable. The fact is that positive (i.e., socialized) charismatic leadership can provide great benefits to individuals and organizations. However, this same power, if uninhibited, can leave a trail of misery and destruction. It is also true that charismatic leadership is just one piece of the puzzle for building a successful organization and mobilizing follower support. Each perspective contains some truth.

Like many things in life, charismatic leadership can be a force for good or for bad. It all depends on whether it is used properly. Students and young managers who aspire to positions of leadership should take time to learn more about the components of charismatic leadership. They should develop key skills (such as effective public speaking, visioning, and active listening) and study important charismatic leaders (both positive and negative). Most important, aspiring charismatic leaders must develop a strong ethical foundation. Without it, a charismatic leader can very easily use his power in a personalized as opposed to a socialized manner.

This discussion also serves as a reminder that charismatic leadership is not the only factor that matters. Becoming a successful leader requires a variety of skills. Problem solving, negotiation, conflict management, delegation, and task structuring are examples of noncharismatic skills that contribute to a leader's success. We must remember that leaders can only do so much to inspire and motivate employees. Factors such as job duties, working conditions, and compensation affect employee motivation as much as or more than charismatic leadership. Similarly, the social and political climate, macroeconomic conditions, industry, and market forces all contribute to a company's financial bottom line more than charismatic leadership.

In the long run, charismatic leadership is here to stay. It is essential that we understand this important style of leadership and make sure that its power is used for good.

See also: Mission Statements; Public Relations and Reputation Management

Reference

Zaleznik, A. 2004. "Managers and Leaders: Are They Different?" *Harvard Business Review* (January).
Further Reading: Bass, B. M. 1985. *Leadership and Performance beyond Expectations.* New York: Basic Books; Conger, J. A., R. N. Kanungo, and associates. 1988. *Charismatic Leadership: The Elusive Factor in Organizational Effectiveness.* San Francisco: Jossey-Bass; House, R. J. 1977. "A 1976 Theory of Charismatic Leadership." In *Leadership: The Cutting Edge,* ed. J. G. Hunt and L. L. Larson, 189–207. Carbondale: Southern Illinois University Press; Howell, J. M., and B. J. Avolio. 1995. "Charismatic Leadership: Submission or Liberation?" *Business Quarterly* 60: 62–70; Khurana, R. 2002. "Curse of the Superstar CEO." *Harvard Business Review* 80: 60–66; Weber, M. 1947. *The Theory of Social and Economic Organization,* trans. A. M. Henderson and T. Parsons. New York: Free Press.

Michael E. Brown

CHINESE CURRENCY

The low prices, critics say, put unfair pressure on U.S. manufacturers, who cannot compete on the "China price" of goods such as textiles, electronics, and other manufactured goods. ("China Rejects" 2005)

The renminbi is undervalued by up to 40 percent, and . . . it gives Chinese exports an unfair advantage. (Bei 2006, 1)

(China) Currency reevaluation could help reduce the trade surplus in the short term; but in the long term, it is production costs that decide whether a country would enjoy a trade surplus. (Bei 2006, 1)

In *Business Week*, on December 6, 2004, there was a special report titled "The China Price" (Engardio and Roberts 2004) which claimed that *the China Price* are the three scariest words in U.S. industry. In general, these three words mean 30–50 percent less than what you could possibly make something for in the U.S. in the worst case, and they mean well below your cost of materials. It has been a big factor in the loss of 2.7 million manufacturing jobs since 2000. In addition, while U.S. consumers binge on Chinese-made goods, the U.S. global merchandise trade and current account deficits hit annual rates of $900 billion in the fourth quarter of 2005, which amounted to 7 percent of the U.S. gross domestic product (GDP), twice the previous record of the mid-1980s, while on the other hand, China's global current account surplus soared to about $150 billion in 2005, about 7 percent of its GDP. China has become the second largest surplus country in the world, slightly behind Japan and far ahead of all others.

Many critics in the United States blamed China's currency exchange policy for the trade imbalance between the two nations. They have long charged that China manipulates its currency to make its exports cheaper and imports into China more expensive than they would be under free-market conditions. This chapter attempts to review the various issues raised by China's present currency policy and tries to give some answers. The questions include, What are the economic concerns raised by the United States over China's currency policy, and what are China's concerns? What caused the U.S.–China trade imbalance? Is China's currency policy to blame? Is China manipulating its currency policy to obtain unfair competitive advantage?

HOW CHINA'S CURRENCY POLICY OPERATES

Before we discuss the nature of the issue, let us first review how China's currency policy works and why such policy has raised concerns, especially in the eyes of U.S. manufacturers and labor unions.

Unlike most developed economies, such as that of the United States, China does not allow its currency to float, that is, let its exchange rates be determined by market forces. Instead, from 1994 until July 21, 2005, China maintained a policy of pegging its currency (the renminbi or yuan) to the U.S. dollar at an exchange rate of roughly 8.28 yuan to the dollar (see Figure C.1). Under this system, the Chinese central bank buys or sells as much currency as is needed to keep the yuan–dollar exchange rate at a constant level.

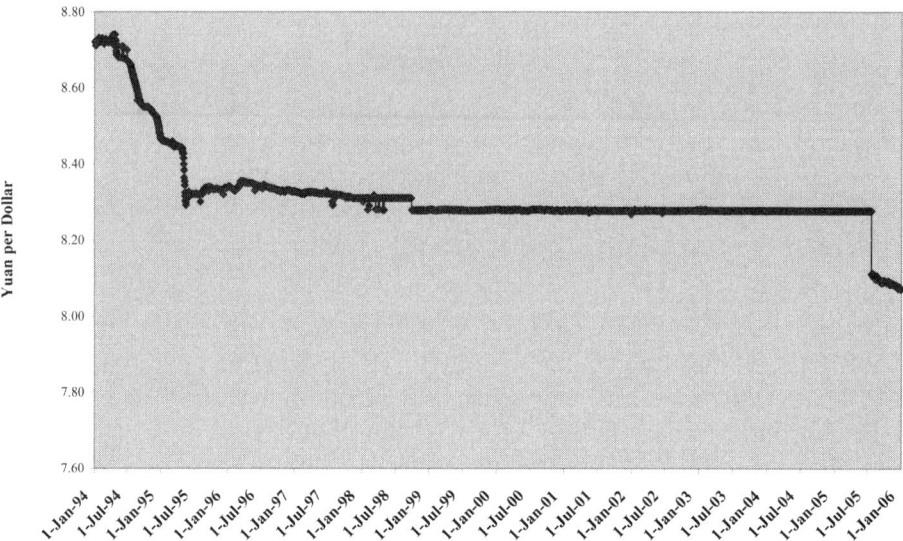

Figure C.1 Yuan–dollar exchange rate.
Source: Federal Reserve Bank.

FIXED VERSUS FLEXIBLE EXCHANGE RATE REGIMES

A flexible exchange rate regime is what occurs when the exchange rate is market determined (by demand and supply of currencies), rather than by establishing a level for it. Examples of nations with flexible exchange rates include Australia, Japan, Switzerland, and the United States. A fixed exchange rate regime means that the country pegs its currency at a fixed rate to a major currency or a basket of currencies, where the exchange rate fluctuates within a narrow margin. Examples of nations with fixed exchange rates include Morocco, Saudi Arabia, India, Thailand, and China.

Using the Chinese yuan as the representative foreign exchange to explain the differences between the two regimes, suppose that the exchange rate is ¥8.28/$1 (this was the exchange rate before China's July 2005 currency reform) at the moment and that the demand for Chinese yuan far exceeds the supply (i.e., the supply of U.S. dollars far exceeds the demand) at this exchange rate. The United States experiences trade deficits. Under the flexible exchange rate regime, the dollar will simply depreciate to a new level of exchange rate, say, ¥4.97/$1, if the claim that Chinese yuan is undervalued by 40 percent is true. At this exchange rate, the excess demand for Chinese yuan (and thus the trade deficit) will disappear.

Now suppose that the exchange rate is fixed at ¥8.28/$1 under a fixed exchange rate regime, and thus the excess demand for Chinese yuan cannot be eliminated by the exchange rate adjustment. For the central bank to maintain the peg, China must increase its foreign reserves by buying dollars from the public in exchange for Chinese yuan. As long as the Chinese central bank is willing to accumulate dollar reserves, China can continue to maintain the peg. As a result, China's foreign reserves grew rapidly during recent years.

There is little consensus among economists and policy makers whether floating or fixed exchange is preferable. Both systems, and the many hybrid systems in between, have their advantages and disadvantages. Furthermore, since countries differ so significantly in their economic and demographic conditions, an exchange rate regime that suits one country may not be suitable for another.

A possible drawback of the flexible exchange rate regime is that exchange rate uncertainty may hamper international trade and investment, as in the case of the United States. On the other hand, proponents of the flexible exchange rate argue that as long as the exchange rate is allowed to be determined by market forces, external balance will be achieved automatically. Consequently, the government does not have to take policy actions to correct the disequilibrium (and thus maintain policy flexibility) since it will be corrected by the so-called international invisible hand.

Proponents of the fixed exchange rate argue that a fixed exchange rate provides stability between the country and the partner to which it is linked. This reduces risk and uncertainty in the price of goods, services, and capital between the two countries. The drawback to greater stability is less policy flexibility. In the U.S.–China case, while the United States loses no policy flexibility from China's peg, China has to use monetary and fiscal policy to offset changes in the business cycle to maintain the peg and therefore would find its currency peg under pressure when economic conditions change.

U.S. CONCERNS OVER CHINA'S CURRENCY POLICY

The primary alternative to China's currency policy would be a floating exchange rate, as the United States maintains with the euro. Under a floating exchange rate system, the relative demand for the two countries' goods and assets would determine the exchange rate of the yuan to the dollar. If the demand for Chinese goods or assets increased, more yuan would be demanded to purchase those goods and assets, and the yuan would rise in value to restore equilibrium.

At the prevailing exchange rate of China, the yuan is widely regarded as undervalued according to many U.S. policy makers, business people, and labor representatives. Ernest Preeg, senior fellow at the Manufacturers' Alliance, estimates that the yuan is undervalued by as much as 40 percent against the dollar. The Institute for International Economics estimates that the yuan is 15–25 percent undervalued, and Goldman Sachs Economic Research Group has estimated that the yuan is 9.5–15 percent undervalued.

In the eyes of U.S. manufacturers, a cheap yuan gives China's exports an unfair price advantage and is accelerating the movement of manufacturing jobs to China. When a fixed exchange rate causes the yuan to be undervalued, it causes Chinese exports to the United States to be relatively inexpensive and U.S. exports to China to be relatively expensive. As a result, U.S. exports and the production of U.S. goods and services that compete with Chinese imports fall. Many of the affected firms are in the labor-intensive manufacturing section such as toys and games, textiles and apparel, shoes, and consumer electronics. These products compete with small and medium-sized firms in the United States, especially makers of machine tools, hardware, plastics, furniture, and tool and die. The U.S. critics claim that an undervalued Chinese currency may contribute to a reduction in the output of such industries.

To illustrate why an undervalued yuan will increase China–United States exports, suppose that the production cost of a Thomas the Tank Engine toy is ¥100 in China, and the production cost of the same toy in the United States is $15. Now suppose that the current exchange rate is ¥8.01/$1. Converting the production cost in China to U.S. dollars, it will cost China $12.48 (=100/8.01) to produce the toy. It is obviously cheaper to make the same toy in China. Therefore U.S. retailers (like Wal-Mart) will import the toys from China, rather than using their own domestic product. If these situations happen a lot, China–United States exports will increase as a result.

If the exchange rate is undervalued by 40 percent, as claimed by some critics, then by appreciating the yuan by 40 percent, the new exchange rate will be ¥4.81/$1. Suppose that the production costs of the two countries remain the same: the production cost of the toy in China is now $20.79 and thus will lose its competitive advantage over the U.S. domestic product. On the basis of the above example, to the point of the U.S. critics, it seems that China deliberately manipulates its currency and therefore artificially maintains its export advantages over U.S. domestic products.

The U.S.–China trade deficit seems to confirm the above arguments. U.S. global trade and current account balance deficits reached annual rates of $900 billion in late 2005, about 7 percent of the total American economy. Table C.2 shows the U.S. trade deficit with China from 1986 to 2005. From this table, we can see that China had a bilateral surplus of around $202 billion with the United States in 2005.

When a fixed exchange rate is equal in value to the rate that would prevail in the market if it were floating, the central bank does not need to take any actions to maintain the peg. However, when economic circumstances have changed, for the exchange rate peg to be maintained, the central bank needs to supply or remove as much currency as is needed to bring supply back in line with market

Table C.2 U.S. Trade Deficit with China (billions of dollars).

Year	U.S. trade deficit with China
1986	−1.7
1990	−10.4
1995	−33.8
2000	−83.8
2001	−83.1
2002	−103.1
2003	−124
2004	−162
2005	201.6

demand, which it does by increasing or decreasing foreign exchange reserves. Thus any time net exports increase, foreign exchange reserves must increase by an equivalent amount to maintain the exchange rate peg. This is the current situation for the Chinese central bank. At the prevailing exchange rate peg, there is excess demand for yuan and excess supply of dollars. So the central bank must increase its foreign reserves by buying dollars from the public in exchange for newly printed yuan. Therefore U.S. critics regard the massive rise in China's foreign exchange reserves in recent years as more evidence that the yuan is undervalued.

As seen in Figure C.2 (actual numbers not shown in the figure), China's foreign reserves (i.e., the foreign currency—in this case, U.S. dollars—deposits held by the Chinese central bank) grew from $22 billion in 1993, to $168 billion in 2000, to $819 billion at year-end 2005. China's foreign exchange holdings rose by 49 percent in 2004 (over the previous year) and by 34 percent in 2005. From the figure, we can see that both cumulative foreign exchange reserves and the current account balance were rising rapidly, especially over the last several years.

In addition to the above-mentioned implications of undervalued yuan to U.S. international trade and U.S.–China trade deficit, critics of China's currency peg argue that the low value of the yuan has had a significant effect on the U.S. manufacturing sector, where 2.7 million factory jobs have been lost since July 2000. They claim that the rapid increase of imports from China has caused these job losses.

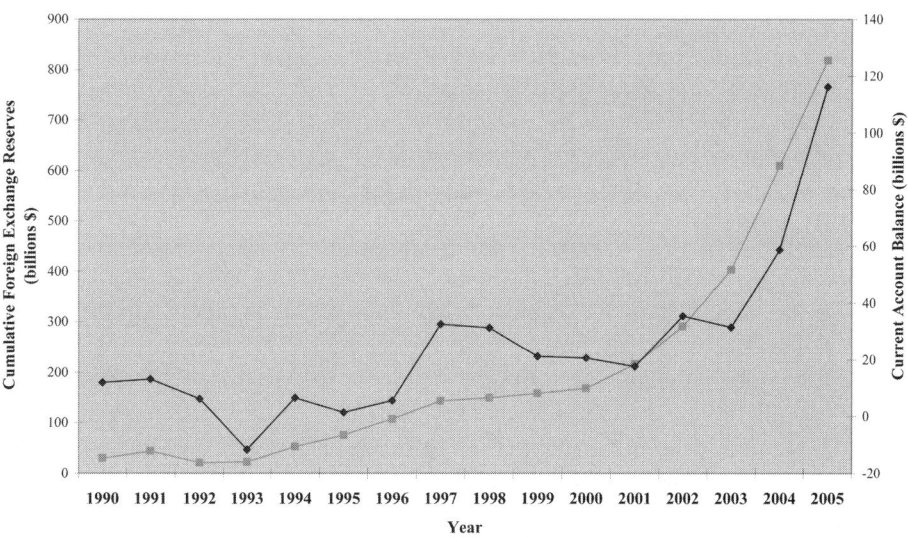

Figure C.2 China's foreign exchange reserves and overall current account surplus (1990–2005).

Source: Economist Intelligence Unit, International Monetary Fund, and People's Bank of China.

CHINA'S CONCERNS OVER CHANGING ITS CURRENCY POLICY

If the yuan is undervalued, then Chinese exports to the United States are likely to be cheaper than they would be if the currency were freely traded, providing a boost to China's export industries. However, an undervalued currency makes imports more expensive, hurting Chinese consumers and Chinese firms that import parts, machinery, and raw materials. In sum, such a policy benefits Chinese exporting firms at the expense of nonexporting firms, especially those that rely on imported goods.

Despite all the accusations that China was deliberately holding down the yuan, the Chinese government has many concerns over changing its currency policy. Chinese officials claim that China adopted its currency peg to the dollar to foster economic stability and investor confidence, a policy that is practiced by a variety of developing countries. They have expressed concern that abandoning the current currency policy could spark an economic crisis in China and would be damaging to its export industries, in particular.

In addition, Chinese officials contend that appreciating the currency could increase imports and diminish domestic food prices and, at the same time, reduce agricultural exports, therefore lowering the income of farmers. Internally, China would not be pressured into changing its currency policy since over 70 percent of the population of China is farmers.

Moreover, Chinese officials contend that the Chinese banking system is too underdeveloped and burdened with heavy debt. The combination of a convertible currency and a poorly regulated financial system is seen to be one of the causes of the 1997–1998 Asian financial crisis. They contend that during the Asian crisis, when several other nations sharply devalued their currencies, China held the line by not devaluing its currency. This convinced officials that China's currency peg was one of the main reasons why China's economy was relatively immune from crisis and that keeping the peg was important to maintaining stable economic growth.

U.S.–CHINA TRADE IMBALANCE: IS CHINA'S CURRENCY POLICY TO BLAME?

Since critics of China's currency peg often point to the large and growing U.S.–China trade imbalance as proof that the yuan is significantly undervalued and constitutes an attempt to gain an unfair competitive advantage over the United States in trade, it is important to examine whether China's currency policy is to blame for the U.S.–China trade deficit.

There are a number of factors that are important to consider when analyzing the bilateral trade deficit. First, although China had a $202 billion trade surplus with the United States in 2005, its overall trade surplus was $102 billion. That is, China had a trade deficit of $100 billion in its trade with the world, excluding the United States. If the yuan is undervalued against the dollar, it should also be undervalued against the other currencies, yet China runs trade deficits against some of those countries. The largest trade deficits in 2005 were with Taiwan, the Association of Southeast Asian Nations, and Japan.

Second, many Chinese exports to the United States are really reexports of materials China imports from somewhere else, especially from East Asia, that have moved their production facilities to China to take advantage of China's abundant low-cost labor. China imports raw materials and components (much of which come from East Asia) for assembly in China. As a result, China tends to run trade deficits with East Asian countries and trade surpluses with countries with high consumer demand such as the United States. Much of the increase in U.S. imports (and hence the rising U.S.–China trade deficit) is a result of China becoming a production platform for many foreign countries, rather than unfair Chinese trade policies. This suggests that the bilateral trade deficit may be independent of China's currency policy.

In sum, Chinese officials argue that appreciation of the yuan will not solve the problem of the U.S.–China trade deficit. They agree that currency reevaluation could help reduce the trade surplus in the short term, but in the long term, it is production costs that decide whether a country will enjoy a trade surplus. The reality is that China's current labor and production costs are low, which has attracted many multinational companies to the country. These companies import raw materials and export finished products with added value, and this leads to high value of exports and low value of imports (and thus the trade surplus of China). Rather than decrying China's exchange rate, they argue, Washington policy makers should turn their attention to the task of permanently raising U.S. worker productivity, the only solid basis for long-lasting increases in worker incomes and benefits.

CHINA'S 2005 CURRENCY REFORMS

In July 2005, China adopted currency reforms. Instead of pegging the yuan to the dollar, the yuan is now theoretically fixed against the weighted average value of the currencies in its basket: primarily the dollar, euro, yen, and Korean won. Theoretically, every time the exchange rates in the basket appreciate or depreciate against the dollar, so will the yuan, according to the new currency policy. Since July 2005, the yuan has depreciated about 4 percent against the dollar over that time (see Figure C.1 for details and current exchange rates).

U.S. treasury officials praised China's currency reforms. However, they stated that China had failed to implement fully its commitment to make its new exchange rate mechanism more flexible and to increase the role of market forces to determine the yuan's value.

Chinese officials have said that China would push forward steadily with reform of the yuan. However, they argued that it is still not the time for a more flexible regime as conditions are not yet ready.

In a semiannual report on international economic and exchange rate policies, Treasury Secretary John W. Snow said that overall, China's record on currency and economic matters was "deeply concerning," but "in the final analysis," the administration was "unable to conclude that China's intent has been to manage its exchange rate regime for the purposes of preventing effective balance of payments adjustment or gaining unfair competitive advantage in international trade" (U.S. Treasury Department 2006).

SUMMARY

The current debate among U.S. policy makers over China's currency policy has been strongly linked to concerns over the growing U.S. trade deficit with China over the past few years. U.S. critics say that an undervalued yuan gives Chinese imports an unfair advantage over goods made in the United States.

Most economists agree that China's currency would appreciate against the dollar if allowed to float. Forcing the Chinese to reevaluate the yuan might temporarily benefit some manufacturers, but it would not address the long-term needs of the American economy, which requires improvements in worker productivity.

Chinese officials are reluctant to change their currency policy, largely because it has facilitated economic stability, a contributing factor to China's rapid economic growth over the past several years. They contend that given the poor state of China's banking system, a move toward a fully convertible currency could spark an economic crisis in China, though in the long run, it is in its own interest to commit to "enhanced, market-determined currency flexibility" (U.S. Treasury Department 2005, 2).

See also: The Dollar; Dumping; Foreign Direct Investment; Trade Surpluses and Deficits

References

Bei, Su. 2006. "Appreciation of Currency 'Will Not Cut Trade Surplus.'" *China Daily* (April 21): 1.

"China Rejects U.S. Currency Criticism." 2005. *CNN News Online* (May 19). Available at: http://edition.cnn.com/2005/BUSINESS/05/18/china.yuan/index.html.

Engardio, Pete, and Dexter Roberts, with Brian Bremner. 2004. "The China Price." *Business Week Special Report* (December 6).

U.S. Treasury Department. 2005. *Report to Congress on International Economic and Exchange Rate Policies.* Washington, DC: U.S. Treasury Department.

U.S. Treasury Department. 2006. "Statement of Treasurey Secretary John W. Snow on the Report on International Economic and Exchange Rate Policies." Available at http://www.treasury.gov/press/releases/js4250.htm. Accessed May 10, 2006.

Further Reading: Congressional Research Service. 2006. *China's Currency: Economic Issues and Options for U.S. Trade Policy.* Washington, DC: Library of Congress; Klein, E. 2003. "Politicians Discover Where the Jobs Went." *Fairfield County Business Journal* 42, no. 37 (September): 39.

Xin Zhao

CORPORATE SOCIAL RESPONSIBILITY

The idea that the wealth and power firms control obligates them to a certain standard of behavior is not new. Charles Dickens, for example, decried the problems of industrialization and exploitation of workers in England in several of his novels and stories. Who could forget Scrooge's perspective on the poor in *A Christmas Carol*:

> "I wish to be left alone," said Scrooge. "Since you ask me what I wish, gentlemen, that is my answer. I don't make merry myself at Christmas, and I can't afford to make idle people merry. I help to support the establishments I have mentioned: they cost enough: and those who are badly off must go there."
>
> "Many can't go there; and many would rather die."
>
> "If they would rather die," said Scrooge, "they had better do it, and decrease the surplus population. . . . It's enough for a man to understand his own business, and not to interfere with other people's. Mine occupies me constantly. Good afternoon, gentlemen!" (Dickens 2001, 13)

Karl Marx and Frederick Engels crafted *The Communist Manifesto* in the mid-nineteenth century, again criticizing the control that firms and owners had over the factors of production and the subsequent adverse effects on workers. A few decades later, the American capitalist Andrew Carnegie wrote *The Gospel of Wealth,* in which he argued that the rich have a moral obligation to share their wealth. Over the past several decades (particularly since the general collapse of Socialist economics), the movement to hold firms to behaviors and actions that extend beyond making a profit has gained substantial strength. More and more, shareholders, outside interest groups, and other organization stakeholders are pressing companies to act in a socially responsible way. Firms ignore this at their peril. Consider the following two cases.

In July 1996, *Life* magazine published an article on child labor in Pakistan and featured prominently a photograph of a 12-year-old boy stitching a Nike soccer ball. For years, Nike had outsourced production of shoes and apparel to Japan, then Taiwan and South Korea, and finally to Indonesia, China, and other low labor cost countries. Activists had begun to attack Nike's practices and stories detailing wages (in some cases, 19 cents per hour), working conditions (women could leave the company barracks only on Sunday), and safety issues (workers in some factories were exposed to hazardous chemicals). An Ernst and Young analysis concluded that "thousands of young women, most under 25, [were] laboring 10½ hours per day, six days a week, in excessive heat and noise and in foul air, for slightly more than $10 a week" (Vogel 2005, 79). Criticism may have reached its apex when the comic strip Doonesbury used a week of strips to focus on Nike's labor practices. At first, Nike executives insisted that since the work was performed by subcontractors, the company could not be responsible for these conditions, but it became clear that this position was damaging the firm's reputation—and sales.

At about the same time, Royal Dutch/Shell had received permission to dispose of an aging North Sea oil storage facility called the Brent Spar in deep marine waters. This permission had followed several years of studies assessing the impact of various disposal options, including on land. Overall, the studies had indicated that deep sea disposal was the safest and most economical approach.

Nonetheless, as the Brent Spar was being prepared for transport and disposal, activists from Greenpeace boarded and occupied the rig, set up a floating TV station, unfurled a flag that called to "Save the North Sea," and pledged to remain on board until the decision to dispose at sea was revoked. Greenpeace justified this by arguing that Royal Dutch/Shell had grossly underestimated the amount of toxic material in the Brent Spar. The activists claimed that the storage facility had over 100 tons of sludge, including oil, arsenic, cadmium, PCBs, and lead, as well as over 30 tons of radioactive material. Dumping the platform would be an environmental disaster and would also set a precedent for like disposal of other platforms. The publicity that developed from the occupation of the platform had a severe effect on Royal Dutch/Shell, particularly in Germany, where a boycott of the firm's service stations reduced revenues by up to 50 percent. Moreover, 200 facilities were damaged, including a firebombing and shootings (Steger and Killing 2002; Watkins and Passow 2002).

These two stories illustrate how firms may find that their decisions are no longer theirs alone or that they are not strictly business decisions. Parties outside the firm increasingly call for actions that reflect obligations beyond profit. This idea of obligation is often called *corporate social responsibility* (CSR) and over the past several decades has become increasingly important to organizations as they try to avoid the damage to reputation and business that missteps like those described above can bring. However, there is also a strong and growing counterargument to some versions of CSR. In this chapter, we will inquire into two theories of how firms are supposed to behave, key topics in CSR, and the problems with applying these theories to real-world issues.

WHAT IS CORPORATE SOCIAL RESPONSIBILITY (CSR)?

What does the firm owe to society? Some have argued that since the modern corporation is supported by social structures and institutions (i.e., corporations exist because of law), then those firms owe something to society in return. A typical definition of CSR requires that firms go beyond simple compliance with the law and engage in actions that further some social good beyond the specific interests of the firm (McWilliams et al. 2006). This has formed a debate with two main streams.

The first is exemplified by the work of Milton Friedman, Nobel laureate from the University of Chicago. In a widely cited article in the *New York Times Magazine,* Friedman laid out the doctrine that has now come to be named for him. In essence, Friedman argues that the sole responsibility of the firm is to make a profit and the only legitimate actions of managers are those that seek that outcome. His reasoning is straightforward: a corporation is a venture formed by investors that has specific standing under law as an artificial person. This limits the liability to the investors and allows contracts to be made by representatives of the firm on its behalf. Obviously, a firm is not really a person, so it cannot act or be ethical—only managers of the firm can. The executives of the firm are hired by the owners (investors) to manage the organization and achieve a satisfactory return. Therefore the managers are agents of the owners and are responsible for the effective use of the firm's resources. Friedman shows that if a manager is to exercise social responsibility in any meaningful way (as defined above), then she must act in a way that is contrary to the interests of the owners; that is, to the extent that the manager spends firm resources to further nonfirm goals, she is spending others' money, and this is a violation of the agency responsibility. This is not to say that firms cannot invest in projects that improve local communities, but to Friedman, this makes sense only if, ultimately, those investments provide a return to the firm in forms like better employee recruitment and retention. Thus investments may have social benefits, but the first measure of legitimacy is how the investment affects firm profits (Friedman 1970).

The alternative is to view the firm as a social institution and managers not as agents of owners, but as trustees of resources, the use of which are to be balanced to reflect the fact that firms have stakeholders other than owners. These typically include employees, customers, suppliers, local communities, and increasingly, external advocacy groups. Thus the investments and expenditures firms make should address the needs and concerns of all stakeholders, creating "a moral imperative for managers to 'do the right thing,' without regard to how such decisions affect the firm's performance" (McWilliams, Siegal, and Wright 2006, 3). Thus, while the concerns of shareholders are important, they are not exclusive, and to satisfy the concerns of nonowners, profits may have to be directed away.

THE CASE FOR CSR

Perhaps the major driving consideration behind the CSR movement is that attention to social concerns can ameliorate the perceived excesses or failures of capitalism and globalization. In most developed countries (such as the United States, Canada, countries of the European Union, and Japan), the social institutions of government, law, and regulation are well developed enough to cover many of the choices open to firms. However, in developing countries, this is not always true. Particularly with respect to labor rules, workers' rights, and environmental standards, developing countries have less complete standards and regulations. In the eyes of some, this opens the door to exploitation by firms that locate production facilities in those countries. This is complicated by the desire of governments in these countries to grow economically, which has, by some accounts, led them to turn a blind eye toward violations of the laws that exist. Thus, CSR advocates argue, firms have an obligation not to take advantage of failed institutions when they harm people in those countries. The Nike example used previously is a clear illustration of how taking advantage of differences in working conditions can be interpreted. However, as Nike modified its practices and standards, some have come to argue that the company imports athletic shoes—but exports higher labor standards. Globalization can become a mechanism for firms and interest groups to affect global working standards (Vogel 2006).

BUSINESS IN SOUTH AFRICA: HOW ACTIVISTS HELPED END SEGREGATION

The practice of apartheid, or racial segregation, had been official policy in South Africa since 1948. It required that every person in South Africa be classified by race, prohibited mixed marriages, and led to the physical segregation of whites, blacks, Indians, and so-called coloreds (or those of Egyptian, Malay, Khoisan, and other backgrounds). Blacks and coloureds had to carry special identification documents and were prohibited from entering white towns. The Separate Amenities Act authorized racially separate services such as beaches, buses, universities, restrooms, hospitals, and the like. Blacks were not permitted to own or operate businesses in white areas without a special permit, nor could they work or enter white areas without a pass. The separate educational systems were funded very differently, with the black educational system receiving about 10 percent of the funds per student as white schools. Ultimately, the South African government established so-called homelands, consisting of about 13 percent of the land area of the country, where blacks were forcibly resettled during the 1960–1980 period.

These practices, coming as they did after the United States had passed through its own problems in developing civil rights, led to a backlash by activists against firms that conducted business in South Africa. Many of the early activists were religious organizations who brought their protests to annual meetings of major corporations with plants or divisions in South Africa. The reasoning was straightforward: if the firms could be convinced to withdraw from South Africa, the resulting economic pressure would force the South African government to reconsider its apartheid policies. According to Tim Smith, executive director of the Interfaith Center for Corporate Responsibility, "We get a lot more attention holding several thousand shares of company stock and a little faith than with just faith alone" ("Financial Desk" 1981).

Although the early movement was often regarded with hostility by firm executives, the pressure to change mushroomed. Researchers have found that shareholder resolutions on divestiture and exit from South Africa were, by far, the most common in the 1980s and early 1990s. By the mid-1980s, AT&T, General Motors, Coca-Cola, Apple Computer, PepsiCo, and nearly 170 others had agreed to end operations. These decisions were amplified by federal legislation that prohibited new investment in South Africa.

Apartheid was abolished in South Africa in 1990–1991. The government of F. W. DeKlerk pledged to find a compromise position between minority whites and majority blacks. This included recognizing the legitimacy of the African National Congress, which, three years later, won the first open elections in South Africa. Was social activism and pressure on U.S. firms a factor in this outcome? To be sure, South Africa faced enormous pressures from international opinion (such as condemnation by most European governments and the selection of Bishop Desmond Tutu, an outspoken South African critic of apartheid, as the Nobel Peace Prize recipient in 1984), an increasingly militant resistance inside the country, the rise of AIDS, and the marginalization of the white minority. However, it is widely argued that economic pressure was also a key part of the decision to reform, particularly as unemployment, resulting in part from the withdrawals, had exploded prior to DeKlerk's election.

Similarly, many are concerned about the increase or growth in the difference between the rich and the poor; that is, "since 1979, 40 per cent of the total growth in disposable income has gone to the richest 10th of the population, while the share taken by the poorest 10 per cent has fallen by a third" (Timmins 2004, 3). This inequity is seen by some as the result of globalization and the elimination of jobs in developed countries as high-paying industry positions are replaced by lower-paying service jobs. On a more global scale, international trade is argued to marginalize poor countries, with benefits flowing to the wealthier nations. Paul Hawken (2000), a well-known environmental businessman, in commenting on the protests at the 1999 World Trade Organization (WTO) meeting in Seattle, said, "Global corporations represent a new empire whether they admit it or not. With massive amounts of capital at their disposal, any of which can be used to influence politicians and the public as and when deemed necessary, all democratic institutions are diminished and at risk. Corporate free market policies, as promulgated by the WTO, subvert culture, democracy, and community, a true tyranny. . . . Seattle was not the beginning but simply the most striking expression of citizens struggling against a worldwide corporate-financed oligarchy."

Third, even in or among developed countries, regulation and governance can lag behind perceived needs. This can happen in several ways. As our experience with environmental law shows, creating regulations is time consuming and subject to negotiation and compromise. From some perspectives, whatever law emerges from the process may be late and/or incomplete. For example, the issues in the Kyoto Accord addressing greenhouse gas emissions were developed at the Earth Summit in Rio de Janeiro in 1992 and formalized in the accord in 1997. While the accord has been ratified by many nations, some, including the United States and Australia, have not yet done so, citing inequities in the structure of the agreement. Given the time required to develop regulations like this, many groups advocate more direct action to accomplish the desired ends now. This is the rationale behind the efforts of groups like Greenpeace in their campaigns to stop the testing of nuclear weapons in the Pacific or mining in Antarctica.

Relatedly, markets may not account for the management of public goods, such as the environment, very effectively because the value of such is very difficult to determine or price. Here, private costs may not reflect true social costs. Thus, prior to legislation like the Clean Water Act, firms did not have to account for the social costs pollution caused downstream from the emission source. What costs might those be? Some are relatively easily calculable, such as the economic loss to marina owners or farmers when the river became unusable for boating or irrigation. Others may be more difficult: how do we account for the value lost by a homeowner on the river? The loss of fisheries and endangering of species? The rippling effects of pollution on other elements of the food chain? The aesthetic loss to people who love rivers? All of these are difficult, if not impossible, to value in a traditional economic fashion. This is why regulation emerges: it can at least address these issues (i.e., make the argument that they are important without necessarily having to value them in a free market way). And since regulation is sometimes slow, CSR advocates step in to fill the gap.

Finally, advocates of CSR often argue that firms can do well by doing good, that is, accomplish both social responsibility and profitability goals at the same time. This is also termed *enlightened self interest* and is the focus of most contemporary writing in the popular press on why firms should engage in it. David Vogel (2005) cites about one dozen popular and textbooks that support the idea that caring capitalism, integrated economic, social, and environmental approaches, and strategic philanthropy result in lowered costs and increased profitability. Most frequently, research indicates that CSR initiatives that improve corporate reputation may lead to effects such as more leads, customers, and so on (McWilliams et al. 2006).

THE CASE AGAINST CSR

It is difficult on one hand to argue against social responsibility: to oppose CSR is to risk being perceived as advocating that firms become less just or fair. However, there are thoughtful critiques of the social responsibility platform from several perspectives. We will examine some here.

First, the notion of what constitutes responsible behavior is vague, a position that writers on both sides of the argument admit. In 1970, Milton Friedman called the discussions "notable for their analytic looseness and lack of rigor" (Friedman 1970, SM17). In 30 years, the situation did not improve much: Hutton termed the concept *fuzzy,* which keeps the discussion stuck in definition and redefinition of terms. Coelho and colleagues suggested with tongue in cheek that this inexactness is "part of the charm" of the call for CSR as it can be applied very broadly. They noted that the definitions in use include compliance with law and regulation, ethical behavior, philanthropy, a higher fiduciary duty, and even a larger sense of responsibility to do the right thing, whatever it may be (Hutton 2000; Coelho et al. 2003).

It is also unclear to whom such behavior is owed. At a minimum, according to the Friedman principle, corporate shareholders must be satisfied. However, the opposing theories calling for accountability to a larger stakeholder group leave the relevant group or groups ill-defined. The definition of relevant stakeholders (aside from shareholders) ranges from customers, employees, and suppliers to "anyone who is directly or indirectly involved with the corporation: employees, citizens, shareholders, NGOs [nongovernmental organizations], unions and government agencies, in short: the social and physical environment" (Maessen, van Seters, and van Rijkevorsel n.d., 12). This is a large group, indeed!

This inexactness makes planning for or assessing the extent to which actions are considered to be responsible difficult. An excellent illustration of how problems with defining CSR can lead to very different interpretations of which firms are acting properly comes from the ethical investing field. In ethical investing, individual investors like you and me as well as institutional investors such as insurance and pension funds decide to place funds only with firms or mutual funds believed to be conducting business responsibly. One of the best known examples of this was the decision by many to avoid investing in firms that were doing business in South Africa when the government still practiced apartheid.

This boycott forced many firms to change their approach to doing business in South Africa—if they continued at all. The boycott also motivated firms to put pressure on the South African government to end apartheid, which, ultimately, it did. Today, we can find large numbers of mutual funds that screen investments based on CSR practices. The assumption is that if CSR works, these firms (and funds) should be better performing. However, the screens that fund managers use vary widely. Many exclude firms in the tobacco or alcohol industries, while some (fewer) exclude firms in the nuclear power and military fields. The key question is, What makes participation in these industries intrinsically irresponsible? Perhaps the answer is clearer cut in the case of tobacco, but it is not in the alcohol industry, where physicians have determined that moderate consumption of wine or other products may improve health. Likewise, firms that provide for national security and energy needs are often fulfilling important social requirements—what makes them socially irresponsible? Conversely, the ethical funds have also been criticized for being too inclusive. Paul Hawken has pointed out that more than 90 percent of firms on the Fortune 500 are included in at least one socially responsible fund. This includes firms such as Wal-Mart, Exxon-Mobil, and Haliburton, firms that have elsewhere and often been criticized for ethical lapses in labor and environmental practices. The point is this: if virtually all major firms are included in ethical funds, then either there is no problem with corporate social responsibility, or the definition of what is responsible has been diluted too much to be useful (Vogel 2005).

An extension to this problem flows from the argument that CSR can be financially beneficial to firms, an effect that should show up in profitability. However, the results are mixed. David Vogel argues that this lack of evidence stems from the sheer number of definitions (or variables) used in the studies. Other works show that the strongest effects are in firm reputation, but not necessarily in profitability. What this means is that the business case for CSR is not clear cut—it may not help, but if reputation is involved, *not* acting responsibly may hurt.

Another aspect of the lack of definition in stakeholder perspectives is purely practical. Who should be counted among stakeholders, and what weight will they carry in the decisions? Put differently, how are managers to define and evaluate the right thing to do when so many can lay claim to a role in the process? How can managers distinguish between private objectives on the part of stakeholders and claims of responsible action? This is, in a sense, what happened in the Brent Spar problem discussed above. Greenpeace members acted to prevent the deep sea disposal of the oil platform on environmental grounds, but it is clear that other motives were in play as well. Greenpeace used interventions like these to elevate their profile because this led to greater monetary contributions. Indeed, in the years just before the Brent Spar incident, donations had dropped off by about 20 percent annually. When the Brent Spar plan was discovered, one member argued to a Greenpeace coordinator that "this will be a big story for the summer. It has everything you need for a real scandal: visually interesting, symbolic, and a strong opponent." Greenpeace's communications director believed that a confrontation had the potential to generate sizable new donations

(Steger and Killing 2002). This is not to argue that Greenpeace members did not have real concerns about the advisability and impact of the Brent Spar disposal option but that stakeholders may have a variety of motivations for the positions they take that may have little to do with responsible action.

Another point to consider here is that the arguments made by stakeholders may not be based on reason and facts, but on emotion, values, and opinion. This was an explicit outcome of the program Shell developed after the Brent Spar incident to try to understand how better to manage similar decisions in the future. As one Greenpeace member also put it, "I don't care about scientific arguments. I don't care if there are ten or a thousand tons of hazardous waste on the platform. The question is, how does society cope with their waste?" (Steger and Killing 2002, 8). The problem here is that values and opinion are often irreconcilable, suggesting that there may be no good way to satisfy all participants.

Finally, determining what is the right or even just best approach before taking action can be difficult. Again, to use the Brent Spar, Shell had conducted a number of studies to build cost/benefit analyses that considered the potential for problems in each of the disposal scenarios. Land disposal was considered excessively hazardous because what waste was on board would now have to be sequestered on land, the risk of breakup increased significantly as the platform moved into shallower waters (with the associated risk of contamination of coastal waters), and many workers would be exposed to hazardous material in the decommissioning and cleanup processes. Deep sea disposal was estimated to have little environmental effect because of the depth of the site and because natural sources of the material in the Spar were already present in much greater quantities. The counterargument from Greenpeace stressed the magnitude of the waste problem (i.e., how many tons of waste were involved) and the effect this would have on the ocean ecosystem. Ultimately, the Brent Spar was decommissioned on land. It turned out that Greenpeace had vastly overestimated the amount of waste (156 tons actual vs. 5,500 tons estimated). The total cost of the project was $65.6 million, or about four times the projected expense of deep sea disposal. Which approach was the right one?

A much more disturbing example comes from efforts to change labor laws to protect children. In Bangladesh, India, and Nepal, for example, children as young as 8 or 10 years old were working in the textile and carpet weaving industries, often under deplorable conditions. Nongovernmental organizations like the South Asian Coalition on Child Servitude (SACCS) lobbied importers in the West, manufacturers, and governments to end this practice. SACCS developed Rugmark, the certification that carpets were produced without child labor. In the United States, the 1993 Harkin Bill was designed to prohibit the import of any products manufactured with child labor. Collectively, measures like these were successful in forcing manufacturers to deeply reduce, if not end, child labor practices. A success? Perhaps not: subsequent work by UNICEF and independent researchers has shown that many of the children displaced from these jobs have been forced to turn to begging and prostitution to survive (Amin et al. 2004). Was this the right outcome?

SUMMARY

That firms and managers are responsible to their stakeholders for the decisions they make is, as we have seen, attractive. Certainly, at a bare minimum, firms must observe the Friedman principle, particularly in that managers must obey existing law. The extent to which they owe greater service to their stakeholders is unclear, so what should firms do to be responsible? Advocates can probably make a very strong case for expecting extra consideration with respect to labor rights and environmental law when the local institutions of government are weak, but even then, selecting the right course is difficult. It is interesting in this context to note that maximizing returns to shareholders may not be as one sided as it appears. Shareholders are the very last in line when it comes to sharing the revenues of the firm. Debt holders, suppliers, workers, and all others to whom the firm owes money must be satisfied first. Only then can shareholders claim any residual profits, so if they are satisfied then, by definition, all those whose claims come before must also be satisfied. Moreover, long-term strategic considerations suggest that firms cannot perpetually give short shrift to those primary claimants. Would clear definition of the obligations to other stakeholders and a longer-term perspective be sufficiently responsible? It seems like a good starting point, but the lessons of the past several decades clearly teach that executives must be sensitive to how their decisions can be interpreted in several ways, and not always as they intended. Thus part of being socially responsible in any sense is being able to manage the message of the action—particular stakeholders may not warrant an increased share of revenues, but they clearly require increased managerial attention.

See also: Ethics in Business at the Individual Level; Personal Success without Selling Your Soul; Price Gouging

References

Amin, Shahina, M. Shakil Quayes, and Janet M. Rives. 2004. "Poverty and Other Determinants of Child Labor in Bangladesh." *Southern Economic Journal* 70: 876–892.

Coelho, Philip R., James E. McClure, and John A. Spry. 2003. "The Social Responsibility of Corporate Management: A Classical Critique." *Mid-American Journal of Business* 18: 15–24.

Dickens, Charles. (2001, 1843). "A Christmas Carol." In *A Christmas Carol and Other Stories*. New York: Modern Library.

"Financal Desk, Watchdogs of Corporate Ethics." *New York Times,* March 5, 1981, D1.

Friedman, Milton. 1970. "The Social Responsibility of Business Is to Increase Its Profits." *New York Times Magazine* (September 13): SM17.

Hawken, Paul. 2000. *The WTO: Inside, Outside, All Around the World.* Available at: http://www.co-intelligence.org/WTOHawken.html.

Hutton, Will. 2000. "Toward a Juster Capitalism." *New Statesman* (November 6): R5.

Maessen, R., P. van Seters, and E. van Rijkevorsel. "Circles of Stakeholders: Toward a Relational Theory of Corporate Social Responsibility." Working paper. Tias Business School, Tilburg University.

McWilliams, Abagail, Donald S. Siegal, and Patrick M. Wright. 2006. "Corporate Social Responsibility: International Perspectives." *Journal of Business Strategies* 17 (Spring): 1–7.

Spar, Debora L. 2002. *Hitting the Wall: Nike and International Labor Practices.* Case 9-700-047. Cambridge, MA: Harvard Business School.

Starkey, Ken, and Sue Tempest. 2004. "Bowling Along: Strategic Management and Social Capital." *European Management Review* 1: 78–83.

Steger, Ulrich, and Peter Killing. 2002. *The Brent Spar Platform Controversy (A).* Case IMD004. Lausanne, Switzerland: International Institute for Management Development.

Timmins, Nicholas. 2004. "Unpalatable Choices Lie Ahead' in Quest for More Equal Society." *Financial Times, London* (October 22): 3.

Vogel, David. 2005. *The Market for Virtue: The Potential and Limits of Corporate Social Responsibility.* Washington, DC: Brookings Institution Press.

Vogel, David. 2006. "The Market for Virtue: The Impact of Corporate Social Responsibility." *Multinational Monitor* 27:37–41.

Watkins, Michael, and Samuel Passow. 2002. *Sunk Costs: The Plan to Dump the Brent Spar (A).* Case 9-903-010. Cambridge, MA: Harvard Business School.

Further Reading: Foley, John, with Julie Kendrick. 2006. *Balanced Brand: How to Balance the Stakeholder Forces That Can Make or Break Your Business.* San Francisco: Jossey-Bass; Frederick, William C. 2006. *Corporation, Be Good! The Story of Corporate Social Responsibility.* Indianapolis: Dog Ear; Vogel, David. 2005. *The Market for Virtue: The Potential and Limits of Corporate Social Responsibility.* Washington, DC: Brookings Institution Press.

Alfred G. Warner

CORPORATE TAX SHELTERS

A fundamental objective of the federal tax law is to raise revenues to cover the cost of government operations. Ordinarily, Congress will set annual budgets, based on anticipated revenues, to plan expenditures and create a balanced budget. Until recently, the last balanced budget was in 1969. Beginning in 1970, there were 28 straight years of deficits. The budget was again balanced from 1998 through 2001, but since 2002, the federal budget has run at a deficit.

The internal revenue code (IRC) comprises numerous code sections, complete with abrupt twists and sudden stops. It has been a complaint of American taxpayers that the tax code is too complicated, often defying logic. Even trained professionals can be baffled by the complexity of a tax return. Recently, the Internal Revenue Service (IRS), the governmental body charged with collecting taxes and auditing tax returns for compliance, has stated that their mission is to simplify the tax code. However, ask any tax professional, and he will tell you that to date, simplifying the tax code has seemingly resulted in three additional binders of tax code.

The IRS distributes more than 649 types of tax forms, schedules, and instructions (Hoffman et al. 2006). That being said, there often is a reason behind every oddity that occurs in the tax code, whether it is an economic, social, or political reason. An example is how the federal government has tried to encourage charitable giving to nonprofit organizations. An individual's ability to deduct his charitable contributions from his taxes is a social practice that Congress has encouraged through tax deductions. Another example would be research and development credits. These credits are given to encourage organizations to develop innovative ideas and processes.

VARIOUS REASONS FOR TAX CODE

Social

Home mortgage deduction. Encourage society to purchase homes by subsidizing the interest cost.

Charitable contribution deduction. Encourage society to give to charities.

Adoption tax credit. Encourage and help subsidize adoptions.

Retirement plans (IRA, 401(k), etc.). Create means to save and encourage retirement planning.

Hope and Lifetime Learning credits. Encourage students to attend higher educational institutions by subsidizing a part of the cost.

Economic

Section 179. Allows for an immediate write-off of an asset, rather than depreciating it over a period of time. This allows a company to recoup its investment faster.

The "S" election. Allows small corporations to avoid double taxation.

Political

Tax incentives for farmers. Special income averaging and depreciation methods for the farming industry.

Oil and gas exploration. Expense drilling and development costs immediately, rather than capitalizing and amortizing over a period of time.

Other

Dividend received deduction (DRD). Grants relief to corporations from triple taxation of income and dividends.

Like-kind exchange. Allows for the deferral of tax on capital gain transactions that occur from trading property and not receiving cash.

Natural disasters. Usually involve charitable contribution incentives for donations to charities. Often adjust tax-filing dates to assist and encourage compliance. Examples are 9/11 and Hurricane Katrina.

BACKGROUND

During the thriving 1990s, business in the United States was growing at unprecedented levels, breaking many corporate earning records. Between 1988 and 1998, corporate revenues grew 127 percent, from $292.5 billion to $666.4 billion. The surge also had a positive impact on the U.S. Treasury. Throughout this time period, reported corporate taxable income increased by 99 percent, or from $94.5 billion to $188.7 billion (Crenshaw 1999). So why did corporate taxes not keep pace with corporate revenues? Experts say that this was due to the emergence of complicated tax shelter plans.

HOW DID THE TAX SHELTER INDUSTRY START?

In the 1990s, during a period of startling corporate growth, it became a strategy of tax departments in many large companies to find solutions to lower the tax liability that would be due on substantial taxable income. Managers aggressively reviewed their budgets for ways to lower cost, and no expense was bypassed. It seemed logical that if all expenses listed on an income statement were fair game, then tax expense would eventually become a focus for cost-conscious managers.

The industry was not started by the invention of tax shelters; corporate managers did not seek out accountants' and lawyers' advice on how to shelter income, but the industry really started with accounting and law firms creating tax shelter plans and promoting them to their high net worth individuals and corporations with substantial taxable income. It was during this time period that many companies' best tax professionals were recruited by large accounting firms for their technical expertise.

The incentive was the ability to earn higher incomes by designing and marketing these tax shelter plans (Rostain 2006). There were penalties in place, 20 percent of money received for implementing the tax shelter, but many firms had feasibility studies performed which proved that the profits created far exceeded the penalties that could be incurred. These marketed tax shelters would create sizeable tax write-offs and, consequently, bring in substantial fees for their implementation. It may cost $200,000 to purchase the services required to set up and execute these schemes, but if they save the company $2 million in taxes, it is worth the expense.

During the 1990s, a peculiar situation developed where, by strict application of the IRC, tax professionals were able to create paper losses that a corporation would be able to use to offset income. This strange phenomenon caught the eye of the IRS in the late 1990s as they began discover the flourishing industry of marketed tax planning packages that enabled corporations to lower their total taxable income and, ultimately, pay less in taxes. In 1999, Stanford law professor Joseph Bankman projected the cost to the U.S. Treasury to be at $10 billion (Stratton 1999). It is reasonable to expect the current cost to have grown greater since that time.

Total corporate taxes paid as a percentage of the entire amount of taxes collected by the IRS have fallen significantly over the past two decades as corporations have found and exploited loopholes in the IRC. These loopholes allow them to reduce their total tax bill, usually by concealing revenues or accumulating additional expenses. For example, a corporation is taxed on its net income, which is generally calculated by taking total revenues received less total expenses incurred to generate the income. By lowering revenues or amassing additional expenses, you can lower your net income and, effectively, your total tax due. These loopholes manipulate the IRC in ways that were never intended by Congress. Tax sheltering methods can be legitimate or illegitimate. Naturally, there are two sides to this debate. On one hand, if a given transaction follows the letter of the law, then how can it be considered abusive or unethical? Conversely, it is justifiable to deem transactions that contain no economic gain, aside from lowering an entity's tax liability, as fraudulent tax reporting.

WHAT IS A TAX SHELTER?

There is no clear definition that characterizes all tax shelters. The purpose of a tax shelter is "to reduce or eliminate the tax liability for the tax shelter user" (Committee on Governmental Affairs 2005, 1). The definition of a tax shelter would include both legitimate and illegitimate actions. The controversy centers on what is considered tax planning and what is considered abusive tax sheltering.

There are many instances written into the IRC that allow a company to structure a transaction that will reduce the tax liability of the organization. It is reasonable for a person to plan his affairs so as to achieve the lowest tax liability. Judge Learned Hand is cited as saying, "There is not even a patriotic duty to increase one's taxes" (*Gregory v. Helvering*, 1934). It is reasonable to believe that if these taxpayers follow the IRC, they should be rewarded for their proper planning and work. For years, tax minimization tactics have been used and have afforded taxpayers the ability to properly plan transactions to achieve the least tax consequences. However, it should be noted that these minimization tactics have been done using acceptable, practical procedures. The argument next focuses on whether these transactions ordinarily contain substance and motivation on some economic level to justify performing the transaction.

Abusive tax shelters can be categorized as financial mechanisms with the sole purpose of creating losses to deduct for tax purposes (Smith 2004). These complex transactions produce significant tax benefits in ways that were never intended by the tax code. These benefits were never expected by the underlying tax logic in effect and, in essence, are transactions used only to avoid or evade tax liability.

Since there is no firm differentiation between legitimate and illegitimate tax planning, it is hard to tell where the line is. A working definition of an abusive tax shelter is a "corporate transaction involving energetic paper shuffling aimed at having favorable tax consequences along with no, or next to no, economic consequences other than the tax consequences" (Shaviro 2004, 11). The purpose of these types of transactions is to create transactions that will generate tax losses that can be offset against other taxable income. There is no economic sense to these transactions, except to generate these losses and reduce the total tax liability.

At its core, the IRS is the agency exclusively responsible for detecting any transaction with the sole purpose of eliminating or avoiding taxes. The IRS, through audits of filed returns, and the U.S. Treasury have begun to spot and publish legal regulations on transactions they consider abusive. These mandates warn taxpayers that use of such listed transactions may lead to an audit and assessment of back taxes, interest, and penalties for using an illegal tax shelter.

The IRS requires that under certain circumstances, certain transactions be reported and disclosed to the IRS as potentially illegal tax shelter transactions. A listed transaction is a transaction that the IRS has determined to have a potential for tax avoidance or evasion. In addition, transactions that are similar in their purpose to the listed transactions require similar disclosure. The IRS uses several distinctive judicial doctrines to determine if a transaction is legitimate or abusive in nature.

WHY TAX SHELTERS ARE HARMFUL

When enacting changes to the tax code, Congress is often directed by the concept of revenue neutrality. Revenue neutrality is the idea that new legislation will neither increase nor decrease the net revenues produced under existing laws and regulations. In other words, the total revenues raised after new tax laws are passed should be consistent with revenues generated under the prior tax laws. One taxpayer will experience a decrease in tax liability, however, at another taxpayer's expense.

When corporations engage in illegitimate tax sheltering schemes, they, in reality, steal from the U.S. Treasury. Over the years, billions of tax dollars have been lost. Recently, the IRS and Congress have taken a firm position with legislation to impede tax shelters that have been identified. It is estimated that legislation to prohibit certain shelter transactions, specifically lease-in lease-out shelters and liquidating real estate investment trust transactions, have saved taxpayers $10.2 and $34 billion, respectively (Summers 2000).

AN EXAMPLE OF A TAX SHELTER TRANSACTION

A corporate taxpayer agrees to purchase property from a foreign entity for $101 in exchange for $1 cash and a 10-year interest payment only loan of $100 at 10 percent. The corporation will be required to make annual payments of $10 on the loan for interest. Subsequently, the foreign entity leases the property back from the corporation to use during the period for $10 per year. At the end of the 10-year period, when the balance on the loan is due, the corporation will sell the asset back to the entity for $100, thus retiring the debt to the foreign entity.

What is the benefit of this transaction for the corporation? The $10 lease revenue received negates the $10 annual interest expense, allowing the corporation to operate this transaction without cost. In addition, they will receive additional depreciation expense over the 10 years they own the asset. Foreign assets that are used for these types of transactions typically involve governmental infrastructure, for example, water and sewer systems. These assets have no value to a U.S. corporation and would never be abandoned by the foreign government entities from which they are purchased. This is a good example of a transaction that has no economic purpose and is solely performed to reduce tax liability (Smith 2004).

It is important to note why transaction schemes like the aforementioned are difficult for the IRS to contest. The purchase of assets and claiming depreciation is allowable under the current IRC and is altogether different from not reporting income that is received from an individual's side business. It is more difficult to disallow a deduction that is in compliance with the tax code then to substantiate the omission of earned income as a violation of the IRC.

When corporate taxpayers do not pay their respective tax liabilities, the result is lower revenues for the U.S. Treasury, which ultimately causes or escalates a government's deficit. Congress, the U.S. Treasury, and individual U.S. taxpayers are dependent on corporations paying their fair share of the tax bill to maintain government operations. Shortages in tax revenues can make fiscal planning difficult when budgeted income falls short of what was anticipated and pledged for various governmental programs.

To maintain tax revenue collections, Congress has only a couple of options: raise corporate taxes or raise individual taxes. Buried deep in the corporate tax shelter controversy is their effect on individual taxpayers. A side effect of a corporation engaging in fraudulent tax practices is that the federal government redistributes the tax burden, ordinarily, back onto the remaining taxpayers, who would otherwise enjoy a tax reduction. To say it differently, the rest of the population picks up the tab for the use of abusive corporate tax shelters.

WHY TAX SHELTERS CAN BE BENEFICIAL

During the Reagan administration, President Reagan cut corporate tax rates as part of his monetary policy. The United States was a leader worldwide in lowering its tax burdens on corporations as a way to facilitate economic growth, and during the mid-1980s, the United States's tax rates were the lowest around the world. However, this started a sequence of events where many industrialized countries around the world began cutting their tax rates by an average of 30 percent in response, according to the Organization for Economic Co-operation and Development (OECD), a group of 30 countries that work to address economic and social issues.

Twenty years later, many counties around the globe have surpassed the United States in its tax-cutting policies. Federal and state corporate taxes average 39.3 percent, approximately 10 percentage points higher than the OECD average ("Let's Make a Deal" 2005). To look at it from a different angle, a corporation in the United States has Uncle Sam as more than a one-third shareholder.

Indeed, of the 30 wealthiest countries in the world, the United States now levies the highest corporate income tax rate on its businesses. In 1996, these 30 countries' average corporate tax rate was 38–30 percent in mid-2004. Overall, global corporate tax rates fell over 20 percent during this time period (Edwards 2004). Although U.S. individual tax rates decreased during this time period, corporate tax rates have remained unchanged.

Furthermore, the effects tax rates have on U.S. businesses go beyond cutting the tax piece of the profits out of a corporation's net income. The world has become a global marketplace, where executives and managers not only compete against their rivals next door, but on the other side of the world. Higher corporate tax rates place U.S. companies at a competitive disadvantage when compared to their foreign counterparts. Higher tax rates produce increased pressure to maintain or lower costs.

Imagine two identical corporations located in the United States and Ireland. Ireland's corporate tax rate is 12.5 percent. These two companies have the same gross sales and administrative costs and, with all other factors being the same, report the same net income. However, the corporation in Ireland is allowed to keep an additional 27.5 percent of its income in comparison to the one located in the United States (40 percent vs. 12.5 percent tax rates). This additional income can be used for additional research and development costs, higher employee wages, or greater dividend payouts for stockholders. To gain greater market share, the Irish corporation is better situated to compete on price and can still produce the same net income after taxes as the American with lower prices.

Having one of the highest tax rates in the world is self-defeating because it encourages American corporations to engage in questionable tax practices as a means of staying competitive globally. Many legal and accounting firms are hired primarily for the purpose of creating arrangements that enable the company to pay little or no tax. With real tax benefits achieved by moving operations to countries like the Cayman Islands, Bermuda, and other international tax havens, many CEOs and boards of directors feel that it is their duty to get involved with these practices.

SOLUTIONS TO ABUSIVE CORPORATE TAX SHELTERS

With high tax rates versus foreign competitors, a potential solution would be to lower the corporate tax rate imposed on U.S. corporations. If a primary reason to engage in questionable tax practices is to become more competitive versus global competition, a tax rate that is more in line with other similar industrial countries could alleviate the pressure that causes corporation managers to investigate these practices. A lower flat tax rate for all industries could not only benefit corporations, but also their employees, who would work for more competitive organizations. A result would be more jobs and job security. In addition, with the need for tax shelters removed, decreasing the use of phony transactions and bringing into the United States income that was held offshore would create a windfall of revenue for the U.S. Treasury.

When President Reagan first initiated corporate tax cuts as part of the Tax Reform Act of 1985, other countries responded by lowering their tax rates. It is reasonable to expect this same activity to occur again should the United States lower its corporate tax rates, but it probably cannot afford to lower them much more. Only a tax-free situation would ensure that corporations would not find motivation to investigate tax shelter activities.

Another option would be to require that a corporation's *book income* be equal to its *tax income*. Corporations are allowed to maintain two sets of books: book and tax. Book income is what is reported to shareholders, while tax income is what is reported to the IRS for taxation purposes. Many transactions deductible for book purposes are not deductible for tax and vice versa. An example of this is the depreciation expense. Differing methods are required to be used when computing depreciation expenses for book and tax purposes. Generally, tax depreciation allows you to write off the value of an asset much quicker than book. This generates a higher book income and a lower tax income. These types of differences occur quite frequently because book and tax income do not agree.

This encourages managers to perform transactions that show a lower tax income, and therefore a lower tax liability, while still reporting the higher book income to the shareholders. In other words, they are able to realize the best of both worlds. To remedy this problem, making tax income equal to book income would once again deter tax departments from creating loopholes in the tax code designed specifically to maintain book income but lower tax income.

CONCLUSION

Embedded in the IRC are numerous tax-planning possibilities for taxpayers. Many corporations have taken tax planning a step too far, infringing on what may be out of bounds in the field of tax planning. Arguments can be made on both sides of the debate as to why corporations should or should not engage in such activities, but the fundamental reason why abusive tax sheltering is detrimental is its redistribution of the tax burden. In addition, tax-sheltering methods should be considered abusive and rejected in their entirety when they offer a benefit that is inconsistent with the purpose of the tax code.

See also: Corporate Social Responsibility; Government Subsidies; Sarbanes-Oxley Act

References

Committee on Governmental Affairs. 2005. *The Role of Professional Firms in the U.S. Tax Shelter Industry.* Washington, DC: U.S. Government Printing Office.

Crenshaw, Albert B. 1999. "When Shelters Aren't Aboveboard: IRS, Hill Step Up Efforts As Improper Deals to Help Firms Cut Taxes Rise." *Washington Post* (November 23): E01.

Edwards, Chris. 2004. "Corporate Tax Tangle." *Washington Times* (July 11): B03.

Gregory v. Helvering, 69 F.2d 809, 810 (2nd Cir. 1934), aff'd, 293 U.S. 465 (1935).

Hoffman, William H., William A. Raabe, James E. Smith, and David M. Maloney. 2006. *West Federal Taxation: Corporations, Partnerships, Estates and Trusts.* 2006 ed. Belmont, CA: Thomson South-Western.

"Let's Make a Deal." 2005. *Wall Street Journal* (December 28): A14.

Rostain, Tanina. 2006. "Sheltering Lawyers: The Organized Tax Bar and the Tax Shelter Industry." *Yale Journal on Regulation* 23: 77.

Shaviro, Daniel N. 2004. *Corporate Tax Shelters in a Global Economy.* Washington, DC: AEI Press.

Smith, Hedrick. 2004. *Tax Me If You Can.* VHS. Boston: PBS. A Frontline coproduction with Hendrick Smith Productions.

Stratton, Sherly. 1999. "Treasury Responds to Critics of Corporate Tax Shelter Proposals." *Tax Notes* 84: 17.

Summers, Lawrence H. 2000. *Tackling the Growth of Corporate Tax Shelters.* Washington, DC: Office of Public Affairs, Department of the Treasury.

Further Reading: Shaviro, Daniel N. 2004. *Corporate Tax Shelters in a Global Economy.* Washington, DC: AEI Press; Sherman, Richard W., and Thomas M. Brinker Jr. 2006. "Tax Shelter Reporting Requirements: Am I My Brother's Keeper?" *Journal of International Taxation* 17: 38–47; Smith, Hedrik. 2004. *Tax Me If You Can.* VHS. Boston: PBS.

Keith C. Farrell

CREDIT CARD MARKETING TO COLLEGE STUDENTS

On college campuses, the term *credit* once exclusively referred to the number of credits or courses taken by students each semester; now it also refers to the use of revolving credit.

The increased access to and use of credit cards among college students is well documented. Most studies suggest that over 70 percent of college students possess an average of two credit cards and carry a median balance of $3,400 (Pinto et al. 2004; U.S. Congress 2002). Nellie Mae (2004) reports that 76 percent of undergraduates began the school year in 2004 with a credit card. Why are college students relying on credit? Is the new form of college credit a good thing?

There are different viewpoints on whether this use of credit is good or bad. Since most states allow 18-year-olds to obtain a credit card without parental consent or proof of employment, there is concern that students will come to campus and obtain a credit card for the first time with no guidance regarding the proper use or misuse of credit. This fact has been substantiated by many college students themselves, who believe that they do not have enough credit education to use credit properly (Norvilitis and Santa Maria 2002).

On the other hand, there are many positive benefits to using credit cards. In fact, credit cards are now negotiable instruments, more widely used than checks. When used properly, credit cards allow college students to establish credit, cover emergency expenses, and be financially independent.

Should students have access to credit cards? Are they setting themselves up for problems after graduating? Should students be protected from credit card marketers?

CREDIT CARDS AND COLLEGE STUDENTS: WHAT IS THE CONNECTION?

College students have grown up in a world of plastic. Since they were very young, these individuals have used plastic as a way of paying for products and services. During playtime as toddlers and young children, messages were sent to them by toy makers that plastic was a good way to buy things. For example, to be the winner of the once popular board game Mall Madness, little shoppers had to be the first to spend the most on their credit cards and make it back to the parking lot. Toddlers playing pretend grocery store pay for their purchases with a plastic card instead of cash.

Today, these young consumers are such heavy users of debit and credit cards that Visa USA has named them Generation Plastic, or Gen P (Associated Press 2006). According to Visa, paying with plastic via either debit or credit cards now accounts for 50.4 percent of spending among consumers 18–24 years old. An important distinction needs to be made between debit cards and credit cards. Debit cards allow users to withdraw money directly from a banking account and do not accumulate debt. Credit cards, however, are a type of revolving credit. They enable consumers to purchase goods and services now and pay for them later at some point in the future. Credit cards have scheduled monthly payments for bills owed and charge interest on balances that are not paid in full at the end of the month.

There has been a proliferation of credit cards in the United States, enabling consumers to constantly ratchet up their spending on goods and services. According to the Nielson Report, consumers used credit cards for $1.75 trillion in purchases in 2005 (Associated Press 2006). The American Bankers Association Education Foundation (2004) reports that four out of five American adults carry more than nine credit cards each, and the number of cards people carry is rising.

The growth of credit cards on college campuses is consistent with the general use of credit in society. What is alarming about this trend is that for most coeds today, debt has become a fact of life. Owing to the high price of college, the total amount of financial assistance provided to students has more than tripled since the early 1990s, and most of the increase can be attributed to student loans (Redd 2004). There has been a growing gap between the ticket price of a college education and a family's ability to foot the bill. On average, two out of every three college graduates face some form of conventional educational debt (e.g., federal student loans), seek expensive private loans, and/or turn to credit cards to finance their education (Schemo 2002). For students who take out loans, the average debt is estimated to be $19,202 (National Center for Education Statistics 2004). This highly leveraged situation has caused college-age consumers to be nicknamed Generation Debt. Anya Kamentz (2006, 1) reports in her recent book, *Generation Debt: Why Now Is a Terrible Time to Be Young*, that this generation is "starting their economic race 50 yards behind the starting line."

WHY ARE COLLEGE STUDENTS TARGETED BY CREDIT CARD MARKETERS?

College students are an untapped market for credit card companies. They are desired customers for three key reasons. First, they provide a consistent stream of revenue for credit card companies. Students often do not have a steady source of income. Many students rely on student loans to help finance their education. Therefore students often rely on credit cards to help pay their tuition, books, and living expenses. They often keep outstanding balances on their cards. Nellie Mae (2004) reported that the average outstanding balance on undergraduate credit cards was $2,169. Second, although most states allow 18-year-olds to obtain a credit card without parental consent or proof of employment, many students use their parents as unofficial guarantors and turn to them to step in and assist them with meeting their monthly payments. Third, while college students' brand loyalty is somewhat fickle, their loyalty to credit cards is stronger than most other products or services. In a recent study of current college students and postgrads, credit cards were the third highest category for brand loyalty (Hein 2003). On average, a student will retain a credit card for approximately 15 years. The popular press reports that two-thirds of all adults still possess the very first card they received.

UNDERGRADUATE STUDENTS AND CREDIT CARDS IN 2004

Summary Statistics

- Seventy-six percent of undergraduates in 2004 began the school year with credit cards. This is an 8 percent decrease from the 83 percent with cards reported in 2001.
- The average outstanding balance on undergraduate credit cards was $2,169, a reduction of 7 percent from 2001, when the average balance was $2,327, and the lowest average balance reported since 1998.
- More than half of undergraduates with credit cards carried balances lower than $1,000.
- Undergraduates reported freshman year as the most prevalent time for obtaining credit cards, with 56 percent reporting having obtained their first card at the age of 18.
- As students progress through school, credit card usage swells. Ninety-one percent of final year students have a credit card, compared to 42 percent of freshmen. Fifty-six percent of final year students carry four or more cards, while only 15 percent of freshmen carry that many. Final year students carry an average balance of $2,864, while freshmen carry an average balance of $1,585.
- Undergraduates reported direct mail solicitation as the primary source for selecting a credit card vendor; the second most common source was referral from parents.
- Seventy-four percent of undergraduates reported using credit cards for school supplies (paper, notebooks, etc.), the number one reported use of cards; the second most common usage of credit cards reported by undergraduates was a tie between textbooks and food, with 71 percent reporting these as charged expenses. Slightly less than 24 percent reported using credit cards for tuition.
- Twenty-one percent of undergraduates with credit cards reported that they pay off all cards each month; 44 percent say that they make more than the minimum payment but generally carry forward a balance; 11 percent say that they make less than the minimum required payment each month.
- Students estimating their outstanding credit card balances in a survey reported lower average balances than the average credit card balance outstanding at the credit bureaus.
- Students from the Northeast had the lowest outstanding average balances, while students from the Midwest had the highest balances.

Source: Nellie Mae, *Undergraduate Students and Credit Cards in 2004: An Analysis of Usage Rates and Trends* (Braintree, MA: Nellie Mae, 2005). Available at: http://www.nelliemae.com/library/research_12.html.

ARE CREDIT CARDS A GOOD THING FOR YOUNG PEOPLE?

As Steve Bucci (2006, 11) states in Credit Repair Kit for Dummies, "Good credit. Bad credit. Damaged credit. Repaired credit. No matter how you define it, credit is a big part of your life. Got a credit card? No doubt, more than one."

Credit cards have become part of the mainstream of college life. And make no mistake about it: credit is not a bad thing. It is an unavoidable part of life, but the important thing is how it is used.

There are many good reasons for a student to have a credit card. First, credit cards gives protection on purchases. Customers can stop payment on a credit card account for unsatisfactory receipt of products or services. Second, credit cards allow customers to shop online. College students and their entire age group do shop more via the Internet than any other generational group. Third, credit cards help students establish a credit history and keep a good credit rating. A good credit history is important after graduation, when graduates attempt to rent apartments, buy cars, apply to graduate schools, and so on. It is important to remember that credit follows an individual into the future. Employers often review credit reports prior to hiring an employee. In addition, credit reports are consulted when evaluating employees for promotion, reassignment, or retention. Problems with credit cards, such as late or missed payments, stay on one's credit report for seven years. Finally, credit cards provide some security in the case of an emergency. They provide a financial cushion to students who may be short on cash in the event of problems associated with housing, transportation, and so on.

But there is a downside to using credit cards, and young people need to be well equipped to deal with the realities of using credit cards. First, students must beware of the temptations created by credit cards. Our roadways and TV screens are plastered with slogans such as "buy now, pay later." These promotions feed directly into our American consumerism and materialistic attitudes. It is well documented that consumers tend to spend more money when using plastic. Students must realize that credit is not free money. They must remember that credit cards provide the opportunity to obtain something now that must be paid for in the future

---

TRUE COST OF ONLY MAKING THE MINIMUM PAYMENT

Consider this situation:

You are short on cash and charge your gas, snacks, and entertainment on your credit card for three months. After charging $60.00 a week for three months, you owe $720 on your credit card. Now assume that you never use this card again (you actually cut up the card). Your card offers 18 percent interest. How long will it take you to pay off the balance if you *only pay the minimum payment every month* (which is approximately 4 percent of your balance)?

If you only pay the minimum payment each month, it will take you 74 months to be rid of your debt. And remember, that is if you *never* charge another dime on your card. Over that time period, you will pay $347.66 in interest on your initial loan of $720. The total amount of money paid back to the credit card company will be $1,067.66.

For more information, see http://www.bankrate.com/brm/calc/minpayment.asp.

COMMENTS FROM COLLEGE STUDENTS IN A FOCUS GROUP ABOUT THEIR USE OF CREDIT CARDS

- "I have had to learn the hard way about credit."
- "I'll never be able to pay off my credit card bills!"
- "I have no choice, with the cost of college—I have had to use my credit card to help pay for my tuition and books. Now I am in over my head."
- "I better get a good job when I graduate—if not, wow, I am in big trouble!"
- "I know I am in over my head but I just can't resist things—like at the mall."
- "I try to be good—but then I get carried away. It is just so much easier than carrying cash."
- "I am not worried about my bills. My mom and dad always help me out if I get in trouble."
- "It is so easy to get a credit card. We get offers all the time, in the mail or over the phone. At the mall. Even on campus. All the giveaways. They are everywhere. I know kids that even fake their name just to get the stuff."
- "I know my card is just supposed to be for emergencies. That is what my parents told me. I am always using it for other things. I am always so short on cash."

Source: P. M. Mansfield and M. B. Pinto, "Protecting College Students from Credit Card Marketers: Is Legislation Effective?" (working paper, Penn State–Erie, Sam and Irene Black School of Business, 2006).

As recommended by the College Board (n.d.), students should take charge of their cards. Make no mistake about it: credit cards are really high-interest loans. It is important to understand all the fine print associated with credit cards. What is a finance charge? What is an annual fee? What is a cash advance fee? What is a late payment fee? Most people are not aware that if one misses a payment on one credit card, other credit card companies may raise one's interest rates. Carrying a monthly balance can be (and most often is) very costly: not paying the entire balance on a monthly credit card bill will result in interest charges being applied to the account. Finally, debt causes anxiety. Users often think about what they owe and worry about paying off the debt. The media has reported the horror stories of students who have so much credit card debt that they have turned to suicide to solve the problems they face. Young people need to be well equipped to deal with the realities of using credit cards.

DO WE NEED TO PROTECT STUDENTS FROM CREDIT CARD MARKETERS?

Credit card companies aggressively market college students with unsolicited offers both on and off campus. Walk onto any college campus and you will see flyers handed out in bookstores, bulletin board advertisements, tables set up in student unions, and even affiliations with on-campus groups such as fraternities or alumni groups. Some higher education administrators, legislators, and consumer advocates believe that credit card marketers need to be banned from college campuses. Unfortunately, college students are solicited by credit companies off campus, too.

Where do students acquire most of their credit card offers? Industry reports state that for the overall U.S. population, there were approximately 4.29 billion direct mail credit card offers mailed in 2003, an average of 40.2 per household per year (Albergotti 2003). Sixty-nine percent of households received 4.8 solicitations monthly, and 90 percent of the direct mail offers came from the top 10 credit card issuers ("Behind" 2004; "Lesson" 2004). According to a recent study by Mansfield and Pinto (2006), college students acquire 32.9 percent of their credit card offers through direct mail (see Table C.3).

If it is true that students receive most of their credit card offers through direct mail, then why all the fuss about banning solicitation on college campuses? Some people believe that the easy access to credit cards on campuses has created a nightmare for college students who find themselves heavily in debt and struggling to meet their minimum monthly payments while attempting to maintain full-time course loads. The problem is that students simply have too many alternative avenues to acquire cards. As evident from Table C.3, students acquire cards from multiple sources.

In their research, Mansfield and Pinto (2006) found no significant differences in card sources between schools that allowed on-campus solicitation and those that did not. So if banning credit card solicitations on campus does not affect students' ability to acquire or use credit cards, then what must be done?

SUMMARY

We live in a society fueled by consumer spending, where customers place a great deal of importance on what is fast, easy, and convenient. We prefer a pay-at-the-pump type of lifestyle. The use of plastic to make purchases is a normal part of everyday life.

Table C.3

Source of card*	
Parents gave it to me	17.7%
Internet offer	8.9%
Direct mail offer	32.9%
TV offer	0.0%
Campus bulletin board	0.8%
Campus bookstore insert	1.6%
Booth/table on campus	2.4%
Telemarketing offer	1.5%
Retail store	19.1%
Bank	8.6%
Other	6.3%

*Total number of credit cards reported on in study = 1,562.

Therefore it is critical for today's youth to get smart about money and learn basic personal finance principles. In 1995, Jump$tart Coalition for Personal Financial Literacy determined that the average high school graduate lacked a basic understanding of the principles involved with earning, spending, saving, and investing. Now, 10 years later, youth are no better off. According to Lewis Mandell, professor of finance and managerial economics at SUNY Buffalo School of Management, "Despite the attention now paid to the lack of financial literacy, the problem is not about to resolve itself any time soon" (Jump$tart 2006).

The bottom line is education. Parents play the most important role in shaping a child's and/or adolescent's financial habits and values. Most children say that they learned the most about how to manage money from their parents. Are parents effective educators of financial literacy? Unfortunately, many parents also live by the "see, want, borrow, buy" motto!

Schools, like parents, also educate children about consumption-related activities. Starting at the elementary school level, educational institutions also can play a very important role in improving the financial literacy of youth. These institutions need to reassess the financial education programs provided to students. Financial education should be considered an integral part of the No Child Left Behind movement in the public school system, making sure that children have not only the academic skills to succeed in life, but also the necessary financial skills.

See also: Blogs; Marketing of Alcohol and Tobacco; Marketing to Children; Marketing to Women and Girls

References

Albergotti, R. 2003. "Fewer Credit-Card Solicitations Are in the Mail." *Wall Street Journal* (November 5, eastern edition): D2.

American Bankers Association Education Foundation. 2004. Available at: http://www.aba.com/Consumer+Connection/CNC_aboutef.htm.

Associated Press. 2006. *Young Consumers Leading the Charge: "Generation Plastic" Reaches Increasingly for Credit, Debit Cards.* Available at http://www.msnbc.msn.com/id/10826914. Accessed June 4, 2006.

"Behind 2003's Direct-Mail Numbers." 2004. *Credit Card Management* (April 1): 20.

Bucci, Steve. 2006. *Credit Repair Kit for Dummies.* Hoboken, NJ: John Wiley.

College Board. n.d. *Credit Card Smarts: Take Charge of Your Cards.* Available at: http://www.collegeboard.com/student/plan/college-success/9139.html. Accessed June 4, 2006.

Hein, Kenneth. 2003. "Marketers Pull an 'F' in the Knowledge of College." *Brandweek* 44(44): 14–15.

Jump$tart. 2006. "Financial Literacy Shows Slight Improvement among Nation's High School Students: Jump$tart Survey Reveals Modest Gain." News release (April 5). Available at: http://www.jumpstart.org/fileuptemp/2006GeneralReleaseFinal%202.doc. Accessed June 4, 2006.

Kamentz, Anya. 2006. *Generation Debt: Why Now Is a Terrible Time to Be Young.* New York: Riverhead Books.

"A Lesson in Student Finance." 2004. *Credit Card Management* (September 1): 8–10.

Mansfield, P. M., and M. B. Pinto. 2007. "Marketing Credit Cards to College Students: Will Legislation Protect them from Excessive Debt?" *Marketing Management Journal* 17(1):112–122.

National Center for Education Statistics. 2004. "Debt Burden of College Students." Available at: http://nces.ed.gov.

Nellie Mae. 2004. *Undergraduate Students and Credit Cards in 2004: An Analysis of Usage Rates and Trends.* Available at http://www.nelliemae.com/library/research_12.html. Accessed September 19, 2005.

Norvilitis, J. M., and P. Santa Maria. 2002. "Credit Card Debt on College Campuses: Causes, Consequences, and Solutions." *College Student Journal* 36: 356–63.

Pinto, M. B., P. M. Mansfield, and D. H. Parente. 2004. "Relationship of Credit Attitude and Debt to Self-Esteem and Locus of Control in College-Age Consumers." *Psychological Reports* 94: 1405–18.

Redd, K. E. 2004. "Lots of Money, Limited Options: College Choice and Student Financial Aid." *Journal of Student Financial Aid* 34(3): 29–39.

Schemo, D. J. 2002. "More Graduates Mired in Debt, Survey Finds." *New York Times* (March 8): A18.

U.S. Congress. Senate. Committee on Banking, Housing, and Urban Affairs. 2002. *The Importance of Financial Literacy among College Students (2002).* 170th Cong., 2d sess. Washington, DC.

Further Reading: Kamentz, Anya. 2006. *Generation Debt: Why Now Is a Terrible Time to Be Young.* New York: Riverhead Books; Manning, Robert D. 2000. *Credit Card Nation.* New York: Perseus Books.

Mary Beth Pinto

D

DEFICITS

When conversation turns to the economy, one of the most popular topics of discussion is the government deficit. Newspaper columnists, TV pundits, and, of course, politicians never tire of talking about the size of the deficit and what it means for the economy. Big deficits are considered bad—except that back in the 1950s and 1960s, they often were considered good. Big deficits depress the economy because they drive up interest rates—except that back in the 1950s and 1960s, the usual argument was that deficits stimulated the economy by encouraging people to spend more. So which is it: are deficits good or bad? Do they depress or stimulate the economy? To answer those questions, we have to answer a more fundamental question: exactly what is the government deficit? Once we know that, we can proceed to the more interesting questions of how deficits affect the economy and whether they are good or bad.

DEBT AND DEFICITS: WHAT ARE THEY?

The deficit is the addition to the outstanding stock of government debt, so to understand what the deficit is, we first have to understand what government debt is. The government undertakes many activities, from national defense to providing medical insurance. To pay for them, the government usually collects taxes. Sometimes, though, the government prefers to postpone collecting part of the taxes it needs and instead borrows funds by selling government bonds to the public. Those bonds, just like corporate bonds, represent a loan the government has taken out and eventually will repay. The person who buys a government bond hands over money to the government and in return gets a bond stating the amount of the loan (the principal, or face value, of the loan), the interest rate that will be paid on the loan, and the date when the principal will be repaid (the maturity date of the loan). The money paid to the government by the buyer of the bond is that person's loan to the government, and the bond is the contract stating the terms of the loan. The government debt is the total amount of bonds that the government has issued but not yet repaid.

TYPES OF GOVERNMENT DEBT

Governments issue several types of debt, which can be classified in various ways. One classification is by the type of government that issued the debt. In the United States, the main divisions are federal, state, and local debt; local debt can be divided further by type of locality, such as county or city.

A second classification of government debt is by maturity at the time of issue. When we talk about a 10-year bond or a 30-year bond, we are talking about the length of time between the date when the bond was first issued and the date on which the principal will be repaid. Federal debt is divided into three convenient maturity categories. Treasury *bills* have initial maturities of one year or less (three-month bills, year bills, etc.); treasury *notes* have initial maturities between 1 and 10 years; and treasury *bonds* have initial maturities longer than 10 years. State and local government securities generally are just called *bonds,* irrespective of the initial maturity. A *perpetuity* is a bond with an infinite maturity, which means that the principal is never repaid and interest payments are made forever. The British government once issued some perpetuities, calling them *consols.*

A third way of classifying government securities is by the source of the revenue to repay them. *General obligation bonds* will be repaid with revenue collected by taxing the public; *revenue bonds* will be repaid with revenue collected from specific user fees such as bridge or highway tolls. This way of classifying debt is used only for state and local debt.

Whenever current government expenditures exceed tax revenues, the government borrows the difference by selling new bonds to the public. In such a situation, the government budget is said to be in deficit. The amount of new debt issued in a given period of time (such as a calendar year) constitutes the deficit for that period. In contrast, when expenditures are less than tax revenues, the government budget is in surplus. At any time, the deficit is the negative of the surplus and vice versa.

HOW MUCH GOVERNMENT DEBT IS THERE?

At the end of 2005, there was about $7.9 trillion of federal debt outstanding. Of that, 42 percent ($3.3 trillion) was held by federal agencies and trust funds, which means that the government owed almost half the debt to itself. Such internal debt is only a bookkeeping device for tracking the flows of funds within the federal government. An accurate analogy would be a household in which one child borrowed money from a sibling. That kind of intrafamily debt has no bearing on the family's net indebtedness and is ignored by credit rating agencies, banks, credit card companies, and so forth. The situation with respect to intragovernment debt is exactly the same: as far as the economy is concerned, that debt does not exist. It has no implications at all for the economy or public welfare. Unfortunately, popular discussions of the debt frequently fail to distinguish between internal and external government debt and thus overstate the relevant number, which is the amount of federal debt held by private investors. At the end of 2005, that amount was about $4.6 trillion. State and local governments also issue debt, and they have about $2 trillion in outstanding debt, most of which was held by private investors. Thus the total amount of privately held government debt was about $6.6 trillion at the end of 2005.

As a fraction of the total size of the U.S. economy, called gross domestic product (GDP), government debt is not especially large by historical standards. GDP was about $12.5 trillion in 2005, nearly twice the size of the privately held government debt for the same year. In contrast, at the end of the Second World War, outstanding federal debt alone was slightly larger than GDP. So when people worry about the size of the debt, they often fail to put the current situation in historical context.

The foregoing numbers on the amount of outstanding government debt are the numbers one would see in the newspaper. They must be adjusted before they can be used to discuss the effect of debt on the economy.

The most important adjustment is for inflation. The nominal value of a bond is the price in dollars that it would fetch on the open market. The real value of that same bond is the number of units of output that it can buy. If DVD movies cost $20 each, then the real value of a $200 bond is 10 DVD movies. In other words, if you sell your bond, you will receive in return enough cash to buy 10 DVDs. If, however, the prices of all goods double, so that DVDs now cost $40 each, then the bond's cash value now buys only five DVDs. The bond's nominal value is unchanged by inflation and remains at $200. Its real value, however, is changed. Real values are what matter because what people care about is how many goods their paper assets can buy. That is precisely what the real value of a bond measures. Adjusting official debt and deficit figures for inflation can change the measurement of the debt's size by a substantial amount. In 1947, for example, official federal government statistics reported a surplus of $6.6 billion. However, inflation that year was almost 15 percent. That inflation reduced the value of outstanding debt by about $11.4 billion. That reduction was equivalent to an additional surplus because it reduced the real value of what the federal government owed its creditors. The true surplus, therefore, was about $18 billion, nearly three times as high as the official figure. Another example is the decade of the 1970s, during which the official numbers showed a federal deficit every year, but the inflation-corrected numbers indicated a real budget surplus in exactly half those years.

Another adjustment is for changes in interest rates. The value of outstanding debt changes as market interest rates change. To see what is involved, suppose that you buy a one-year $10,000 treasury bill (equivalently, you make a loan of $10,000 to the federal government) at 10:00 a.m. The bond carries an interest rate of 10 percent, which means that you will be paid $1,000 in interest when the bond matures one year from now. At 11:00 a.m., the Federal Reserve announces a change in monetary policy that causes one-year interest rates to fall to 9 percent. Your bond now is worth more than when you bought it an hour ago because you could now sell the bond to someone else for more than $10,000. The reason is that anyone who wants to lend $10,000 for one year now will find that new bonds pay only 9 percent, meaning an interest payment in one year of $900. Your old bond, however, has a 10 percent rate locked in and will pay $1,000 interest for sure. That makes your bond's sales value higher than its stated value of $10,000. These kinds of changes happen continually, day in and day out. As a result, the market value of the outstanding government debt fluctuates from day to day, even if there is no inflation, and even if the government issues no new debt and retires no outstanding debt. The sales, or market, value of outstanding debt will be greater than the stated, or official, value if interest rates have fallen on average since the debt was issued and will be smaller than the par value if rates have risen. The difference between official and market value of the outstanding debt is typically a few percentage points. Unfortunately, market values for the total outstanding government debt are not readily available. Governments do not report them, and newspaper reports rarely mention them.

THE ECONOMIC EFFECTS OF GOVERNMENT DEBT

To see how government debt may affect the economy, we need to understand how government debt affects the flow of net income to the people lending money to the government. When the government borrows, it promises to repay the lender. To make those repayments, the government ultimately will have to raise extra taxes, beyond what it needs to pay for its other activities. The economic effect of government debt depends heavily on how taxpayers perceive those future taxes. Perceptions are difficult to measure, and neither economists nor others understand exactly how people form their perceptions. As a result, economists still disagree on the economic effect of government debt.

A simple example will help illustrate the situation. Suppose the government buys $1 trillion worth of goods and services every year and pays for them entirely by collecting taxes. The government's budget is balanced because revenues equal expenditures. Suppose that the government decides to change the way it finances its expenditures but does not change the amount being spent. In the first year, the government reduces taxes by $100 billion and replaces the lost revenue by selling $100 billion worth of bonds that mature in one year and carry an interest rate of 10 percent a year. In the second year, the bonds mature, and the government pays the $100 billion principal and the $10 billion of interest. Taxes in the first year are $100 billion lower (the government is running deficit) but in the second year are $110 billion higher (the government is running a surplus). How does this rearrangement of the timing of tax collections affect people? In the first year, people give the same total amount of revenue to the government

WHAT DEBT IS THE RISKIEST?

There is an inconsistency in popular discussions of government debt compared to other types of debt. Corporations and households both issue debt (i.e., borrow money). Corporate debt outstanding was about $5.0 trillion in 2004 (as of this writing, the latest year for which figures are available), not much below the amount of privately held government debt. Household debt is even larger. In 2004, households' total credit market debt stood at $9.6 trillion, 50 percent larger than the privately held government debt.

Commentators regularly express concern that government debt represents a risk to the economy, once in a while express similar concerns about household debt, and virtually never even mention corporate debt. In fact, household and corporate debt can represent an economic risk in some rather rare circumstances, but government debt virtually never represents such a risk. In a deep recession, debtors may become unable to repay their debts and be forced to default on them. That, in turn, can make financial institutions insolvent and lead to a collapse of the financial system. Such a mechanism seems to have been the reason the recession of 1929 became the Great Depression of 1932. Deflation made existing debt increasingly costly to repay, leading to widespread defaults on debt.

The banking system came under great pressure and eventually collapsed with the banking panic of 1932. This sort of thing happened from time to time up through the Great Depression but has not happened since, largely because of regulatory changes and an improved understanding by the Federal Reserve System of how to conduct monetary policy in the face of such circumstances. In contrast, default by any level of government in the United States has been exceedingly rare, and the federal government has never defaulted on its debt obligations.

as they did when they paid only taxes, but now $100 billion of the total payment is in the form of a loan that will be repaid in the second year, with an extra $10 billion in interest. On this account, people may feel richer because they seem to be paying less in total taxes over the two periods. This year, they pay $900 billion in taxes and $100 billion in loans for the same $1 trillion total that they were paying before the government decided to issue debt. Next year, however, it seems they will be better off than before. They will pay $1 trillion in taxes, but they will receive $110 billion in repayment of their first-year loan. Their net payment in the second year will be only $890 billion. This seems like a good deal, but unfortunately, it will not turn out that way. When the second year arrives, people will find that their net payment is $1 trillion, just as if the debt never had been issued. Why is that? To pay the $110 billion in principal and interest, the government must come up with an extra $110 billion in revenue, so it must raise taxes by that amount. Those extra taxes exactly cancel the payment of the principal and interest. The government gives with one hand and takes away with the other. The net result is that people do not really get back the $100 billion they lent the government or the $10 billion in interest on it, and the loan is equivalent to having paid the $100 billion in taxes in the first year. The same result holds from any maturity of debt, whether it is a 1-year bond, as in the previous example, a 10-year bond, or even a bond with an infinite life.

Note, by the way, that the government cannot beat the mathematics by refinancing old debt with new debt. If the government tried to repay existing debt, including the interest on it, by issuing new debt, the amount of debt would grow at the rate of interest. In our example, in the second year, the government owes $110 billion in principal and interest on the debt issued in the first year. The government could raise the revenue by issuing $110 billion in new debt. It then would have to pay $121 billion in principal and interest in the third year ($110 billion in principal and $11 billion in interest, assuming that the interest rate stays at 10 percent for simplicity). Thus the debt would grow by 10 percent every year that the government issued new debt to repay the old debt. The problem is that interest rates generally exceed the growth rate of the economy, so in finite time, the government would reach a point where it was issuing debt equal in value to the entire GDP of the economy. After that, it would not be able to issue any new debt because the government would be promising to repay more than could possibly be available to it, and the scheme would come to an end.

There are two major factors determining how government debt affects the economy. One is the kind of taxes the government uses to collect revenue, and the other is the way that people perceive the future taxes implied by current debt. It is easiest to start with people's perceptions in a simple case and then move on to the more complicated case that actually confronts us.

Suppose for a moment that taxes are very simple. In particular, suppose that the government uses what are called lump sum taxes to finance everything it does. A lump sum tax is one whose amount is independent of anything the taxpayer does. For example, he could draw a number out of a hat, and that would be his tax, irrespective of whether he was rich or poor. Actual taxes are more complicated, usually being based on income, consumption, or some form of wealth. The taxpayer has some influence over how much of those kinds of taxes he pays because he can control how much income, spending, and wealth he has. For the moment, though, concentrate on the simple, even if unrealistic, case of a lump sum tax. In that simple case, government debt is unlikely to have any significant effect on the economy. People generally try to estimate their future income, and of course, what they care about is their income after taxes. That means that in effect, they try to estimate their future taxes. As we have seen already, any government debt issued today implies extra taxes at some time in the future. If people are aware of that fact, then they will see that any reduction in today's taxes brought about by the government issuing new debt is going to be offset by more taxes in the future. Our example above showed that the offset is exact.

The question is whether people recognize at least approximately that the offset is exact. If they do, then bond finance is equivalent to tax finance, as our example above showed. In that case, government debt has no effect on anything important, a property known as Ricardian equivalence after David Ricardo, the economist who first discussed it. If people do not foresee all the future taxes implied by government debt, then they feel wealthier when the debt is issued but poorer in the future when, unexpectedly, they have to pay higher taxes to finance the principal and interest payments. They then are likely to increase their consumption spending today and perhaps work less today. In the future, when the inevitable taxes arrive, they will have to reduce their consumption spending and increase their work effort. So if people do not correctly perceive the future taxes implied by current debt, they will alter their economic behavior when debt is issued or retired and thus affect the economy.

The situation becomes more complicated when we extend our examination to include the fact that taxes are not lump sum. Taxes in the real world take some fraction of the tax base, which is the thing taxed: income for an income tax, consumption purchases for a sales tax, and so on. To keep the discussion simple, restrict the story to an income tax by supposing that that is the only kind of tax the government uses. (The principles are the same for other taxes, so nothing important is lost by this simplification.) The problem with taxes that are not lump sum, such as an income tax, is that they have positive marginal tax rates. The marginal tax rate is the fraction that you must pay in tax on the next dollar of income that you earn. A proportional income tax, for example, levies a fixed tax rate on your income, no matter how high or low your income is. If the marginal rate were 20 percent, then you would pay 20 cents on every dollar that you earn, whether you earn $10,000 or $10 million. Everybody would pay exactly 20 percent of his income in taxes. This is the so-called flat tax. Some state governments levy that kind of income tax. A graduated or progressive income tax is one whose tax rate rises with the income of the taxpayer. The federal income tax is that type of tax. Somebody earning $20,000 has a marginal tax rate of 15 percent, so if he earns another dollar, he will pay 15 cents of it to the federal government in tax. In contrast, someone earning $200,000 has a marginal rate of 35 percent and will pay in tax 35 cents of the next dollar he earns. For our purposes, it is sufficient to consider a proportional income tax, with the same marginal tax rate for everyone.

The important thing about marginal tax rates is that they affect people's economic behavior. People's choices depend on the tax rate they face. Think of someone trying to decide whether to work an extra hour. Suppose he earns $30 an hour. If there were no tax, then one more hour of work will earn him $30, pure and simple. If, in contrast, he is in the 15 percent tax bracket, he will get to keep only 85 percent of his extra $30 dollars, which is $25.50. The other $4.50 goes to the government as tax. Thus the effective return to working another hour is not the stated $30, but the after-tax earning of $25.50. It is less attractive to work an hour for $25.50 than for $30, so fewer people would end up deciding to work when there is a tax compared to when there is not. The same reasoning holds for investment. People will be less likely to make the next investment (e.g., buying a new machine for their machine shop) because the return on that investment is reduced by the tax.

So what does all this have to do with government debt? Remember that debt rearranges taxes over time. It therefore also rearranges the incentive effects associated with those taxes. For example, if the government reduces taxes today by issuing debt, in reality, the taxes it reduces will be income taxes, not lump sum taxes. Thus, by issuing debt, the government will reduce the disincentive effects of taxes today and increase them tomorrow. As a result, the government will affect the timing of people's economic decisions. The effects of rearranging disincentive effects over time get to be quite complicated, but the important thing for our discussion here is that precisely because debt does rearrange taxes and has disincentive effects over time, it has real effects on the economy. The situation becomes even more complicated if people cannot figure out exactly what the new timing will be after debt is issued. No one really knows when the government will collect the taxes to repay a new 30-year bond. It may decide to retire the bond early, or it may decide after 30 years to replace it with another bond, say, a five-year note, thus postponing the repayment by five years. In the face of such uncertainty, figuring out exactly what the incentive effects will be can become extremely complicated.

Unfortunately, there is no reliable way to discover people's expectations about taxes, so we have to use statistical methods to learn the effect of government debt on the economy. Even though economists have been studying this issue for more than 30 years, they have not yet reached a consensus. Statistical measures of the effect of debt on economic activity are straightforward in principle but difficult to carry out in practice. Overall, though, the evidence is that debt's effects are not strong. Some of the evidence even favors Ricardian equivalence (no effect of debt at all) as a close approximation. For example, Figure D.1 shows two plots. One is the federal deficit as a share of GDP, and the other is the real (inflation-adjusted) interest rate on three-month treasury bills. There is no obvious relation between the two series. The statistical correlation between them is a virtually nonexistent –4 percent.

A related issue is the desirability of deliberately using deficits to influence the path of the economy. If taxpayers fully anticipate and perceive the effects of

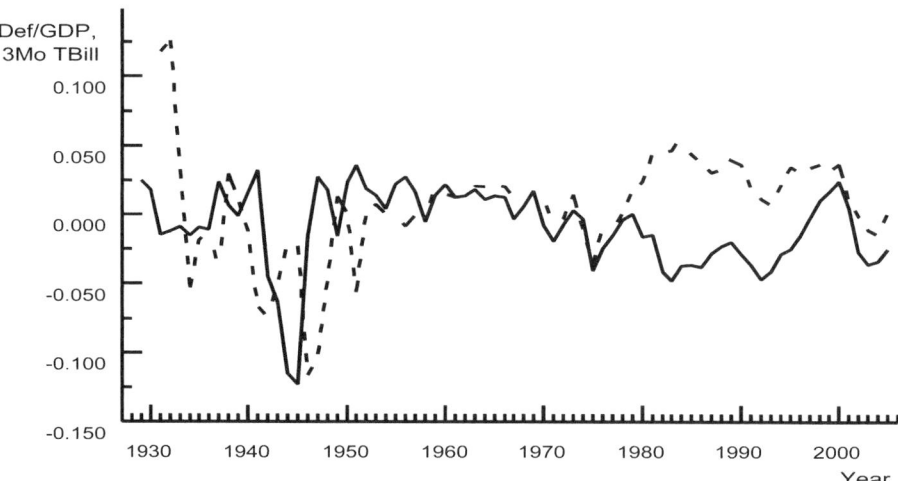

Figure D.1 Federal deficit to gross domestic product ratio and the real interest rate on three-month treasury bills.

Source: Congressional Budget Office, President's Council of Economic Advisers.

deficit and tax finance (Ricardian equivalence), no such thing can be done, of course, because deficits do not affect anything important. If taxpayers do not, though, deficits do have effects, as we have just seen. Therefore it might seem desirable to run up deficits in recessions to encourage people to spend more and run up surpluses in booms to restrain spending. The problem is that these seemingly desirable effects arise for undesirable reasons: the taxes distort choices, and on top of that, they fool people into thinking that they suddenly have become wealthier (and conversely for surpluses). Is it desirable to influence the path of the economy by using a policy that is effective because it deliberately misleads the public? Such a proposition seems difficult to justify. Another problem is that any desirable effects are accompanied by other effects that might not be deemed desirable. When equivalence is incomplete, changing the stock of debt outstanding also changes the interest rate in the same direction. In particular, running a deficit in a recession would raise interest rates, which would reduce investment and economic growth, which in turn would reduce output in the future. Thus using deficits to stimulate the economy now to ameliorate a recession comes at the cost of reducing output later. Whether that is a good exchange is not obvious and requires justification.

See also: The Dollar; Inflation; Interest Rates; Stock Market Predictions

John J. Seater

THE DOLLAR

To be generally accepted as money, a thing (gold, silver, beads, checks, or electronic impulses linked to a government or financial institution) must have three characteristics:

1. It must function as a unit of account; that is, people must be used to measuring or keeping score with it.
2. It must serve as a medium of exchange; that is, people must be willing to provide goods or services in trade for it.
3. It must be a store of value; that is, it must not be rendered worthless or nearly so in a short period of time.

In the early years of the United States, most money was gold or silver coins. This was also true in the rest of the world. Before 1914, it was not necessary to have a passport to travel between countries, nor was it necessary to exchange the money of your country for that of the one you were visiting, because your gold coins of a certain weight had exactly the same value as theirs did.

At the time of the creation of the Federal Reserve System, which occurred on December 23, 1913, when President Woodrow Wilson signed the Federal Reserve Act into law, about half of the broad money supply of the United States was currency in circulation: coins and bank notes. In 2006, the Federal Reserve reported that coins and currency accounted for only 10 percent of a broad measure of the money supply.

Thus is should be obvious from the huge drop in the share of coins and currency in the broad money supply that most of what we call money in the United States today is a deposit of some sort that can be accessed by writing a check or using electronic means. Checks have been declining as a way of accessing deposits as electronic banking has grown in popularity. Of course, analysts have been predicting the advent of the cashless, checkless society for over 40 years, and we are still a long way from that happening.

THE U.S. DOLLAR IN INTERNATIONAL TRANSACTIONS

Every three years since April 1989, the Bank for International Settlements (http://www.bis.org), which is known as the central bankers' central bank, conducts a survey of foreign exchange trading around the world. This is the single best source regarding the importance of the U.S. dollar internationally.

The final report on the April 2004 survey covered the data from 52 central banks and monetary authorities globally. It reported that average daily trading of international currencies was $1.9 trillion, a 57 percent increase from April 2001 measured at current exchange rates. The report showed that 89 percent of these trades had the U.S. dollar on one side. The euro was involved in 37 percent of trades, the Japanese yen was in 20 percent, and the British pound sterling was in 17 percent. The most common trading pair was the U.S. dollar and the euro, which accounted for 28 percent of global turnover. Next was the dollar–yen at 17 percent and then the dollar–sterling pair at 14 percent.

The most active trading center was the United Kingdom, where 31 percent of the total took place. Next came the United States at 19 percent, Japan at 8 percent, Singapore and Germany at 5 percent each, Hong Kong at 4 percent, and Australia and Switzerland at 3 percent each.

These trading volumes are staggering. As the total world economic output in 2004 was about $36 trillion, this means that the total value of the world's annual production was traded every 18 days. The U.S. economy produced $11.7 trillion in goods and services in 2004, so it took only six days to trade the total value of the U.S. economy.

Various types of so-called derivatives contracts have grown in volume far more rapidly than traditional foreign exchange trading. These contracts are based on the underlying values of the currencies involved or on interest rates for loans in these currencies, which is why they are called derivatives.

Daily trading in April 2004 in these instruments was $2.4 trillion, a 74 percent increase at current exchange rates. Interest rate derivatives were trading at an average daily $1.1 trillion pace, while exchange rate derivatives traded at a $1.3 trillion daily average. Most of this trading occurred in London or New York.

It is all designed to reduce risks, although many people worry that it may increase risk. The total net value of all the contracts in June 2004 was $221 trillion. That is more than five times total world output each year.

HOW THE VALUE OF THE U.S. DOLLAR HAS CHANGED SINCE 1971

From July 1 to 22, 1944, as World War II raged throughout Europe and the Asia-Pacific region, an intrepid group of representatives from 44 countries, led by the famous economists Lord John Maynard Keynes of the United Kingdom and Harry Dexter White from the U.S. Treasury, met in the United Nations Monetary and Financial Conference at the Mount Washington Hotel in Bretton Woods, New Hampshire. Out of these deliberations came the very important international institutions known today as the International Monetary Fund and the World Bank, which have their headquarters across the street from each other in Washington, D.C.

The delegates agreed on a system that would tie the value of all currencies of member countries to the U.S. dollar. The U.S. dollar was pegged to gold at a rate of one troy ounce of gold equal to $35. Thus most currencies were tied to the U.S. dollar, and no one worried a lot about its value. This system worked quite well until 1965 as the U.S. had low inflation, and so the dollar's value was changing very little. This was known as a period of stable foreign exchange rates.

The system began to unravel after 1965. U.S. inflation rates picked up as first President Johnson and then President Nixon tried to fight the Vietnam War and expand social programs at the same time. While no one has been able to devise a model to predict relative currency movements in the short to medium terms, virtually all economists and foreign exchange experts agree that over the long run, currencies move against each other based on their relative rates of inflation. A country's currency value declines if its inflation rate increases.

With higher U.S. inflation—meaning a lower value for the dollar—this meant that the free market price of gold rose well above $35 an ounce. While only foreign central banks could exchange dollars for gold at this official rate, many of them did so because, with the dollar's value lower, paying only $35 for an ounce of gold was a bargain.

Although there is no particular economic significance to how much gold the U.S. government owns, politicians became alarmed at the outflow of the precious metal by 1971. More significantly, President Nixon and his advisors were convinced that he would never be reelected because inflation, as measured by the consumer price index, was forecast to hit 4 percent, and the federal budget deficit was expected to exceed $20 billion. (How quaint those concerns appear now that we have learned the destructive impacts on the U.S. economy of 10 percent inflation in the late 1970s and early 1980s and survived federal budget deficits of $157–412 billion in the 2000s.) In any case, after a series of meetings with his top advisors at Camp David, Maryland, President Nixon went on national television and announced a package of wage and price controls in an effort to stem the rise in inflation. President Nixon also suspended the conversion of the dollar to gold.

It was 1973 before the dollar was again free to trade against the currencies of other countries. Figure D.2 shows what has happened to the international value

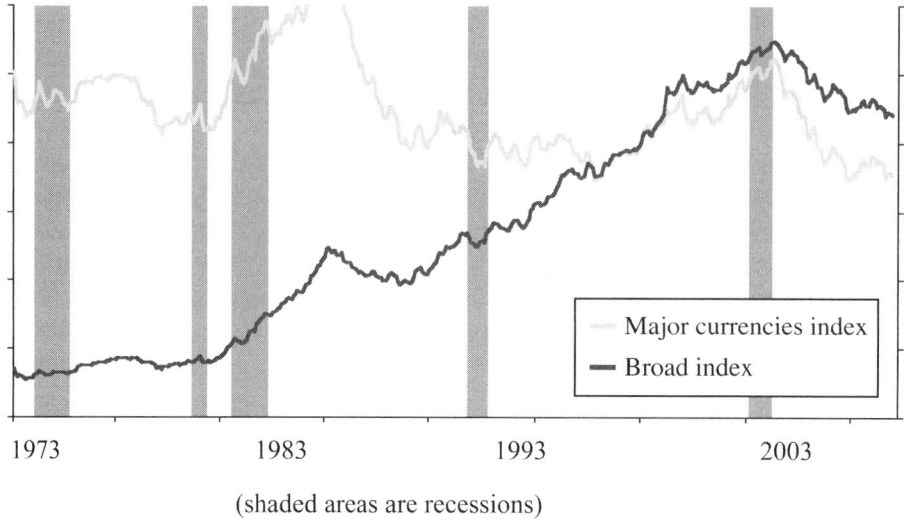

(shaded areas are recessions)

Figure D.2 Foreign exchange value of broad and major currencies with an index 1/1997 = 100.

of the dollar since the 1970s. Two measures, or indices, are used to gauge the movement of the dollar's value. Both indices are weighted by the share of the country or currency in U.S. exports and imports. The bigger the share a country has of U.S. exports and imports, the greater the weight of its currency in the equation. The weights are changed every year as new trade patterns emerge. These changes are made only once a year, unless there is a major revision of the trade flow data, which would necessitate another revision.

The major currencies index (green line) includes seven currencies that trade widely in currency markets outside their home countries. These are the Canadian dollar, euro, Japanese yen, British pound, Swiss franc, Australian dollar, and Swedish krona. The rationale behind the broad index (blue line) is to include every country that accounts for at least 0.5 percent of U.S. exports or imports. This adds 19 countries to the major currency index. They are China (by far the most important addition given its share of U.S. exports and imports), Mexico, South Korea, Taiwan, Hong Kong, Malaysia, Singapore, Brazil, Thailand, India, the Philippines, Israel, Indonesia, Russia, Saudi Arabia, Chile, Argentina, Colombia, and Venezuela.

The chart shows that against major currencies, the U.S. dollar shot up after the election of President Reagan (in 1980) to a peak in March 1985. The broad measure shows that the U.S. dollar appreciated quite substantially after 1985 and peaked at the end of the 2001 recession. Even today (2006), its value remains above 100 (107.9 on September 22, 2006).

THE PLAZA AGREEMENT AND THE LOUVRE ACCORD

Perhaps the most dramatic and, at least for a while, most successful coordinated international efforts to change and then maintain the foreign exchange value of the U.S. dollar were the Plaza Agreement and the Louvre Accord. Both occurred in President Reagan's second term and involved the same players.

As shown in Figure D.2, the dollar rose sharply in late 1984 and until March 1985. This was not too surprising as the U.S. economy in 1984 grew at its fastest pace (adjusted for inflation) since 1951, a huge 7.2 percent. With relatively low taxes and the strongest growth rate in the developed world, foreign investors rushed to buy dollars to invest in the United States.

But a higher-valued dollar hurt U.S. exports and made imports more attractive to U.S. consumers. So U.S.-based manufacturers and labor unions screamed to Congress for help. Treasury Secretary James A. Baker III and his aide, Deputy Secretary Richard G. Darman, organized a meeting of the G-5, the group of five countries (the United States, Japan, Germany, the United Kingdom, and France) with the largest economies at that time.

The meeting was held at the Plaza Hotel in New York City on Saturday, September 22, 1985. In attendance were Secretary Baker and his counterparts from the other four countries, along with the heads of the central banks of all five countries. Paul A. Volcker was the chairman of the Board of Governors of the Federal Reserve System at the time.

At the end of the meeting, the group issued a document that surprised financial market participants. They called for an "orderly" depreciation of the U.S. dollar. The German and French representatives agreed to tell the other members of the European monetary system (Italy and the Netherlands were the two largest ones) about the plan to sell U.S. dollars beginning on Monday, September 24. This was necessary because those other countries had to spend considerable amounts of money on the effort.

After the agreement, the dollar dropped quickly and sharply. This was viewed as a great success for the attendees at the Plaza meeting.

By early 1987, the same group decided that it was time to try to stabilize the dollar. At the time, the French Ministry of Finance was headquartered in a wing of the Louvre, the rest of which houses the world famous art museum.

They hosted a dinner at the Louvre on February 21, 1987, at which the 19 participants agreed to try to stabilize the foreign exchange value of the dollar. They finalized the Louvre Accord, as it is known, the next day and issued the G-6 Communiqué. Canada was the sixth country.

They had agreed on secret trading ranges for the U.S. dollar against the other five currencies. This worked reasonably well for a few months, but because it required the United States to keep interest rates on short-term loans among banks too high for domestic conditions and forced the other five countries to keep theirs too low for their domestic situations, the system was doomed to fail.

It cracked spectacularly with the huge global decline in stock markets on October 19, 1987. By then, Alan Greenspan had replaced Paul Volcker at the Federal Reserve, and he and his colleagues on the Federal Open Market Committee wasted no time cutting interest rates and promising banks and brokerage firms that the Federal Reserve would provide all the liquidity needed to prevent another episode like the Great Depression of 1929–1933. They succeeded admirably, and the U.S. economy barely wobbled, and stocks regained nearly all their losses by early 1988.

The Japanese were not so lucky. They had to keep interest rates too low for domestic conditions. This led to a bubble in stock prices and real estate values that peaked on December 31, 1989. Japanese stock prices and real estate values remain far below these levels, and it was 2007 before Japan finally shook off most of the effects of the collapse. That was a high price to pay.

The lesson is that trying to manage the foreign exchange value of a currency is easier tried than accomplished. Something has to be given up to keep a currency high or low, and when that something becomes too costly, the agreement can fall apart.

The lesson is that the U.S. dollar's value against foreign currencies does fluctuate over time. To say the dollar is weak or strong is to beg the question, compared to when? For example, the dollar's value in 2006 was not out of line with the range of its value in the past 30 years.

PRESSURES ON THE U.S. DOLLAR FROM TRADE FLOWS

The balance of payments for every country in the world is exactly the same, namely, zero. This is because of the iron rule of international accounting—in other words, it is a matter of definition. If we had all the data perfectly measured, then a country with a trading deficit on goods and services would have an exactly offsetting inflow of capital (investments) resulting in a capital surplus.

The current account balance is the value of goods and services a country exports minus the value of goods and services a country imports. An alternative way of thinking about it is that when it is negative, it measures how much of a country's investment is due to savings by foreigners, and when it is positive, it measures how much of a country's savings is invested abroad.

The U.S. current account has been in deficit for all but one quarter (the first quarter of 1991) since 1982. That anomaly was caused by the fact that the United States made a profit on the first Iraq war. The Germans, Japanese, Kuwaitis, Saudis, and others contributed so much to the U.S. defense budget that it exceeded our costs of driving Saddam Hussein's forces out of Kuwait.

The current account deficit was 6.6 percent of U.S. GDP in the second quarter of 2006, which is very high by both historical U.S. and international standards. Such a high deficit does two things. First—as mentioned previously—it motivates foreign holders of dollars eventually to invest those dollars in the United States by purchasing land, stocks, bonds, and U.S. companies and building factories in the United States. Second, with so many dollars being in the world economy, it puts downward pressure on the international value of the dollar. Indeed, notice from the chart that the dollar's international value was falling in the 2000s, just as the current account deficit was hitting record levels. A lower-valued dollar will actually help to trim the current account deficit by making U.S. exports to foreign countries cheaper and foreign imports to the United States more expensive.

HOW CHANGES IN THE FOREIGN EXCHANGE VALUE OF THE U.S. DOLLAR AFFECT YOU

The most obvious implications of a change in the value of the U.S. dollar are to people who travel abroad. For example, when the dollar rises against the euro, the traveler finds hotels and meals cheaper than before in all the countries that use the euro. As the euro has been relatively strong the past few years, more people have switched their travel plans to Mexico or places in the Caribbean, where currencies have depreciated against the dollar.

Business firms with international operations notice two things when the value of the dollar changes. As it goes down, they will find export demand growing, as goods and services produced in the United States will be cheaper than before. They will also find that profits earned in other countries whose currencies have appreciated are larger than before when translated into dollars.

Consumers will also notice price changes on imported goods. For example, a Volvo will become much more expensive if the Swedish krona appreciates against the dollar.

So changes in the international value of the dollar are more than a curiosity—they can affect both businesses' and consumers' wallets and pocketbooks.

See also: Chinese Currency; Foreign Direct Investment; Inflation; Interest Rates; Saving

Further Reading: Funabashi, Yoichi. 1989. *Managing the Dollar: From the Plaza to the Louvre.* 2nd ed. Washington, DC: Institute for International Economics; Loretan, Mico. 2005. "Indexes of the Foreign Exchange Value of the Dollar." *Federal Reserve Bulletin* 92 (Winter): 1–8.

James F. Smith

DOWNSIZING

From the early 1800s until the era of the New Deal legislation in the 1930s and the age of the industrial revolution, the U.S. workforce was focused on entrepreneurial spirit. The 1930s shifted the focus of employment from the individual business owner to large businesses. The New Deal legislation regulated the increasingly employer-dominated workforce. Business contracts between employers and employees became more formal, and employees had trust in their employers based on implied long-term commitments, insurance, workers' compensation, and pension plans. The consensus on organization size was that bigger is better. The focus on increased profits through growth continued through the prosperous postwar years, until the United States entered a period of financial turmoil. Faced with the oil embargo, the savings and loans debacle, and the crash of the stock market in 1987, organizations shifted focus from balancing stakeholder satisfaction to maximizing shareholder profits. New pressures from foreign low-cost competitors, mergers creating inefficient business clusters, new technologies replacing humans, and the creation of the European Union led large organizations to examine their management and compensation structures and ultimately led to the start of downsizing.

What is downsizing? What are the causes of downsizing? Who is affected by downsizing, and to what extent are different classes of employees affected? Is it a necessity for firms to lay off employees to stay ahead? Also, is downsizing ever good for the laid off employees? Leading economists believe that the media does not always portray the role of downsizing truthfully. Scientific studies show that there may be damaging results to employees spared from layoffs. Is downsizing bad economically, socially, and physically?

THE WHAT AND WHY OF DOWNSIZING

Downsizing refers to a "deliberate decision to reduce the work force that is intended to improve organizational performance" (Kozlowski 1993). During the 1980s and early 1990s, numerous large U.S. corporations announced their intention to implement both major restructuring (industrial change) and downsizing. The string of announcements abated during the prosperous late 1990s and into 2000 and returned again as the economy stalled in 2001.

The American Management Association International (1997) listed the following reasons that firms chose to downsize their workforce: firms chose to lay off employees in response to short-term business decline, to combat forecasted economic downturns, to lead to better staff utilization, to adapt to mergers, to adjust for automation and advancing technologies, and to source or transfer work abroad. Downsizing occurs because of (1) an intentional decision; (2) a reduction in personnel, often disproportionately in the management ranks; (3) efficiency and/or effectiveness objectives; and (4) changes in work processes. Again, the primary purpose of downsizing is to lower operating expenses by employee elimination to show a greater profit for the company.

Downsizing can be an effective tool if used correctly. However, firms must be careful to avoid sending the wrong messages to employees, clients, shareholders, and the media.

MYTHS ABOUT DOWNSIZING

Although there is a multitude of literature regarding layoffs both from an employer and employee perspective, there are still many untruths that circulate through the business world. We suggest that there are certain myths that create false impressions during a downsizing (Workforce Management 2002). In short, what you think you know about layoffs might hurt your business or put undue stress on you if you are an employee who is downsized. Here are the myths that they identify.

Myth 1: Jobs Are Secure at Firms That Are Doing Well Financially

As stated, corporate America has shifted focus from stakeholder satisfaction to shareholder maximization. This shifting focus means that not only sick firms downsize. Today, healthy companies are boosting earnings by reducing costs through fewer salary dollars. Large firms are no longer using layoffs as a reaction to economic downturns, they are using them to restructure for profit maximization.

Although large corporations are not alone in restructuring/downsizing efforts, small companies tend to retain employees longer. In these companies, there is substantial investment in training and developing employees as well as increased costs in recruiting and hiring replacements. Smaller corporations tend to protect their capital and human resource investments over a longer period and seek to maximize profits through other outlets.

Myth 2: Companies That Are Laying Off Workers Are Not Hiring New Ones

As firms use downsizing more to shape themselves for the future, instead of reacting to economic downturns, downsizing does not necessarily mean a net reduction in the workforce. Firms are often simultaneously firing and hiring to reduce slack and rehire new skills. As companies lose workers in one department, they are adding people with different skills in another. This flexibility is possible due to temporary and contract labor. Employers can cover vacant positions with little to no employment commitment to temporary workers, while inventorying their knowledge, skills, and abilities.

Myth 3: Downsizing Employees Boosts Profits

In a survey conducted by the Society for Human Resource Management and supported by the S&P 500, profitability does not necessarily follow downsizing. In only 32 percent of reported cases did firms who downsized indicate that the layoffs improved profits (Baumol et al. 2003). However, despite the mixed performance of downsizing, downsizing announcements led to increases in security prices: "stock price gains among [the ten top corporate downsizers] averaged over 130 percent from 1990 to 1995, as compared with only 86 percent for the S&P 500 companies overall" (Baumol et al. 2003) This perceived increase has powerful implications for corporations focused on maximizing shareholder interest.

Myth 4: Downsizing Employees Boosts Productivity

To increase net profits, companies in the past have leaned toward job elimination, with the theory being that fewer employees would cut payroll costs and force the remaining workers to work harder. However, the recent study on downsizing by the American Management Association showed that only one-third of the companies achieved both immediate and long-term cost reductions and profit increases by eliminating jobs. The rest (66%) showed no gain; some even showed a loss. Fewer than 40 percent boosted worker productivity by job elimination. The remaining 60 percent showed either no productivity gain or a productivity loss (Woodruff 1998).

Myth 5: Downsizing Employees Has No Effect on Quality

Many people overlook the reduction in quality resulting from the downsizing process. This reduction in quality is even more prevalent when firms do not take the proper steps to ensure a smooth transition period. Many senior employees leave due to application of early retirement incentives, which results in the loss of institutional memory. In combination with early retirement, voluntary workforce reductions (buyouts) result in the most marketable employees leaving, stripping valuable knowledge, skills, and abilities from the organization. In addition, early retirements and voluntary reductions lead to too many people quitting and to a staff shortage, creating deadlines that are impossible to meet.

Myth 6: There Are No Adverse Effects on Those Who Remain after Downsizing

It is common to believe that stress-related medical disorders are more likely for those laid off than for those who remain. Workers who remain employed at downsized companies are just as likely to suffer adverse health consequences.

Myth 7: The Costs of the Number of Employees Let Go Is the Total Cost of Downsizing

To evaluate the total cost of downsizing, both financial and nonfinancial factors must be taken into account. Managers must calculate the present value of all costs and benefits associated with the cuts, including severance packages, lower employee productivity due to talent loss, eventual rehiring expenses, and future rightsizing costs. The value created should exceed the effects of lower employee morale and the potential damage to the firm's reputation. In knowledge-based or relationship-based businesses, the most serious cost is the loss of employee contacts, business foregone, and lack of innovation.

Myth 8: Training Survivors during and Following Layoffs Is Not Necessary

Training survivors is critical to success following a layoff. To facilitate a successful downsizing project, managers must communicate to remaining employees, clients, shareholders, and the media the extent of, and the reasoning for, the downsizing. Additionally, take steps to ensure that remaining employees feel a sense of job security and have the training necessary to take on any new responsibilities resulting from the downsizing.

THE EMPLOYEE LEFT BEHIND

To understand the potential impact on remaining employees when an organization downsizes, let us first look at typical employee reactions. It is helpful to understand so-called survivor syndrome, or the behavior of those who remain in the organization after layoffs. Too many companies focus entirely on assisting those who are leaving the organization in finding new jobs, providing severance packages, and counseling for adjustment. It is the layoff survivors—those who stay in the organization—who need attention so that they can adjust and remain productive employees. Some major reactions to downsizing that can have significant negative impact on the organization include the following (Howard n.d.):

- *Reduced risk taking.* This usually takes the form of reluctance to take on new challenges or introduce new products or ideas and fear of proposing changes.
- *Lowered productivity.* Survivors tend to become consumed by seeking information and reassurance, rather than by productivity.
- *Thirst for information.* An unquenchable need for any type of information, whether formal communications or through the company grapevine, is shown.
- *Blaming others, usually management.* Everyone is looking for someone else to blame. It is the opposite reaction from a sense of empowerment, that is, someone else is in control, someone else is to blame. Typically, everyone looks up in the organization for faultfinding.
- *Justifying the need for a layoff.* To live with themselves, typically, a group of survivors tries to justify the layoff decision. These are generally the people who took part in the decision-making process—managers and human resource people.
- *Denial.* A common response is to deny the feelings of layoff survivors. It is particularly common among upper managers to deny the feelings of fear, insecurity, sadness, frustration, and so on, typical of the survivor syndrome.

So how, then, do firms minimize the effects of downsizing on employee morale?

THE REMAINING EMPLOYEES (MCKEE 2004)

If you are among the lucky employees who survived downsizing, studies show that you are twice as likely to die from heart disease. The increased risk of heart-related death is five times greater among people who do not lose their jobs for over four years following a major downsizing. The increased insecurity that results after downsizing, in combination with the increased workload and added pressure to produce higher-quality work, can trigger fatal cardiovascular disease. Those with preexisting cardiovascular disease are at highest threat and should avoid excessive and chronic stress. In addition to cardiovascular disease and hypertension, added workload in combination with feelings of loss of control in decision making may lead to panic attacks, ulcers, and assorted stomach ailments (e.g., acid reflux, irritable bowel syndrome, migraines, and depression). These ailments, which are often controlled by rest and medication, rage out of control as employees are afraid of being frequently absent because such behavior might be assumed to increase their likelihood of being laid off in the future. Studies show that these illnesses are most prevalent in workers older than 50 and can be as high as 14 times higher than in their younger coworkers.

IS DOWNSIZING A GOOD OR BAD STRATEGY?

Downsizing as a strategy to improve business has been practiced by U.S. companies since the early 1970s. Downsizing got its bad name in the late 1980s and 1990s, when it became synonymous with massive job cuts in recessionary times. Downsizing as a strategy got mixed up with the negative connotations and multiple definitions associated with downsizing. These definitions have even stumped researchers. The three main components of downsizing are as follows:

- Most companies that downsized had been financially underperforming (as compared to the industry average) prior to doing so.
- On average, downsizing did not improve financial performance (it went neither up nor down).
- There was a short-term gain in productivity, but this gain was not sustained beyond the first year.

Bad downsizers are those companies that use the tactic frequently for short-term cost reductions derived from culling the head count. Often, when they discover that desired results have not been achieved, they repeat the downsizing process without modifying it or examining why it did not succeed. This form of downsizing tends to be an unthinking reaction to a sudden drop in demand for services without any serious thought to the outcome or the objective. With an eye on the bottom line, those most likely to see the door first are male, middle-aged middle managers. Without the critical forethought, these organizations suddenly find themselves without the necessary knowledge or experience to weather the next phase.

Good downsizers are those organizations that shed staff usually as a one-off event and as part of a broad growth strategy. Good downsizers focus on a problem and a plan and a commitment to future growth. When a company's main reason for downsizing is cost cutting, and there is little in the way of strategic focus, there is no demonstrable improvement in financial performance. Those companies that use downsizing to improve productivity, improve marketing strategies, and improve corporate direction and as part of a broader strategy will show a significant upturn in financial performance.

THE RIGHT WAY TO DOWNSIZE

Corporations committed to downsizing assign management to downsizing committees. This is a tough job for anyone, but in order to properly determine how many employees to lay off, these committees are extremely important. Committees answer the following tough questions (Osterio Group n.d.):

- How many of our staff are retirement-eligible and are likely to take a buy-out option?
- What can we outsource to another company to remove the head count overhead costs from our income statement?
- What are the head count benchmarks for comparable functions in similar industries and companies?
- How do we share the pain across the board in light of the fact that some departments may need to be upsized while others must be downsized?
- Is it possible to have a temporary layoff, rather than a permanent one?

After answering these tough questions, and determining if downsizing is the correct course of action for their business, it is time to tell the employees. It is key to minimize the negative impact on your employees who will be displaced. Assist by providing services to help them find other employment. Secure counselors who can help employees work through the pain and fear of change. Provide good employees with professional letters of recommendation and referrals to other companies. Whenever possible, offer severance packages and/or extend health-care benefits so that the employees' families are cared for. Create support groups for employees where they can vent their frustrations, talk about their fears, and gain strength from others. Realize that the whole person's body, soul, and spirit are affected by such a traumatic change in life.

Also, once the decision has been made to downsize, communicate early and often with all affected people. Tell employees everything about the layoff that you possibly can, and allow them to ask questions. Honesty and empathy are keys to all communications. Acknowledge feelings of hurt, anger, fear, and frustration. Remember that the way you treat the employees who are laid off will speak volumes to those who will remain. If you are deceptive, underhanded, or cruel, you probably will not have to worry about another round of downsizing because the employees that survived the first round of layoffs will begin to look for other employment immediately.

Finally, after the downsizing has occurred, treat your remaining employees as if they are the most valuable resources that you have because that is precisely what they are. Realize that a 20 percent reduction in your workforce means a 20 percent increase in workload for those that remain. It is very likely that your employees' workloads were full to begin with, so be sensitive to potential problems with stress, burnout, and other negative impacts on employees and their families as overtime increases.

IBM RETRAINING TALENT (HAMM AND ANTE 2005)

IBM, once known for its employment for life policy, has undergone major downsizing and restructuring over the last two decades. Employees at technology companies have been hard hit by downsizing pressures as the reduced cost of labor in places like India, Pakistan, and China make outsourcing very attractive. IBM is helping to reduce the fears of these employees by establishing a multi-million-dollar worker retraining fund. The Human Capital Alliance fund will be made available to workers whose current positions are those most threatened by outsourcing. IBM is doing extensive analysis to determine demand in the short- and long-term future of on-demand computing to help train and place these threatened employees. IBM is not backing down from its plans to outsource job overseas; it has, however, made an effort to match the number of positions outsourced with staff in the United States. Although shareholders like what outsourcing does to a bottom line, corporations cannot ignore the public relations aspect of the outsourcing movement. IBM's public image was substantially damaged when it reduced its workforce by tens of thousands in a few short years; this move is trying to rebuild its reputation.

Downsizing is an unfortunate aspect of organizational life. When handled properly, you can maintain a reputation for being both professional and fair, secure employee commitment, and position yourself for growth when business picks up again in the future. If you have to downsize, do it right.

See also: Corporate Social Responsibility; Employee Loyalty and Engagement

References

American Management Association International. 1997. *1997 AMA Survey: Corporate Job Creation, Job Elimination, and Downsizing*. Available at: http://www.amanet.org. Accessed February 16, 1998.

Baumol, William J., Alan S. Blinder, and Edward N. Wolff. 2003. *Downsizing in America: Reality, Causes, and Consequences*. New York: Russell Sage Foundation.

Hamm, Steve, and Spencer E. Ante. 2005. "Beyond Blue." *Business Week* (April 18): 68.

Howard, Jennifer M. n.d. *Can Teams Survive Downsizing?* Available at: http://www.quality digest.com/may/downsize.html.

Kozlowski, S.J.W, G. T. Chao, E, M. Smith, and J. Hedlund. 1993. "Organizational Downsizing: Strategies, Interventions, and Research Implications." In *International Review of Industrial and Organizational Psychology*, ed. C. L. Cooper and I. T. Robertson. New York: John Wiley.

McKee, Maggie. 2004. *Downsizing Raises Risk of Death in Workers*. Available at: http://www.newscientist.com/article.ns?id=dn4706.

Osterio Group. n.d. *Downsizing Staff the Right Way*. Available at: http://www.osterio.com/downloads/downsizing.pdf.

Woodruff Imberman. 1998. "Using Incentive Plans to Boost Productivity in Manufacturing." *Journal of Management* 50: 80.

Workforce Management. 2002. *13 Myths and Facts about Downsizing: What You Think You Know about Layoffs Might Hurt Your Business*. Available at: http://www.workforce.com/archive/article/23/34/04.php.

Further Reading: Applebaum, Eileen, Annette Bernhardt, and Richard J. Murnane. 2003. *Low-Wage America: How Employers Are Reshaping Opportunity in the Workplace*. New York: Russell Sage Foundation; Atwood, Jane, Ethel Coke, Christine Cooper, and Kendra Loria. 1995. *Has Downsizing Gone Too Far? A Review of the History and Results of Downsizing*. Available at: http://www.iopsych.org/downsize.htm; Deal, Terrence E., and Allan A. Kennedy. 1999. *The New Corporate Cultures: Revitalizing the Workplace after Downsizing, Mergers and Reengineering*. New York: Perseus.

Dawn M. Slokan

DRUG (PRESCRIPTION) COSTS

Few issues have created such controversy as the rising cost of prescription medicine. News reports often quote examples of patients, especially seniors, who cannot afford their medications. The pharmaceutical industry and advocacy groups maintain very different positions as to why prescription drug costs are so high in the United States compared to other countries. This entry examines the costs and related issues, one at a time, from both the industry and consumer advocate perspectives.

RESEARCH AND DEVELOPMENT

Industry Standpoint

Pharmaceutical companies contend that searching for new drugs, or the next cure, can be a costly venture. Often, it may take hundreds and possibly thousands of concepts to create one drug that makes it to market. Cost estimates of researching both successes and failures range from $500 to $800 million. An estimate released in a study by economists at Tufts University stated that on average, it takes almost 15 years to bring a new drug compound to the market. Only 1 compound out of 5,000 ever makes it to market. Only 30 percent of drugs that make it to market will ever recoup their research and development costs (Clayton 2005). The cost and risk involved are very high. This is one way the industry justifies the high cost of medicine.

The U.S. Food and Drug Administration (FDA) maintains a strict and lengthy process to approve a medication for use. After filing a patent for a new compound, the drug manufacturer has approximately 20 years to research, receive FDA approval, and market the new drug. This process often leaves only five or six years to profit from the extensive research before generic manufacturers can challenge the patent. Therefore a company can be limited in the time it has to recover its investment.

DRUG REVIEW STEPS (U.S. FOOD AND DRUG ADMINISTRATION N.D.)

1. The sponsor holds preclinical (animal) testing.
2. An investigational new drug application outlines what the sponsor of a new drug proposes for human testing in clinical trials.
3. The sponsor holds phase 1 studies (typically involving 20–80 people).
4. The sponsor holds phase 2 studies (typically involving a few dozen to about 300 people).
5. The sponsor holds phase 3 studies (typically involving several hundred to about 3,000 people).
6. The pre–new drug application (NDA) period begins, just before a NDA is submitted. This is a common time for the FDA and drug sponsors to meet.
7. The submission of an NDA follows, which is the formal step asking the FDA to consider a drug for marketing approval.
8. After an NDA is received, the FDA has 60 days to decide whether to file it so it can be reviewed.
9. If the FDA files the NDA, an FDA review team is assigned to evaluate the sponsor's research on the drug's safety and effectiveness.
10. The FDA reviews information that goes on a drug's professional labeling (information on how to use the drug).
11. The FDA inspects the facilities where the drug will be manufactured as part of the approval process.
12. FDA reviewers will approve the application or find it either approvable or not approvable.

The pharmaceutical industry defends its position on research and development costs by demonstrating that all top companies in a variety of industries are research and development–intensive. The pharmaceutical industry relies on new drugs to keep an income stream from which they can continue to search for new drug compounds. Pharmaceutical companies invested roughly $33.2 billion in research and development in 2003, which is a 23 percent increase since 2000 (Clayton 2005).

The U.S. government offers some help, but in terms of overall development, the industry maintains that it faces most of the burden. The industry maintains that roughly 91 percent of all drugs brought to market were fully funded by the industry, with no help from the National Institutes of Health, which conduct government-funded research (GlaxoSmithKline 2005).

Consumer Advocate Standpoint

Consumer advocate groups contend that the numbers pharmaceutical companies tout regarding the cost of research are overstated. A report was released showing how the $500 million figure that the industry uses as a benchmark for new drug development is wrought with flaws and overestimates. The report referenced showed that the actual $500 million figure is incorrect and purely a mathematical estimation. The report stated that the true cost of researching and developing was much less (Public Citizen 2001).

Anti-industry groups also illustrate that the pharmaceutical companies receive certain advantages, for example, tax breaks, for doing the research and development. These government tax breaks could lower a pharmaceutical firm's tax burden considerably. The amount of tax incentives companies receive is a closely guarded secret among the industry. One such tax break involved incentives for pharmaceutical companies that built manufacturing facilities in U.S. territories. Many major manufacturers opened facilities in Puerto Rico to take advantage of this opportunity. Under this incentive plan, the industry's average tax rate was believed to be around 26 percent, as compared to roughly 33 percent for all other major U.S. industries (Greider 2003). Advocates for lower drug prices cite examples such as these to show that pharmaceutical companies do receive some benefit for the heavy investment in research and development.

Consumer groups also dispute claims that the pharmaceutical industry pays for most of the research into new cures. The advocate groups believe that the National Institutes of Health often conduct the most basic and risky research, and the pharmaceutical companies only begin researching once an opportunity during the government research is discovered.

NEW MEDICINE OR OLD TECHNOLOGY

Industry Standpoint

Recent television advertisements quote lines such as "Today's medicines, financing tomorrow's miracles." This sums the industry view that to discover new treatment, the cost of medication must remain at its current level. The industry invests heavily into research and development and needs to have adequate income to fund these ventures. New treatments for every disease from AIDS to cancer are being researched.

The industry trade group PhRMA believes that these new cures are not only improving patient lives, but are also reducing the overall cost of health care. One study showed that treating patients with the latest medicines actually reduced their nondrug medical spending, for example, on hospitalization. The study specifically showed that for every extra dollar spent on new medicine, a corresponding decrease of $7.20 could be found in other health-care costs (PhRMA 2005). Therefore the industry believes that it is not only funding future cures with the current price of medication, but also helping to reduce the overall cost of health care with these new treatments.

Consumer Advocate Standpoint

Consumer groups respond to the pharmaceutical companies' suggestion that they are searching for the next cure by showing that many of the drug companies' newest products are simply brand extension drugs rather than new chemical entities. The new drugs offer extended release (XR), controlled release properties to existing drugs (CR), or a combination of two readily available drugs into one pill. This allows for patent extension and continued profits from a drug that is about to become generically available. The producer simply changes the pill to make it time released and does clinical research to show benefits of doing the drug under these new formulations. The FDA would likely approve the XR or CR version, which then becomes a market drug with extended patent protection. Advocacy groups see a serious decline in the number of compounds being studied to treat or cure new diseases or new ways to treat existing conditions. In fact, most widely advertised products are often product line extensions based on existing chemical entities. The industry is providing fewer new drug entities and increasing its output of current brand extensions. In fact, according to one report released in 2002, only 15 percent of new drugs developed between 1989 and 2002 were made of new chemical compounds, and over half of the new drugs brought to market were product line extensions (Public Citizen 2001).

MARKETING AND ADMINISTRATION COSTS

Industry Standpoint

Many believe that perhaps the reason drug costs are so high is that pharmaceutical companies spend a lot of money on product promotion. Pharmaceutical companies refute this argument by stating that they spend far more on research and development than on marketing a drug. Pharmaceutical companies maintain that they are not as heavily involved in advertising as companies such as Coca-Cola.

In an effort to help get their messages to patients, pharmaceutical companies have launched direct-to-consumer (DTC) campaigns to help the patient understand if a drug may be right for him. This information is then to be shared between the patient and his physician to see if the drug is appropriate. The cost of DTC is relatively low as compared to other industry advertising of products. One industry estimate shows that only 2 percent of U.S. drug costs are attributed to DTC advertising (Greider 2003).

The majority of all sales expenditures for marketing are for the salespersons each company employs. They act as consultants on particular disease states and promote medications using clinical data to demonstrate why their products are superior. The sales representative is trained as an expert and is versed in the latest clinical research, bringing the newest information to physicians to help them treat their patients. It is the strong belief of the pharmaceutical companies that the most effective way to keep physicians abreast of the latest clinical data is through this type of selling (McKinnell 2005). The physicians simply do not have time to keep up with every new publication and study.

Consumer Advocate Standpoint

Responding to the industry view of the fair proportion spent between marketing and research and development, advocates point to some interesting information. One study found that eight of nine pharmaceutical companies studied spent twice as much on marketing, advertising, and administration as on research and development (Families USA 2002).

The high compensation and expenditures on marketing, advertising, and administration fuel the argument that research and development would not have to suffer if price controls were implemented. The administration costs are extremely telling when the top officers of a pharmaceutical company have their salaries and bonuses published annually by the SEC (Security and Exchange Commission). The generous salary packages are one of the excesses the advocacy groups point to as a necessary area of reform to reduce the cost of prescription medication. Some executives make over $200 million a year with bonuses and salaries (McKinnell 2005). This amount comes very close to what advocates believe the real cost is of developing a new medication. Hypothetically, cutting high compensation of executives could pay for the development of new drugs.

Advocates state that DTC campaigns are an unnecessary cost and create more confusion for patients. To the consumer advocate groups, this is money that could be better spent to help reduce the overall cost of the medicine.

Pharmaceutical companies are known for their salespersons or detail persons, who sell medicines directly to physicians. These sales representatives number in the thousands throughout the United States. Consumer advocates believe that many doctors find little value in this type of promotion and find representatives to be bothersome and a nuisance on a busy day.

IMPORTATION

Industry Standpoint

One of the hottest issues in pharmaceuticals is the possibility of seniors seeking cheaper medications from other countries such as Canada. To afford their medications, many people feel forced to bring cheaper medicines into the United States from other countries.

The pharmaceutical industry maintains that drug importation is illegal and is in violation of the Federal Food, Drug, and Cosmetic Act. The industry cautions against the importation of prescription drugs by consumers. Drugs manufactured outside the United States are not subject to the same FDA safety regulations. Therefore there are no assurances that medications acquired from foreign pharmacies are chemical equivalents of U.S. medications. Sometimes the medications received from foreign pharmacies may be counterfeit. Since the FDA does not regulate these medications, there is no recourse for the patients who have been wronged by such a transaction. The online foreign pharmacies often have waivers that must be acknowledged by patients, stating that they have no recourse if they receive incomparable medications through the transaction.

Not only can importation be unsafe, but the foreign medications are not always cheaper than U.S. medications. In general, generic medications are cheaper from U.S. than from foreign pharmacies.

GENERIC PRICE COMPARISON (U.S. FOOD AND DRUG ADMINISTRATION 2004)

One-Month Supply Shipping Charges from Canada Not Included

Drug	United States	Canada
Amiodarone	$41.89	$134.90
Verapamil	$43.97	$93.95
Diltiazem	$127.99	$145.00
Warfarin	$20.69	$24.90
Lisinopril 20 mg	$16.19	$97.90

Consumer Advocate Standpoint

The problem is obvious to consumer advocate groups, who cite numerous examples of seniors organizing bus trips and traveling hours to Canada to buy their prescriptions. To consumer advocates, this practice shows that there is a major problem with the price of U.S. prescription medicines.

There is a certain trade-off that exists when a patient must look to other means by which to acquire his prescription medicines. Often, a patient may simply not be able to afford all of his prescriptions, and the only alternative to importation is to not take his medicine. This is very dangerous. To many, this danger far outweighs the risk of using a foreign pharmacy.

Another concern is that the FDA process for inspecting drugs is not perfect. The prescription drug Vioxx was associated with serious and sometimes fatal cardiac events in a small population of patients. Vioxx was an FDA-approved drug and had met all the requirements to be marketed. Some groups believe that the FDA process is industry-friendly and that pressure from a company will hasten a product's approval. This makes the industry's argument against importation moot. Political resistance to establishing price controls in the United States is intense. European countries, such as Germany and England, do allow drug importation. In the United Kingdom, at least eight prescriptions under the National Health Service are filled by imports from countries like France and Spain, where drug prices are cheaper. This has been estimated to save the government $130 million a year (Public Citizen 2001).

Though generic drugs may be cheaper in other countries, such as Canada, advocate groups point to the fact that in many cases, branded prescription drugs (newer medicine that is still under patent protection) are many times cheaper.

BRANDED PRICE COMPARISON (*INTERNATIONAL MEDICATION* N.D.)

Cost Comparison: United States and Canada

Price of Medication and Shipping for a Three-Month Supply

Drug	United States	Canada
Plavix	$397	$213
Lipitor	$214	$162
Actos	$542	$377
Zocor	$423	$231
Celexa	$281	$138

PRICE CONTROLS

Industry Standpoint

Why do branded medicines cost more in the United States? Government-imposed price controls are one option to help control the cost of medication. Canada has imposed a countrywide price for each medication. Under this system, the price of medications is specifically regulated. The belief is that more patients have access to the best medications.

The pharmaceutical industry maintains that government restrictions would severely limit the research and development potential. One study shows that the United States accounts for roughly 70 percent of the world's new medical therapies (Clayton 2005). The industry points to the low percentages of innovation and new drug introductions in countries subject to price controls. From an industry standpoint, price controls are not the solution to improving access to the newest medications. The industry points out that prices are lower in countries with socialized medicine, a type of system repeatedly rejected by Americans.

The industry believes that using medications is actually cost-effective for the consumer as they prevent costly surgeries or other hospital care caused by a preventable event. For instance, paying for a high blood pressure medication is cost-effective when compared to paying for hospitalization following a heart attack caused by uncontrolled high blood pressure.

Consumer Advocate Standpoint

Advocate groups argue for price controls by showing the effectiveness that the U.S. government has in negotiating prices for medications for its veterans and military personnel. The government set a price for branded and generic drugs that companies must meet. This allows for every veteran and active soldier to have access to necessary medication. Advocates believe that the government can go one step further and institute this type of system for the country's seniors so that they, too, can have access to necessary medicine.

In comparison to other developed countries, consumer advocates show that the United States pays more for prescription drugs than any other country. In the United Kingdom, patients pay roughly 69 percent of the cost patients pay in the United States. The difference is the same for patients in Switzerland. Germans pay 65 percent, Swedes pays 64 percent, the French pay 55 percent, and Italians pay only 53 percent (Public Citizen 2001).

Advocates point to the success of Canada's Patented Medicine Prices Review Board, which puts a ceiling on prices for all drugs. Many of the drugs purchased in Canada are purchased by the government. This allows access for low-income and elderly patients. This system is very similar to how the United States purchases medications for military personnel, but Canada implements controls on a much wider scale.

PROFITS

Industry Standpoint

The pharmaceutical industry is currently profitable. The industry maintains that the high profitability is necessary to attract new investment for further research and development. For the year 2006, Fortune magazine ranked industries in terms of most profitable. The pharmaceutical industry ranks fifth on the profit list behind crude oil production, Internet services and retailing, commercial banks, and network equipment (CNNMoney 2006). The pharmaceutical industry cites examples of charity toward underprivileged individuals. The industry estimates that in 2003, it distributed approximately $16 billion worth of free samples to U.S. physicians' offices (Greider 2003). This provided patients access to the newest treatments for all types of illness.

The industry further demonstrates acts of giving in Third World nations, where patients have no possible means of paying for such medication. In these cases, the industry freely dispenses the necessary medications to those in need. Instances of giving in times of disaster can also be found. Emergency shipments of medications have been sent to victims of the recent tsunami as well as to U.S. hurricane disaster victims.

The industry trade group PhRMA has presented some figures which show that the cost of medicine is in line with the increases in overall health-care spending. Pharmaceuticals accounted for only 11 cents of every health-care dollar spent. In fact, PhRMA suggests that the overall cost of prescription drugs has remained roughly 10 percent of overall health-care costs for the past 40 years (Clayton 2005).

Consumer Advocate Standpoint

Consumer advocates believe that pharmaceutical profits are a clear example of the excess that exists in the industry. The pharmaceutical industry consistently ranks among the top in terms of profitability. For a 10-year span ending in 2001, the industry was the most profitable in the United States and, on average, was five and one-half times more profitable than the average of other Fortune 500 companies (McKinnell 2005).

The industry spends a tremendous amount of money to protect its interests as well. For instance, the industry in 2002 had approximately 675 lobbyists in Washington, D.C., to promote industry-friendly legislation. This amounts to seven lobbyists for every U.S. senator (Public Citizen 2003).

Though the industry may at times be charitable, advocacy groups are quick to identify what they feel is a much larger issue. The rate at which prescription costs are rising is increasing greatly. For the last several years, the amount Americans are spending on prescription drugs has increased 15 percent each year. This is twice the rate of overall health-care spending and five times the rate of inflation (Public Citizen 2001).

CONCLUSION

The issue of prescription drug costs in the United States remains very complicated. In many cases, the information supporting either side can be confusing. For every study that promotes an industry stance, a consumer advocate group has information that argues just the opposite. The government is little help when trying to find answers to the problem of high medication costs. Both sides of the argument frequently cite studies from the National Institutes of Health to support their own viewpoints. Regardless, it is imperative that patients always have access to all medications. Pharmaceutical companies have various discount programs designed to assist financially struggling patients in receiving medicine at reduced cost. Some companies even give medications at no cost to patients who can prove that their situation leaves no way of paying for the medicine. Though these programs can be complicated and time consuming, they can help alleviate the burden of prescription drug costs until definitive research can be conducted to find permanent solutions to this problem.

See also: Health Care Costs; Universal Health Care

References

Clayton, Anne. 2005. *Insight into a Career in Pharmaceutical Sales,* 7th ed. Deerfield, IL: Pharmaceuticalsales.com Inc.

CNNMoney. 2006. *Fortune 500: Our Annual Ranking of America's Largest Corporations.* Available at: http://money.cnn.com/magazines/fortune/fortune500/index.html. Accessed July 1, 2006.

Families USA. 2002. *Profiting from Pain: Where Prescription Drug Dollars Go.* Available at: http://www.familiesusa.org/assets/pdfs/PPreort89a5.pdf. Accessed June 6, 2006.

GlaxoSmithKline. 2005. *The Value of Medicines: Beyond the Basics.* Brentford, Middlesex, UK: GlaxoSmithKline.

Greider, Katharine. 2003. *The Big Fix: How the Pharmaceutical Industry Rips Off American Consumers.* New York: Public Affairs.

International Medication Program Price List. n.d. Available at: http://www.wecaremedicalmall.com/prices.htm. Accessed July 7, 2006.

McKinnell, Hank. 2005. *A Call to Action: Taking Back Healthcare for Future Generations.* New York: McGraw-Hill.

PhRMA. 2005. *What Goes into the Cost of Prescription Drugs?* Available at: http://www.phrma.org/files/Cost_of_Prescription_Drugs.pdf. Accessed June 1, 2006.

Public Citizen. 2001. *Rx R&D Myths: The Case against the Drug Industry's R&D "Scare Card."* Available at: http://www.citizen.org/documents/ACFDC.PDF. Accessed May 30, 2006.

Public Citizen. 2003. *2002 Drug Industry Profits: Hefty Pharmaceutical Company Margins Dwarf Other Industries.* Available at: http://www.citizen.org/documents/Pharma_Report.pdf. Accessed July 1, 2006.

U.S. Food and Drug Administration. 2004. *U.S./Canadian Price Comparisons October 2004.* Available at: http://www.fda.gov. Accessed July 8, 2006.

U.S. Food and Drug Administration. n.d. *From Test Tube to Patient: The FDA's Drug Review Process: Ensuring Drugs Are Safe and Effective.* Available at: http://www.fda.gov/fdac/special/testtubetopatient/drugreview.html. Accessed July 8, 2006.

Further Reading: Greider, Katharine. 2003. *The Big Fix: How the Pharmaceutical Industry Rips Off American Consumers.* New York: Public Affairs; McKinnell, Hank. 2005. *A Call to Action: Taking Back Healthcare for Future Generations.* New York: McGraw-Hill.

Brandon Kramer

DRUG TESTING IN THE WORKPLACE

Many employers have adopted drug screening as an important tool for dealing with rising safety concerns, health costs, and increased litigation. These companies believe that employees who use drugs increase the risk of workplace accidents, potentially harming both the drug user and his coworkers, and, in some cases, their customers. Employer costs associated with these accidents may include medical expenses for injured workers, increased workers' compensation premiums, and the legal costs associated with law suits filed by injured workers or the public. Employers are also concerned that the ability of employees to actually perform their jobs may be impaired by drug use and that employees who use drugs have higher absenteeism, more sick days, and lower overall productivity in the workplace than those employees who do not use drugs. These concerns drive the use of employee drug testing programs.

Drug testing in sports is conducted because of concerns over the health risks to athletes. Ironically, however, in professional sports—the sports workplace—drug testing has also been prompted not by concerns of lack of productivity, but just the opposite, namely, concerns that some athletes may be enhancing their performance and getting an unfair advantage over their peers by taking or using illegal substances. Thus there are different issues regarding drug testing in the sports workplace than in other workplaces.

The primary controversy in the general workplace is whether or not employers should be allowed to test potential or current employees, without reasonable cause or suspicion of substance abuse and without evidence that their work has been, is, or will be affected by it. Is drug testing a good idea for businesses? Or does such testing constitute an unreasonable invasion of privacy of individual employees? There are different points of view on these issues.

In professional sports, the primary controversy seems to be whether or not drug testing is effective, and whether it is fair to test for some drugs and not others. In addition, there is evidence that some Americans believe that it is not cheating unless you get caught. With the rather pervasive use and abuse of performance-enhancing drugs in many professional sports, should we just ignore the issues as long as we get better performances and, consequently, better entertainment value from our athletes? Or should we clean up all sports and adopt universal drug-free policies with strict enforcement in all professional sports? Again, there are differing opinions and perspectives.

ARGUMENTS FOR DRUG TESTING IN THE WORKPLACE

According to the U.S. Department of Labor, drug use in the workplace costs businesses between $75 and $100 billion each year for lost time, accidents, health care, and workers' compensation costs. Sixty-five percent of all accidents on the job are directly related to drugs or alcohol. Substance abusers are absent 3 times more often and use 16 times as many health-care benefits as nonabusers (U.S. Bureau of Labor Statistics). According to the U.S. Department of Health and Human Services, substance abusers are six times more likely than their coworkers to file a compensation claim. In addition, the National Institute on Drug Abuse reports that 74 percent of drug users are employed either full time or part time, and 23 percent of drug users use drugs while on the job.

Statistics from the Ohio Bureau of Workers' Compensation show that 77 percent of illicit drug users and 90 percent of alcoholics are employed, primarily in the construction, commercial truck driving, and manufacturing industries. Furthermore, the Ohio Bureau's statistics show that employee drug abuse is expensive and has significant negative effects on employers (David 2006):

Productivity: Substance abusers are 33–50 percent less productive.
Absenteeism: Substance users are absent about three weeks or more per year and are tardy three times more often than nonusers.
Accidents: Substance abusers are three to four times more likely to have an accident on the job and are five times more likely to file a workers' compensation claim.
Medical claims: Substance users file three to four times more costly medical claims.

Employee theft: An estimated 50–80 percent of all pilferage, theft, and loss are due to substance-using employees.

With these sobering statistics, it is easy to see how drug abuse may affect the financial welfare of a company, and why drug testing has become the norm in many workplaces. And it is important to know that most companies have a choice of whether or not to administer drug tests. Since the adoption of the Drug-Free Workplace Act of 1988, federal contractors (with contracts of $25,000 or more) have been required to certify that their workplace is drug-free. The act does not require drug testing, but it does specify that contractors must have drug-free policy statements and provide awareness programs for all employees. Regulations adopted in 1990 and 1991 by the U.S. Department of Transportation and the U.S. Department of Defense, respectively, required government contractors in those industries to begin drug testing employees and applicants for employment in safety-sensitive positions. Beyond these federally mandated, safety-sensitive positions, there are no federal mandates on employers to conduct drug tests.

Over the last two decades, many U.S. employers have chosen to use drug tests for preemployment screening as well as for testing current employees. There are statistics that appear to indicate that such testing is working. For example, the incidence of positive drug tests in the combined U.S. workforce (including both the federally mandated, safety-sensitive workforce and the general workforce) has been steadily decreasing in the United States. This would seem to indicate that there is less drug use in the workplace.

ANNUAL POSITIVITY RATES OF EMPLOYER DRUG TESTS (FOR COMBINED U.S. WORKFORCE; MORE THAN 7.3 MILLION TESTS FROM JANUARY TO DECEMBER 2005)

Year	Drug positivity rate (%)	Year	Drug positivity rate (%)
1988	13.6	1997	5.0
1989	12.7	1998	4.8
1990	11.0	1999	4.6
1991	8.8	2000	4.7
1992	8.8	2001	4.6
1993	8.4	2002	4.4
1994	7.5	2003	4.5
1995	6.7	2004	4.5
1996	5.8	2005	4.1

Source: Quest Diagnostics Inc., *Drug Testing Index,* 2005, http://www.questdiagnostics.com/employersolutions/DTI_05_2005/dti_index.html.

Likewise, the percentage of positive preemployment tests in the general workforce has steadily decreased over the last five years. This provides evidence that having the preemployment test itself is sending a signal to applicants, resulting in fewer drug users applying for positions where they know preemployment drug testing will be conducted.

ANNUAL POSITIVITY RATES BY TESTING REASON (FOR GENERAL U.S. WORKFORCE)

Table D.1

Testing reason	2005	2004	2003	2002	2001
Follow-up	9.6%	10.0%	9.6%	10.3%	11.3%
For cause	28.3%	27.8%	28.2%	25.9%	26.1%
Periodic	2.4%	1.9%	2.2%	2.7%	3.4%
Postaccident	5.8%	5.7%	5.7%	5.9%	6.0%
Preemployment	3.9%	4.1%	4.1%	4.3%	4.4%
Random	6.6%	7.1%	6.6%	6.5%	7.0%
Returned to duty (after recovery)	6.0%	5.5%	5.6%	5.6%	5.3%

Source: Quest Diagnostics Inc., *Drug Testing Index,* 2005, http://www.questdiagnostics.com/employer solutions/DTI_05_2005/dti_index.html.

There are numerous stories and anecdotal evidence of the effectiveness of drug testing in the workplace. For example, in the November 2004 issue of Inc. magazine, one business owner related his experience with implementing a drug testing program in his trucking business. He wound up losing about 25 percent of his workforce, but he concluded that the drug testing did work. The accident rate declined, along with the incidence of petty theft. In addition, the drug testing program made his company more attractive to insurers and allowed him to obtain a policy from a better insurance provider. Likewise, the lower accident rate would result in lower workers' compensation costs in the future (Brodsky 2004).

But the owner also got an unexpected result from the drug testing program. In his words,

> Even more gratifying was the response from the employees who remained: they thanked us. They said they felt safer. Only then did I begin to appreciate the real importance of having a drug-free company. It wasn't just about reducing our liability, or even keeping someone from getting hurt, as much as we wanted to do both. It was also about creating a better working environment for the other employees, the ones on whom we depend most heavily, the people we absolutely must figure out how to keep. (Brodsky 2004)

In the workplace of organized sports, there are different forces at work than in the general workplace. First of all, it is clear that organized sports now constitute a substantial industry in the United States and other nations. Top athletes can now earn huge sums of money from lucrative contracts, endorsements, and sponsorships. Sports teams (employers of athletes) may also garner substantial sponsorship dollars because of the entertainment value of their teams—often enhanced by the presence and performance of star athletes. Thus there is considerable emphasis on athletes performing at their best since it benefits both the employer (the team owners) and the employee (the athlete).

Since the beginning of organized sporting events, athletes have looked for aids to help them compete. Advances in science and technology have been applied to improve athletes' performance. Training regimens, clothing, shoes, and sports equipment have all improved. Likewise, nutrition for athletes has improved. Athletes have also benefited from advances in science, namely, performance-enhancing supplements to help increase strength, speed, agility, and so on, such as anabolic steroids and stimulants. When it became obvious that these supplements could create an unfair advantage as well as endanger the health of the athlete, bans on these began to surface.

In 1928, the International Amateur Athletic Federation was the first international agency to ban doping. Several other sports federations followed with their own bans, but none were effective because no drug tests were conducted. It was not until the 1960s that advances in science allowed for the first drug tests for athletes. In 1966, the International Cycling Union first tested for banned substances. The International Olympic Committee began testing for amphetamine use in 1968 and adopted tests in the 1970s for anabolic steroids, amphetamines, and ephedrine, and tests in the 1980s for testosterone, beta-blockers, diuretics, and marijuana. When Ben Johnson tested positive for steroids and was stripped of his gold medal in the Seoul Olympic games, it brought the world's attention to the doping problem in athletics (Todd and Todd 2001).

The 1990s saw the adoption of the Anabolic Steroid Control Act in the United States, which criminalized nonmedical uses as well as possession and distribution of anabolic steroids. A World Conference on Doping in Sport was held in 1999, and one of its outcomes was the creation of an independent agency called the World Anti-Doping Agency. In 2000, the United States created its own agency, the U.S. Anti-Doping Agency (USADA), to take over the testing and enforcement of the U.S. Olympic Committee rules. For the Sydney games, blood samples were taken for the first time, and athletes were tested before the games began (Todd and Todd 2001).

In 2003, the Bay Area Laboratories Co-Operative (BALCO) scandal hit the media. An anonymous college coach provided the USADA with the names of U.S. and international athletes who were using an undetectable steroid. The substance was subsequently identified as tetrahydrogestrinone (THG), and the source of the drug was identified as Victor Conte, president of BALCO. Since that time, 39 of BALCO's clients have been subpoenaed, including Olympic gold medalist Marion Jones, National Football League player Bill Romanowski, and Major League Baseball player Barry Bonds (Woolf 2005). Such was the magnitude of this scandal that U.S. president George W. Bush in his 2004 State of the Union address said,

To help children make right choices, they need good examples. Athletics play such an important role in our society; but, unfortunately, some in professional sports are not setting much of an example. The use of performance-enhancing drugs like steroids in baseball, football and other sports, is dangerous; and it sends the wrong message, that there are shortcuts to accomplishment and that performance is more important than character.

So tonight I call on team owners, union representatives, coaches and players to take the lead, to send the right signal, to get tough, and to get rid of steroids now.

The recent doping scandal in the Tour de France (cycling) has brought further international attention to the issue of drug testing in sports. Nearly all major professional sports in the United States have adopted drug testing, but each has its own policies and rules. It is also interesting to note that in the National Basketball Association, the National Football League, the National Hockey League, and Major League Baseball, drug testing policies are governed by each sport's collective bargaining agreement. Thus players' unions and management negotiate over the terms of employment, including drug testing policies, which become part of collective bargaining agreements (Woolf 2005).

PUNISHMENT FOR FIRST-TIME OFFENSE OF DOPING IN ORGANIZED SPORTS (2005)

Table D.2

IOC	NCAA	MLB[a]	NBA	NFL	NHL
two-year ban	365-day ban, one-year loss of eligibility	10-day suspension	five-game suspension, must enter steroid program	four-game suspension, must test clean before returning to play	no policy

Source: Richard D. Woolf, "Banned Substances in Organized Sports," *Strength and Conditioning Journal* 27 (2005): 88–93.

Note: IOC, International Olympic Committee; NCAA, National Collegiate Athletic Association; MLB, Major League Baseball; NBA, National Basketball Association; NFL, National Football League; NHL, National Hockey League.

[a] From Bloom (2006).

For all the reasons noted by President Bush, drug testing is the norm in organized sports in America.

ARGUMENTS AGAINST DRUG TESTING IN THE WORKPLACE

While drug abuse is a national problem, it may not be as severe as many people believe. Reports by the National Institute on Drug Abuse (NIDA) show that illegal drug use in America peaked in 1979, with 14 percent of all Americans over the age of 12 reporting having used some illegal drug in the previous month. By 1996, the figure had fallen to 6 percent, with the large majority of users citing marijuana use. The NIDA also reports that only 3 percent of all random drug tests are positive.

Many people also claim that drug users are less effective than other employees. However, a 1994 study by the National Academy of Sciences found that employees who use drugs off the job were no more likely to be involved in accidents on the job than other employees. They also found no consistent relationship between drug use and productivity. When the U.S. Postal Service randomly chose over 4,000 new hires for a drug test, and then tracked their performance, it found that 87 percent of those who tested positive became employees in good standing, compared to 91 percent of those who passed the test.

One simple explanation for these results may be that most employees who use illegal drugs do not use them on the job. They confine their use to evenings and weekends, just like coworkers who use alcohol, and their performance at work is not affected by their drug use.

Another argument against drug testing is that drug testing of any kind brings privacy issues into play and can create employment practice liability exposures. For example, if someone is terminated because of off-premises drug use that does not affect her performance in the workplace, she may have a claim for invasion of privacy. Furthermore, an employee may claim that the way in which his specimen was collected or the test was conducted was defective and file a suit for wrongful termination, or even defamation.

The problem is further complicated by the fact that state laws vary widely with respect to privacy protection. For employers to avoid liability, they must be consistent and precise when implementing and enforcing drug testing policies. They must also be careful not to violate the Americans with Disabilities Act (ADA). The ADA specifically protects recovered drug addicts from discrimination such that an employer may not require a drug test of a former addict without specific cause.

Drug tests themselves are also subject to suspicion and have differing rates of effectiveness. Whether it is a urine, blood, or hair test, it may still give a false-positive, subjecting the employer to liability if it wrongly disciplines or dismisses an employee. It is also critical that an employer involve an independent medical review officer in the testing process to avoid these potential liabilities.

All these requirements may argue against drug testing when applying cost-benefit analyses. Furthermore, there is evidence that drug screening may not be cost-effective in some industries. A January 2005 article from the Journal of Substance Abuse Treatment suggested that drug abuse–based absenteeism is, at best, an incidental cost to businesses and an insufficient reason for justifying the significant investment required to achieve a drug-free workplace. A February 2004 article from Health Services Research also concluded that the positive results from drug testing could only be seen in certain industries, with the strongest evidence of effect in the construction industry. And even in the construction industry, the net cost savings were small.

In particular, small business owners may find that the costs of drug testing are prohibitive. Ninety-five percent of Fortune 500 companies now conduct preemployment drug screening. But over 60 percent of employed drug users work for small companies, many of which do not do drug testing. Furthermore, low unemployment makes it harder to banish all drug users from the workplace; employers may loosen up their drug policies if they have a lot of vacancies to fill.

Another argument against drug testing is that not all drugs are being screened by the tests. Drug enforcement agencies report that at least 25–30 percent of drug abuse in the workplace now involves prescription drugs, which are not always detected by standard drug screens. Is it fair to punish an employee who only smokes marijuana on the weekend, when a coworker comes to work impaired from abusing prescription drugs but escapes detection in the drug test?

Some of the same arguments against drug testing in the typical workplace also apply to the sports workplace. Athletes argue that drug testing is an invasion of privacy and that they are defamed by positive drug tests. They also argue that not all drugs are being screened, so that many athletes can still beat the tests. Several studies are confirming that this is true. Testosterone and THG as well as growth hormones are still quite popular with athletes and often avoid detection by drug tests.

But one additional argument against drug testing is unique to the sports workplace. Since professional athletes are paid handsomely, they can make the economic argument of restraint of trade if they are prohibited from participating in their profession because of a positive drug test. Their potential earning power through lucrative endorsement contracts may be severely impacted by an accusation of doping.

Controversy over drug testing in the workplace will not die down anytime soon. In the meantime, proponents of drug testing can take heart that new technologies are being developed to do better screening in both the typical workplace and the sports workplace and that nearly every major U.S. sport has recently revised its drug testing policies. Furthermore, there is increasing international interest in developing universal drug policies in organized sports. The civil libertarians among us can breathe easier knowing that as the tests get better, fewer privacy rights will be infringed. And free-market enthusiasts should be thrilled to know that while nearly every major bicycle manufacturer has had at least one sponsored athlete test positive for a banned substance in the past four years, very few companies have given any indication of backing away from pro team sponsorships, even in the aftermath of the Tour de France doping scandal.

See also: Corporate Social Responsibility; Ethics in Business at the Individual Level

References

Bloom, Barry M. 2006. *Report: Tentative Labor Deal Reached.* Available at: http://mlb.mlb.com/NASApp/mlb/news/article.jsp?ymd=20061022&content_id=1720750&vkey=news_mlb&fext=.jsp&c_id=mlb.
Brodsky, Norman. 2004. "Just Say Yes." *Inc.* 26: 67–68.

Bush, George W. 2004. "The State of the Union by the President of the United States." *Congressional Record* 150: H20–H23.

David, Patricia. 2006. "Screening Can Cut Down on Liabilities." *Occupational Health and Safety* 75: 24, 26.

Todd, J., and T. Todd. 2001. "Significant Events in the History of Drug Testing and the Olympic Movement: 1960–1999." In *Doping in Elite Sport: The Politics of Drugs in the Olympic Movement,* ed. W. Wilson and E. Derse, 65–128. Champaign, IL: Human Kinetics Publishers.

U.S. Bureau of Labor Statistics. Available at: http://www.bls.gov. Accessed September 18, 2006.

Woolf, Richard D. 2005. "Banned Substances in Organized Sports." *Strength and Conditioning Journal* 27: 88–93.

Further Reading: Buti, Tony. 1999. "Drug Testing in Sport: Legal Challenges and Issues." *University of Queensland Law Journal* 20: 153–85; Hubbartt, William S. 1998. *The New Battle over Workplace Privacy: Safe Practices to Minimize Conflict, Confusion, and Litigation.* New York: American Management Association; International Olympic Committee. 2005. *Fact Sheet: The Fight against Doping and Promotion of Athletes' Health: Update—December 2005.* Available at: http://multimedia.olympic.org/pdf/en_report_838.pdf; National Collegiate Athletic Association. 2006. *NCAA Drug Testing Program.* Available at: http://www2.ncaa.org/portal/legislation_and_governance/eligibility_and_recruiting/drug_testing.html; Staudohar, Paul D. 2005. "Performance-Enhancing Drugs in Baseball." *Labor Law Journal* 56: 139–49.

Randy C. Brown

DUAL EARNERS

In the majority of families with two parents today, both the mother and father work. In fact, it is almost expected that both parents work because many people believe that it takes two incomes for a family to get by today.

It was not always this way. Sitcoms from the 1950s like *Leave It to Beaver* or *I Love Lucy* showed the husband working but the wife remaining at home to take care of the household and manage the kids. These sitcoms reflected the reality of the time: mothers, especially, just did not work away from the home.

But that began to change in the 1960s to where, today, having both parents work is the norm, rather than the exception. What happened? Why are so many parents now working at a paying job? Is it a necessity with today's prices and expenses, or are some other factors responsible for the shift? Also, are families always better off financially with two working parents?

WHY?

The increase in two-parent working families is largely the result of mothers trading in their aprons for briefcases and cash registers. The percentage of married mothers with children at home who work jumped 70 percent from the 1960s to the 2000s. Women now make up almost half the workforce, compared to only 30 percent in the 1950s (U.S. Census Bureau 2005).

The reasons behind this change can be divided into two forces: those that have pulled mothers into the paid labor force, and those that have pushed them. Among those on the pull side is the changing nature of jobs. Jobs today require much less muscle power and more brainpower than jobs in the past. The heavy lifting that once was a part of many jobs is today being done by machines or technology. The simple fact is that women can qualify for more jobs now because physical strength, which is an advantage for most men, is no longer an important requirement for a large number of jobs.

At the same time, educational opportunities have opened for more women. It may be hard to realize today, but it was not that long ago that few women went to college. Many parents thought, What's the point? Their daughters would just get married, have children, and be stay-at-home moms. What a difference in today's economy. With more jobs open to women and able to be done by women, females are now flocking to colleges and universities to get the necessary education. In fact, more than half of students on campuses are now women (National Center for Education Statistics 2005). Today's women have more of the training and smarts required for the modern workforce.

Women have also been pulled into the job market by the strength of job creation. Particularly during the 1980s and 1990s, the U.S. economy created jobs at an unprecedented rate. A total of 38 million jobs were generated during these two decades (U.S. Commerce Department 2006). Simply put, to fill their job ranks, businesses more and more had to turn to women.

Women, and especially mothers, have been pushed into the workforce by two forces. One is the fact that women are having fewer children. The national birthrate has been dropping for almost 40 years and hit an all-time low in the 2000s (Centers for Disease Control and Prevention 2006). Some of this reduction may have to do with the greater number of job opportunities outside the home for women. As women have seen more openings in the workplace, they may have been motivated to have fewer children so they can, indeed, work more. Nonetheless, the point is that today's woman has more time available to work because she has fewer children to raise.

Second, some mothers have been pushed into the workforce as a result of their husbands earning less money. Our economy has gone through big changes in the decades since World War II. Millions of manufacturing jobs have been lost, wages have stagnated for many occupations, and foreign competition has forced many companies to cut costs. These changes have caused many workers—particularly factory workers—to lose their jobs or have their hours cut back. Often, the wives of these workers have taken jobs to replace the income lost by their husbands.

WHO IS GETTING AHEAD?

Look around any neighborhood and you can reach a quick conclusion about the number of workers in each household. More times than not, the larger homes with more vehicles, bigger yards, and more appliances, TVs, and computers inside are owned by households where both parents work. So it is easy to get the idea that incomes from two working parents are needed to attain an adequate standard of living today.

However, this is a case of where appearances, or comparisons, can be deceiving. Look at Figure D.3. It shows the average income over the past 50 and more years for married couple families where the wife worked (ww) and married couples where the wife did not work (not ww). The dollar amounts in the figure have been adjusted to account for changes in prices each year. The adjustments mean that the dollars in each year can purchase the same amount of consumer products and services. In other words, all the dollars have the same purchasing power.

The numbers bounce around a bit, but one fact is clear: incomes for both household groups have not gone down. Both incomes of households with two working parents and one working parent are higher in the 2000s than in the 1950s. Indeed, they are higher in the 2000s than in any other decade.

In one important way, the income numbers in Figure D.3 do not fully reflect how much the dollars buy in recent years because families have been getting smaller. There were 17 percent fewer people in families in 2000 than in 1970 and 24 percent less than in 1950 (U.S. Census Bureau 2005). So the family income numbers in 2000 are higher, on a per person basis, than the income numbers in earlier years.

So why might many single-earner households feel as if they have fallen behind if the statistics say they have not? There are two answers. First, recognize

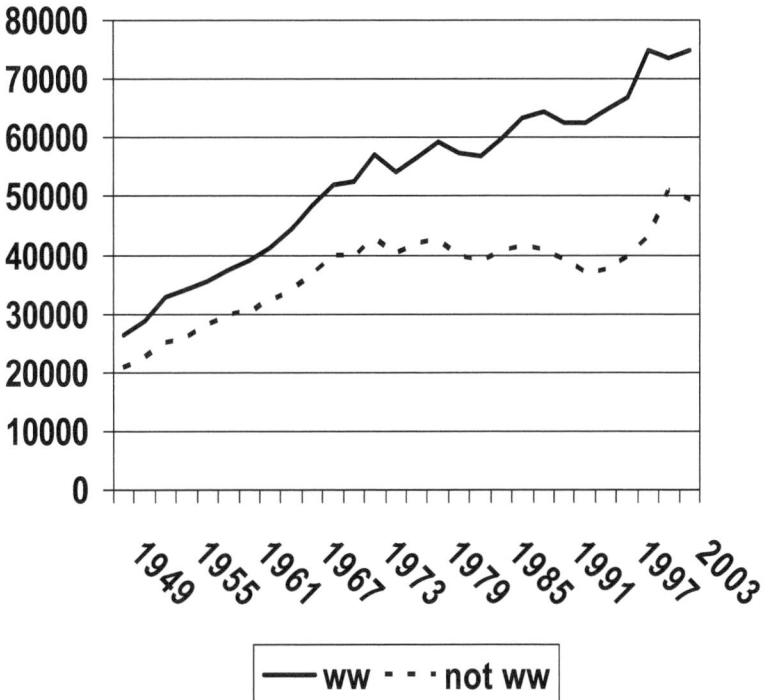

Figure D.3 Median family income of single-earner and dual-earner households.
Source: Original data from the U.S. Census; adjustments made by the author.

that the income numbers in Figure D.3 are averages. The specific average used is the median, which, in this case, is the income value that is exceeded by half the households and not met by the other half of households. This means that many households of both types could have experienced a decline in income in recent years. Studies show that the incomes of many single-earner households, where the worker has only a high school education or less, have not kept up with rising prices in recent decades. So there certainly are some single-earner households who have fallen behind.

The second reason is that single-earner households have, in fact, fallen behind when compared to dual-earner households. Again, look at Figure D.3. Notice that the gap between the incomes of single-earner and dual-earner households has widened between the 1950s and 1960s and more recent decades. The gap actually quadrupled between 1950 and 2000. So, relative to dual-earner households, households with one worker have gotten poorer.

DUELING COMPARISONS: ABSOLUTE VERSUS RELATIVE

Most of us like to periodically take stock of where we are in life. Indeed, experts think that it is a pretty good idea to every so often see where you are in life's path and how close you are to your goals.

In essence, this means answering the question of how you are doing. But the answer must include, Compared to what? There are at least two possibilities for the *what*: yourself and others.

If you use yourself as the *what*, or reference point, this means judging your progress over time by periodically looking at measures of your own economic well-being. This is called an *absolute* comparison. For example, if you use income earned as the measure, this would mean comparing your income in different years.

If you do use income as the economic measure, one important adjustment must first be made. Dollars in different years must be adjusted for their differing *purchasing power*. Dollars earned in years when prices were higher are worth less than dollars earned in years when prices were lower.

To make these *purchasing power* adjustments, use the inflation calculator located on the U.S. Bureau of Labor Statistics Web site (http://data.bls.gov/cgi-bin/cpicalc.pl). Type $1.00 in the first line, and in the second line, specify the year you earned that dollar. Next, hit the Calculate button. The answer will show the purchasing power of that dollar in the present year.

For example, if you enter $1.00 and 1995, the answer shows $1.31 for 2006. This means that $1.00 earned in 1995 is the same as $1.31 earned in 2006. The 1995 dollar is worth more in 2006 because prices were lower in 1995 than in 2006. Therefore, if you earned $30,000 in 1995, that would be like earning $30,000 × 1.31, or $39,300, in 2006. So in comparing your salary in 1995 to your salary in 2006, if you earned $30,000 in 1995, you would actually want to use $39,300 for the comparison to whatever you earned in 2006.

The second kind of comparison is *relative*. Here you compare your salary in some past year to someone else's salary in that same year, make that same comparison today, and then judge whether you have gotten closer to or further away from the other person. Before making these comparisons, it is best to adjust the dollars in different years for their purchasing power, as shown in the above two paragraphs.

As an example, suppose that you have the following incomes for yourself and John Jones, *after* adjusting the dollars for their differing purchasing powers:

	1995	2006
You	$39,300	$50,000
John Jones	$45,000	$55,000

The difference between your adjusted income and John Jones's adjusted income is 1995 was $5,700, and in 2006, the difference is $5,000. So based on a *relative* comparison, your situation has gotten better relative to John Jones's.

As seen in comparing dual-earner and single-earner households, absolute and relative comparisons can give different conclusions. Using an absolute comparison, the average income of single-earner households has not fallen, but using a relative comparison, single-earner households have fallen further behind dual-earner households.

Which comparison is better? There is no correct answer because each gives different information. However, surveys show that most Americans judge their own progress against the progress of others. We apparently live in a keeping-up-with-the-Joneses society.

A big reason behind the growing income gap between dual-earner and single-earner households is education. A higher percentage of dual-earner households have at least one worker with a college degree than single-earner households. Since, in our high-tech economy, the greatest income gains have been going to people with college training, two-income households have been getting bigger income boosts.

ARE TWO WORKERS BEST?

Since dual-worker households have more income and have benefited from larger increases in their incomes in recent years, is it best for both parents to work whenever possible? There is no easy yes or no answer to this question because working for pay gains a family some things at the expense of other things. Trade-offs have to be considered and evaluated.

Clearly, by getting a paying job, a parent earns more money for the family, and with that additional income comes an ability to have more. For instance, the extra income could be used to buy a bigger house, an additional car, and more TVs, computers, and iPods. Or some of the money could be saved and invested for children's college education or parents' retirement. The point is, money does buy things that we value.

But by having a second parent work, additional expenses may be created, and some other things that are valuable may have to be given up. When both parents work, babysitting or child day care expenses may have to be paid, an extra car and clothes may have to be purchased, and definitely, more taxes will be owed to the government.

DECIDING IF A SECOND JOB IS WORTHWHILE

Deciding whether a parent should take a paying job involves much more than looking at the prospective paycheck. It means comparing the benefits from the job, which certainly do include the paycheck, to the additional costs associated with the parent moving from home to the workplace.

For example, imagine that Joe works full time for a construction company. His wife, Susan, has remained at home taking care of their two preschool children and managing the household. Susan surely is working; she is just not working for pay. Susan has a degree in accounting and is considering taking a job with a local accounting firm. The job pays $50,000 and also includes medical and retirement benefits valued at $8,000 annually.

Susan and Joe should try to estimate the costs of the following items associated with Susan working before making a decision about the job:

1. annual child care expenses for the two children
2. additional yearly expenditures on clothes for Susan (Susan will have to purchase suits for when she meets clients)
3. additional annual food expenses if Susan eats her lunch in restaurants
4. additional annual transportation costs—maybe Susan and Joe will have to buy a second car for Susan to drive to work
5. additional annual household costs if Susan works—maybe Joe and Susan will hire a cleaning service and eat out more
6. additional annual taxes paid—Susan and Joe will have to pay taxes on Susan's $50,000 salary; depending on Joe's income, taxes could take one-fourth to one-third of the $50,000

Suppose that the total of these six costs is $27,000 annually. This means that instead of gaining $58,000 ($50,000 salary plus $8,000 in benefits), Susan effectively clears only $31,000, or just a little over half of the original gain.

Susan could take the $31,000 net gain and express it on an hourly basis. For instance, if she works an average of 40 hours per week, 50 weeks per year, her hourly net pay is $31,000/2,000, or $15.50 per hour.

Therefore, Susan and Joe will have to decide if Susan earning $15.50 per hour is worth the time away from the children and the more hectic life usually accompanying households with two working parents. The couple should determine what additional material goods they could purchase as well as what savings they could accumulate with the extra money. Maybe the $31,000 net pay would allow the couple to add on a third bedroom or start a college fund for the children. How do the benefits of these improvements compare to the losses from less time at home? Only Susan and Joe can decide.

One important thing that is given up when both parents work is time. Time spent at work means less time available for managing the home, cooking, cleaning, and, very importantly, being with children. Some of this time can be bought back, for example, by hiring a cleaning and lawn service, eating out or buying prepared meals, and having clothes professionally laundered. Of course, these services cost money, so their cost reduces the net gain from working. But it is impossible to replace a parent's time with his or her child. Many dual-earner families consider the lost time with their children to be the biggest cost of all from working.

So parents face a choice—after all, economics is about making choices—and it is one of the most important choices they will make. In families where there are two parents and young children, is it better for both parents to work, earn more money, and be able to provide more material goods for their children and perhaps save more for their children's future education? Or is it better for one parent to not work, stay at home, keep the household running, and be there for the children, but at the same time giving up a larger home, more material goods, perhaps an extra car, and some investments for college?

It is a tough choice, especially in our material-oriented society, where families are frequently driven to keep up with their neighbors. It is a choice outsiders cannot make, yet it is one they can help in framing.

PUBLIC POLICY

Is there a role for public policy in this decision? Not really, if by this is meant some government official will tell families how many workers they can have. But government policy can influence the playing field in the comparison of single- versus dual-worker families. Specifically, government tax policy can have a big role.

To show this, I have to take a little detour into explaining how the federal income tax works. The income tax has not one, but several tax rates. Different tax rates are applied to different parts of a taxpayer's income. For example, a tax- payer with $70,000 of taxable income will have that income divided into three parts, and each part uses a different tax rate. Furthermore, the tax rate rises with each successive part, or slice, of taxable income. So if the $70,000 is divided into parts consisting of the first segment of $15,000, the second segment of $45,000, and the third segment of $10,000 (the segments do not have to be of equal size), the tax rate will be lowest for the first $15,000, higher for the second $45,000, and higher still for the last segment of $10,000.

Now, here is the rub for families with two workers. Say Jason is working full time and earns $45,000 in taxable income. His wife, Ellen, is considering taking a part-time job, which will earn her $15,000 in taxable income. In calculating their federal income tax, Ellen's income will not be considered separately and divided with a mix of lower and higher tax rates applied. Instead, Ellen's income will be stacked on top of Jason's and taxed at the highest tax rate that applies to the family! So there is an extra tax penalty for Jason and Ellen if Ellen decides to work.

For some, but not all, families, there are some ways to reduce or eliminate this penalty. But tax experts say that there are only two real ways to rectify this situa- tion: either eliminate the multiple tax rates of the federal income tax system and have one rate that applies to all income, or let the income earned by a second worker in a family start from the bottom of the tax rate scale, just like the income of the first worker.

SUMMARY

The average family with both the husband and wife working has more income and has the ability to buy and save more than the average family with only one working parent. Furthermore, the income gap between two-parent working families and one-parent working families has widened in recent years.

This is not to imply, however, that the average family with only one working parent is worse off today than their counterparts were years ago. They are not. Today's average family with one working parent has more resources and material goods than ever before. Yet, relative to dual-earner families, single-earner families have fallen behind. So an important issue in deciding whether it takes both parents working today to have an adequate standard of living is selecting the basis of comparison. If the comparison is to single-earner families of the past, the answer is no. If the comparison is to dual-earner families today, the answer may be yes.

Of course, life is about more than material goods and bank accounts. A major cost for families with two working parents is time. With both parents working, there is less time for household chores and, very importantly, less parental time available with children. Dual-earner households may have more material possessions, but they may have less time to enjoy them.

Money versus time: that is the big trade-off for families in evaluating how many parents should work. In fact, it may be the trade-off for the modern family.

See also: Downsizing; Income Tax, Personal; The Middle Class

References

Centers for Disease Control and Prevention. 2006. *National Vital Statistics Report.*
National Center for Educational Statistics. 2005. Available at: http://nces.ed.gov.
U.S. Census Bureau. 2005. Available at: http://www.census.gov.
U.S. Commerce Department. 2006. Available at: http://www.bls.gov.
Further Reading: Blau, Francine, Marianne Ferber, and Anne Winkler. 1998. *The Economics of Women, Men, and Work.* Upper Saddle River, NJ: Prentice Hall.

Michael L. Walden

DUMPING

Dumping is selling an imported product for less in the United States than the seller charges for a comparable product in the seller's own domestic market. This kind of activity is illegal in the United States, even if it does not reduce competition. Antidumping is part of a broader set of laws that deal with so-called unfair trade practices. Antidumping laws can allow the U.S. government to impose taxes, called tariffs, on foreign-made products that have been found to have been dumped. Additional tariffs, called safeguards, can temporarily be imposed to offset surges in imports of a particular product.

WHO DUMPS?

Dumping has been illegal in the United States since 1921, but dumping cases have become more common in recent decades. More antidumping tariffs are now imposed globally in a single year than were imposed over the entire period of 1947–1970 (Blonigen and Prusa 2003). U.S. firms that compete with imports are the main beneficiaries, and they are also the main political proponents of antidumping law. High tariffs against dumping are a way to circumvent the limits on tariff levels agreed to by members of the World Trade Organization.

All buyers of imports and close domestic substitutes are harmed by antidumping laws. U.S. antidumping law applies to all trading partners, including its North American Free Trade Association partners, Canada and Mexico. Some of the more controversial cases have involved Canadian and Mexican products. The basic U.S. antidumping law was amended in 2000 by the Continued Dumping and Subsidy Offset Act, better known as the Byrd Amendment. The Byrd Amendment was found to violate the rules of the World Trade Organization, and it was repealed by Congress in January 2006.

THE BYRD AMENDMENT

The Byrd Amendment allows firms that file antidumping cases to receive the revenue from the tariffs imposed on import companies found guilty of dumping. Thus the victim is rewarded twice by (1) reducing competition they face from imports and (2) receiving tariff revenue. The United State has been the only country to resort to this unusual practice, and it was challenged immediately by other member countries in the World Trade Organization (WTO). The WTO ruled in 2000 that the amendment violated the rules of the WTO, and it authorized other WTO members to retaliate against the United States by imposing tariffs against U.S. exports. After the U.S. Congress refused to change the law, the European Union, Canada, and Japan imposed large tariffs against U.S. exports in 2005. Finally, in January 2006, Congress repealed the law but insisted on continuing payments to U.S. firms through 2007. Foreign sanctions against U.S. exports remained in place.

Some strange developments have occurred under the Byrd Amendment. In the case of wooden bedroom furniture dumped by Chinese firms, some American furniture companies have been simultaneously paying tariffs on furniture they import and sell in America and receiving payments from complaints they filed under the Byrd Amendment against dumping of furniture.

In the early experience with antidumping, American firms were the most frequent filers of complaints. Over time, Canada, the European Union, and Australia became more frequent filers, and by the late 1980s, these four traders accounted for more than 90 percent of antidumping cases filed in the world.

Recently, firms in other countries have become more frequent complainers, and since 2000, the four traditional filers accounted for only 33 percent of the cases. China and India have become more frequent filers, and since 2000, India has filed more cases than any other country. American firms that were once the most frequent complainers about dumping have become some of the most frequent targets of antidumping cases. The United States is the world's largest trading nation, and its economic size influences the number of cases in which American firms are involved. When data are adjusted for the volume of a country's trade, the prominence of U.S. firms is reduced.

East Asian countries, especially China, South Korea, and Taiwan, have been the most common targets of antidumping cases. The U.S. steel industry has generated more antidumping complaints than any other industry. These cases have pitted domestic steel producers against important steel-using firms. Steel users have organized a lobby, claiming that tariffs have destroyed more jobs in steel-using firms than they have saved in steel-producing firms. Other prominent dumping cases in the United States involved Canadian lumber, cement from Mexico, wooden furniture from China, and chemicals and electrical products.

ENFORCING ANTIDUMPING

How is the U.S. antidumping law administered? U.S. firms claiming to be harmed by dumping can initiate action by filing a complaint with the U.S. Department of Commerce (DOC) against specific foreign dumpers. As the result of an investigation, the DOC has ruled in favor of dumping in 94 percent of recent cases filed. In determining whether the price charged in the United States is too low, the DOC rarely compares the price charged in the United States with a price charged in the supplier's home market. Instead, the DOC makes its own estimate of cost of production in the supplier's market. In effect, dumping in the United States becomes pricing below cost of production as estimated by the DOC.

If the DOC rules in favor of dumping, the case moves to the U.S. International Trade Commission (USITC) to determine whether U.S. producers were harmed by dumping. The USITC has found injury in 83 percent of recent cases. In assessing injury, the USITC staff is guided by a peculiar asymmetry in the law. The USITC is asked to estimate the damage done to U.S. producers by dumping, but it is not allowed to take into account the gain to U.S. buyers from paying lower prices for products affected by dumping. If harm is found, the USITC estimates the amount of dumping and recommends a remedy to the president. It is usually a tariff whose level is related to the dumping amount, and it is imposed for an indefinite period against firms guilty of dumping. The tariff is retroactive to the day the dumping complaint was filed. Consequently, imports from accused firms often stop even before cases are resolved. On the basis of the high percentage of successful cases, U.S. firms competing with imports have a strong incentive to complain about imports.

IMPACTS

What are the economic effects of the U.S. antidumping law? Domestic producers gain in the same way they gain from any tariff. Competition from imports is reduced, and domestic producers can charge a higher price for their products. Foreign suppliers who are not accused of dumping and do not face the dumping tariff also gain from the reduction in competition.

Consider the example of steel. Say that antidumping tariffs are imposed on certain foreign steel producers. All steel producers in the United States and foreign steel suppliers not subject to antidumping tariffs gain from antidumping tariffs. Because of reduced competition, domestic producers are able to raise their steel prices. Since both domestic steel and imported steel are more expensive, all buyers of steel in the United States are harmed by antidumping laws. Since the United States is a net importer of steel, the total value of losses to buyers of steel exceeds the gains to domestic steel producers. Many of the steel buyers are businesses that use steel in their own production, and an association of steel users has become a vocal opponent of steel tariffs in recent years.

Similar impacts occur from other antidumping examples. In the case of Canadian lumber, antidumping has increased the cost of a key component of housing. In the Mexican cement case, antidumping restrictions magnified shortages of cement following the hurricanes that hit the Gulf Coast in 2005. For all antidumping cases combined, losses to U.S. buyers have exceeded gains to domestic producers by an estimated $2–$4 billion per year. Antidumping has become one of the costliest forms of trade protection for the United States, and for the world as a whole (Blonigen and Prusa 2003).

JUSTIFICATION

If antidumping laws are harmful for the nation, are they merely special interest legislation for U.S. producers, or can they be justified in some other way? One possible rationale is that antidumping prevents foreign companies from achieving monopoly power in the U.S. market. It has been suggested that foreign dumpers might charge low prices to drive all U.S. rivals out of business. Without rivals, they would then raise prices to monopoly levels. However, this argument has two weaknesses. First, if the predatory firm succeeds in destroying all current rivals, it has no way of blocking entry by new firms once it raises its price. Second, real-world cases of monopoly achieved by this strategy are extremely rare. If the goal is to prevent lower prices for foreign made products from leading to monopoly control, there is no reason to have a special law against foreign firms. Antitrust laws, which are laws against monopolies, could be enforced equally against both domestic and foreign companies who might acquire monopoly power.

There is an additional practical argument against the U.S. antidumping law. The administration of the law is said to be systematically biased toward finding dumping, even when there is none. Lindsey and Ikenson (2002) have constructed examples in which the DOC procedures produce prices in the United States that appear to be lower than in the supplying foreign country, even when the true prices are identical in the two countries. They conclude that the anti-dumping law is just a standard form of protectionism.

DUMPING REFORM

Short of completely repealing the U.S. antidumping law, are there ways to reform the law that would better serve producers, consumers, and society in general? First, the antidumping law could be modified to make it consistent with general antitrust policy. In that case, price differences would not be illegal unless they also increased the monopoly power of the dumping firm. For example, if a South Korean firm is one supplier of imported steel among many, lower prices charged by that firm would not necessarily be illegal. Its illegality would be judged in terms of its contribution to monopoly power in the U.S. market for steel. Retailers who offer discounts to students and senior citizens do not violate domestic antitrust law, even though they charge different prices for the same product. Price differences by foreign firms could be judged by the same standard as price differences by domestic firms.

A second reform would allow the DOC and USITC to estimate the consumer gains from dumping and compare them with domestic producer losses. Instead of evaluating exclusively the losses and harm to domestic producers, the agencies would evaluate dumping in terms of the general public interest of both buyers and sellers of products. By this broader standard, dumping that harms U.S. producers but provides greater benefits to U.S. buyers would not be illegal.

A third reform is to reduce barriers faced by American exporters, especially in countries that charge different prices for their products in their home and foreign markets. Dumping can only occur if buyers in the lower price market are prevented from reselling the product in the higher price market. If Korean firms tried to dump steel in the United States, and buyers could resell the cheap steel in Korea, their scheme would not be profitable, and an antidumping case would not be necessary. Thus negotiating to reduce trade barriers facing exports from the United States would discourage dumping in the United States.

Antidumping laws and all laws that protect producers against unfair trade practices face the possibility of penalizing perfectly legitimate behavior by sellers. Is it unfair to invent a new and better product that harms producers of traditional products? Was it unfair to introduce automobiles, which replaced horses and buggies, or computers, which replaced typewriters? The new competition from automobiles and computers must have appeared to be unfair to the traditional producers, and they were definitely harmed. Candle makers may have considered natural sunlight to be unfair competition, and sellers of irrigation equipment may consider rainfall to be an unfair rival. However, if all practices that harm traditional producers are judged to be unfair and illegal, consumers will not be served, and there will be no economic growth.

See also: Chinese Currency; Foreign Direct Investment; Trade Surpluses and Deficits

References

Blonigen, Bruce, and Thomas Prusa. 2003. "Anti-Dumping." In *Handbook of International Trade,* ed. E. K. Choi and J. Harrigan, 251–84. Oxford: Oxford University Press.

Lindsey, Brick, and Daniel Ikenson. 2002. *Anti-Dumping 101: The Devilish Details of Unfair Trade Law.* Trade Policy Analysis No. 20. Washington, DC: Cato Institute.

Further Reading: Campbell, Doug. 2006. "Trade Wars." *Regional Focus* (Spring): 20–23; Drope, Jeffrey, and Wendy L. Hansen. 2006. "Anti-Dumping's Happy Birthday?" *World Economy* 29: 459–72; "EU Further Punishes U.S." 2006. *Wall Street Journal* (May 1): A10.

Thomas Grennes

E

EDUCATION AND ECONOMIC COMPETITIVENESS

In a modern economy, education is of great importance in determining the productivity of workers. The skill and productivity of workers are crucial to the productivity of firms and industries. In turn, it is productivity that determines which firms will succeed and which industries will be competitive in regional and international trade. In this entry, the focus is on the role that education of individuals plays in economic productivity and competitiveness. It is based on a new way of looking at education that developed in economics a little more than 50 years ago. It has invigorated both research and policy debates. This modern analysis has been no less than a shooting star in the academic world, and it shows no sign of burning out.

EDUCATION, SCHOOLING, AND HUMAN CAPITAL

Education is a little like oxygen: it is odorless and colorless. You cannot see it, smell it, or touch it. It is best observed in action in people at work solving problems. Education occurs through schooling and experience, that is, through both guided and individual learning. Acquiring education is an economic process itself because it consumes buildings and materials as well as the time of teachers and students. All of these are scarce resources that could be used in other ways. Hence it is important to understand how education increases economic output and wages and how education itself is created.

Human capital was discovered in the 1950s during the search for the source of increased productivity in national economies. When economists added up the number of units of inputs and outputs over several decades, they discovered that there was a phenomenal increase in output per hour of work and per machine. Search for the source of increased output per unit of input led to the conclusion that the market productivity of the so-called human agent had increased. It was only a step from this conclusion to the analysis of the relationship between schooling and wages. The early wage equations showed that an additional year of schooling increased wages 5 percent or more. College graduates were earning 30–60 percent more than high school graduates each year they worked. This differential generated a handsome return on investment in additional schooling. Educational investment is typically made in young people in a period of schooling and yields a payoff in a lifetime of use—hence the term human capital.

The high wage premium for schooling was too broad a finding in the sense that economic research appeared to show that the content of schooling could be ignored: it was productive at all levels and in all kinds of schools. It did not seem to matter what the native ability (raw human capital) or personal drive of the student was, or the vigor of his or her peers. Increased productivity appeared to have been universally associated with schooling. Even crudely correcting for the variations among schools, households, and individual students, the major findings held. The conclusion was and is that human capital has been an extremely important source of productivity.

There is at least one major failing with this explanation of productivity: schooling is more productive in some economies than others. The institutional arrangements often called "law and order" facilitate the increased productivity arising from education. The business climate has to be right for even well-trained and well-motivated workers to be productive. For example, a satisfying workplace exchange between employees and employers is important. This is sometimes referred to as industrial peace. It may be provided by unions that represent the tastes and preferences of workers or by an astute employer. Another law-and-order factor is the ability to freely negotiate contracts. The courts play a role in economic productivity because contracts frequently need to be interpreted in settling disputes between the contracting parties. Law-and-order issues also include freedom from government confiscation of assets and from exploitive taxation.

Human capital is important in the economy. Labor receives approximately three-fourths of the total income of the economy. This is nearly three times the amount of income generated by physical capital. Before 1945, growth was thought to be largely the product of increasing the amount of physical capital in the economy. This earlier belief is the source of the present emphasis on saving and investment. By inventing the term human capital, labor and its improvement became a form of investment to be considered on a conceptual par with physical capital.

FORMAL SCHOOLING

Schooling is the most visible input in the process of becoming educated. The Founding Fathers were very concerned that the electorate be literate so that the people could participate intelligently in the electoral process. In colonial

America, most schooling was provided by church groups. In Puritan New England, schools were supported by a parish-wide tax. The level of literacy was high, even in the absence of a national system of free schools. But the call for free schooling was very strong. As new territories, counties, and states were formed in the West, school districts were laid out, and legal provision was made for funding them—a novel development in the world at the time. Compulsory attendance at these schools was legislated in most states. Of course, quality and expenditure differed according to local option and in response to regional tastes and racial policies. By the opening of the twentieth century, the United States led the world in mass schooling.

By 1910, the national public high school movement was gathering strength. Following the pattern established by elementary education, public high schools were first introduced in New England and then swept across the country. They were set up sooner and more completely outside the Old South, where the 12th grade of public school was not universal until about 1945. In contrast to Europe, where most of the schools were organized as national systems, U.S. schools were made up of a multitude of small, independent districts funded largely by local property taxes. The U.S. system was (1) open and forgiving of student failure, with little or no occupational tracking for young students; (2) responsive to local needs and tastes; (3) based on an academic yet practical curriculum; (4) under public control; and (5) based on gender-neutral admission. Enrollment in both elementary and high schools in the United States has continued to grow continuously, but it was even more rapid in Europe. By the 1970s, the level of schooling of youth was almost as high in Europe as in the United States.

In the United States, the percentage of people over 25 with high school degrees continued to grow decade by decade, as older persons retired and were replaced by young people with more years of schooling. Currently, younger and older cohorts have about the same number of years of schooling. This has led some analysts to conclude that the growth in productivity arising from schooling may be nearly over. In the past few decades, the proportion of young people graduating from high schools has dropped, perhaps partially the result of large-scale immigration.

Maybe more ominous for future economic productivity, the United States generally stands only mid-range internationally on a number of standardized academic tests. U.S. educational performance was an acute national issue when the Russians took the lead in space technology in the 1960s. It was a concern with the startling development of the Japanese economy in the 1980s and has reemerged since 2000 with the rapid growth of Chinese exports. Analyses of the growth of economic output across nations suggest that education has probably played an important role, but firm conclusions are hard to make because comparing growth internationally requires great effort to develop dependable measures of the forces at work.

The growth and funding of higher education has been quite different from K–12 schools. Private payment for teaching services in the form of tuition is much more important at the college level. In addition, many old-line private universities and a few large public universities have accumulated large endowments through gifts from their alumni. These now fund a substantial number of scholarships for current students. State governments began to subsidize college attendance more than a century ago. This has allowed them to set their tuition below the level of costs for many enrollees. The federal government's first support for higher education came in the Morrill Act of 1852 through an allocation of land to new state universities. These were originally intended to serve the "sons of mechanics and farmers," signaling an interest in equality of opportunity. The Morrill Act is perhaps the earliest legislative mention of the wage advantage of schooling.

Federal support for college education is now made largely to individual students rather than to institutions. The GI Bill for veterans of World War II is the most famous of these programs. More recent additions have been the provision of grants and federally insured loans.

Over the last 50 years, college and university enrollments have risen more than fivefold in the United States. Currently, close to 60 percent or more of all persons aged 18–24 years enroll in an institution of higher education each fall. The proportion of persons completing four or more years of college has increased about threefold over the same half century. In 1950, the ratio of college graduates in the workforce to nongraduates was in the neighborhood of 1 to 19. The present ratio is close to 1 to 6, and for presently enrolled college students, the ratio could rise to 1 to 3. This puts the United States at the top of the range internationally. For some, it suggests that Americans may be overeducated.

WHAT MAKES A WORKER PRODUCTIVE?

A productive worker is one who is healthy, interested in work, and has acquired the skills required in his or her assigned tasks. Productivity is based on a number of components arising from family, culture, and schooling and the interaction of these with experience.

Health is one of these components. Health is partially a matter of heredity, but it is also a product of habits acquired largely at home. A personality that is positive and outgoing can also affect productivity. A desire to please, something that may or may not be instilled by parents, can be a major source of output. Raw energy and drive also are important and largely uninfluenced by schooling. Employers searching for new recruits even at the BA level inquire about the candidate's attitudes and desire to succeed, sometimes almost ignoring the college transcript. Sociologists in the nineteenth century identified a cultural element they believed contributed to differential rates of economic growth that they labeled the Protestant work ethic. Today, high rates of economic activity are identified with a number of different ethnic and religious groups. While it is difficult to quantify its importance, this is another element not greatly affected by schooling.

Cognitive skills are essential to worker productivity. Cognitive skills include (1) verbal skills that make it possible to follow printed instructions, (2) quantitative skills that allow the worker to use numbers and numerical processes in deciding how to carry out an assignment, and (3) reasoning skills that are useful in comprehension, composition, and problem solving. Most standardized school tests are based on these three skills. Test scores explain an important portion, but not all, of the variation in success in school. They have a strong positive correlation with wages of workers. But it is possible that test scores and market productivity both reflect high native intelligence and positive personality factors.

Two additional components related to a productive worker are probably based on a combination of personality and cognitive skills. One is entrepreneurial ability (enterprise-man-ship, if there were such an English word), meaning the ability to outline alternative courses of action, evaluate risks, and make decisions and the willingness to live with the consequences. The returns to entrepreneurial activity are especially strong during periods of rapid growth and change, when new ways of organizing production are rewarded. Another factor related jointly to personality and cognitive skill is personal flexibility: the ability to change work location or acquire a new skill or find employment in a new industry in response to changing market conditions. This has become an important factor as the geographic size of labor markets has expanded in the past 50 years and as the pace of change has increased.

DEMAND FOR SKILLS AND THE DETERMINATION OF MARKET WAGES

Many of the items just mentioned have to do with the supply of worker characteristics, but the demand for these characteristics is also important. Labor demand is a function of the technology used in production and consumers' changing demand for commodities. Over time, the development of particular materials, machines, and fuels has reduced the demand for brawn relative to brains. Perhaps the best example is the relative decline in farming that occurred as consumers increased their demand for nonfarm goods. The portion of the workforce engaged in farming has fallen from near 50 percent a century ago to 3 percent or less today.

Even more important were the host of mechanical inventions that reduced the demand for skills acquired through apprenticeships. These also increased the demand for general academic skills acquired in school. Perhaps the most dramatic example of this force in the past 50–70 years is found in the household. Under older technologies, wives and daughters did a large share of the food preparation, clothing construction, and home decoration. Girls and young women stayed home and worked as apprentices. But now, many of the traditional home-produced goods and services come from factories. With rewards from work at home low and opportunities for work in the market high, women now go to school and compete for almost every class of job in the nation. In fact, women now constitute more than 50 percent of all college students in the United States, and the percentage continues to climb.

The demand for and supply of labor of a particular skill level determines the wage for that skill level in the market. Generally, higher-skilled jobs pay more than lower skilled ones. For example, jobs that require a college degree usually pay more than those that require only a high school diploma, in the neighborhood of

50 percent more. The ratio of wages could be reasonably expected to decline as the proportion of college graduates increased, if only supply mattered. But demand for higher skills has also been increasing as fast as the relative supply of students with more schooling.

There have been some interesting variations in relative wages over the past 60 years. The premium paid to college over high school graduates narrowed during World War II, a time at which the national emphasis was on massive increases in output of standardized products and manpower was diverted to the armed forces. The wage premium for college graduates began to increase slowly after the end of the war. But increases in college enrollments spurred by the Vietnam War draft reduced the college wage premium for a time. It has since recovered as technological change has led to high wages for those who have the ability to acquire computer skills. A short-run example of this force can be seen in the wages paid programmers in the run up to the year 2000, at which time all data files had to be identified with four digits rather than two.

International trade is another way in which changing technology and world labor market balances can affect relative wages in the United States. In the past several decades, production techniques have made labor with lower levels of schooling more valuable in manufacturing in many countries. This has led to greater levels of imports of cheap manufactured goods. These imports have in turn reduced the wages of U.S. laborers that produce these same goods. Thus part of the current wage premium for U.S. college graduates is a result of changes in international labor supplies and production techniques. World labor conditions have become a stimulus for more college enrollment in the United States.

Not all occupations benefit equally from conventional schooling. Jobs based on physical performance are still based largely on direct practice and participation. These occupations include musical performance, acting, and professional sports. If it were not for the fact that U.S. colleges have developed a minor league system for some sports, there would be little direct payoff to aspiring professional athletes who attend college even today. Few universities outside the United States enroll them. Until recently, many youthful American baseball players honed their skills in club teams, much as they still do the world over for soccer.

PUBLIC POLICY ISSUES FOR KINDERGARTEN THROUGH 12TH GRADE

Public taxes continue to provide the major portion of funding for elementary and high schools, although individual private students receive most of the benefits from schooling. Even charter schools and student vouchers are supported by taxes when students enroll in approved schools organized by private companies. The usual justification for public support of the education of private individuals is that students and their parents by themselves might underinvest because (1) they are not well informed of the benefits of schooling, (2) parents may not be willing to afford the cost of schooling at the time their children are young, and (3) there may be positive benefits from schooling that are captured by the community and not by the individual student. Public funding has given the U.S.

population nearly universal access to schooling. In turn, universal schooling can be credited with the maintenance of a more or less common language and culture across a large nation formed from people of many different backgrounds.

The downside of public school funding is that childless families are required to pay taxes from which they may believe they receive little or no direct benefit.

HOW DOES THE U.S. EDUCATIONAL SYSTEM STACK UP AGAINST OTHER COUNTRIES?

International competition is a major force in today's economy. As never before, U.S. workers are directly competing with workers in foreign countries. Increasingly, it is the brains of U.S. citizens against the brains of citizens of other countries. In this kind of world, a nation's educational system becomes vitally important.

So how well does the U.S. education system perform? As the table shows, the United States compares favorably with other countries on standardized test scores. In fourth and eighth grades, the U.S. scores are higher than for their international counterparts. However, although the reading scores of U.S. high school students are better than those of foreign students, U.S. high school scores are lower in math and science.

While U.S. students are at or above the international average, they are not at the top. Students in some Asian countries—Japan, South Korea, and Hong Kong (now a part of the People's Republic of China)—typically do better.

There is also a concern for the international competitiveness of U.S. college graduates. Although American colleges and universities are rated the top in the world, there is a worry that U.S. college students are not pursuing disciplines that have the most influence on the competitive position of a country. Many economists think that the future success of countries will be largely guided by the scientific training of their most highly educated workers. In 2003, only 18 percent of bachelor's degrees and 14 percent of graduate degrees in U.S. colleges and universities were awarded in the sciences. This compares with rates of over 30 percent in countries like Germany, South Korea, Japan, and the United Kingdom. And while it is true that college graduation rates are higher in the United States, the concern is whether U.S. students are acquiring degrees in the disciplines needed for the United States to go head-to-head with other countries in the global economic race.

Standardized test scores, 2003

	United States	*International*
Fourth-grade math scores	518	495
Fourth-grade math scores	504	467
Eighth-grade science scores	527	473
High school reading scores	495	488
High school math scores	483	489
High school science scores	491	496

Source: U.S. Department of Education, *Digest of Educational Statistics*, 2005.

Older parents whose children have finished public school may come to feel that the schools are adding unproductive frills at their expense. This could lead to conflicts over bond issues and to underfunding of schooling, as seen from students' parents' point of view. When this occurs, parents are left to support private tutors and pay for other activities. Of course, the other side of this coin is that parents with young children may seek elaborate schools beyond the level they would be willing to fund if they had to pay the full bill. The divergent points of view lead to friction in the process of making public decisions. The line between private and public responsibility for schooling inevitably shifts back and forth, sometimes covering extras such as sports teams, music lessons, and after-school child care, and other times not.

One way to conceptually resolve much of the possible conflict between families with school-aged children and older families is for school district residents to think of public schooling as a fund from which the student borrows and then repays as a taxed adult. This way of looking at public schooling may explain why even communities heavily populated by retired people generally fund respectable public schools.

Often, support for school funding is advocated on the grounds that better schools will increase employment locally. For example, better schools might attract businesses whose managers want their children to attend good schools.

Other proponents of more local spending sometimes argue that once a student is schooled, she or he will stay in the school district and become a magnet for new plants and firms the community would like to attract. This argument comes very close to claiming that human capital built through public schools belongs to the district. As a general rule, good schools by themselves do not raise the level of economic activity within the district appreciably, primarily because schooled individuals are free to migrate and often do so in large numbers. Fortunately for young people, their mobility has virtually never been restricted just because they were educated at so-called public expense. But it is possible that attention to migration may dampen a local district's willingness to fund public schools.

If free, compulsory schooling increases the wage opportunities of the poorest people and the funding is borne heavily by the well-off members of the district, incomes may be more equal than in the absence of public funding. Some analysts believe that public schooling is the most important societal means for making incomes more equal, even more important than the cash transfers of public welfare. A current manifestation of the concern with income distribution is with the so-called digital divide, in which computer instruction is seen by some to be a vital component for equalizing opportunity.

Another income transfer motivation is seen in the proposals to share the tax bases of rich and poor districts within a state. Within the United States, there have been legal suits in 44 of the 50 states to equalize funding by transferring school funds across district lines. These suits are controversial for several reasons. Among them is the uncertain impact the transfer of funds may have on the willingness of school districts to increase tax levies. The issues are far from being resolved at present.

One of the most serious problems at the K–12 level is the variation in the effectiveness with which public educational services are delivered. School districts that have a reputation for being very effective sometimes seek to limit the immigration of students from outside the district. Others are sometimes labeled as failed schools, as measured by standardized end-of-year student achievement tests. Two approaches have been used to deal with this problem. One is to create new schools that compete with traditional public schools. In some states, charter schools license a small number of private schools to receive public funds. In others, vouchers are given to students, who then use them to enroll in private schools regulated by public authorities. Making publicly gathered funds available to private firms may sound a little unusual at first. But the same kind of apparatus is used to provide for the private construction of public highways as well as defense hardware and most public buildings.

Another policy measure provides for state intervention in the administration of local public schools that have a high portion of students who have failed to make acceptable progress. No Child Left Behind legislation is the federal entry in this approach, but it is not yet clear how the law will work and whether this is the beginning of a sizeable infusion of federal funds into K–12 schooling. One of the truly difficult problems facing school reform organized around student test scores is to separate instructional failures of the school district from different educational needs of students. The home environment of the student is almost always acknowledged to have an important effect on the rate at which the student learns. But little attention has been given to distinguishing between the problems in school instructional services versus the special needs of failing students that may arise in the home. If poor test performance is primarily a problem that lies with the student and not with the school, only a substantially enriched environment can reasonably be expected to raise scores. Many analysts believe that learning skills must be augmented at a very early age if a substantial impact is to be achieved.

PUBLIC POLICY ISSUES FOR HIGHER EDUCATION

Should the United States support a goal to enroll all high school graduates in an accredited college or university? To achieve such a goal, more subsidization of college attendance would be required. What would the return on this kind of public investment earn? The recommendation to expand enrollment usually is based on an assumption that the wage differential for the new graduates will be as high as it has been for the average of previous graduates. Supporters note that nonmarket returns, such as the higher probability of working in a pleasant environment, are a benefit to college graduates that have gone unmeasured. Also, more diplomas will open up the chance for advancement to people who otherwise might be excluded from better opportunities. This is also one of the arguments that underlies efforts to provide for a wider diversity in selective colleges.

Some oppose greater subsidization of college on the grounds that reducing the cost of a good usually means that it is less appreciated. They note that the academic level of college instruction may already have fallen, at least in some institutions, due to the presence of students who are more interested in the pleasant interlude between childhood and work than they are in scholarship. Also, wage differentials between the average college and high school may represent returns to personal and scholarly attributes that have not been fully identified in making comparisons between high school and college graduates.

Future students are concerned about the rising cost of tuition. For a number of years, it has increased at roughly twice the rate of inflation. In some state systems, the level of tuition is kept low as a matter of public policy. In a few states, there have been calls to limit the increases in tuition to maintain the opportunity for students and their families to afford a college experience. Even though there is no national policy on tuition, it would be useful to think about the determinants of tuition.

In a progressive economy, where productivity increase is the general rule, some products are not amenable to technical change. Haircuts are a good example. The market costs of inputs used by the industry rise as real wages rise. Without an increase in the price of a haircut, it would be uneconomic to produce it. This may also be the case for mail delivery and university instruction, both of which are heavily dependent on the time of suppliers. Policy efforts to put a ceiling on tuition would probably not work, just as putting a limit on the price of haircuts would not. Perhaps the force most likely to arrest the steady increases in tuition would be to place a greater responsibility for learning on the student's own efforts, such as by greater use of the computer and taped lecturers. But a shift to more individual learning would also require new institutional arrangements for certifying the student's progress.

SUMMARY

Much of the massive increase in productivity in the U.S. economy has been made possible by investments in human capital. Schooling is the most important form of this investment, but it is not the only form. Better public health, lower rates of child mortality, and attention to good nutrition have also increased the productivity of persons as workers as well as in their role as consumers. On-the-job training is still very important in the lifetime earnings of workers, even though many formal apprenticeships have been replaced by general schooling. Much of the investment in good habits, good health, and strong motivation comes in families and could be regarded as private investment. Even much of the investment in public schooling can be regarded as essentially private in form: the student benefits from public funding of schooling as a child. Later, he or she pays it back in the form of taxes to support schooling for the next generation.

A student who either under- or overinvests in his or her own schooling forgoes income later in life. It is not easy to formulate dependable expectations on future wages or to estimate what schooling can do to support the individual's personal cultural life. It is the responsibility of the individual student to identify his or her interests and capabilities in formulating schooling objectives. If one is to do well in school, it is important to seek a clear understanding of the connection between study and future productivity. In an era of human capital, every individual has become responsible for formulating improved estimates of costs and returns concerning his or her own personal capital.

See also: Glass Ceiling; Salary Disparity

Further Reading: Barro, Robert J. 2001. "Human Capital and Growth." *American Economic Review* 91: 12–17; Cameron, Steven V., and James J. Heckman. 1993. "Nonequivalence of High School Equivalents." *Journal of Labor Economics* 11: 1–47; Hanushek, Eric A. 1986. "The Economics of Schooling: Production and Efficiency in the Public Schools." *Journal of Economic Literature* 24: 1141–77; Hanushek, Eric A. 1996. "School Resources and Student Performance." In *Does Money Matter? The Effect of School Resources on Student Achievement and Adult Success,* ed. Gary Burtless, 43–73. Washington, DC: Brookings Foundation; Hanushek, Eric A., and Dennis D. Kimko. 2000. "Schooling, Labor-Force Quality and the Growth of Nations." *American Economic Review* 90: 1184–1208; Lazear, Edward P. 2002. *Education in the Twenty-first Century.* Stanford, CA: Hoover Institution Press.

Dale M. Hoover

EMPLOYEE LOYALTY AND ENGAGEMENT

Until the 1980s, most U.S. workers and employers adhered to an implicit social contract that exchanged lifelong employment for loyalty and productivity from employees, as long as the economy remained strong (Baron and Bielby 1984). More recently, three developments indicate a shift away from this philosophy. First, in the name of efficiency, many firms have restructured businesses and laid off employees independent of economic cycles. Second, labor markets have come to be viewed as more volatile, and job tenure continues to become shorter. Finally, there has been an increasing externalization of employment as more work is being done by temporary employees, independent contractors, consultants, and strategic partners (Kunda et al. 2002).

Beginning in the 1980s, the employer-employee relationship changed, as many firms engaged in extensive downsizing and restructuring activities. Between 1979 and 1993, employment totals of the Fortune 500 companies in the United States declined annually from 16.2 million employees in 1979 to 11.5 million in 1983 (Useem 1984). Additionally, throughout much of the 1990s, despite strong economic growth, the number of regular jobs eliminated in U.S. companies on an annual basis increased from 100,000 in 1989 to nearly 700,000 in 1999 ("Future of Work" 2000). While earlier job cuts targeted mainly blue-collar workers in manufacturing companies, the more recent job cuts targeted white-collar employees, including middle managers, in a wide range of industries (Casio 1993).

Statistics also show that there has been a significant decline of perception of employment security in U.S. firms during the past 20 years. In 1987, 26 percent of firms offered job security to over 80 percent of their employees; this number declined to only 9 percent in 1996 (Farrell et al. 2006). Among those employees who have job security, there is still a decline in their job tenures with a particular employer, especially for professional service industries. As a result, there is also a growing perception of uncertainty among employees and speculation about whether the implicit contract between employers and employees, which promised job security to loyal and productive employees, has been repealed (Cappelli 1999).

There are also increasing uses of newer forms of employment modes that do not involve traditional security or loyalty, but involve new forms of commitment and responsibility. For example, currently, various types of nontraditional workers or contingent workers account for between 25 and 35 percent of the total workforce, and this number continues to grow (Farrell et al. 2006). With contingent workers, employers provide opportunity rather than security; employees provide task contribution rather than loyalty—both are not and cannot possibly be obligated to maintain a long-term relationship. In addition, globalization is causing a large number of job losses. Many manufacturing jobs, for example, are being outsourced to outside of the United States. Manufacturing reduced from accounting for 32 percent of the total U.S. employment in 1975 to 21 percent in 2005. Service jobs are also being outsourced due to the application of new technology to enable physical separation of service provider and service consumer (such as the increasing outsourcing of call centers); some predict that up to 10 percent of service jobs have a potential to be outsourced (Farrell et al. 2006).

Overall, there seems to be a divergence of practices and views toward loyalty: some continue to believe that loyalty is good for both employers and employees, while others opt for market transaction and flexibility. This entry aims to explore these different perspectives.

WHY TRADITIONAL LOYALTY CAN BE GOOD FOR EMPLOYERS

The importance of employee loyalty has been emphasized in the traditional bureaucratic management model, often with the condition that the external environment needs to be relatively stable or predictable. It is also highlighted in many new high-commitment/high-performance human resource management (HRM) models in the past 20 years, where the assumption is that traditional employee loyalty contributes to higher performance outcomes, even in a turbulent environment. So what are the benefits of employee loyalty for companies?

First, with expected long-term employment, there is a predictable pattern of career path inside the firm, which encourages workers to work hard today and stay committed to the firm to enjoy the benefits tomorrow. Owing to the expected long-term tenure with the firm, workers can develop a sense of belongingness and a high level of trust and may be willing to contribute wholeheartedly to the firm. Therefore companies are able to reap the benefits of the continuous hard work of workers. In fact, a growing body of research argues that a high-trust, high-commitment work environment, which is based on a quid pro quo arrangement of providing high job security in exchange for an engaged and productive workforce, can enhance organizational performance (Osterman et al. 2001). Engaged and committed employees are willing to learn new skills, share their knowledge and offer ideas and suggestions, and care about quality and productivity (Osterman 2000). Likewise, where the work performed is central to the organization's purpose or where there is a significant risk of error that cannot be shifted to the employee, it is in the firm's interest to create longer-term employment relations that build trust and commitment (Lautsch 2002).

To the contrary, firms that frequently downsize, especially when out of cost reduction, tend to enjoy short-term efficiency by sacrificing remaining employees' long-term trust and productivity (Heckscher 2007). Workers who expect to be laid off tomorrow cannot possibly be motivated to work hard today. Instead, they may even engage in counterproductive behaviors if they feel that their psychological contract is violated. Of those who remain employed tomorrow, they may still feel threatened and stressed about the fact that the day after tomorrow, they may be laid off as well. As a result, even the morale and commitment of those employees who are lucky today are greatly hurt.

Second, security and loyalty can be cost-effective because there is less direct cost devoted to recruiting, selecting, and training new employees. Turnover can be very detrimental to the firm, especially for service industries, where turnover rates tend to be especially high, and new employees' lack of competence may have an immediate consequence on customer outcomes due to their direct interaction with customers. Customers are often frustrated by prolonged service time due to the on-the-job training of the employee who is serving them. In addition, employees' lack of experience and competence often annoys customers and drives them away. In fact, statistics show that the average cost of turnover is 1.5 times the annual salary of a replaced employee, or $55,977 per employee (Spherion 2003).

Third, with employee loyalty, firms may be able to develop firm-specific human capital (the knowledge, skills, and abilities of employees) and social capital (the idiosyncratic social relationship/ways of communication/trust among workers) that may lead to high performance that otherwise would not be achieved. Specificity refers not just to the extent of specialized knowledge and skills of employees, but to the degree to which these skills are transferable across employers. The more specialized the skills of employees for a specific employer, the deeper and more dependent the relationship (Williamson 1981). It is in the interest of both employees and the employer to ensure a secure and committed working relationship. For example, with higher trust among workers and between workers and the employer, higher quality of products and services is more likely to be achieved. In addition, with common language and strong networks, employees are better able to share knowledge and stimulate innovation. On the contrary, when firms expect that employees are not going to stay for a long time, they are more reluctant to train employees, particularly for generic skills that would increase their employability elsewhere. Also, when workers are constantly threatened with losing their jobs, they may not help other employees and may even hurt them to make themselves look better.

Fourth, a longer stay of workers also provides opportunities for employers to observe the performance of workers and develop and promote the best, who can best contribute to the firm. In fact, even in firms that employ contingent workers, most still keep a small portion of winners and provide them with job security and advancement opportunities to retain the best workers and develop core competencies of the firm (Heckscher 2007).

WHY TRADITIONAL LOYALTY CAN BE GOOD FOR EMPLOYEES

The assurance of job security may also prove beneficial for employees, particularly for those who value stability and predictability. Many employees may fear that increasing uncertainty, along with the lack of job security, are undermining the well-being of workers and their families (Osterman 1987). According to Maslow's human needs hierarchy, security is one of the most basic needs of human beings. The incomes and benefits from work determine living standards for American employees more than in other countries (Freeman and Rogers 1999). Employers are the primary source of many important benefits, ranging from health insurance to pension plans that increase in value based on continued loyal service (Kochan et al. 1994). For many employees, leaving a job may also mean losing health insurance and, if they are not vested, losing a pension. With future job security and the predictability of career path, workers know how to get ahead, and when to plan starting a family, buying a house, paying for children's college, and saving for retirement (Heckscher 2007). Therefore, in general, people need to be paid a premium to be willing to assume risks if they have a choice.

On the contrary, owing to the increasing uncertainty of many job positions, there is an increasing level of stress among workers and a decline of job satisfaction among workers with or without job security. This is exacerbated by an increase in the cost of living: many workers count on their work earnings to support the daily expenditures of the family; when they lose their job, they cannot even make ends meet. Therefore job security is particularly desired among those who do not have it, are least skilled and least employable, and make the least amount of money.

There is also a significant cost associated with changing jobs that many employees may prefer to avoid. The costs to search for a new position, along with possible moving expenses and the disruption to family life, can be substantial. In addition, there is no guarantee that the next position will provide higher wages or improved benefits. In fact, many employees who are forced to look for new employment, particularly lower-skilled employees who have been with a company for a long period of time, often find it difficult to find a position that pays a comparable compensation (Freeman and Rogers 1999).

WHY TRADITIONAL LOYALTY CAN BE BAD FOR EMPLOYERS

However, loyalty in a traditional sense is not always good for employers, especially in today's turbulent environment. The concept of functional turnover describes situations in which companies can benefit by losing employees who are bad performers or are no longer needed due to factors such as technological change, changes in customer demands, and product specialization. Indeed, there are situations where companies do not want employees to be loyal or do not want to commit to employees because that contradicts the needs of the increasingly dynamic and complex environment, which calls for more adaptability and innovation by companies. There are several reasons.

First, under the traditional security mode, employees who work together all the time tend to become very similar, which inhibits their inclination to think out of the box and come up with innovative approaches. Therefore there is an increasing trend of hiring consultants, contractors, and temporary workers to bring in fresh ideas and technical expertise that are not possible or are too expensive to cultivate in-house.

Second, facing increasing cost reductions, many companies may not be able to afford security. Owing to the ever-increasing cost of competition in the global market, companies may target only a certain core employee group (those who are most valuable for and unique to the company) and provide them with security and good benefits, and employ more flexible employment modes toward the peripheral workers (Lepak and Snell 1999). This corresponds to the emerging differentiations of mission-critical functions and mission-supportive functions in companies and the application of different strategies toward workers in the two functions.

In these highly changing times, organizations also adopt a core-peripheral model to enhance their flexibility. Today's highly competitive markets and demanding customers exert pressure on firms to create customized products and responsive services. We are also in the midst of a long-term technological revolution, which is continually changing how, where, and when we work (Heckscher 2001). Skills that were in high demand last year can be obsolete today. Oftentimes, organizations need to quickly adapt to environmental pressures and thus can only be loyal to a small group of core employees. With skills and demand changing so rapidly, organizations may find it more effective to look for needed skills on the open market, rather than developing them internally. As such, companies are able to excel at their core competencies, while at the same time reduce costs and be adaptable to external changes. In fact, studies show that companies who employ at least 10 percent temporary workers have higher financial and share-price growth (Spherion 2003).

Third, it is dysfunctional to retain bad performers or employees who are no longer needed for a lifetime. Good performers today may no longer be good performers tomorrow, and employees who add core value to the firm today may not be valuable tomorrow. Therefore voluntary turnover of these employees may avoid the companies being at fault by firing them. In addition, a tenure system may actually turn good performers into bad performers due to their lack of motivation to keep up with their jobs. Thus having a core and noncore differentiation among different workers can help maintain a sense of competition and crisis among workers, which will continuously motivate them to work hard to be the winners.

WHY TRADITIONAL LOYALTY CAN BE BAD FOR EMPLOYEES

While some employees value stability, others may prefer mobility and flexibility. Additionally, a growing number of individuals may be unhappy with corporate life and see few long-term benefits for being loyal to one employer.

These employees may view the old employer-employee relationship as outdated and view corporate life as exploitive and stifling, forcing people to play politics and be subject to the whims of managers. These individuals view themselves as free agents and shun loyalty by marketing their skills to the highest bidder. They advocate a postindustrial vision of economic individualism, in which free agents would act as entrepreneurs and capture a fair portion of their market value (Barley and Kunda 2005).

Even employees who used to believe that employers are responsible for providing them with job security and a clear career path are starting to change their mind-set given the changes in the workplace. In fact, while in 1999, 86 percent of these traditional workers reported that they were fearful of job change, this number dropped down to 72 percent in 2003. Also, while in 1999, the vast majority (96%) of workers believed that career advancement is the responsibility of employers, in 2003, this number dropped to 86 percent (Spherion 2003). On the other hand, there are more and more so-called emergent workers who want control in their own careers and expect employers to provide resources and opportunities for them to learn and develop. They define loyalty not in a traditional, longevity way, but in a way that reflects their value, contribution, and self-development (Heckscher 2007; Spherion 2003). But why is the meaning of loyalty changing for workers?

First, people may realize that they have different pursuits at different points in their careers. By being able to flexibly switch their jobs, rather than being tied to a particular company, employees are able to pursue different experiences that are considered meaningful for their lives. In fact, more workers report that they become self-directed, self-motivated, and self-reliant with increasing employment flexibility (Spherion 2003). Among emergent workers, 95 percent reported that they were very eager to explore different opportunities (Spherion 2003). Indeed, some people use job changes to get an advancement, both in terms of position level and income level, because there is often limited opportunity within a single company.

Second, with employment flexibility, employees are able to continuously develop themselves. People have the opportunity to obtain different skill sets, work with different people, and face different challenges in different companies, all of which are not likely to be available if they continue to work within a single company. Therefore, with employment flexibility, employees are also more able to manage their employability and subsequent career advancement.

Third, the increasing flexible market also contributes to the job flexibility of employees, particularly skilled employees. To them, losing a job may not be viewed as a big deal; in fact, many of them choose to end a job because they believe that they will not have any problem finding a job elsewhere in a relatively short time period.

SUMMARY

The construct of employee loyalty has a long-standing tradition in the world of work. Yet, over the last 25 years, we have witnessed the emergence of alternative perspectives on the value of employee loyalty. What was once an implicit concept that employers and employees alike adhered to has become less taken for granted. Depending on one's point of view, there are clear advantages and disadvantages to employee loyalty for employers as well as for employees.

See also: Charismatic Leadership; Violence in the Workplace

References

Barley, S. R., and G. Kunda. 2005. "Contracting: A New Form of Professional Practice." *Academy of Management Perspective* 19: 1–19.

Baron, J. N., and W. T. Bielby. 1984. "The Organization of Work in a Segmented Economy." *American Sociological Review* 49: 454–73.

Cappelli, P. 1999. *The New Deal at Work: Managing the Market-Driven Workforce.* Boston: Harvard Business School Press.

Casio, W. 1993. "Downsizing: What Do We Know? What Have We Learned?" *Academy of Management Executives* 7: 95–104.

Farrell, Diana, Martha A. Laboissiere, and Jason Rosenfield. 2006. "Sizing the Emerging Global Labor Market." *McKinsey Quarterly* 3.

Freeman, R. B., and J. Rogers. 1999. *What Workers Want.* New York: ILR Press.

"The Future of Work: Career Evolution." 2000. *The Economist* (January 29): 89–92.

Heckscher, C. 2001. "Living with Flexibility." In *Rekinndling the Movement: Transforming the Labor Movement in the 1990s and Beyond,* ed. R. Hurd, H. Katz, and L. Turner, 59–81. Ithaca, NY: Cornell University Press.

Heckscher, C. 2007. *White-Collar Blues: Management Loyalties in an Age of Corporate Restructuring.* New York: Basic Books.

Kochan, T., H. Katz, and R. McKersie. 1994. *The Transformation of American Industrial Relations.* New York: Basic Books.

Kunda, G., S. R. Barely, and J. Evans. 2002. "Why Do Contractors Contract? The Experience of Highly Skilled Technical Professionals in a Contingent Labor Market." *Industrial and Labor Relations Review* 55: 234–61.

Lautsch, B. A. 2002. "Uncovering and Explaining Variance in the Features and Outcomes of Contingent Work." *Industrial and Labor Relations Review* 56: 23–43.

Lepak, D. P., and S. A. Snell. 1999. "The Human Resource Architecture: Toward a Theory of Human Capital Allocation and Development." *Academy of Management Review* 24: 31–48.

Osterman, P. 1987. "Choice of Employment Systems in Industrial Relations." *Industrial Relations Review* 26: 48–63.

Osterman, P. 2000. "Work Reorganization in an Era of Restructuring: Trends in Diffusion and Effects on Employee Welfare." *Industrial and Labor Relations Review* 53: 179–96.

Osterman, P., R. Kochan, R. Locke, and M. Piore. 2001. *Working in America: A Blueprint for the New Labor Market.* Cambridge, MA: MIT Press.

Spherion. 2003. *The Rise of the Emergent Workforce.* Available at: http://www.spherion.com/downloads/pov/POV_Main_(LR-BW).pdf.

Useem, M. 1984. *The Inner Circle.* New York: Oxford University Press.

Williamson, O. E. 1981. "The Economics of Organization: The Transaction Cost Approach." *American Journal of Sociology* 87: 548–77.

Further Reading: Cappelli, P. 1999. *The New Deal at Work: Managing the Market-Driven Workforce.* Boston: Harvard Business School Press; Freeman, R. B., and J. Rogers. 1999. *What Workers Want.* New York: ILR Press; Schier, T. J. 2002. *Send Flowers to the Living:*

Rewards, Contests, and Incentives to Build Employee Loyalty. Flower Mound, TX: Incentivize Sol.

Ying Hong, William Castellano, and David Lepak

ENTERPRISE RESOURCE PLANNING SYSTEMS

Enterprise resource planning (ERP) systems have been in existence since the 1980s, and companies have experienced many problems and challenges implementing these systems. The success rate in implementing an ERP system has improved but is still below 28 percent (EyetoIT 2004). Owing to the low success rate, many organizations are wondering if ERP systems are really worth the trouble and expense. Within organizations, especially those with failed systems, there is tremendous controversy regarding the usefulness of ERP systems.

In the 1980s, companies were under pressure to produce new products faster and to reduce costs to compete in a global economy. They felt that an ERP system would solve their problem of gaining and maintaining a strategic and competitive advantage. Companies rushed to implement these systems with the hope they would solve all their problems. Organizations have moved toward acquiring and implementing package software, rather than building a similar application of their own. Companies realized that it was cheaper to purchase an ERP software application, knowing that the cost of development had already been paid by a vendor. When successful, these packaged business software applications allow companies to automate and integrate the majority of their business processes, share common data and practices across the enterprise, and produce and access information in a real-time environment.

In today's environment, why can every company not implement a successful ERP system? Why do ERP projects cost more to develop? Why are implementation scheduled dates missed? Why are users not adequately trained to process data in an ERP system? Why do ERP conversions not run smoothly? The answers to these questions are found in a few important implementation issues. Each of these issues is unique and has a significant impact on the successful implementation of any enterprise system. Each item is just as important as another, and each contains a unique set of challenges. Even though they are not in any order of importance, they must be addressed and resolved to have a successful ERP implementation. In each section of this entry, the controversial aspects of ERP and potential problems will be identified, and proactive solutions will be provided.

CORE BUSINESS PROCESSES MUST BE ALIGNED CORRECTLY

Because of the pressures of global competition in the last 20 years, businesses are constantly streamlining their processes to be more efficient. Many companies assume that their core business processes (e.g., sales order processing, purchase order creation, accounts receivable processing, etc.) are efficient and do not need any review or improvement. Prior to implementing any enterprise system, it is assumed that business processes are already standardized, efficient, and running smoothly.

Business processes have an impact on various organizational functions. Business processes are interwoven among departments. With the use of information technology, reviewing and correcting business processes, sometimes referred to as business engineering, is a lengthy process and normally takes months to complete. Companies are reluctant to begin this effort because it costs money in overtime, takes time away from producing product, and does not immediately impact profits.

Because business engineering is a complete rethinking and reshaping of business processes, companies recognize that communication is the starting point to understanding their business processes. They must break down the walls, both real and imaginary, that separate different departments within a company. Departments must not only address their normal day-to-day workload, but they must also allow additional time to review these processes. All core processes are analyzed; recommendations are made and changes are implemented to ensure that they are current and efficient. If the existing business processes are not efficient and running smoothly, issues will occur during the design of the ERP system.

A survey indicated that the success rate of a business engineering effort in meeting goals is mixed. Thirty-two percent of the companies surveyed considered their projects very successful. Forty-five percent felt that their projects were somewhat successful, and the remaining 23 percent said that their business engineering efforts were not very successful or unsuccessful (Curran and Keller 1998). In summary, companies that completed the business engineering effort did improve communication to employees regarding change, and the companies focused on compelling reasons for changing their business processes (possibly to reduce costs, improve customer response, or bring products to market faster).

THE BEST ORGANIZATIONAL STRUCTURE, PROJECT LEADER, AND FUNCTIONAL TEAMS MUST BE CHOSEN

The organizational structure must be established early in the project. The structure consists of a steering committee, a project leader, and various functional teams. An organizational hierarchy, similar to the one shown in Figure E.1, can provide structure to a complex project.

Because the scope of ERP projects impacts many functions in an organization, a steering committee must be formed. The committee is composed of senior management, who oversee and recommend the acquisition of an ERP application and monitor the progress of the project. They select an ERP project manager and functional team leaders and resolve major implementation issues that affect the organization.

The project manager reports to the steering committee and is responsible for coordinating the entire project effort, interfacing with functional teams, and providing progress reports to the steering committee. The project manager is responsible for delivering an ERP system that satisfies the business objectives. The system must be implemented within budget and on the scheduled due date. The project manager's experience is vital in leading the implementation effort. If an individual is chosen who is new to project leadership, it will add more challenges to an implementation that is already full of complex issues.

Figure E.1 Organizational structure.

The functional teams are composed of a team leader and full-time or part-time individuals who are knowledgeable with the particular process. Some individuals may be members of more than one team because they are knowledgeable with the process and are able to ensure that the interface to their primary functional team is transparent.

Because the functional teams are responsible for implementing their particular segments of the overall project, they must work closely together during the development. In some cases, functional teams are relocated to another department or the central area to discuss and develop their portions of the application without interruption.

The functional teams are responsible for documenting their business processes and ensuring that their processes are included in the application package and that there is an understanding of how to use the software. They are responsible for testing and interfacing their portions of the project with other functional teams. They will be heavily involved with the training and education of others within their functions and will assist with postimplementation problems.

The individuals on the functional teams are in a cross section of personnel who are knowledgeable of their particular functions. Supervisors or managers of key departments, such as order processing, sales, production, and accounting, must also be represented on the team. Each functional team should include an information technology representative to assist in design and testing of the project. The functional teams cannot be composed entirely of information technology personnel. The enterprise software decision is a business decision and not an information technology decision. As a result, personnel from critical areas of the business, such as order entry, inventory control, and transportation logistics, must be members of the functional teams. Their input will be valuable, especially during the design, conversion, testing, and implementation phases of the project. Too many times, the business professionals leave all of the decision making to the information systems staff.

ERP PROJECT LEADER AND FUNCTIONAL TEAM LEADER SKILLS

The ERP project leader and functional team leaders must have resource management, project management, risk management, and change management skills.

Project leaders and functional team leaders must be able to recognize the strengths of each functional team member and assign tasks that utilize these strengths. The functional team leaders must be able to identify these capabilities in all team members and be able to delegate and empower people to do tasks.

The ERP project leader must possess skills to manage a complex project, control costs, and implement a project on time. The functional team leaders must be able to identify where manpower is needed and how many resources are required. They should be knowledgeable of business processes and understand the relationships between business functions and their processes. They must be excellent communicators. They should possess verbal and written communication skills. They have to be able to conduct presentations to senior management and use their interpersonal skills to listen to and work with other team members.

Leaders must be able to anticipate what might go wrong with a project. They must be able to identify risk, assess its complexity, and manage the solution. It is human nature to resist change, especially when the changes affect processes into which employees have poured their hearts and souls for 20 years. Project and functional team leaders must be able to manage change to ensure a smooth transition to the new system. The leaders must be able to rally support for the new system during the development of the project, and especially when the project is implemented. The buy-in and support of senior management, the ERP project leader, and the functional team leaders are vital to ensure an efficient transition. If there is a total buy-in from all team members, questions such as Why was this product chosen? and How will this software ever work in our department? will be avoided.

The number of full-time and part-time team members will vary with the size of the ERP project. Part-time members have to juggle their functional team responsibilities with their day-to-day activities. If the day-to-day activities begin to consume all their time, progress will begin to suffer on the ERP implementation.

Business and information technology consultants may also be used to support the entire ERP implementation effort. Consultants should be contracted to provide expertise in areas that are unfamiliar to people within the organization.

THE SUPPORT OF SENIOR MANAGEMENT IS ESSENTIAL

It is critical to the success of any ERP implementation to have the support of senior management of the organization. Lack of adequate senior management support is probably the most common cause of failure. The questions that confront many ERP project implementations are When should top management be involved? and How can top management be used effectively?

Initially, senior management is involved during the prioritizing of all projects at the beginning of the corporate planning cycle. Management approves an estimated budget prepared by the project leader. The budget includes hardware and software application costs and internal and external manpower requirements.

During project development, periodic reviews allow senior management to be informed of the progress and resolve important issues that have surfaced during the entire project. The primary reason management is involved in review sessions is to make decisions that impact the project. The project team leader and functional team leaders can ask senior management for their opinion on key issues. The reason that this is done is twofold: it ensures the leaders that senior management understand the project and that senior management can communicate the project status to other top management employees. Failure to use top management during the early phases of development may result in delays and complications later in the project life cycle, when decisions are assumed to be resolved.

Keeping senior management informed should not be taken lightly. They have approved the investment in an ERP project and should be aware of the project status. They must be kept informed if the project is on schedule or starting to fall behind. If it is behind schedule, the project manager must explain the reason and what steps will be taken to bring it back on schedule.

Top management can also serve as a cheerleader when the project is close to implementation. Top management can be used effectively when emphasizing the critical nature of the project to all employees who are going to use the system. They can emphasize the importance of where it fits into the company's overall strategic planning and how it is going to benefit the organization. They will emphasize the importance of the project and encourage all employees to support the project and the efforts of the functional teams. They make it clear that employees must use the new system. It is hoped that users will understand the importance of the project and strongly encourage the buy-in by all users to have a successful project implementation. Top management can encourage users to assist the project team in any way possible and to ask questions of the project team to clarify any system questions. Without the communications coming from senior management, the end users may resist the change and knowingly provide obstacles to hinder the efforts of the functional teams (GEAC 2003). By speaking to the employees of the organization, top management can divert skepticism and criticism from the project team by employees who resist change. The open communications between end users and all teams cannot be stressed enough to answer any user questions and obtain their support prior to and after the project implementation date.

THE BEST CONSULTANTS MUST BE CONSULTED TO ASSIST IN PROJECT IMPLEMENTATION

The best-qualified consultants should assist the project team leader and functional teams during critical phases of the implementation (Robinson 2002). Consultants are paid a great deal of money, and they must be used effectively during the project. An organization should treat consultants as outside employees. The consultants' résumés should be reviewed prior to selection. Consultants should be treated as employees, but with the understanding that when the project is complete, they are not available on a full-time basis, unless this is contractually negotiated prior to the implementation. Companies fail to realize that consultants must be managed just like internal employees. This means that an internal employee must know what the consultant is doing and review the results of what he has done. The hourly rate for consultants varies from $100.00 to $250.00, with added travel and lodging expenses. It is easy for companies to fall into the trap of throwing away dollars to consultants. The cash outlay to consultants can be a bottomless pit, resulting in cost overruns and lost benefits.

Organizations must understand that the tasks performed by consultants should be clearly defined and reviewed for completeness. Internal employees must review the design and testing results performed by the consultants. When consultants complete their assigned tasks and leave their assignment, the in-house information technology staff is left with the work done by the consultants. If their work is ignored and testing is not reviewed, added cost will incur when the consultants return to complete their assigned work.

Consultants are not employed by an organization, but by a consulting firm, who assigns them to the organization. When the consultants have completed their defined tasks, they will be assigned to another account. If consultants are not supervised and they commit errors during the design and testing process, the consultants must return to correct their mistakes. If there is a significant difference in time between when the error occurred and when it was detected, the original consultant may have left the organization and been assigned to another customer account. As a result, the error may be corrected by an individual who may not be familiar with the original task, causing delays in solving and correcting the problem.

ENTERPRISE RESOURCE PLANNING PROJECT COSTS MUST BE CONTROLLED

Most ERP projects cost more to implement than originally planned. During a company's budget planning process, when an ERP system is initially suggested as a planned project, estimates of the amount of money needed are established. The estimates are prepared with the best intentions to include all required expenses for the project development period and for future years. Even though these estimates are well thought out and include most of the major expenditures, many other expenses will be left out and surface during project development. Senior management and the project leader must understand that there will be unforeseen expenses that occur during the development of an ERP project. It is up to the project leader or an individual assigned to monitor the project expenses to identify, track, and summarize all costs. Changes in project cost must be communicated to senior management during briefing sessions.

If an ERP system is more than 50 percent developed and unplanned costs are beginning to increase, a major decision of whether to continue with the project must be addressed. When an organization has spent a great deal of money in time and effort, the decision to stop development is extremely difficult. There are conflicting views between management and the project leader. Normally, the project leader feels that the project can be implemented successfully, even though the costs have exceeded the planned budget. Management, on the other hand, must weigh the project team's enthusiasm against the continuing cash outlay. Many times, the development is too far along to stop. Too much money has been invested in hardware, software, and manpower costs to turn back. In most cases, management will give the OK to continue the project, recognizing that a cost overrun will occur. If management decides to stop or postpone the development of the project, morale of all individuals will be affected by the delay. Restarting the project at a later date will result in significant pressure placed on the new project team to implement the project on time and within budget.

The solution to ERP cost overruns is not easy to identify. Tasks, such as providing ample time for ERP development and testing, are difficult to estimate. Doing a better job of detailed planning in the early stages of development will help to further detect potential areas where cost overruns may occur. Setting aside contingency funds for unplanned expenses is another possible solution.

It is unfortunate, but in many cases, the training and education costs are reduced to cut costs. It is clearly an issue of "pay me now or pay me later." If training and education costs are reduced or even eliminated, the problem will surface again when the project is implemented. Users will not have a thorough knowledge of the system and how it works because they have not been educated properly.

RISKS INVOLVED WITH THE PROJECT MUST BE IDENTIFIED

Every ERP project has risk, and it should not be ignored. Failure to identify and manage risk (or just ignoring it) results in higher project costs, missed project completion dates, and failure to attain the expected planned benefits. Functional teams must understand the source and type of risk. Once these two items are identified and subsequent actions taken, risk will be minimized.

Figure E.2 describes a risk assessment matrix for large projects. The matrix indicates that there is risk associated with technology, the application software, and user requirements. Degrees of risk can be categorized as low, medium, or high. Enterprise resource planning projects are normally considered high-risk projects because they impact many functions of the business and take a great deal of time and manpower to implement. The matrix indicates that if the organization has a high familiarity with the technology and the application software, but the user requirements are not defined, the degree of risk is very high. Projects that fall into this category have a very good chance of being unsuccessful if they are not managed effectively. If the organization is familiar with the technology and software, and the user requirements are defined, the project would be classified as being low risk.

Technology and application software have a significant impact on risk. If the technology is considered leading edge, and it is not currently being used in the

	Requirements are not defined	Requirements are defined
High Familiarity with Technology or Application Area	Low-Medium Risk	Low Risk
Low Familiarity with Technology or Application Area	**Very High Risk**	Medium-High Risk

Figure E.2 Risk assessment matrix for large projects.

Source: Adapted from Jeffrey Hoffer, Joey George, and Joseph Valacich. 2002. *Modern Systems Analysis and Design*, 6th ed. Upper Saddle River, NJ: Prentice Hall.

organization, the functional teams must be trained and educated with the new technology. Likewise, if the application software is new, the risk increases because all members of the functional teams, along with all users who will be using the system, must understand the software and be trained on the new application.

Throughout the development of an ERP implementation, project teams must constantly focus on identifying risk, assessing the level of risk, taking corrective action, and managing each risk factor. If the risk issues can be identified, then the risk can be managed.

REALISTIC IMPLEMENTATION SCHEDULES MUST BE ESTABLISHED, AND ADEQUATE RESOURCES MUST BE PROVIDED

The implementation due date can be established from many sources. Implementation dates may be predetermined because of strategic business goals, state or government regulations, or business cycle requirements. Any one of these scenarios will generate hardship on the project team to establish a realistic date. The unfortunate reality is that when the project leader assigns an implementation due date, senior management casts the date in stone, with no possible room for delays or extensions. The pressure from senior management may cause project team members to compress the schedule to implement the project sooner. Functional team members will work longer hours to make up for any delays. If the longer work day stretches over an extensive period of time, it will cause project members to burn out. If this occurs, team members will not think clearly, will continually make mistakes, will become emotionally drained, and will become short tempered with other project team members (Ligus 2004).

Normally, additional staff are not available to be added to the project, so consulting services have to be acquired to offload tasks from existing team members. The addition of a consultant will cause increased project cost, which adds more complexity to the issue. It is hoped that management will understand this dilemma and be open minded to any unforeseen problems that could cause a project extension. An ERP project implementation may be delayed if employees are asked to work unrealistic hours over an extended period of time and if the project is viewed by senior management as a trivial task.

ALL PROJECT TEAM MEMBERS MUST BE EDUCATED AND TRAINED

The education and training of all project team members involved with the ERP implementation is required. Education begins at the top of the organizational hierarchy, with the steering committee receiving a high-level overview of ERP concepts and how the application will be used in the organization.

The level of education increases for the ERP project leader and the functional teams. The ERP project leader must have a broad knowledge of what is included in the application package. He must have an understanding of how each business process interfaces with other functions of the package. He must have a general understanding of the underlying technology used to support the application package. If the project leader does not have the technical background, he must rely on information technology personnel to provide the correct infrastructure to support the package.

Each functional team must have a complete understanding of all features of their business process. For example, the sales order processing team must know which application screens are used to enter a sales order, which individual elements are required on each screen, and which screens should be accessed to ensure that the sales order was entered correctly.

Training must be conducted for all employees who have a direct involvement with the day-to-day operation of the system. Training is associated with the physical use of the hardware that is required to enter data into the system, so each user must attend as many hands-on training classes as deemed necessary to maintain his particular business process. Training classes can be attended offsite at a vendor's location and conducted by a training specialist, or training can be conducted on-site by either an internal team member who has attended the training session or an external consultant who is contracted to train a group of users.

Training and educational costs are always underestimated. If the project is behind schedule, training classes may be canceled. In this case, users are asked to train themselves using other training methods. Training tools, such as tutorials and interactive training manuals (combination of tutorials and computer-aided instruction), can be used. These methods tend to be less effective than participating in group training sessions, where several functional users are trained at one time.

CONVERSION PROCEDURES MUST BE TESTED, AND POSTIMPLEMENTATION SUPPORT MUST BE PROVIDED

Conversion is the task of loading existing data into the new software application package and is critical to the implementation process. Because it is a critical component of an ERP project, time must be spent planning and testing the conversion to the new system. Each functional team must test and approve their portion of the system. The entire system must be tested to ensure that all business processes interface correctly. Failure to test all portions of the system will lead to postimplementation problems (Piasecki 2004).

The data in an ERP system is dynamic, which means that it changes on a daily basis. Customer sales orders, purchase orders, inventory stock updates, and accounting transactions are examples of dynamic data (Kogent-MML Ltd. 2004). Dynamic data must be tested prior to implementation to ensure that the data are error-free when the cutover date arrives. Customer sales and purchase orders must be matched against existing orders to ensure that all information is correct. If there are errors in the quality of the data, these must be corrected prior to the implementation date. Failure to correct these problems will result in system integrity issues as well as added costs.

Even though the ERP system is tested and the conversion from the existing system to the new system runs smoothly, it is a foregone conclusion that postimplementation problems will be encountered. It is hoped that these problems will be minor and will require little effort to solve. Functional team members must be available to answer any questions and resolve any problems.

After the system has become stable, the functional team members can return to their original jobs and will be an important resource to answer any questions that other functional users may have. Because of their extensive involvement throughout the project, the functional team members are considered resident experts and are available to assist others in their business functions.

CONCLUSIONS

To avoid controversy during and after an ERP implementation, learn from the successes and failures of others. Organizations should make sure that their core business processes are streamlined and running smoothly. Discuss the business process reengineering effort with other organizations that have successfully implemented an enterprise package solution.

Organizations have to manage their consultants and supervise them. When the consultant's assignment is finished and he is no longer available for help, someone in the organization must understand the work he did. An internal team member should have been appointed to work with the consultant at all times. This member will then take the responsibility of understanding what the consultant did after he leaves.

Organizations must realize that all ERP projects have a high degree of risk. Look for the signs: if a business process is very complex, then there is high possibility that it contains some degree of risk. Functional teams have to identify all areas where they feel that there could be potential risk issues and manage them closely.

Users have to be educated on the new system and trained on the new application. The education and training budget should not be reduced because the project is over budget. If the training budget has the possibility of being cut or reduced, the project leader should stress to senior management that it is a "pay me now or pay me later" situation. If the training budget is reduced, implementation problems will likely occur because users will not have a complete understanding of the application. User frustration normally results when users are trying to do their job with a system that has not been thoroughly explained to them.

The project leader should keep senior management informed of the progress of the implementation and ask for their opinion to solve problems. Senior management's role is to make decisions and provide corporate leadership to the ERP implementation team and all users. They can also assist the implementation team by communicating the importance of the ERP project to all employees. By providing timely updates, organizational resistance to the project can be minimized.

Traditionally, ERP projects cost more to implement. Because of the scope and complexity of an ERP implementation, there are numerous areas where costs may not be identified. All project costs should be monitored and controlled. Internal accounting staff should be used to track these costs and provide project reporting.

There are many other issues associated with an ERP implementation. If an organization recognizes and addresses these issues, a smooth transition to a new enterprise system will be achieved.

See also: Strategic Planning; Technological Connectivity

References

Curran, Thomas, and Gerhard Keller. 1998. *SAP R/3 Business Blueprint.* Upper Saddle River, NJ: Prentice Hall.

EyetoIT. 2004. *Project Success Rates Drop in 2004.* Available at: http://www.eyetoit.com/2004/11/project_success.html. Accessed July 5, 2006.

GEAC. 2003. *5 Tips for Successful Business Performance Management Software Implementations.* Available at: http://www.geac.com. Accessed May 27, 2006.

Kogent-MML Ltd. 2006. *How to Implement ERP/MRPII Systems Successfully.* Available at: http://www.mml-net.com/howto/how_to_system_imp.html. Accessed June 29, 2006.

Ligus, Richard G. 2004. *The 12 Cardinal Sins of ERP Implementation.* Available at: http://www.rockfordconsulting.com/12sinart.htm. Accessed May 27, 2006.

Piasecki, Dave. 2004. *Software Selection and Implementation Tips.* Available at: http://www.inventoryops.com/software_selection.htm. Accessed May 27, 2006.

Robinson, Phil. 2002. *ERP (Enterprise Resource Planning) Survival Guide.* Available at: http://www.bpic.co.uk/erp.htm. Accessed July 7, 2006.

Further Reading: Hoffer, Jeffrey A., Joey F. George, and Joseph S. Valacich. 2005. *Modern Systems Analysis and Design.* Upper Saddle River, NJ: Prentice Hall; Olson, David. 2004. *Managerial Issues of Enterprise Resource Planning Systems.* New York: McGraw-Hill/

Irwin; Verville, Jacques, and Alannah Halingten. 2001. *Acquiring Enterprise Software.* Upper Saddle River, NJ: Prentice Hall.

Robert J. Nelson

ENVIRONMENTAL DEGRADATION

Environmental issues tend to elicit emotional responses from people across the political spectrum. Popular commentary on the environment exacerbates this tendency by highlighting alarming findings, quoting the more extreme (and hence newsworthy) viewpoints and ignoring the complexities inherent in understanding environmental problems. While commentary of this type is useful for fostering interest and prompting discussion, it can confuse the issue when it comes time to consider difficult societal choices related to environmental policy. Economics provides a set of analytical tools that, when properly employed, can help organize our thinking on environmental issues and help in the design of solutions.

In this entry, I will introduce and describe some of these tools. First, I will contrast the popular notion of the cause of environmental problems with a more precise definition employed by economists. Second, I will describe how economists think about the trade-offs between increased material prosperity and a cleaner environment and use this notion to define pollution management goals. Finally, I will describe some examples of environmental policy tools that economists favor.

THE CAUSE OF ENVIRONMENTAL DEGRADATION

Popular debates on environmental problems often begin by drawing sharp distinctions between polluters and people who suffer because of pollution and do not get far before the different sides are labeled as right or wrong, good or bad, just or unjust. In many instances, this takes on an us versus them flavor, in which a large, faceless entity (often a corporation) is the unjust them inflicting harm on us. Sometimes this simple dichotomy is close to accurate. In 1989, when the intoxicated captain of the Exxon Valdez oil tanker ran his ship aground in Alaska's Prince William Sound and spilled millions of gallons of crude oil into the pristine environment, there was little doubt about who to blame or who should pay for the cleanup. In other cases, popular rhetoric aside, the issue of right and wrong is less clear. For example, in the eastern United States, almost all sulfur dioxide pollution comes from a relatively small number of coal-burning electricity-generating plants. Sulfur dioxide emissions are the primary cause of acid rain, which destroys forests, poisons lakes and streams, and can have negative impacts on human health. So are the large electricity plants the blame? In one sense, yes, because they produce the emissions. But in another sense, people who use electricity are to blame—which is everyone. So the them in the blame game is us: we both cause the environmental damage (through our use of electricity) and suffer its consequences (reduced enjoyment of forests, lakes, and streams).

A second example can help further illustrate this point. One of the main water quality problems in the United States today is elevated ambient levels of nitrogen and phosphorous in lakes and streams. These chemicals cause fish kills. They threaten human health by contaminating drinking water. They cause unsightly and odorous algae blooms in streams. The main sources of nitrogen and phosphorous loading are crop production (fertilizer runoff), livestock raising (waste management leakage), and golf courses and homeowners (lawn fertilizer runoff). So who is to blame? Farmers, or people who eat? Golf course owners, or people who enjoy a green lawn? Once again, to a degree, we all contribute to and suffer from nutrient pollution.

The point is a general one: while for some specific environmental problems, it is easy to assign blame, in most cases, blame is elusive or widespread when we look beyond the obvious. This realization has important consequences for how we think about pollution and public policy responses to it. If, in general, environmental degradation is not the result of wrongdoing by a knowingly unjust

THE U.S. ACID RAIN PROGRAM

In spite of the attractive features of incentive-based environmental regulation of the type advocated by economists, there have been relatively few large-scale examples of this type of policy. An exception to this is the U.S. Acid Rain Program, which put in place the world's first large-scale transferable emission permit regulatory scheme. The program was established by Title IV of the 1990 Clear Air Act Amendments and was designed to reduce emissions of sulfur dioxide primarily from coal-fired electricity-generating plants in the eastern United States. The regulatory goal (begun in 1995) was to reduce aggregate emissions of sulfur dioxide to nine million tons annually by year 2000 and beyond, a reduction of over 50 percent from 1980 levels. This was to be established by a transferable emission permit scheme (also known as a cap and trade program) targeted initially at the 263 dirtiest generating units and later expanded to include all significant sources of sulfur dioxide emissions. Most of the nine million annual emission permits were allocated freely to the polluting sources based on historical emission rates, with a small number held back each year by the U.S. Environmental Protection Agency for the purpose of selling them in an auction (to ensure that there would always be a willing seller of permits).

More than 10 years after the program went into place, it has been judged a success by nearly every measure. Emission reduction targets have been met and, in some cases, exceeded. Trading volume has increased each year of the program, with over 12 million allowances per year transferred between firms in 2000. This flexibility in meeting industry-wide emissions reductions has led to estimated compliance cost savings of 30–40 percent over alternative policy considered by Congress in the years preceding the program. A robust market for permits has developed, with the price per ton ranging between $100 and $200 for most of the program, with prices increasing to over $400 per ton in recent years.

entity, but instead is a by-product of our entire society, policy should be aimed at managing the problem, rather than punishing the perpetrators.

This point bears repeating. Punishment of polluters might be a means toward the end of reducing pollution, but it should not be an end in and of itself when a society has shared blame for its environmental problems. With some notable exceptions, economists adopt the view that pollution is an undesirable outcome of economic activity. Its existence is not evidence of immoral or malicious behavior; rather, it is the result of the amoral forces of supply and demand. This viewpoint is useful for two reasons: first, it allows us to focus on examining the trade-offs between the desirable (material well-being) and undesirable (environmental degradation) aspects of economic activity, without engaging in distracting moral debates; second, it allows us to consider a range of policy options that concern themselves first and foremost with reducing pollution with the least reduction in material well-being, rather than punishing wrong behavior.

AN ACCEPTABLE LEVEL OF ENVIRONMENTAL DEGRADATION?

Designing policy to combat environmental degradation requires first determining what an acceptable level of pollution is, and then designing a specific policy to obtain that level. In this section, I discuss how the tools of environmental economics can be utilized to think about the so-called correct level of pollution. As with the case of assigning blame, economists' approach to this is seemingly at odds with popular rhetoric. If pollution is bad, should not we pursue policies aimed at eliminating pollution completely? Given this, how can we define an acceptable level of pollution?

Economists approach this problem by considering trade-offs between the benefits and costs to society as a whole of reducing pollution, relying critically on the concept of marginal analysis. Marginal analysis simply involves looking at things incrementally. In considering the question of an acceptable level of environmental degradation, economists ask the question, At current levels of emissions, would the benefit of reducing pollution by a small amount outweigh the costs? If the answer is yes, the step should be taken and the question asked anew. Conceptually, then, the economist's recommendation is to incrementally reduce pollution until the benefit of the last reduction just offsets the costs, and then go no further. In this way, we can define the correct level of environmental degradation as one that balances the benefits of reduction with the costs of achieving the reduction.

This process requires that we obtain a sense of the benefits and costs to society of reducing pollution, and this will be context-specific. Consider again the example of sulfur dioxide emissions by coal-fired electricity plants in the eastern United States. In general, plants can reduce emissions in three ways: by switching from eastern-produced high-sulfur coal to western-produced low-sulfur coal, by installing scrubbers onto smokestacks to catch sulfur before it is emitted, or by shutting down. The first is somewhat costly in that it involves purchasing and transporting coal via rail across the continent but can reduce emissions at a plant by perhaps 30–40 percent. The second is more costly in that it involves a large capital expenditure but can reduce emissions by 90 percent. The latter reduces emissions completely at the cost of no electricity produced.

Through markets for electricity, these costs are borne by society as a whole. Thus it is relatively inexpensive for society to remove 30 percent of emissions, but it becomes progressively more expensive to remove more. The incremental benefits of sulfur dioxide reduction consist of the environmental improvements that occur when emissions are reduced. The physical improvements are determined by the resilience of natural systems. While high levels of acid rain will certainty kill forests and poison streams, low levels can be absorbed with little notable impact. Thus initial reductions from a high emission baseline that move the natural system away from the threat threshold will have large environmental benefits, while subsequent decreases will have less dramatic benefits. The acceptable level of environmental degradation in this case is determined by society's willingness to accept incrementally higher electricity prices in exchange for incrementally improved forest and stream health. Since the cost of complete emission reduction is very high (ceasing electricity production from coal altogether) and the incremental benefit of zero emissions is very low (due to natural resilience in forest and stream systems), there is likely to be some correct level of sulfur dioxide emissions greater than zero but less than the nonregulated baseline.

This story is static in that it considers the relative costs and benefits of sulfur dioxide reduction given current electricity generation technology. Over time, however, technology can improve. For example, if alternative methods for producing electricity cheaply without burning coal become available, it will become relatively cheaper to prevent sulfur emissions simply by switching from coal to the alternative. To a degree, this has occurred. Over the past 20 years, technology improvements in wind turbines have caused the cost of electricity generated from wind to fall by 90 percent to the point that the cost per kilowatt hour of electricity generated at installed plants by coal and wind are roughly comparable.

The sulfur dioxide case illustrates a general point that is central to how economists think about an acceptable level of environmental degradation. At any point in time, there will be costs and benefits to society associated with pollution reductions, and striking a balance between these determines the best level of reduction. As time moves on and technology improves, environmental degradation should be reduced. These two definitional notions link to the final section on how economists think about environmental policy.

DESIGN OF ENVIRONMENTAL POLICY

As with much concerning the environmental debate, economists view the design of environmental policy somewhat differently than how it is conveyed in the popular media. As I have noted, economists focus more on the goal of balancing the competing desires of more material wealth with a cleaner environment, rather than the punishment of wrongdoing. A precise articulation of this was given in the previous section: economists are interested in determining a level of pollution reduction that balances costs and benefits, encouraging technology developments that shrink the cost of pollution reductions, and finding ways to achieve these goals with the least reduction in society's material well-being. Economists have proposed policy strategies based on economic incentives designed to achieve these goals. Popular debates on environmental policy tend to emphasize a coercive approach to policy, in which legislation or executive order establishes acceptable behavior for polluters, and deviations from this are punished with fines or other sanctions. Economists, by contrast, prefer a subtler type of regulation, in which firms are provided with incentives to reduce pollution and do so because it is in their interest. Two types of regulation have gained favor with economists: emission taxes and transferable pollution permits.

Emission taxes are based on the simple idea that firms be required to pay a fixed tax for each unit of pollution they emit into the environment. Thus firms may freely choose their level of emissions but will do so knowing that there are financial consequences of being a high polluter. Because of this, it is in polluters' best interest to find ways to reduce their emissions. Thus, rather than prescribing particular actions, an emissions tax can unleash creative forces among polluters, allowing each to pursue emission reductions according to its unique circumstances. There is an added bonus to this type of policy: because polluting firms can avoid tax payments by avoiding emissions, they have incentives to seek out and deploy cleaner production methods, thereby pushing forward the technological advances that can ultimately lead to both a cleaner environment and greater material wealth.

This is an important point: the ability both to grow materially and maintain the environment depend critically on the development of production technologies that are both affordable to use and environmentally friendly. For this reason, economists consider policies that encourage firms to invest in this type of development to be inherently superior to those that do not. Importantly, most types of coercive regulation do not provide this type of encouragement in that once the prescribed behavior is met, firms have no additional incentive to seek further emission reductions.

The second type of regulation favored by economists is a system of transferable emission permits. In this type of regulation, the government determines the target level of emissions per year and distributes a number of certificates equal to the emission target to the polluting firms. If a firm emits a unit of pollution, it must turn in a certificate. Thus firms need to possess enough certificates each year to cover their emissions or face steep fines. Importantly, the certificates may be traded among the polluting firms. Firms with fewer emissions (and hence less of a need for the certificates) can earn additional profits by selling excess certificates to firms with larger emissions. In this way, a market for pollution rights arises, and the total amount of pollution is capped at the total number of available certificates. Like the tax case, firms have incentives to reduce their emissions, allowing them either to purchase fewer or sell more certificates and thereby improve their bottom lines. For the same reason, a system of transferable pollution permits also will encourage firms to seek out and deploy cleaner production technology. Finally, the government can precisely control the overall level of emissions by its allocation of total certificates.

CONCLUSION

My objective in this entry has been to convey an understanding of how economists view problems related to environmental degradation. Popular and policy debates on environmental issues and solutions should include several viewpoints, and I am in no way advocating a strictly economic approach to discussing and analyzing these problems. What I am suggesting, however, is that the economist's way of thinking about the issues can provide a perspective that is often lost in the emotional rhetoric surrounding environmental issues. By using the analytical tools of economics, we can identify the sources of environmental degradation and consider solutions absent the usual moralizing, thereby contributing disinterested logic to a field that often lacks precisely this perspective—and helping to achieve outcomes consistent with societal goals.

See also: Corporate Social Responsibility

Further Reading: Ellerman, D., P. Jaskow, R. Schmalansee, J. P. Montero, and E. Bailey. 2000. *Markets for Clean Air: The US Acid Rain Program.* Cambridge: Cambridge University Press; Oates, W. E. 2005. *The RFF Reader in Environmental and Resource Policy.* 2nd ed. Washington, DC: RFF Press.

Daniel J. Phaneuf

ETHICS IN BUSINESS AT THE INDIVIDUAL LEVEL

Businessmen and women do not enjoy very good reputations in our society. In recent years, countless newspaper headlines have brought to light many high-profile corporate scandals and recounted the misdeeds of corporate executives. Undeniably, much of the bad press is deserved. However, movies and television shows so often portray businesspeople in a negative light that it seems like all businesspeople are unethical and manipulative scoundrels. But do businesspeople deserve such bad reputations? Can you be ethical in business and still get ahead? Does virtue pay, or do nice people finish last? Do you have to sell your soul to advance? We will examine both sides of the debate.

HISTORY OF THE TOPIC

Doubts about the ethical intentions and actions of businesspeople are nothing new. Many ancient thinkers were concerned about the negative influence of business. For example, Aristotle was concerned that greed for money was a vice that could easily overwhelm and consume a person. In most ancient societies, the norm governing economic transactions between individuals was to make an equal exchange of goods and services. The concept of a profit was unseemly because it meant that one party was taking advantage of the other. It was thought that there was only a fixed amount of resources available for all persons in a society. Therefore profit was seen as taking more than a fair share, which meant fewer resources for someone else.

In medieval times, the influential Roman Catholic Church continued to distrust businesspeople and commercial activity. Much of what took place in business went against church teachings. Avarice or greed for money was considered one of the seven deadly sins. Charging interest on a loan (a standard business practice) was also considered sinful. Ancient thinkers called this practice usury, and the Roman Catholic Church prohibited it. The Roman Catholic Church was not the only religion that eyed business activity with caution. For example, both Judaism and Islam have prohibitions that govern many business dealings, including money lending and commercial transactions.

It was not until the growth of Protestantism that the ethics of businesspeople was seen in a more favorable light. For John Calvin, business success and financial wealth were not the result of greed or unethical conduct. To the contrary, they were seen as a sign of divine favor bestowed on the elect, those individuals who were predestined for heaven. In other words, being successful in business was not something to be ashamed of; rather, it was a sign of God's approval. The influential philosopher Adam Smith, the father of modern capitalist thought, further legitimized business conduct by outlining how a market system based on self-interest promoted the common good of society.

During the nineteenth and twentieth centuries, many critics decried the ethical practices of prominent business leaders. In the early 1800s, John Jacob Astor built his fortune in the fur trade but was widely denounced for bribing politicians, using alcohol and cheap trinkets to secure favorable dealings with Native Americans, and for other unscrupulous business dealings. John D. Rockefeller's Standard Oil Company revolutionized the oil industry in the late 1800s. However, many critics were concerned with Rockefeller's cutthroat and monopolist business tactics. The government eventually agreed, and the U.S. Supreme Court broke up the Standard Oil Company in 1911.

SOME FAMOUS BUSINESS CRITICS AND REFORMERS

- *Mary "Mother" Jones* was a critic of business and a crusader for labor rights during the late 1800s and early 1900s.
- *Arthur Levitt* served as chairman of the Securities and Exchange Commission from 1993 to 2001. Levitt was an advocate for investor protection and a champion of many reforms during his tenure.
- *Ralph Nader* is a consumer advocate (and former presidential candidate) whose 1965 book *Unsafe at Any Speed* took aim at the automobile industry for its poor safety record. Nader remains a leading critic of political corruption and big business greed.
- *Upton Sinclair's* most famous work was *The Jungle,* an exposé of the meatpacking industry published in 1906. He was one of a group of critics called *muckrakers* who took aim at corruption in business and politics during the late 1800s and early 1900s.
- *Ida Tarbell* was a muckraker who published a best-selling criticism of John D. Rockefeller and his Standard Oil Company in 1904.

In the twentieth century, growing social concern about the ethics of business-people translated into increased government regulation of business. The misery caused by the collapse of many businesses and financial institutions during the Great Depression brought new regulations designed to reform the conduct of business. The trend toward increased regulation would remain throughout the rest of the century. In particular, the 1960s and 1970s was a time when many new social and economic regulations were passed.

The 1980s and 1990s brought about a shift to a more hands-off approach to government regulation of business. However, in response to many ethical lapses and transgressions, particularly among Wall Street firms during the 1980s, the U.S. Sentencing Guidelines were established in 1991 to encourage companies to be more proactive in managing the ethical conduct of their employees. These guidelines call for reduced penalties and fines for companies that run into legal trouble but have an effective corporate ethics program in place.

HIGHLIGHTS FROM THE FEDERAL SENTENCING GUIDELINES

According to the U.S. Sentencing Guidelines (U.S. Sentencing Commission n.d.), there are seven components of an effective ethics and compliance program:

1. Establish standards and procedures to prevent and detect criminal conduct.
2. Ensure that organizational authorities are knowledgeable about the content and operation of the compliance and ethics program and exercise reasonable oversight with respect to the implementation and effectiveness of the compliance and ethics program.
3. Use reasonable efforts not to hire or give substantial authority to any individual whom the organization knew, or should have known through the exercise of due diligence, to have engaged in illegal activities or other conduct inconsistent with an effective compliance and ethics program.
4. Take reasonable steps to communicate periodically and in a practical manner its standards and procedures, and other aspects of the compliance and ethics program, by conducting effective training programs and otherwise disseminating information appropriate to such individuals' respective roles and responsibilities.
5. Take reasonable steps to ensure that the organization's compliance and ethics program is followed, including monitoring and auditing to detect criminal conduct; evaluating periodically the effectiveness of the organization's compliance and ethics program; and having and publicizing a system, which may include mechanisms that allow for anonymity or confidentiality, whereby the organization's employees and agents may report or seek guidance regarding potential or actual criminal conduct without fear of retaliation.
6. Promote and enforce consistently the organization's compliance and ethics program throughout the organization through appropriate incentives to perform in accordance with the compliance and ethics program and appropriate disciplinary measures for engaging in criminal conduct and for failing to take reasonable steps to prevent or detect criminal conduct.
7. After criminal conduct has been detected, take reasonable steps to respond appropriately to the criminal conduct and prevent further similar criminal conduct, including making any necessary modifications to the organization's compliance and ethics program.

In the aftermath of the bull market and Internet boom of the late 1990s and early 2000s, many high-profile business scandals came to light, starting with the collapse of Enron in late 2001. These scandals helped drive opinions about the ethics of businesspeople to new lows and encouraged a new round of government regulation of business. Among the most significant of these reforms was the Sarbanes-Oxley Act, which reformed corporate governance, increased internal controls, and improved the quality and transparency of corporate financial reporting.

Overall, concern about the ethics of businesspeople is not a recent development; rather, questions have always surrounded the ethical conduct of business. Next, we will examine both sides of the fundamental controversy in more detail. Is business ethics an oxymoron? Or can an individual be a successful and ethical businessperson at the same time?

ARGUMENTS FOR THE ETHICAL CONDUCT OF BUSINESS

Most business ethics research shows that unethical behavior in the workplace exists but is not the norm. Positive, cooperative behavior is fairly common in the workplace. The majority of workers that cut ethical corners are reported to their superiors. Most employees trust their companies' management and rate their ethical leadership as strong. Taken together, this research suggests that the vast majority of businesspeople quietly go about their work in an honest fashion.

Consider the number of business transactions that you engaged in recently. Did you buy gas, groceries, or clothes? Did you go out to dinner? What else did you purchase? Were you cheated by an unethical businessperson? For most of us, the reality is that we engage in hundreds of transactions with businesses each year without coming in contact with an unethical businessperson. The same holds true for the people we work with. Although we might occasionally encounter a coworker who behaves unethically in the workplace, most of the people with whom we work play by the rules while doing their jobs.

Furthermore, compared to the days of the no holds barred capitalism of the past, societal expectations and tighter regulations make it harder for today's businesspeople to commit wrongdoing. In most cases, companies are legally responsible for the conduct of their employees. Many large companies have formal ethics and compliance programs designed to promote ethical conduct and prevent unethical and illegal practices. The U.S. Sentencing Guidelines have encouraged companies to set up effective ethics and compliance programs. All this means that it is much more difficult for an individual to act unethically in the workplace.

Ultimately, the argument that one can be ethical and successful in business rests on the twin pillars of trust and fairness. Trust and fairness are the keys to building successful relationships with customers, bosses, employees, and coworkers. When employees trust their bosses and coworkers and believe that they are being treated fairly, they are more satisfied, motivated, and committed to their work. Unethical behavior destroys trust and violates our sense of fairness. Most people believe that it is unfair when bad people succeed or unethical behavior goes unpunished.

Consider the case of former Sunbeam CEO Al Dunlap. Dunlap earned the nickname "Chainsaw" because he had a long track record of slashing jobs and ruthlessly cutting costs during his tenure in a variety of companies. Although investors loved Dunlap because his tactics delivered higher share prices, many others criticized Dunlap for unethical tactics that had a devastating impact on workers and their families. So it was no surprise that when Dunlap was fired from Sunbeam for accounting irregularities, fined by the Securities and Exchange Commission, and barred from holding an executive position in a publicly traded company ever again, many people took satisfaction in his demise. It violates our sense of basic fairness to see so-called bad people get ahead. Wrongdoers may get ahead in the short term, but in the long run, someone somewhere is likely to blow the whistle and put a stop to the unethical behavior.

The message is clear: individuals can and do commit wrongdoing in business. However, it has become increasingly more difficult to get away with because society expects businesspeople to behave more ethically and responsibly. Newspaper headlines scream of ethical lapses by businesspeople, and the corporate executive is likely to be portrayed as the villain on television and in the movies. But remember that for every Martha Stewart whose reputation has been tarnished by ethical misdeeds, there are plenty of Oprah Winfreys who are known for building successful businesses without any cloud of suspicion or suggestion of impropriety.

EVIDENCE AGAINST THE ETHICAL CONDUCT OF BUSINESS

Recent corporate business scandals are proof enough that unethical people can and do get ahead in the business world. Although executives from Enron, Adelphia, WorldCom, and many other companies were ultimately caught and punished for their misconduct, how is it possible that these corrupt individuals were able to reach the highest levels of corporate America in the first place? How many other executives have committed transgressions that have gone undetected?

One executive who fooled many people was former Enron chief financial officer (CFO) Andrew Fastow. Fastow was highly regarded in his profession. He was even hailed as CFO of the Year by *CFO* magazine. However, much of Fastow's success was in fact accomplished using unethical business practices. Ultimately, he pleaded guilty to charges of wire and securities fraud, but for many years, Fastow was successfully able to pull the wool over the eyes of many people. Fastow, like many other business leaders who figured prominently in the recent wave of business scandals, was an upstanding citizen and a pillar of the community. What causes good people to do bad things? Critics contend that the business environment has a corrupting influence on people, even good people, for a variety of reasons.

First, some argue that our current business system is fundamentally flawed. The lure of enormous salaries, bonuses, and stock options creates a tremendous incentive for people to engage in risky, unethical behavior. In publicly traded companies, pressures from investors can cause employees to take ethical shortcuts to satisfy stockholders who demand a quick return on their investments. The concerns of other stakeholders (such as employees, communities, suppliers, and the natural environment) are often ignored compared to the needs of stockholders.

Although most of these pressures are likely to be felt by executives, high-level business leaders put pressure on lower-level employees to perform. The message "deliver results or lose your job" is not uncommon. For example, consider former GE CEO Jack Welch's imperative that each business at GE needed to be "number one or number two" in every line of business. If not, then GE would get out of (i.e., sell or close) that business. For many hardworking men and women trying to support their families, the prospect of losing a job is a motivating force to deliver results, sometimes by any means necessary.

There has been quite a bit of research demonstrating that an unethical workplace environment can corrupt good individuals. Most employees learn appropriate ethical standards in the workplace from their coworkers and peers. If an individual believes that everyone else is doing it, then he is likely to emulate the same behavior (for better or for worse). Even though many companies have taken steps to create formal ethics and compliance programs, some companies have not. Others have implemented them but do not manage them effectively. In fact, research shows that when employees believe that their companies have created an ethics program just to protect top management from blame, unethical behavior in the organization actually increases.

Another pressure comes from our desire to fit in. In companies that are highly cohesive, loyalty is valued, and dissent is discouraged. In such environments, individuals might be more likely to compromise their individual ethical standards to preserve group harmony and avoid making waves. This can lead to unethical conduct in the workplace.

The corporate environment can also desensitize an individual to the ethical implications of decisions. As Dennis Gioia, a recall coordinator for the Ford Motor Company during the 1970s, discovered, even well-intentioned people can end up missing obvious ethical warning signs in a business environment where ethics is not routinely discussed. Gioia was a recall coordinator at the time when Ford manufactured a car called the Pinto. The Ford Pinto was an economy car which had a serious design flaw that compromised its safety. In low-speed crashes, the Pinto would burst into flames when struck from behind, causing serious injury or death to those inside it. Gioia had many opportunities to recall the Ford Pinto but failed to do so, in large part because he did not think that the problem was particularly serious. However, looking back on his time at Ford, Gioia acknowledged that he should have recalled the Pinto. For Gioia, studying car crashes and looking for design flaws had become routine for him. Horrific Ford Pinto accidents were just numbers that he tracked and did not necessarily merit special attention. He became desensitized to the fact that his job involved life and death decisions for Ford Pinto owners, their passengers, and anyone else who shared the road with a Ford Pinto. Gioia's tale is a warning to any businessperson that the routine of corporate life can obscure the ethical implications of everyday decisions.

Overall, companies are in business to make money. Business schools drill into their students that the primary goal of business is to maximize shareholder wealth. Investors demand financial results. Most companies reward employees for financial, not ethical, performance. In this environment, it is very easy for ethical standards to get compromised. It is no surprise that businesspeople engage in unethical conduct.

RECONCILING THE PERSPECTIVES

Now that we have presented both sides of the debate, can we reconcile them? We know that many years ago, bad behavior in business went unchecked. There were very few regulations governing business conduct. The good news is that today, social expectations and government regulation require businesspeople to be more mindful of the ethical implications of their decisions. Unethical behavior can ruin companies, careers, and even lives. In a post-Enron world, most companies would rather prematurely terminate an ethically questionable employee rather than risk damage to the company's reputation by offering him or her a second chance and giving the person the benefit of the doubt.

On the other hand, all human beings are vulnerable to wrongdoing, and businesspeople are not immune to these pressures. Without a doubt, there will be more ethical scandals in business in the future. However, many other professions have had occurrences of unethical conduct, too. Unfortunately, there have been many accounts of politicians who have taken part in corruption, academic researchers who have committed plagiarism, soldiers who have participated in atrocities, doctors who have committed fraud against health insurance companies, and schoolteachers and religious leaders who have engaged in sexual misconduct with children.

The point is that individuals commit unethical acts in many professions, not just in business. Clearly, unethical behavior in business is a serious problem that needs to be addressed. Individuals pursuing a career in business must not be naïve. The business environment can be very competitive. Individuals must be on guard when entering the business world or face the prospect of compromising their own ethical standards to get ahead. On the other hand, the fact that there are men and women who succeed in business without violating ethical or legal standards supports the idea that business ethics does not have to be an oxymoron. When choosing an employer, individuals should look carefully to find companies that promote and support individual ethical conduct in the workplace and avoid the ones that tolerate ethically questionable performance from their employees.

See also: Blogs; Corporate Social Responsibility; Employee Loyalty and Engagement

References

U.S. Sentencing Commission. n.d. *U.S. Sentencing Guidelines.* Available at: http://www.ussc.gov/2005guid/8b2_1.htm. Accessed July 12, 2006.

Further Reading: Ethics Resource Center. 2005. *National Business Ethics Survey.* Washington, DC: Ethics Resource Center; Gioia, D. A. 1992. "Pinto Fires and Personal Ethics: A Script Analysis of Missed Opportunities." *Journal of Business Ethics* 11: 379–89; U.S. Sentencing Commission. n.d. *U.S. Sentencing Guidelines.* Available at: http://www.ussc. gov/2005guid/8b2_1.htm. Accessed July 12, 2006; Trevino, L. K., and K. A. Nelson. 2003. *Managing Business Ethics: Straight Talk about How to Do It Right.* Hoboken, NJ: John Wiley; Trevino, L. K., and M. E. Brown. 2004. "Managing to Be Ethical: Debunking Five Business Ethics Myths." *Academy of Management Executive* 18: 69–83.

Michael E. Brown

F

FEDERAL RESERVE SYSTEM

The chairman of the board of governors of the Federal Reserve System is often referred to as the second most powerful person in the United States. While the financial media cover every statement of the chairman, most people are unsure of what the Federal Reserve does and why it is considered so important. Many people believe that the Federal Reserve (the Fed) is a department of the federal government such as the Treasury or State Departments. In reality, the Fed is a combination of private and public institutions with considerable independence from the government. Its main responsibilities are to supervise the financial sector, particularly banks, and to conduct what is known as monetary policy, using its tools to affect the level of interest rates and the supply of credit so as to move the economy in the direction the Fed thinks is appropriate. It is the power to influence the economy that gives the Fed its prominence.

BACKGROUND ON BANKING

To understand why the Federal Reserve was created, it is necessary first to understand the business of banking. Commercial banks are the main financial institutions that people and businesses use to hold deposits, such as checking accounts, and to obtain loans to buy cars, purchase houses, or expand businesses. These banks make profits by charging higher interest rates on their loans than they pay to their depositors. Bank deposits are the way that banks borrow the funds that they lend out. Generally, banks promise that depositors can withdraw their funds from the bank with little or no warning to the bank, such as by writing a check or using a debit card to pay for some purchase. The loans that banks make, however, are usually for longer periods of time and cannot be easily turned into cash. Banks help the economy by allowing savers, the depositors, to hold their savings in a convenient form, while indirectly lending in a form, that is, bank loans, that is desirable to borrowers.

Since cash generates no income, a bank keeps only a small fraction of its deposits as cash, referred to as the bank's reserves. But if many depositors demand cash all at once, the bank would have difficulty in honoring its promises, unless it could borrow cash from another bank. Why would the depositors demand cash? This is usually prompted by the fear that the bank has made some bad loans and that the bank does not have enough in assets to pay off all the depositors. Hence the depositors try to convert their deposits to cash before the bank runs out of funds.

If people believe that many banks are in trouble, there will be a general bank panic, and since all banks are facing the same cash shortage, there is no one to borrow from. Banks that cannot honor their promises to depositors must close their doors. Multiple bank failures lead to people distrusting banks, and the benefits of banks transferring funds from savers to borrowers are lost. This possibility is an important reason for countries to create central banks. These are institutions that can lend to commercial banks when the banks need cash to meet the demands of their depositors. They are said to be so-called lenders of last resort. The Federal Reserve System is the central bank of the United States.

ESTABLISHMENT OF THE FEDERAL RESERVE SYSTEM

Central banks started in Europe. These were private banks that were selected to act as the governments' banks, helping to finance government spending, particularly during wartime. The United States experimented with central banks in the late eighteenth and early nineteenth centuries. The First Bank of the United States and the Second Bank of the United States were created to act as banks for the federal government, but neither survived political fights over the desirability of a government-dominated bank. The nineteenth century saw several financial crises that typically were accompanied by large numbers of bank failures. Finally, after the financial panic of 1907, the political forces favoring a central bank were successful, and Congress passed the Federal Reserve Act of 1913, establishing the Federal Reserve System.

The fears of some that a central bank would favor the interests of large cities on the east coast were at least partially allayed by the creation of a system of 12 regional Federal Reserve banks. Each of these banks was a private institution owned by commercial banks. The creation of regional Federal Reserve banks was supposed to allow different regions of the country to have different credit conditions. The board of governors, in Washington, D.C., was the oversight body—in essence, the headquarters of the Fed.

The main role of the new Federal Reserve System was to supply an elastic currency to the country so that the periodic banking panics of the nineteenth century would not be repeated. Federal Reserve paper currency became the paper money of the country. If bank depositors all demanded their funds in currency—called a bank run—banks could turn to the Fed for loans of currency, using their own loans as collateral. When depositors' confidence had been restored, the commercial banks would pay back their loans from the Fed. The Fed also served as the federal government's bank. When taxes were paid or when the government sold new government bonds, the funds were deposited in the Fed. The government then used this account to pay its bills.

STRUCTURE AND FUNCTION OF THE FEDERAL RESERVE SYSTEM

The Federal Reserve Act of 1913 set up the basic structure of the Federal Reserve, which was modified by the Banking Acts of 1933 and 1935. At the top of the Fed is the board of governors. There are seven governors, appointed by the U.S. president and confirmed by the Senate. Once confirmed, governors cannot be fired for policies that the president or Congress dislike and can only be impeached for malfeasance, similar to Supreme Court justices. Governors are appointed to 14-year terms, with a vacancy opening every two years if governors serve their full terms. This means that a one-term U.S. president would appoint two governors. This system was supposed to insulate the board from political influence. In reality, however, few governors serve for 14 years, so a president may get to appoint several governors over a four-year period. As part of a commitment to regional representation, each governor must be from a different Federal Reserve district. The U.S. president appoints one of the governors as the chair for a renewable four-year term. It is customary that if a chair is not reappointed, he or she resigns from the board, even if his or her 14-year term is not finished.

HOW LONG DO GOVERNORS ACTUALLY SERVE?

The term of appointment for a governor is 14 years. Governors can actually serve longer than this if they are initially appointed to fill out a resigning governor's term and then are appointed to their own full 14-year term. For example, Alan Greenspan served as chairman for 19 years. The framers of the Federal Reserve Act thought that the long, nonrenewable terms would make the governors independent of the presidents that appointed them and would mean that a one-term president would only be able to appoint two governors since the terms were staggered, with one ending every two years.

The record of service indicates that these intentions have not been realized. Since 1970, the average length of service for governors, excluding chairs, is less than six years. President George W. Bush appointed more than seven governors in his two terms. While there are several reasons for governors resigning before their terms are up, one important reason is that the job does not pay that well. A governor receives an annual salary of $165,300, and the chairman gets $183,500. These salaries are set by Congress and are similar to salaries of heads of government departments. While the salaries may seem high, the presidents of the regional banks make considerably more, with the highest-paid presidents receiving almost twice the salary of the chairman. Many of the Fed staff make more than the governors. Being a Fed governor is prestigious and may be thought of as an investment in that it leads to a higher-paying job in the financial markets.

The Federal Reserve Board has several responsibilities. It sets the required reserve ratios, the minimum fraction of deposits that all banks must hold in cash. The board also regulates member banks and all bank holding companies and financial holding companies, companies that own one or more banks in addition to other financial services companies. The board administers consumer finance regulations, such as Truth in Lending, that help consumers make financial decisions and oversees the regional Federal Reserve banks, including approving their budgets. In addition, the board has a large staff of economists who analyze data, provide advice on monetary policy, and conduct economic research.

Below the board of governors are the 12 regional Federal Reserve banks. The Federal Reserve Act divided the country into 12 regions and selected one city within each region, after a considerable battle, as the location of a Federal Reserve bank. The 12 banks are located in Boston, New York, Philadelphia, Richmond, Atlanta, Cleveland, Chicago, St. Louis, Minneapolis, Kansas City, Dallas, and San Francisco.

Each regional bank is a separate private corporation. Its shareholders are commercial banks that belong to the Federal Reserve System. Each member bank contributes funds to the regional bank equal to 6 percent of the commercial bank's capital (the difference between the bank's assets and its liabilities). The member banks receive a fixed 6 percent dividend on their shares. Each regional bank has nine directors on its board, six elected by the member commercial banks and three chosen by the Federal Reserve Board. The latter three directors are called the public directors, and one of these is appointed as the chair of the board. The directors choose the president of the regional bank and also set the interest rate that the bank charges commercial banks for loans, the so-called discount rate. Initially it was thought that different Federal Reserve banks would have different discount rates, corresponding to different economic conditions across regions. The integration of financial markets did not make this practicable, and all regional banks now charge the same discount rate. The employees of the regional Federal Reserve banks are not federal government employees, unlike the employees of the board.

The regional Federal Reserve banks are, however, unlike other private corporations. First, they originated in an act of Congress. Second, the shareholders, the member banks, have much less say than in a regular corporation. As noted previously, the shareholders get a fixed dividend, not a share of the profits. While the regional banks' directors appoint the banks' presidents, the boards of governors can veto their choices. Similarly, the regional banks' directors only recommend discount rate changes since the boards can, and often have, turned down these requests. The regional Feds can be best thought of as private-public institutions.

In addition to setting the discount rate, the regional banks are the operational arms of the Fed. The regional banks monitor the reserve accounts to ensure that banks meet their reserve requirements. The commercial bank accounts at the regional Fed banks also play an important role in the system of check clearing. Commercial banks transfer large payments through an electronic system run by the regional banks called FedWire. Currency enters the economy through the regional Feds. When a member bank needs more paper currency or coins, it orders what it needs, charging the amount to its account at the Fed. The regional Feds do most of the legwork involved in bank supervision, conducting bank examinations, and monitoring bank activities.

HOW DO CHECKS WORK?

Most people have a checking account. When someone writes a check on his account to pay for something, the check authorizes the bank to subtract that amount from the person's account and credit it to the person or business to whom the check was written. Suppose John buys a used bicycle from Jack for $100 and pays for it with a check drawn on his account at the Bank of Springdale. If Jack has an account at the same bank, when he deposits the check at the bank, the bank will credit Jack's account with $100 and debit John's account for $100.

What if Jack has an account at a different bank? If Jack deposits the check at another bank in Springdale or the nearby area, say, the Bank of Forestview, this bank will credit his account and send the check to a local institution called a clearinghouse. All the checks drawn on the Bank of Springdale and deposited in the Bank of Forestview will be collected together: assume they total $100,000. All the checks drawn on the Bank of Forestview and deposited in the Bank of Springdale will also be collected: assume they total $80,000. The banks will then send back the deposited checks to the respective bank on which they were drawn, and Bank of Springdale will send the Bank of Forestview $20,000. Each bank will now debit the accounts of the customers who had written checks so that John will see his account fall by $100. If the Bank of Forestview is worried that John's check will not be honored—this is referred to as the check bouncing—it may hold up crediting Jack's account until it knows John has sufficient funds to cover the check.

What if Jack has an account at a bank in a different area, perhaps in a different state? This is where the Fed comes in. Suppose Jack deposits John's check in the Bank of California and that the Bank of Springdale is in North Carolina. The check is sent by the Bank of California to the Federal Reserve bank of San Francisco, which will credit the bank with $100 in its account at the Fed. The check will then be sent by plane to the Federal Reserve bank of Richmond, Springdale Bank's regional Fed bank. The Richmond Fed will debit Springdale Bank's account at the Fed by $100 and send the check to Springdale Bank. Springdale Bank then debits John's account by $100.

Because the paper trail of checks is expensive, the banking system has been trying to convince customers to switch to debit cards and electronic banking. Evidence suggests that this is occurring. The number of checks written in the United States has been falling in recent years, going from 50 billion in 1995 to 37 billion in 2003.

The New York Federal Reserve bank, the largest of the regional banks, has additional operational duties. When the federal government sells new bonds to the public, the New York Fed acts as the agent that sells the bonds. The New York Fed also is the largest gold depository in the world, holding the gold owned by many other countries. It is the New York Fed's gold vault that is robbed in the 1995 movie Die Hard with a Vengeance.

How do the regional banks generate revenue to support their operations? Since they have a monopoly on the printing of paper currency, it should not be surprising that they are profitable institutions. As the economy grows, it needs more paper currency to conduct the increasing volume of transactions that occur. Regional banks purchase U.S. government bonds from the public in exchange for Federal Reserve notes. By the end of 2005, the banks collectively owned almost $800 billion in government bonds. The interest payments from these bonds are the primary source of income for the banks. For 2005, the banks had a collective net income after expenses of about $23.5 billion. Unfortunately for the member banks, most of this ($21.5 billion) is paid back to the U.S. Treasury since the member banks receive only a small amount in dividends ($780 million in 2005). Not surprisingly, the banks have little incentive to limit expenses, and the U.S. Treasury has a strong incentive to try to restrict Fed expenses.

MONETARY POLICY AND THE FEDERAL OPEN MARKET COMMITTEE

While Congress originally stipulated that the Fed's goals were providing an elastic currency and increased stability to the banking system, the Great Depression of the 1930s prompted Congress to insist that the Fed should have broader economic goals. The latest of these mandates is the Balanced Growth and Full Employment Act of 1978, commonly called the Humphrey-Hawkins bill after the senator and congressman who sponsored it. The goals of monetary policy are low unemployment, maximum sustainable economic growth, stable prices (low inflation), and moderate long-term interest rates.

Monetary policy influences the economy by affecting the supply of money and interest rates. A simple way to think of the main goal of monetary policy is that the Fed seeks to keep spending, sometimes called aggregate demand, rising at the same rate as the capacity of the economy to produce goods and services. If spending rises faster, we eventually get rising prices and inflation. If spending rises more slowly, we get, at least initially, an increase in unemployment and slower growth. Because other factors affect spending, such as the confidence of households and the demand for U.S. goods by foreigners, the Fed is often trying to offset the effects of these factors to keep spending on track.

The Federal Open Market Committee (FOMC) is the body that makes monetary policy for the United States. The FOMC has 12 voting members: the seven governors of the Federal Reserve Board, the president of the New York Fed, and four other regional Fed bank presidents who serve one-year terms and then rotate off. The nonvoting regional presidents do, however, attend the FOMC's meetings. The chairman of the board of governors also chairs the FOMC. It is the FOMC that decides on the course of monetary policy under the intense scrutiny of the financial press.

The FOMC meets about every six weeks. Prior to each meeting, three briefing books, named for the colors of their covers, are compiled to help the FOMC. The beige book has reports from each of the regional Federal Reserve banks based on surveys of the economic conditions in their districts. These surveys are mostly anecdotal information collected through phone calls to bankers and businesses across their regions. The beige book may illustrate that some regions of the country are booming, while others are in slumps.

The board's staff puts together the green book that goes out to the FOMC prior to the meeting. This contains data on recent trends in unemployment, inflation, economic growth, and other variables thought to be useful to the FOMC. The green book includes forecasts of these variables up to two years in the future, assuming no change in monetary policy and specific guesses on other factors affecting the economy such as the level of government spending and taxes. Since the FOMC's policies will affect the economy months after their decision, they need to know the likely path of the economy to decide whether a change in policy is needed. Finally, the FOMC receives, just prior to the meeting, the blue book, which gives the staff's beliefs about how the economy will fare under alternative policies. If it is likely that the FOMC will consider raising interest rates, the blue book will give forecasts of how the economy will perform if rates increase versus how it will perform if rates are left unchanged. If the FOMC is likely to be considering lowering interest rates, the blue book will provide forecasts for that decision.

At each meeting, the members of the FOMC, the nonvoting presidents of regional banks, and senior staff members sit around a large table, with support staff sitting elsewhere in the board room. After staff presentations, each governor and bank president has the opportunity to present his views on the economy and indicate what policy he favors. After the chair summarizes this discussion, the FOMC then votes on the alternatives, and this decision is then made public in a short statement at 2:15 p.m. Eastern standard time. It is not uncommon for the financial markets to react quickly to this announcement if it is a surprise, resulting in large swings in interest rates and stock prices.

TOOLS OF MONETARY POLICY

Since 1994, the FOMC announcement has given a specific target for the federal funds rate, the interest rate that one commercial bank charges another on very short-term loans. How does the Fed affect this interest rate? The level of the federal funds rate depends on the demand for and supply of reserves by banks. If banks get more reserves than they need, they lend them out to other banks in the federal funds rate market. This causes the federal funds rate to fall. If banks need more reserves than they have, they borrow them from other banks, and this causes the federal funds rate to rise. The Federal Reserve can cause the federal funds rate to change by changing the supply of reserves that the banks have. If they increase the supply of reserves, the funds rate will fall, and if they decrease the supply of reserves, the funds rate will increase.

How does the Fed change the supply of reserves? The Fed conducts what are called open market operations, the main tool of monetary policy. These operations involve buying or selling government bonds. As noted above, the Fed owns a large amount of U.S. government bonds. Suppose the Fed wants to decrease the funds rate from 6 to 5.5 percent. The Fed would add to its stock of bonds by buying some from banks, crediting the banks' accounts at the Fed for the amount of the purchase. Since the balance in this account counts as reserves, buying government bonds increases bank reserves. The increase in reserves is typically more than the banks want to hold, so they lend reserves out in the federal funds market, increasing the supply of reserves and causing the federal funds rate to fall.

If the Fed wanted to increase the federal funds rate from 6 to 6.5 percent, it would sell some of its government bonds to the banks, debiting the banks' accounts at the Fed and thus lowering bank reserves. The decrease in the supply of reserves would raise the federal funds rate.

There are two other potential tools of monetary policy: the required reserve ratio and the discount rate. The required reserve ratio sets the minimum amount of reserves that banks must hold. While a change in this ratio would likely change the demand for reserves, the Federal Reserve changes the ratio rarely so that it plays little role in current monetary policy. Since 2003, the Fed has set the discount rate at 1 percent above the target for the federal funds rate so that the FOMC essentially sets this rate since it sets the funds rate target. Hence open market operations are really the only tool that the Fed uses to change monetary policy.

HOW DOES MONETARY POLICY AFFECT THE ECONOMY?

Monetary policy is imprecise. The Fed tries to influence the demand for goods and services by changing the federal funds rate target. An increase in the target normally leads to a decrease in the supply of credit and raises short-term interest rates. Banks usually raise the interest rates they charge on loans right after the Fed raises the target for the funds rate. As interest rates increase, some borrowers will decide not to borrow and hence not to make the purchases they had planned. Thus an increase in interest rates would be expected to decrease the demand for cars, appliances, and houses. Moreover, businesses may decide that the higher interest rates make the building of a new plant or the purchase of new equipment unattractive. As spending declines, firms find that sales are not as great as they anticipated, and inventories of unsold goods are higher than desired. This leads to firms reducing production, which slows the growth of the economy.

Similarly, if the Fed believes that the economy is growing too slowly, with little or no sign of inflation, it will lower the target for the funds rate. This will normally set in motion a decrease in other interest rates and make borrowing more attractive. This should increase spending and stimulate growth in the economy.

Of course, the Fed can be wrong in its analysis of the economy and lower or raise interest rates when it should have done the reverse. Some economists, referred to as monetarists, believe that this is too often the case and recommend that the Fed simply attempt to increase the money supply at some constant rate, about 3 percent per year. Their view is that the Fed is not smart enough to stabilize spending and is more likely to make things worse. Naturally, this opinion is not shared by the Fed.

INDEPENDENCE OF THE FED

A continuing controversy is whether the Fed should be less independent of the federal government. It is argued by some that it is undemocratic to have such a powerful tool as monetary policy under the control of people who are not elected and, in the case of the regional bank presidents, who are not even appointed by elected representatives. Because the Fed generates its own revenue, it is not dependent on Congress for an appropriation, and there is limited governmental oversight on its expenditures.

The proponents of an independent Fed point to the dangers of having a central bank under the control of the federal government. There is always the temptation to finance government spending by printing money. Excessive money growth causes inflation, which is undesirable. The structure of the Fed makes this unlikely to occur, and there is little evidence that the Fed has helped finance government spending, at least for the last 50 years.

Of course, Congress has the power to change the Federal Reserve Act and sometimes threatens to do so when it disapproves of Federal Reserve policies. The Fed is mindful of this possibility and takes the political pressures into account when making decisions.

SUMMARY

The Federal Reserve System is a unique combination of private and public institutions. While initially created by Congress to reduce the likelihood of financial panics, its role has evolved over time, and it currently focuses on setting monetary policy to keep inflation low and economic growth robust. Its principal tool to accomplish these goals is the open market operations that allow the buying or selling of government bonds. These operations change interest rates and the supply of credit, which then affects spending and the overall economy.

See also: The Dollar; Inflation; Interest Rates

Web Sites

The latest version of the beige book can be found at http://www.federalreserve.gov/fomc/beigebook/2006/default.htm.

Verbatim transcripts of FOMC meetings, along with the staff presentations, can be found at http://www.federalreserve.gov/fomc/transcripts/transcripts_1980.htm.

Further Reading: Meyer, Laurence H. 2004. *A Term at the Fed—An Insider's View.* New York: Harper Business; Woodward, Bob. 2000. *Maestro: Greenspan's Fed and the American Boom.* New York: Simon and Schuster; Woolley, John T. 1984. *Monetary Politics: The Federal Reserve and the Politics of Monetary Policy.* New York: Cambridge University Press.

Douglas K. Pearce

FOREIGN DIRECT INVESTMENT

Much has been made about American companies putting jobs and factories in foreign countries. This phenomenon, called outsourcing, has stirred concerns about America's competitiveness and the ability of U.S. workers to go head-to-head with foreign workers, many of whom are paid much less.

But perhaps just as important, yet largely unnoticed in the popular press, is the opposite flow of money and jobs. This occurs when foreign companies and foreign investors put funds into the U.S. economy. The money is used to build factories and stores or buy financial investments. With the inflow of money usually come jobs and incomes. This process is technically called foreign direct investment (FDI) or popularly termed insourcing.

THE SIZE AND ORIGIN OF FOREIGN DIRECT INVESTMENT (FDI)

FDI can happen from any country. People and companies from any country can invest in (almost) any other country. For example, there is FDI in China, France, Poland, and Chile. Of course, there is also FDI in the United States, which will be the focus of this entry.

So when we talk about the amount of money foreigners invest in the United States, are we talking a small or large amount? Figure F.1 gives the answer. The dollar amounts in different years in the figure have been adjusted so they have the same purchasing power; therefore they are directly comparable. As can be seen, FDI in the United States is substantial, at $1.6 trillion in 2005. It has also increased substantially in recent years, rising 200 percent from 1990 to 2005.

Who is behind these investments? That information is given in Table F.1, which shows FDI in the United States according to the top countries of origin in

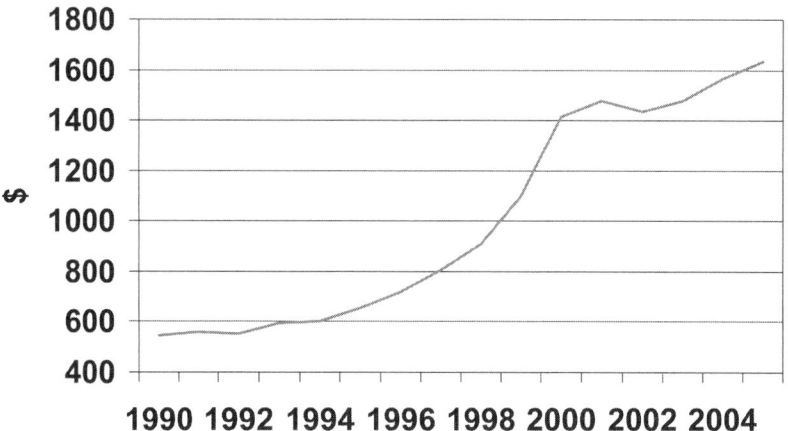

Figure F.1 Foreign direct investment in the United States (2005 dollars in billions).
Source: U.S. Department of Commerce. Available at: www.commerce.gov.

Table F.1 Leading Countries of Origin for FDI in the United States (1990 and 2005).

Country	Share of total FDI in 1990 (%)	Share of total FDI in 2005 (%)
United Kingdom	25.0	17.3
Japan	21.0	11.6
Netherlands	16.3	10.4
Germany	7.1	11.3
France	4.7	8.8
Switzerland	4.5	7.5
Australia	1.7	
Luxembourg		7.1

Source: U.S. Department of Commerce. Available at: www.commerce.gov.

1990 and 2005. In both years, the leading investor countries were all in Europe, of European origin (Australia), or Japan. The biggest changes from 1990 to 2005 have been a reduction in the shares of the two leading countries, the United Kingdom (Great Britain) and Japan, and the replacement of Australia in 1990 with Luxembourg in 2005 as a leading investor country.

WHY DO FOREIGNERS INVEST IN THE UNITED STATES?

What motivates foreigners to invest in the United States, and should we be pleased or worried by the interest of foreign investors? These are important questions that help determine how we feel about FDI.

On one level, we should not be surprised that foreigners want to invest in the United States. The United States is the world's largest economy by far, the biggest in aggregate wealth, and has a stable political system that respects the rights of investors. The U.S. economy has doubled in size in the past 20 years (1985–2005), and its population is among the fastest growing for developed countries. Against this backdrop, any investor would want part of the action in the United States.

Recently, there has been a demographic reason for FDI in the United States. Compared to Europe, Japan, and soon China, the United States is a relatively young country with a growing population. Europe, Japan, and China are aging rapidly, and their populations may even decline in the decades ahead. Older people tend to be savers and investors so that they can ensure an income in their later years. Younger people, by contrast, are usually borrowers so that they can supplement their income to purchase the homes, cars, appliances, and other assets needed for their lives. Therefore it makes sense that countries with older populations will lend—which is another way of looking at investing—to countries with a higher proportion of younger people. Indeed, this is exactly the pattern shown in Table F.1. The greatest source of FDI in the United States is from the aging countries of Europe plus Japan.

Last, there is a practical reason why foreign citizens invest in the United States. For most of the past 30 years, U.S. businesses and consumers have been purchasing more products and services from foreign countries than foreign businesses and consumers have been buying from the United States. In other words, imports to the United States have exceeded exports from the United States. This means that foreign citizens have been accumulating U.S. dollars. Eventually, these dollars have to make their way back to the United States, and they do so as FDI in the United States. This is one reason to expect China, with which the United States now runs a large trade deficit, to soon become a major source of FDI. The Chinese computer giant Lenovo's purchase of IBM's personal computer unit in 2004 is an example of what is likely ahead.

IMPACT OF FDI ON EMPLOYMENT

Like any investment, FDI in the United States creates jobs. But how many jobs, and where are they and what do they pay?

Table F.2 shows the latest data on the distribution of jobs by industry created by foreign investments in the United States. Almost 5.6 million jobs in the United States are directly associated with FDI, accounting for approximately 4 percent of all jobs in the country. Perhaps the most striking feature is the concentration of jobs in the manufacturing sector. Of the 5.6 million jobs, over 2 million of them are in manufacturing. This is 39 percent of the total FDI jobs. In comparison, in 2004, only 10 percent of all U.S. jobs were in manufacturing. An interesting feature of FDI is the growth of production and jobs in foreign-owned vehicle manufacturing factories placed in the United States.

Table F.2 Employment Associated with FDI in the United States (2004).

Sector	Employment	Percent of total
All industries	5,562,300	100.0
Manufacturing	2,169,000	39.0
Wholesale trade	546,300	9.8
Retail trade	697,600	12.5
Information	284,800	5.1
Finance	260,300	4.7
Real estate	42,400	0.7
Professional services	181,000	3.3
Agriculture and mining	71,900	1.3
Utilities	36,800	0.7
Construction	72,200	1.3
Transportation and warehousing	210,700	3.8
Hotels and food service	348,800	6.3
Other	640,500	11.5

Source: U.S. Department of Commerce. Available at: www.commerce.gov.

RISE OF FOREIGN-OWNED AUTO FACTORIES IN THE UNITED STATES

Manufacturing is the leading sector attracting foreign direct investment to the United States, and within manufacturing, vehicle production has become a popular venture for foreign investors. There are now 10 foreign auto companies with factories operating in the United States, and more are planned for the future. Additionally, there are foreign-owned factories producing vehicle parts that then supply their output to the vehicle assembly plants.

Employment in foreign-owned auto factories in the United States has steadily increased since the mid-1990s, rising 52 percent from 1995 to 2005. In contrast, domestic U.S. vehicle assembly and parts factories cut 350,000 jobs between 2000 and 2005, with more reductions expected. However, the gains in foreign-owned vehicle factories have not matched the cuts from domestic plants, so total employment in vehicle production in the United States has continued to fall.

The rise of foreign vehicle production in the United States and the decline of production from domestically owned companies have paralleled their sales trends. American auto companies first trailed their foreign competitors in developing smaller, fuel-efficient vehicles in the 1970s and 1980s. Then they lagged in quality and customer satisfaction in the 1990s and 2000s. American auto companies have not been able to close these gaps, and they are likely destined to become smaller in scale at the same time that foreign producers become larger.

American and foreign vehicle companies have also differed in terms of their locations within the United States. Traditionally, American vehicle companies located their production facilities in the Midwest, in states like Michigan, Ohio, and Indiana. Foreign vehicle companies have sited most of their factories in the South, including Alabama, Texas, and South Carolina. Lower labor costs and access to centers of growing population have been the main reasons pulling foreign factories to southern locations.

Although many Americans may be suspicious of foreign ownership, they have voted with their purchases and dollars in favor of foreign auto companies. The pay and prestige that a foreign vehicle production plant brings to a locality has set off intense competition between states for landing these so-called trophy firms.

FDI employment in the United States also pays well. In 2004, FDI jobs paid an average of $62,959 in salaries and benefits, compared to $48,051 for all U.S. jobs. Hence the average FDI job paid over 30 percent more than the average U.S. job in the country. So foreign investors are not creating low-paying positions in the United States; they are creating just the opposite—jobs that pay at the upper end of the wage scale.

COMPARING INSOURCING AND OUTSOURCING

How does FDI in the United States (insourcing) compare to U.S. direct investment in foreign countries (outsourcing)? Although FDI in the United States has been growing substantially, U.S. investment in foreign countries is still larger. The total value of U.S. investments in foreign countries is almost one-third larger than the corresponding foreign investment in the United States. Also, there are about two jobs in U.S. foreign factories and offices for every one job in the United States in a foreign-controlled company. So, by these standards, it can be said that outsourcing is larger than insourcing.

But before the conclusion is reached that this is bad, consider two counterpoints. First, since the U.S. economy is the largest in the world, it makes sense that U.S. companies will have more operations in foreign countries than foreign countries have in the United States. Second, foreign investments by U.S. companies can be complementary to domestic operations, making the domestic operations more efficient and profitable. Stated another way, putting some jobs in foreign countries, where costs may be lower or where access to important inputs is easier, can actually save jobs at home by making the operating company stronger and healthier.

ARE FOREIGNERS BUYING UP AMERICA?

Although many positive aspects can be stated for FDI, there is one nagging question that frequently bothers people: will foreign investments give the foreign owners control over the U.S. economy? Would these owners then pursue policies that are contrary to the national interests of the United States and its citizens?

From an economic perspective, these concerns are unlikely to be realized. This is because any investor, domestic or foreign, has two main objectives: preserving its investment and earning income on that investment. Pursuing destructive policies that damage the investment or its income-earning ability are simply not consistent with basic investment philosophy.

Another way of answering the question is to calculate the proportion of the U.S. economy that foreigners own. This is found by taking foreign-owned assets as a percentage of all assets in the United States. In 2004, this percentage came to 14 percent. While this is double the percentage in the late 1990s, foreign gains have not come at the expense of domestic ownership. Between 1997 and 2004, foreign-owned assets in the United States increased by $5 trillion, but U.S. domestically owned assets rose by $28 trillion.

THE WORLD IS OUR ECONOMY

It is likely that FDI, both in the United States by foreign citizens as well as in foreign countries by U.S. citizens, will increase in coming years. The reason is simple: globalization. With trade barriers lower and technology making travel and communication among countries in the world easier, we should expect money flows between nations and regions to likewise surge. Just as a century ago, local financial markets in the United States expanded to become nationwide financial markets, world markets are now supplanting national markets. Our perspective of what is normal and common will have to adjust.

See also: Chinese Currency; The Dollar; Free Trade; Trade Surpluses and Deficits

Further Reading: Office of Aerospace and Automotive Studies. 2005. *U.S. Automotive Industry Trends.* Washington, DC: U.S. Department of Commerce.

Michael L. Walden

FREE TRADE

Free trade is one of those concepts espoused by economists that makes perfect sense in the abstract. However, looking a bit closer, we question whether we should support the implementation of free trade principles and policies. It ultimately depends on one's point of view.

WHAT IS FREE TRADE?

Simply, free trade is the exchange or sale of goods or services without adding a tariff or tax. It is common for import taxes to be levied when goods are brought into a country. Often, products that are produced in the country are taxed, sometimes heavily, when foreign manufacturers bring these products into the home country for sale. The notion of free trade says that there would be no additional taxes on foreign imports vis-à-vis domestically produced automobiles.

WHAT IS NONFREE TRADE?

Another label for nonfree trade is protectionism. In this case, tariffs or taxes, trade restrictions, or quotas may be placed on the import of goods and services into a country. This is done to protect the business of the home country from competitors. Opponents of free trade also tend to call this practice fair trade.

On the surface, as a resident of the home country, higher prices for imported goods mean that the home country goods will be purchased and purportedly save jobs in the home country. However, adding tariffs to level the playing field between foreign and domestic competition actually taxes the consumer and causes him to pay higher prices.

BACK TO BASICS

The fundamental laws of trade were first hypothesized in 1776 by Adam Smith in his treatise Wealth of Nations. In this document, he had a simple make-buy argument: do not make at home what you can buy cheaper outside. This applies to countries as well as individuals. Thus, if one country can make shoes (say, Brazil) cheaper than another (say, the United States), then it would make sense for Americans to buy shoes that are made in Brazil. Smith's argument is logical in that we can do the things we do well and buy the goods or services that others do well. This argument makes good sense in the aggregate.

As we can see in Figure F.2, country 1 has a lower cost (C1) than the cost for the product produced in country 2 (C2) for the product being made. If we presume the same profit, X, then the price (P1) of the product produced in country 1 will be lower than the price (P2) of the product produced in country 2. This should be fundamentally good for consumers. However, if a tax (T) is added to the price for the good produced in country 1, as shown in Figure F.4, then consumers will pay the same amount for the product and not realize any potential savings for efficiencies, as seen in Figure F.3.

The example begs the question of what would happen if the tax were not imposed and free trade were enabled. Figure F.4 illustrates the value to the

$$

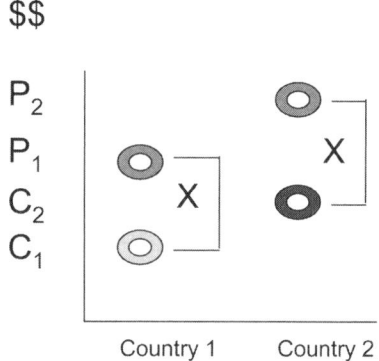

Figure F.2 Illustration of costs and corresponding prices.

consumer of free trade. In the example, both countries produce wine and wheat. However, country 1 produces wheat at a lower cost than country 2. Likewise, country 2 produces wine at a lower cost than country 1. If a consumer was able to buy wine from country 2 and wheat from country 1 (without any interference from tariffs), he would expend less money for both products.

WHAT ARE THE ISSUES THAT PROMPT FREE TRADE AMONG NATIONS?

There are two fundamental factors that prompt nations to engage in free trade. One is buying power (or selling power), and the other is cost.

Consider the trading power of a nation. In our prior example, the more products a trading unit (i.e., nation) has that it can produce at a low cost, the more

$$

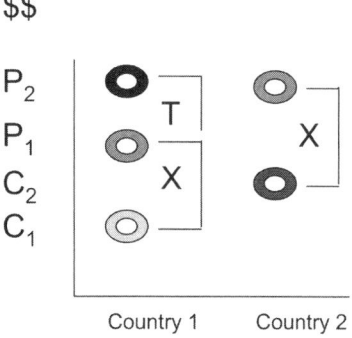

Figure F.3 Illustration of prices under nonfree trade.

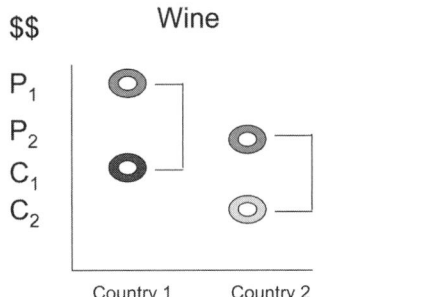
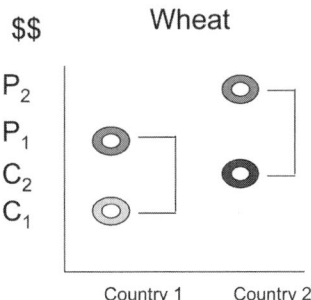

Figure F.4 Tariff-free spending.

opportunities it will have to trade. If each state in the United States was acting independently, it would have to be very efficient at organizing trades that
would take a small number of products and obtain all of the products that the
individual state would need. However, with all 50 states operating without trade
barriers, the movement of goods and services is free flowing. Consumers do not
have artificial pricing increased by taxes. Trading power is enhanced in a free
trade environment.

Cost is the second issue prompting free trade. Think about the possibility
that a truckload of product would need to stop at the border of each state to
continue. In addition to the time lost in the stops, a tax would be charged at each
checkpoint. The total cost of the product in such a scenario would be increased
dramatically. In fact, at one time, the truck transportation cost was estimated
to be double in Europe versus the United States due to border checkpoints, at
which inspections would be made and taxes levied. Therefore we can presume
that total cost in a nonfree trade environment would be higher.

WHERE IS FREE TRADE?

One of the classic examples of an implementation of free trade policies is the
formation of the European Union (EU). The countries in Europe maintained
separate governments, currencies, and standards over centuries. The EU was
formed to enhance political, social, and economic cooperation. As an example,
prior to the formation of the EU, there was no free movement of people from
country to country. Licensing standards for medical and professional personnel
were neither consistent nor even recognized from one country to the next. In
fact, these standards were so different and so ingrained in the laws of each country that it took 17 years to reach agreement on the qualifications for an architect.
Architects, like other professionals, could not move freely from one country to
another. Once the EU was established, architects could move from one country
to another since they would be licensed in all of the countries in the EU. Licensing standards for doctors and other medical personnel were among those that
would be harmonized, or standardized.

Uniting Europe was done for two stated reasons: preventing another world war and creating an economic unit as strong as the United States. The issues in the EU were many and the task was very daunting in the beginning. Issues included a difference in tax rates (i.e., high in the United Kingdom and low in southern European countries), government (i.e., monarchy vs. democracy), currencies (each country with its own currency), and wages (i.e., high in the heavily industrialized countries and low in other countries). The common currency, the euro, only came into use officially in 1999, and many of the other issues are either unresolved or recently resolved. So we might say that the jury is still out on the EU's success.

The North American Free Trade Agreement (NAFTA) was launched in 1994. Canada, Mexico, and the United States formed the world's largest free trade area. Unlike the EU, there is no supraorganization over the independent participants. The agreement called for the elimination of duties on half of all U.S. goods shipped to Mexico and Canada immediately and for the phasing out of other tariffs over a period of 14 years. The treaty protected intellectual property and also addressed the investment restrictions between the three countries.

Several reports have been published that address the progress of the NAFTA agreement 10 years later. The Yale Economic Review reports that during the five years before NAFTA, Mexican gross domestic product grew at 3 percent ("NAFTA 10 Years Later" 2004). However, after the agreement, this rate increased to a high of 7 percent. During the 10 years post-NAFTA, exports from the United States to Canada increased by 62 percent, and exports to Mexico increased by 106 percent. Canada's success with NAFTA is also well established.

WHAT ARE THE ISSUES?

There are a number of issues and questions regarding free trade. The issues concern the economy, the political situation, and social issues.

LOSS OF JOBS AS A PERSONAL ISSUE

The steel business was a major industry in Buffalo, New York, employing nearly 60,000 at its peak. The purchase of Lackawanna Steel by Bethlehem Steel was critical for location and access to the Buffalo and Detroit auto plants. Power was inexpensive due to the proximity to the Niagara Power Project, although a strong union position served to increase costs. As the industry gradually left the United States for offshore locations, initially to Southeast Asia, a cry concerning the impact of free trade and the loss of jobs as a result was heard throughout the area. Although that claim can be empirically disproved, it is a tough sell to a family whose father is one of those unemployed, with little prospect for work in another steel plant and few other options.

One question deals with workers' rights. Stories abound of child labor issues and wages of 50 cents per hour. The presumption is that these wages must be at slave labor rates in comparison to the United States. However, wherever globalization has taken place, workers have seen a dramatic improvement in working conditions. Since foreign-owned companies are likely to provide similar conditions to their overseas versus domestic workers, local firms are forced to compete. Foreign-owned companies typically pay more than local businesses and provide a better environment to attract the best possible workers.

Another question relates to the environment. One view is that companies will set up shop at locations where they might avoid environmental constraints. However, this is usually a minor issue in locating a facility. Higher on the list of requirements are tax laws, legal systems, and an educated workforce. Infrastructure, such as transportation and packaging facilities, are also high on the list. Empirical evidence shows that the environmental standards of countries with free trade actually improve and do not deteriorate.

How does free trade affect manufacturing? Free trade is actually an advantage to U.S. manufacturing. Increasing productivity and decreasing costs forces innovation and an increase in profitability. In fact, during the period of 1992–1999, when the overall economy increased by 29 percent, the manufacturing output of the United States increased by 42 percent.

So we need to ask if free trade enables movement of people across borders. Is immigration bad for the United States? The answer is actually no. Immigrants tend to fill gaps in worker shortages and often bring technical skills with them. Furthermore, the National Research Council conducted a study and showed that immigrants and their children actually pay more in taxes than they consume in services (Simon 1995).

What about the phenomenon called brain drain? This is when nations or regions lose skilled or educated workers due to the availability of better-paying jobs elsewhere. Poor countries often educate their population in specific jobs in medical areas and other professions in the hope that they will stay, only to find that some rich countries try to attract them away. The BBC reports that one-third of doctors in the United Kingdom are from overseas (Shah 1998). The report goes on to state that African, Asian, and Latin American nations are plagued by this issue.

Finally, free trade always spurs a discussion on jobs. While imported goods may take some jobs away from a country, they are generally in those industries that are less competitive. More often, technology, monetary policy, and other nontrade factors are those which will cause a loss of jobs. Increasing imports actually increase jobs and serve to make workers more productive. Remember that this effect is in the aggregate, not in specific industries.

WHAT ARE THE VARIOUS PERSPECTIVES?

The benefits to the individual consumer are well documented. As seen in Figure F.4, the individual will pay less overall for goods and services under a free trade economy. Furthermore, he will be able to buy higher-quality goods at lower prices than without free trade. The downside, of course, is that while the long-term benefit is clear, the short term presents problems, especially if one's job is impacted by the movement abroad.

AN EXAMPLE OF THE CURRENCY ISSUE

Assume that a component, say, a circuit board, can be made both in the United States and also in Thailand. The cost is represented in the following table, both with and without tariffs.

Table F.3

	U.S. product	Thai product without tariff	Thai product with tariff
Cost (USD)	100	60	60
Tariff (USD)			50
Final price (USD)	100	60	110

If the U.S. product is used as a component part, the final product will be least expensive if the Thai product is used without a tariff. The idea here is that if there are no tariffs, then the corporation would tend to use the lowest cost raw material. Thus we could assume that under the condition of no tariffs, the final price of the finished good might be as much as $40 less than if the U.S. circuit board were used.

If the U.S. circuit board were used (or the Thai product with tariff), then the final product would cost more. A consumer would have less disposable income and would not be able to buy as many other goods, reducing trade overall.

Since there would be fewer imports, there would be fewer U.S. dollars on the international market, raising the dollar's value. The result is that we would be selling less on the export market and actually decreasing trade.

If we were to use the Thai product without tariffs, the cost of the final product would be less, and we would be able to spend more and buy more imports. This would cause the currency to be lower in value with respect to other countries and encourage export sales. The overall result is an increase in trade.

Countries that engage in free trade, or at least lower trade barriers, enjoy higher standards of living overall. As noted by Griswold (1999), trade moves to those industries where productivity and returns are higher. Thus workers will have more job opportunities at higher wages.

There are also national implications from the value of the U.S. dollar (or the home currency). If trade barriers are imposed, imports are restricted. Americans then spend less on foreign goods, which makes its currency higher with respect to other currencies. Thus any industry that is not protected by tariffs becomes less competitive in world markets, and the United States is less able to export. It is a cycle: restricting imports creates higher currency value, which then inhibits exports.

From the corporate perspective, raw materials may be purchased more cost-effectively, manufacturing becomes more streamlined, and lower costs make products more profitable. When we consider the changes in industries that will make one industry more profitable, we should also examine whether or not a change in one industry places even more pressure on another. In our steel example, if quotas are imposed once steel moves offshore, then automobiles become less competitive domestically.

Continuing with the steel example, some of the "buy American" slogans may be misleading when we examine them further. According to Blinder (2002), the estimated cost of saving jobs by implementing protectionism is staggering. He cites costs of restricting imports in the "automobile industry at $105,000 per job per year, one job in TV manufacturing at $420,000, and one job in steel at $750,000/year." No wonder the steel industry was one of the earliest to leave American shores.

WHAT ARE THE OPTIONS?

One option for free trade is balanced trade. In this model, countries must provide a balance from each country. Neither country is allowed to run deficits at the risk of penalties. Some critics of this approach think that innovation may be stifled.

Another option is called fair trade. In this scenario, standards are promoted for the production of goods and services, specifically for exports from lesser developed countries to well-developed (First World) countries.

Another alternative is an international or bilateral barter program, which would force the matching of imports and exports. Finally, establishing increased credit risk for international loans, especially those brought on by trade imbalance, would lower the volume of uneven trade and look to the economic market for discipline.

WHAT DO YOU NEED TO KNOW?

Artificially constricting competition through tariffs will serve to restrict trade and reduce productivity. Free trade is not a main factor in the loss of jobs. Free trade actually helps to improve productivity.

Be sure you know how free trade or protectionism affects your business. What raw materials or components have import tariffs? What competing products or substitute products have tariffs? Which substitute products for your final product have tariffs? How do these tariffs (or lack thereof) impact the competition in your business? How do they affect the costs?

SUMMARY

Free trade is the movement of goods, services, capital, and labor across boundaries without tariffs or other nontariff trade barriers. The impact of the tariffs is purported to save jobs but actually costs the consumer more for the final goods and services and restricts the competition in a number of fundamental ways, ultimately reducing the overall standard of living.

When you evaluate the empirical evidence, free trade is a good thing. However, in very specific cases, when the issue is personal, free trade may not look as attractive in the short term.

See also: Chinese Currency; The Dollar; Foreign Direct Investment; Rich Country/Poor Country; Trade Surpluses and Deficits

References

Binder, A. S. 2002. "The Concise Encyclopedia of Economics." *The Library of Economics and Liberty.* Available at: www.econlib.org/library/enc/freetrade.html.

Griswold, D. T. 1999. "Trade Jobs and Manufacturing: Why (Almost All) U.S. Workers Should Welcome Imports." In Trade Briefing Paper. Cato Institute.

"NAFTA 10 Years Later." 2004. Available from: www.ita.doc.gov/tdindustry/otea/nafta/coverpage.pdf.

Shah, A. 1998. "Criticisms of Current Forms of Free Trade." Available from: http://www.globalissues.org/TradeRelated/FreeTrade/Criticisms.asp#Braindrainfrompoorcountries torichcountries. Accessed Marh 31, 2006.

Simon, J. L. 1995. *Immigration: The Demographic and Economic Facts.* Cato Institute.

Further Reading: Batra, R. 1996. *The Myth of Free Trade: The Pooring of America.* New York: Touchstone; Irwin, D. A. 2002. *Free Trade Under Fire.* 2nd ed. Princeton, NJ: Princeton University Press.

Diane H. Parente

G

GLASS CEILING

WHAT IS THE GLASS CEILING?

Glass ceiling is a term used to refer to the alleged limits of advancement that minorities experience in the American workplace. It has been observed that the highest-ranking positions in organizations are dominated by heterosexual white males. This observation has led to the theory that minorities within organizations have a limited level to which they can advance. That ceiling for advancement is said to be transparent, or obviously biased, unlike other ceilings, which require various degrees of experience or education. Hence the term glass ceiling has been used to describe this phenomenon.

DOES THE GLASS CEILING EXIST?

The term glass ceiling was first used by Carol Hymowitz and Timothy Schellhardt in the March 24, 1986, edition of the Wall Street Journal to describe the limits of advancement that women face in the workplace (Hymowitz and Schellhardt 1986). When originally used, the term drew widespread criticism because it claimed that women did not achieve high levels of advancement in the workforce because they were consumed by family life or did not obtain the required levels of education and/or experience. Since then, the term and the arguments surrounding it have developed to encompass all minorities in the workplace.

According to a great deal of research, the glass ceiling is a very real characteristic of the American corporate atmosphere. A 1995 study by the Federal

STRATEGIES FOR INDIVIDUALS TO BREAK THROUGH THE GLASS CEILING

- Understand where the glass ceiling begins. While the glass ceiling is most keenly observed at the senior management level, the filtering out of minority candidates for high-ranking positions often begins at the lower levels. Many minorities are often channeled into support or secondary roles, from which high-level advancement can be rare. Minorities are often excluded from various functions inside and outside of the workplace due to racial stereotypes and background differences. Get involved, ask for opportunities outside the ones where minorities are typically found, and be clear about your goals.
- Identify opportunities for promotion. Research the demographics of your company's senior management or board of directors. Does this group include any minorities? Are there any people in the same minority group as yourself? Recognize potential for exclusion: are they mostly family members or in-laws? Did they all go to the same college? Do they belong to the same types of non-work-related social groups?
- Find a mentor. While formal mentoring programs exist in many businesses, feel free to seek out your own mentor, and develop a relationship with that person. The stronger his or her future is in the company, the better the mentor.
- Build a network. Your network begins with your mentor as he or she will help you begin to build internal support within the organization. On your own, or with advice from more senior members of the company, begin to develop interdepartmental relationships with strong employees. Identify any external organizations that exist to support minorities in your profession.

Glass Ceiling Commission found that 97 percent of the senior managers of the Fortune 1000 Industrial and Fortune 500 were white, and 95–97 percent were male. This is not demographically representative, considering that 57 percent of the workforce consists of ethnic minorities, women, or both. In 1990, Jaclyn Fierman (1990) found that fewer than 0.5 percent of the 4,012 highest-paid managers in top companies in the United States were women, while fewer than 5 percent of senior management in the Fortune 500 corporations were minorities. The conclusion reached from studies such as these is that there are invisible barriers that exclude women and ethnic minorities from upper management positions.

Despite evidence to the contrary, many argue that the glass ceiling concept does not exist. Those who argue that the glass ceiling does not exist focus mainly on the status of women and argue that the glass ceiling ignores pertinent evidence that disproves the theory and that it is an unrealistic conspiracy theory that simply reflects women's chosen positions in American society.

One of the forms of evidence that glass ceiling detractors claim is ignored is the education of high-ranking executives. They argue that these executives are more qualified because they have achieved a higher level of education than most women. They argue that women are not well represented in upper-level management because of a lack of women receiving master of business administration (MBA) degrees.

Those who argue against the existence of the glass ceiling also argue that women are not represented in upper-level management because women do not aspire to such positions, partially because of the characteristics of American society. It is argued that men work better in teams and under a chain of command than women, who take less dangerous jobs, are not willing to work long hours like men, and wish to have more maternal positions, such as nurse, childcare provider, or secretary. Of course, the issue of childbirth and maternal instincts are also factors that many claim prevent women from holding high-level positions. Glass ceiling detractors often take as fact that women cannot be highly successful and raise children. Surprisingly, a great number of these types of arguments are being made by women with experience in the business world who do not see themselves as victims. Instead, they deny their advancement potential by claiming that they have decided to make another choice.

Those who argue against the glass ceiling in terms of how it affects ethnic minorities use similar arguments and often expand them to include stereotypes, the most common being that African Americans and Latinos are lazy or would rather perform labor-centered tasks. Other reasons used include a lack of education, inability to understand the English language or Western society, or a desire to hold certain types of positions (e.g., linking Asian Americans to computer and science jobs).

The argument against the existence of the glass ceiling is compelling; however, the enormous disparities between the minority and majority when it comes to senior management positions make the analysis of this issue necessary, whether the concept is seen as bona fide or not. The next section of this entry will focus on issues surrounding the lack of high-level employment among different types of minority groups.

GROUPS AFFECTED BY THE GLASS CEILING

Women

For most of the twentieth century, the levels of education achieved by men and women were disproportionate. However, recent decades have seen the end of unequal access to education in terms of gender. In 2003, 50 percent of the Yale undergraduate class was female, the University of California at Berkley law class of 2004 was 63 percent female, and Columbia University's law class was 51 percent female. Over 45 percent of medical students are women, as are half of undergraduate business majors (Belkin 2003). So how has the discrepancy between men and women in high-ranking positions evolved?

One major and incontrovertible difference between men and women is that women give birth and men do not. This leads to one of the most common reasons given for the existence of a glass ceiling. Many argue that women simply choose other paths than their careers. One example comes from business. A

Harvard Business School survey found that only 38 percent of women from the MBA classes of 1981, 1985, and 1991 were working full-time. Of white men with MBAs, 95 percent are working full-time, while only 67 percent of white women with MBAs have full-time positions (McNutt 2002).

Many women are discriminated against in the workplace. Often, when a woman is hired, she is hired under the assumption that she will leave her job or stop working so hard when she gets married or has children. This type of attitude places women in the types of jobs that can be seen as temporary. Women may be working on small projects instead of being heavily involved with the infrastructure of a corporation. This type of job discrimination may go so far as to place women with college degrees as administrative assistants or secretaries. It is with this type of discrimination that many women's careers begin. Perhaps one of the reasons that women opt out of the workplace to raise children is because of the pressure and stress that comes along with being a woman in the business world.

In addition, many of the same factors that affect ethnic and racial minorities also affect women. The next section addresses these issues specifically.

Ethnic and Racial Minorities

The barriers that ethnic and racial minority managers encounter are common to the experience of other minorities. These barriers operate at the individual and organizational levels. They range from overt racial harassment experienced in the workplace to specific segregation practices. These barriers are believed to be responsible for the lack of ethnic minority senior executives in large organizations.

Bell and Nkomo (1994) have identified three major individual barriers that ethnic minorities experience: (1) subtle racism and prejudice, (2) managing duality and bicultural stress, and (3) tokenism and presumed incompetence.

This subtle form of racism and prejudice does not resemble the outright hostility that American culture has rejected since the civil rights movement of the 1950s and 1960s but instead takes the form of what Essed (1991) has termed everyday racism. This includes acts of marginalization, which refers to the exclusion of African American managers from mainstream organizational life, thus maintaining their outsider status, and problematization, which includes the use of stereotypes to justify the exclusion of African American managers without seeming to be prejudiced or racist.

Another important form of an individual barrier includes racial harassment. Racial harassment occurs when an individual or group of employees is continually subjected to racial slurs, jokes, pranks, insults, and verbal or even physical abuse because of their race. Obviously, threats of violence and abuse are detrimental to any working environment, but racial harassment takes many forms and is often precipitated by fellow employees who are unaware of the harassment they inflict. Racial jokes are a good example of unconscious racial harassment. Another example would include a negative reaction to a news event involving a minority that reflects negatively on that minority's race or ethnicity.

EXAMPLES OF EVERYDAY RACIAL HARASSMENT

- Any type of racialized joke.
- Racial comments about public figures such as politicians, entertainers, athletes, or even criminals, for example, pointing out that the city councilman accused of fraud is "the black one."
- Asking individuals questions pertaining to their entire race, for example, Why do black people like chicken so much? or Why are Asians so good with computers?
- Using phrases that encompass derogatory terms, for example, nigger-lip, Asian eyes, black booty, or black music.
- Any comments or questions pertaining to a physical difference between the ethnic minority and white employees, including skin color, hair, or any other prominent features.
- Displaying symbols that could be racially offensive, whether one individual considers it so or not, for example, a swastika, Confederate flag, or any symbol resembling a racist organization. The display of a logo of a popular sports team may also be offensive. The most objective are those that portray Native Americans in a negative light. The display of this type of symbol may also be considered racial harassment.
- Discussing or using quotes from racist films or music.

The second level of individual barriers is referred to as bicultural stress. As Bell and Nkomo (1994, 47) noted, "in the organizational world, there is little tolerance or appreciation for cultural diversity in terms of behavioral styles, dress, or rich aesthetics representing multiculturality." Bell and Nkomo pointed out that most business environments rely on norms from mostly white Western society that may conflict with other dimensions of these minority managers' normal lives or backgrounds. If the manager is from a non-Western country, this conflict can only increase. The challenge of balancing these contrasting aspects of life often creates stress and tension between the workplace and one's private life. This tension becomes a barrier when ethnic minorities feel compelled to suppress one part of their identity to succeed in one or both of the cultural dimensions in which they exist.

The third level of individual barriers is tokenism. Tokenism is the process of hiring a token number of individuals from an underrepresented minority group to comply with government or organizational affirmative action policies. The people who are token hires are often viewed as representative of their entire race, rather than as individuals. Their performance on the job and their personal lives are carefully examined and taken out of context. Because of these stereotypes and general animosity toward affirmative action policies, many other employees believe that these tokens received their jobs not because of individual merit, but because of their minority status.

The psychological effects of being treated as a token negatively affect job performance. To overcome the stereotypes associated with each ethnic or racial group, the minority employees often feel that they have to perform at a higher level than other employees just to maintain equal status. They also have to spend a disproportionate amount of time validating their existence in the workplace. They are often aware that because they are perceived to represent their entire race, performing poorly will negatively contribute to the negative stereotypes attributed to their ethnic minority.

Entering a work environment is different for ethnic minorities than it is for white men and women. There are often a multitude of factors that must be juggled just to achieve equal status to that of fellow white employees. The disadvantages that ethnic minorities experience in the workplace are prevalent from the first day on the job, and maybe even before.

ORGANIZATIONAL-LEVEL BARRIERS

Bell and Nkomo pointed out various organizational-level barriers that exist for ethnic minorities in the workplace. These include (1) lack of mentorship, (2) unfair promotion and evaluation processes, and (3) segregation into staff-type jobs.

Mentors are important in any large business environment. A mentor helps to increase self-confidence, motivation, career skills, career enhancement, career planning, networking opportunities, and perhaps most importantly, mentors reduce isolation. Mentors are most likely to have mentees who have similar backgrounds. This is perfectly understandable because people tend to sympathize with and coach those in similar situations or from similar backgrounds as themselves. A problem is that mentors may pass over a potential protégé who belongs to an ethnic minority group because of racial stereotypes that may make the mentor see the minority as a risky protégé.

Many employees from ethnic minority groups find it difficult to find mentorship. In 1993, Friedman and Carter found that 53 percent of National Black MBA Association members felt that they did not have the support of a mentor. Without equal access to mentors, ethnic minorities are without one of the most important aspects of successful career advancement. It limits their networking opportunities, exposure within the company, and potential supporters. It also denies them the important basic advantages that a mentor provides as far as career planning and the transition into a new organization.

Over the past 20 years, numerous studies have been done that show that white supervisors rank managers from ethnic minority groups below white managers in their evaluations (Bell and Nkomo 1994). They rank them lower in terms of job performance and how they interact with other employees. Part of this is because of racial stereotypes. If supervisors consider ethnic minority managers to be doing a fine job, then their performance is attributed to the support structure they have around them that makes their job easier. For whites, top performance is attributed to effort and competence. As negative feedback builds, it has a snowballing effect on African American managers as they lose their confidence and begin to question their own abilities. Low performance ratings have negative effects on an individual's own long-term career prospects and self-prescribed potential for advancement within the organization.

There are clear trends in the career paths of the vast majority of CEOs of large organizations. The critical career paths have historically been through marketing, finance, and operations. The people who head companies are often funneled through these departments. Collins (1989) has pointed out that African Americans have been relegated to racialized jobs outside of those departments that produce the most upper-level managers. She suggested that African Americans are often placed in jobs dealing with public relations, community relations, affirmative action, and equal employment opportunity. Among 76 of the highest-ranking African American managers, she found that 66 percent held jobs that dealt with affirmative action or consumer issues. Because of the types of jobs that African American employees are often relegated to, it becomes more difficult for them to advance up the corporate ladder because they do not get experience in the most important functions.

The glass ceiling concept for women and ethnic and racial minorities is hotly contested. Those who argue that it does not exist for women claim that women are not represented in upper management well because they put their families before their careers. The argument against the glass ceiling concept as it concerns ethnic and racial minorities basically hinges on racial stereotypes. Opponents claim that groups like African Americans and Latinos are lazy and that they are not willing to do what it takes to get to the top.

The argument backing the glass ceiling concept for women accepts that many women do choose to leave the workplace to make a family but that those who do not have suffered because of the common misconception and stereotypes surrounding all women. Arguments backing the glass ceiling concept for ethnic and racial minorities claim that basic racist ideas as well as cultural conflicts hinder the ability of people of color to reach upper levels of management. Arguments that the glass ceiling does exist are the most convincing because they are all backed by facts that do indicate, for one reason or another, that minorities are not represented demographically in upper levels of management.

See also: Affirmative Action; Blue-Collar and White-Collar Jobs; Education and Economic Competitiveness; Poverty and Race; Salary Disparity

References

Belkin, Lisa. 2003. "The Opt-Out Revolution." *New York Times* (October 23): 1.

Bell, E., and S. Nkomo. 1994. *Glass Ceiling Commission—Barriers to Work Place Advancement Experienced by African-Americans.* Ithaca, NY: Cornell University Press.

Collins, S. 1989. "The Marginalization of Black Executives." *Social Problems* 36: 317–31.

Essed, P. 1991. *Understanding Everyday Racism: An Interdisciplinary Theory.* Newbury Park, CA: Sage.

Federal Glass Ceiling Commission. 1995. *Good for Business: Making Full Use of the Nation's Human Capital.* iii–iv.

Fierman, J. 1990. "Why Women Still Don't Hit the Top." *Fortune* 122: 40.

Friedman, R. A., and D. Carter. 1993. "African American Network Groups: Their Impact and Effectiveness." Working Paper 93-069, Harvard Business School, Cambridge, MA.

Hymowitz, Carol, and Timothy Schellhardt. 1986. "The Glass Ceiling." *Wall Street Journal* (March 24).

McNutt, L. 2002. *The Glass Ceiling: It Can't Be Shattered If It Doesn't Exist.* Available at: http://www.ifeminists.net/introduction/editorials/2002/1217c.html.

Further Reading: Morrison, A., and R. White. 1994. *Breaking the Glass Ceiling: Can Women Reach the Top of America's Largest Corporations?* Beverly, MA: Perseus; Schulz, M. 2004. *Breaking the Glass Ceiling: Women Police Chiefs and Their Paths to the Top.* New York: McGraw-Hill; Stith, A. 1998. *Breaking the Glass Ceiling: Sexism and Racism in Corporate America: The Myths, Realities, and the Solutions.* Toronto: Warwick.

William M. Sturkey

GOVERNMENT SUBSIDIES

A subsidy refers to an economic benefit from government to individuals or business firms. A subsidy may lower the price of a product or service to individuals or raise the price received by those who produce it. It may also benefit producers by lowering the cost of production. Governments—federal, state, and local—subsidize a wide range of economic activities in the United States. Well-known subsidies include government assistance to farmers, food stamps, college student loans, and economic incentives (such as tax breaks) by state and local governments to attract sports teams and manufacturing or research facilities.

Subsidies began in Great Britain in the 1500s with a grant of money by the British Parliament to the king to finance military expenditures. The money was raised by a special tax. The subsidy concept has long since been generalized and now refers to any economic favor by government to benefit producers or consumers. Though some subsidies may benefit the public at large, many subsidies today do not and frequently, quite appropriately, are referred to as political pork or corporate welfare.

POLITICAL PORK AND CORPORATE WELFARE

In the literal sense, a pork barrel is a barrel in which pork is kept. The term is thought to have originated on southern plantations, where slaves were given a barrel with the remainder of slaughtered hogs—the pork barrel. In the political arena, pork barrel legislation is a derogatory term referring to government spending meant to shore up constituent support in a politician's home state. Pork barrel legislation provides rich patronage benefits to incumbent politicians. Public work projects and agricultural subsidies are commonly cited examples of pork. Increased pork might be ladled out for existing government programs that benefit particular groups such as corn producers, sugar producers, textile manufacturers, or workers in auto factories. It also might go for government spending on a new project, such as a new post office building, where economic benefits are concentrated in a specific congressional district.

Pork barrel projects providing subsidies to favored groups are added to the federal budget by members of the appropriation committees of Congress. The congressional process often provides spending on federally funded projects in the congressional districts of members of the appropriation committee. Pork barrel projects frequently benefit major campaign contributors. Politicians often are judged by their ability to deliver pork to their constituents, and candidates for political office sometimes campaign with the promise that if elected, he or she will secure more federal spending for that state or congressional district.

Pork barrel legislation may also give rise to so-called corporate welfare, which describes a wasteful government subsidy to a large company. The government subsidy may be in the form of grants of money, tax breaks, or some other form of special treatment. Corporate welfare, which benefits particular business corporations, generally comes at the expense of other corporations and the public at large.

Either political pork or corporate welfare, like beauty, may be in the eye of the beholder. For example, the prospect of large numbers of unhappy voters may cause the federal government to bail out a large corporation when it faces bankruptcy. The justification given may be that the loss of jobs and economic activity accompanying bankruptcy is so large that a bailout by the government to avoid bankruptcy would benefit the public at large. For example, some firms in the airline industry may not be able to survive ongoing losses without government subsidies. Such bailouts, however, may not be beneficial. Bankruptcy of less efficient firms is an inevitable feature of a competitive market process, and profit and loss signals lose their ability to channel resources efficiently if business firms are not allowed to fail. Moreover, business firms seeking government aid often succeed when the benefits are highly concentrated on a relatively small group and the costs are borne by taxpayers generally, even if the subsidy is harmful to the public at large. This point is no less important in the case of corporate welfare, where the economic stakes are huge.

What are the main kinds of subsidies in the United States? How do some of the familiar and not-so-familiar subsidy programs work? Why do subsidies typically lead to too much of the subsidized activity being produced and used? Subsidies generally benefit a small group at the expense of the general population, and many are harmful to the general public. How, then, do harmful subsidy programs get enacted into law in a democratic society that makes decisions on the basis of majority vote? The following sections consider these questions and clear up some of the confusion about subsidies.

TYPES OF SUBSIDIES

Subsidies take many different forms and can be classified in different ways.

Money versus In-Kind Subsidies

A subsidy or so-called transfer from the government to an individual or business firm may be in the form of money or in-kind benefit. Well-known money transfers include agricultural subsidies, veterans' benefits, and Medicaid. Common in-kind benefits include food stamps, school lunches, rent subsidies, medical assistance, and other programs that do not involve the exchange of money. In some cases, an in-kind subsidy program may require the recipient to pay some of the cost. For example, the school lunch program is said to be means tested: depending on the parents' income, some students receive free meals, while students from families having higher incomes must pay, but the price paid is below the cost of the meal.

Business Subsidies versus Subsidies to Individuals

Business Subsidies

Federal, state, and local governments subsidize a wide range of producer activities. Farmers, for example, may receive financial assistance when crop prices are low or crop yields are lowered due to drought, hail, or other unfavorable weather conditions. Governments sometimes subsidize large corporations such as auto or steel companies. Assistance may be direct, as in the case of a financial bailout, or it may be indirect, including tariffs and import quotas that limit domestic sales of competing goods from foreign countries.

Quite often, a government subsidy is targeted on a specific business firm. State and local governments may attempt to lure a corporation to locate a manufacturing facility within its borders by providing property tax holidays or other financial incentives. For example, South Carolina, Alabama, and other states have used tax breaks to induce foreign auto companies, including Toyota and Mercedes, to locate manufacturing facilities within their states. Similarly, local governments often subsidize the construction of sports facilities to lure sports teams.

Similarly, large industries may induce the federal government to restrict competition from foreign firms producing similar products. Subsidies of this type include import tariffs on autos, steel, textile products, and agricultural products. An import tariff on autos, for example, means that Ford, General Motors, and other domestic auto producers can charge higher prices for their products in the United States.

The federal government also subsidizes the export of products from the United States to other countries. For example, the export of agricultural products has been subsidized for more than 50 years. The best known program, known as Public Law 480, was first enacted in 1954. The program was begun to reduce stocks of food that the government acquired through its farm subsidy programs. The program reduces the cost of U.S. food in foreign countries. Some of the food is sold to foreign buyers with long repayment periods at low interest rates, a monetary subsidy. Some of the food subsidies are in-kind: the U.S. government donates food products to people in foreign countries in response to devastation caused by floods, earthquakes, famine, and so on. Still other agricultural export subsidies go to private companies and to state and regional trade groups to promote sales of U.S. farm products in foreign countries.

With the exception of subsidies for disaster aid, all export subsidies are inconsistent with free trade between countries. Programs that subsidize exports of U.S. agricultural products help to insulate U.S. farmers from world market prices and often work against the interests of low-income farmers in less developed countries. Moreover, U.S. export subsidies tend to cause recipient countries to retaliate by creating their own export subsidies and thereby foster increased protectionism by producer interests in those countries.

SUBSIDIES FOR SPORTS FACILITIES

Taxpayer subsidies are commonplace for professional sports facilities. In the year 2000, projections indicated that more than $20 billion would be spent on 95 stadiums either built or planned after 1990 (Siegfried and Zimbalist 2000). Local and state governments were to contribute some two-thirds of this amount.

Sports facilities did not always receive taxpayer-financed subsidies in the United States. With a few exceptions for facilities built with the intention of luring the Olympic Games, all major league facilities were constructed exclusively with private funds until 1953.

Why are local and state governments willing to provide the subsidies for sports facilities? Do the benefits outweigh the cost of the subsidies? Public subsidies for new sports facilities typically are justified on the basis of the promised economic benefits that they will bring to the local community. However, there is little evidence to support the argument that the benefits outweigh the costs. Indeed, researchers with no axe to grind have found no positive effect of sports facility construction on economic development (Siegfried and Zimbalist 2000).

If sports stadiums and arenas do not provide an economic payoff to local and state governments, why do they subsidize sports facilities? Why have sports leagues and owners of professional sports teams been so successful in persuading government officials and voters to subsidize their industry? There are at least two reasons. First, the proponents of a sports subsidy typically are able to produce a misleading economic impact statement that appears to support the public subsidy. Such studies, which necessarily entail assumptions and projections of future economic activity, may have unrealistic assumptions not easily proven wrong and methodological errors that are not apparent for those not trained in economic analysis.

Second, and like almost all other special interest legislation, the benefits of subsidies for sports facilities are highly concentrated on those who benefit from the subsidy, while the costs are spread out over the much larger group who bear most of the costs. Only a small proportion of the public in any urban area attend professional sports contests. The benefits to these individuals may be high enough that they become politically active in supporting the obvious interests of team owners and players to promote subsidization. In contrast, the costs of the subsidy are widely dispersed among taxpayers, each of whom may face an increase of no more than, say, $25–50 per year in additional taxes. In this situation, opponents of sports subsidies are unlikely to find it in their interest to actively oppose a referendum that will entail relatively little cost. Hence a referendum to subsidize a sports facility quite often will pass, even though it does not spur economic growth—its stated rationale. The bottom line is that subsidies for sports facilities are prime examples of corporate welfare.

Subsidies to Individuals

Federal, state, or local governments may subsidize a product to increase the use of the product subsidized; such subsidies generally target lower-income consumers and are no less common than producer subsidies. Some consumer subsidies targeting low-income individuals, including food stamps and the school lunch program, have been operating for decades.

Other consumer subsidies of more recent origin are much less dependent on the individuals' incomes. For example, a recently enacted federal program provides an income tax credit for the purchase of hybrid cars—cars with both electric motors as well as internal combustion engines—which is available to all taxpayers. In this case, purchasers of hybrid cars may reduce their federal income taxes by a specified amount in the year that the car is purchased. For example, some buyers of hybrid cars, if purchased during 2006, were able to reduce their 2006 federal income taxes by as much as $3,150.

The hybrid car subsidy ostensibly was begun to reduce U.S. dependence on imports of petroleum. The long-term prospect for hybrid cars remains in doubt, and the huge tax credit required to make hybrids competitive with conventional gasoline-powered cars suggests that the subsidy may not be socially beneficial. It also raises a question as to whether future increases in technology will make hybrid cars competitive with conventionally powered autos. The crucial public policy problem is that temporary subsidies to enable a new technology to become established often become permanent subsidies, even when the new technology does not pan out.

EFFECTS OF SUBSIDIES

Why Do Subsidies Lead to Overproduction and Overuse?

When production of an activity is subsidized, producers increase output. When a business enterprise is operating under competitive conditions—in which it has little ability to influence the market price—it will continue to produce an additional unit of the product as long as the expected return is greater than the cost of producing the unit. For example, if the cost of producing another widget is $10, but the widget can be sold for more than $10, it is profitable to produce the widget. But if it costs more, say, $12, than it can be sold for, say, $10, it is not profitable or socially beneficial to produce it. The profit and loss system in this way provides a check on wasteful production.

However, if the government subsidizes production, a business firm may find it profitable to produce and sell too much. In the above example, a subsidy of $3 per widget makes it profitable to produce and sell another unit for $10, even if it costs $12 to produce: $10 from the buyer plus $3 from the government is more than the cost of production. In this case, the government subsidy overrides the loss signal—the resources used in production are worth more than the value of the product produced! Agricultural subsidies are a good example. Government subsidies to farmers lead to overproduction. This may also be the case for ethanol, a substitute fuel for gasoline. The ethanol subsidy also illustrates how government subsidies generally are supported by vested interests. It is shown in the following section how small groups are able to maintain their transfer programs, whether or not they are beneficial to the public at large.

The Ethanol Subsidy

The far-reaching energy legislation enacted by the U.S. Congress in 2005 illustrates a number of issues related to producer subsidies. With higher petroleum prices and increased uncertainty about oil production in the Middle East, there was increased interest in biomass-derived fuels. Biomass refers to all bulk plant material. One of the first provisions of the 2005 legislation to take effect mandated an increase in the production and use of ethanol, currently made from corn or sugar. Gasohol, a mixture of gasoline and ethanol, is the primary fuel of this type.

Ethanol production recently has become a much more important public policy issue in the United States. However, interest in ethanol as an auto fuel is not new. Congress enacted legislation providing for subsidies for ethanol and other biomass-derived fuels more than 30 years ago, following the Arab oil embargo of 1973. The subsidy was in the form of exemptions from federal excise taxes, which have been in the range of 50–60 cents per gallon of ethanol. The subsidy amounted to more than $10 billion between 1979 and 2000. In 2005, over four billion gallons of ethanol were used in gasohol in the United States out of a total gasoline pool of 1.22 trillion gallons. Corn farmers became staunch supporters of the ethanol program—no surprise because it increases the use and market price of corn.

Most energy experts believe that using corn to make ethanol is not an economically feasible substitute for gasoline. Although ethanol is sold to the public as a way to reduce dependence on oil, the net amount of oil saved by gasohol use, if any, is small. Indeed, widely cited research suggests that it may take more than a gallon of fossil fuel to make one gallon of ethanol. The growing, fertilization, and harvesting of corn and the fermentation and distillation processes that converts corn to ethanol require enormous amounts of fossil fuel energy. Although there is no consensus among energy experts as to whether ethanol production reduces dependence on fossil fuel, there is little doubt that ethanol subsidies are driven far more by congressional lobbying and farm-state politics rather than by the fact that it is a practical, long-run alternative to petroleum.

WHY ARE SUBSIDIES OFTEN HARMFUL?

Government subsidies were originally viewed as a grant of money or special privilege advantageous to the public. More often, however, as in the case of farm programs, subsidies work against the interests of the public at large because they lead to too much production; that is, the cost of production exceeds the value of the product produced. Moreover, the very process through which special interest groups gain an economic advantage through government legislation creates additional waste. Typically, as in ethanol production, a subsidy can be traced to so-called privilege-seeking behavior by those who stand to gain. Privilege seeking occurs when individuals or groups, such as corn farmers or sugar producers, attempt to influence the political process for their own financial benefit.

Why is privilege-seeking behavior harmful from the standpoint of the public at large? It is not easy or cheap to influence the political process—to obtain a government favor. Individuals and groups spend large amounts of time and money on campaign contributions, lobbying, and so on to obtain government subsidies. The time and money to influence the political process to obtain legislation that restricts competition is wasted, at least from the standpoint of consumers and taxpayers generally. The valuable resources used to obtain the subsidy could have been used to produce additional goods and services that would have benefited the public at large.

The sugar program is a prime example of how privilege-seeking behavior can lead to bad public policy. The sugar price support program raises sugar prices to U.S. producers of sugar cane and sugar beets by restricting imports of sugar from Brazil and other countries that can produce sugar more cheaply than the United States can. U.S. import quotas limit the amount of sugar coming into the United States from other countries and keep the domestic price of sugar in the United States higher than the world price of sugar—it has sometimes been twice as high. The cost of the sugar subsidy is borne largely by U.S. consumers and manufacturers of sugar products, who must pay much higher sugar prices than they would have to pay if there were no sugar program. This sugar tax, in the form of higher retail sugar prices, according to the General Accounting Office, costs American consumers some $2 billion per year.

Who benefits from the sugar subsidy? It benefits relatively few U.S. farmers—growers of sugar beets, sugar cane, and corn—and domestic manufacturers of sugar substitutes. It should not be surprising that sugar interests donate large amounts of money to political candidates. The Florida cane-growing company Flo-Sun contributed $573,000 to candidates in recent elections. American Crystal, a sugar beet cooperative in the Red River Valley of North Dakota and Minnesota, donated $851,000 in the 2004 elections.

The sugar subsidy benefits corn farmers as well as sugar producers. How do corn farmers benefit from the sugar subsidy? The sugar price support program not only raises the price of sugar, it also spurs the development and production of sugar substitutes because it makes them more competitive with sugar. For example, U.S. consumption of corn-based sweeteners now is larger than that of refined sugar. The sugar subsidy is defended by lobbyists representing both corn farmers and producers of corn-based sweeteners. The added support for the sugar subsidy helps to maintain what almost all objective analysts agree is a bad public policy.

WHY NOT JUST ABOLISH BAD SUBSIDIES?

Why is it that getting rid of a harmful subsidy is easier said than done? A subsidy program may be proposed for a variety of reasons that are generally misleading and often erroneous. These arguments made by subsidy proponents quite often divert attention from the actual reason. For example, the sugar subsidy, which virtually all objective analysts agree raises the sugar price, is sold to the public as a way to stabilize the sugar market or prevent swings in sugar prices.

Consumers, of course, benefit when prices are low some of the time instead of being high all the time, as they are under the sugar price support program. In reality, the sugar subsidy can be chalked up to favor-seeking by producers of sugar and sugar substitutes.

The sugar program is a classic example of how a government program may last a long time, even though the number of consumers and taxpayers harmed is far, far larger than the number of individuals and business firms benefiting from the subsidy. The direct beneficiaries of the U.S. sugar subsidy, for example, are highly concentrated on the approximately 10,000 domestic producers of sugar and sugar substitutes. Each sugar cane and sugar beet farmer may benefit by thousands of dollars from the sugar subsidy. For example, A U.S. Depart of Agriculture study reported that each 1 cent increase in the sugar price was estimated to average $39,000 per sugarcane farm and $5,600 per sugar beet farm (Lord 1995).

The sugar subsidy program also is highly beneficial to the industry producing high fructose corn syrup, the sweetener used in many soft drinks. It should not be surprising that Washington lobbyists for corn refiners are highly effective advocates for the sugar subsidy. Archer Daniels Midland Corporation (ADM), a large agribusiness firm, for example, is a driving force behind the sugar lobby in the periodic congressional battles over sugar legislation. Although ADM does not directly produce sugar, it does produce high fructose corn syrup. As the sugar price increases, so does the demand for and price of high fructose corn syrup and other sugar substitutes.

The sugar subsidy creates a price umbrella under which ADM can profitably operate to produce the corn sweetener substitute. If there were no price support program for sugar, sugar price in the United States would be much lower, and ADM probably would not be able to produce high fructose sweetener at a price low enough to compete with sugar. Since the benefits of the sugar subsidy are highly concentrated on a relatively small number of sugar farms and agribusiness firms, such as ADM, it is in their financial interest to make sure that well-paid lobbyists exert a lot of pressure in Congress to maintain the sugar subsidy.

While the benefits of the sugar subsidy are highly concentrated on a small number of producers of sugar and sugar substitutes, the cost of the sugar subsidy is divided among 300 million users of sugar in the United States. The average consumer uses only about 100 pounds of sugar per year. Even if the sugar producer subsidy doubles retail sugar price, the cost to the individual consumer is quite small (almost certainly less than $100 annually). What is the implication? Individuals supporting the sugar subsidy can afford to spend huge amounts of money lobbying Congress to maintain the sugar program, but individual consumers cannot afford to spend much time or money fighting the sugar program because the amount of money each spends on sugar is just too small. This is the main reason the United States sugar subsidy has lasted for decades, even though it is harmful not only to consumers buying sugar, but to manufacturers using sweeteners in candy, cookies, and other food products as well.

CONCLUSIONS

The term government subsidy originally referred to a grant of money from the British Parliament to the king to finance military expenditures. Subsidy now refers to a wide range of government favors to business firms or individuals. Current subsidies often face widespread criticism, especially corporate welfare, a derisive term for subsidies made to large business corporations.

A subsidy program may be enacted to benefit individuals or business enterprises. Common subsidy programs to individuals include federal and state education subsidies, food stamps, rent subsidies, medical subsidies, school lunch subsidies, and subsidies to reduce energy use in autos and home heating and cooling systems. Business subsidy programs include subsidies to farmers, agribusiness firms, steel producers, auto producers, textile producers, sports teams, and so on.

While a subsidy may sometimes be warranted, that is, it is advantageous to the public at large, typically, this is not the case. Quite often, the cost of the output exceeds its value—too much is produced from the public's point of view. What explains the prevalence of harmful government subsidies? Most public subsidies can best be explained by favor seeking by narrowly focused producer and consumer groups who successfully further their own interests through the legislative process at the expense of the public at large. In other words, programs presumably enacted to further the public interest frequently transfer wealth from individual consumers and taxpayers to special interest groups—including the auto industry, airline industry, steel producers, textile producers, farmers, ship builders, etc.—even when they are harmful to the public. Ethanol and sugar subsidy programs are prime examples.

In a democratic society operating on a one person–one vote basis, how can a small group of individuals or business firms obtain legislation that benefits them at the expense of the public at large? Economists, using public choice theory, a new subfield of economics, only recently have begun to understand this phenomenon. If the benefits of a subsidy are highly concentrated on a small group and the costs are widely dispersed over the entire population, as is often the case, the subsidy may be enacted and last for a long period of time. Consequently, the burden of proof for any subsidy should be on those who defend it. Citizens in a democratic society should question current and proposed government programs that confer benefits on particular business firms or individuals at the expense of the rest of society.

See also: Corporate Tax Shelters; Sarbanes-Oxley Act

References

Lord, Ron. 1995. *Sugar: Background for 1995 Legislation.* AER 711. Washington, DC: U.S. Department of Agriculture Economic Research Service.

Siegfried, John, and Andrew Zimbalist. 2000. "The Economics of Sports Facilities and Their Communities." *Journal of Economic Perspectives* 14: 95–114.

Further Reading: Hyman, David N. 1999. *Public Finance: A Contemporary Application of Theory to Policy.* 6th ed. Orlando, FL: Dryden Press; Mitchell, William C. 1994. *Beyond*

Politics: Markets, Welfare and the Failure of Bureaucracy. Boulder, CO: Westview Press; Pasour, E. C., Jr., and Randal R. Rucker. 2005. *Plowshares and Pork Barrels: The Political Economy of Agriculture.* Oakland, CA: Independent Institute; Shorts, Jason Lee. 2005. "Sugar Daddies." *National Review/Digital* (July 18). Available at: www.nationalreview. com.

E. C. Pasour Jr.

HEALTH CARE COSTS

Over a half century ago (1950), an average of $424 was spent by every person in the country on health care, and health care spending accounted for only 5 percent of all spending in the economy. In 1980, these amounts had increased to $2,066 and 12 percent, and in 2005, they had jumped to $6,015 and 20 percent. The current amounts for the United States are higher than comparable measures in most other countries.

While spending amounts will rise over time because of general inflation, the spending amounts above have been adjusted for general inflation (the dollar values in the different years all have the purchasing power of dollars in 2005), so we cannot blame the increase in health care spending on the general rise in prices.

Many citizens and policy makers look at the steady climb in health care expenditures and health care's share of the economy with alarm. Is it a result of waste in the health care system, meaning that all we need to do is eliminate the waste, and health care costs will fall? Or are other factors at work that make the rise in health care expenditures more complicated and less ominous?

WE ARE AGING

One simple reason why health care spending is rising is that we are an aging population. In 1950, only 8 percent of the nation's persons were aged 65 years or older, whereas in 2005, 12 percent were. It is a simple fact that older persons use more health care. People in their seventies spend over 6 times more on health care than people in their twenties, thirties, and forties, and folks in their eighties spend 15 times more. Our aging population can account for as much as 25 percent of the increase in health care expenditures per person between 1950 and 2005.

However, this still leaves the majority of the rise in health care spending in recent decades owing to factors other than aging. What are they, and what do they imply for efforts to tame the health care money-eater?

ARE WE GETTING MORE FOR OUR MONEY?

An economic fact of life is that spending on any product or service equals the price charged per unit of the product or service multiplied by the number of units purchased. So, for example, if one hamburger has a price of $1, and you purchase 10 hamburgers, then your spending on hamburgers is $1 (per unit) times 10 (units), or $10.

Therefore, when we notice that total spending on health care is rising, the increase can occur because (1) the price per unit of health has risen, (2) the number of units of health care purchased has increased, or (3) a combination of both has occurred.

We already know that the number of units of health care purchased has been increasing due to the country's aging population. But the quality and scope of health care provided to the entire population has also been increasing. Modern health care, with its high-tech equipment and ever-increasing knowledge, can perform more operations, successfully treat more diseases, and extend healthy life spans to a much greater degree than ever before. Stated another way, modern health care spending can do much more than health care spending in the past. The costs are greater, but so, too, are the benefits.

Some economists therefore argue that because modern health care is accomplishing so much more, its price per unit has actually fallen, and all of the increase in spending is because of the increased consumption of units of health care. Admittedly, while this is a difficult as well as controversial conclusion to reach, it does direct attention away from total spending to its components—price and both quantity and quality consumed.

HEALTH CARE AS A LUXURY GOOD

For well over a century, economists have observed that people will change the amount of products and services they buy when their incomes increase. They will reduce some purchases (secondhand clothes, high fat content beef) but increase the amounts for most others.

This does not mean that people with increased income will increase the amounts bought of products and services to the same degree. They will increase some a little amount, some a moderate amount, and others a lot. In economics lingo, the last category—where purchases increase a lot following an increase in income—is called luxuries.

Economic studies show that one type of spending that people increase markedly when their income rises is health care. This finding makes sense. As people

IS A SINGLE PAYER THE ANSWER?

Many countries have a single-payer health care system, and supporters say that it is a system that guarantees access to health care and controls costs at the same time. They say that it is exactly what the U.S. health care system needs.

A single-payer system is simple. On the cost side, it is financed by taxes collected from the country's citizens. On the benefit side, all citizens are automatically enrolled and eligible for health care. There is no private insurance or worries about not being able to afford care. If a person needs health care, he or she goes to a clinic or hospital, shows some identification, and the care is provided. No money changes hands between the patient and the provider.

In addition, there is no relationship between the amount of taxes paid and the amount of health care received. Taxes supporting the health care system are based on some financial measure of the person, like income (for an income tax) or spending (for a sales tax). Care received is based on need. Also, supporters claim, since profits are taken out of the system, and since the government directly controls how much is spent on health care, waste is eliminated, and costs are controlled. Thus it is argued that the major problems in today's health care system could be avoided by a single-payer system.

Or would they? Notice that with a single-payer system, the direct price consumers pay for health care is zero. Sure, they pay taxes to support the system, but they pay the same taxes regardless of how much health care they use. So with a zero price, consumers are motivated to use more health care then when they face some positive price for accessing care. But if more health care is used, the costs of the health care system rise, which means that taxes would have to be increased to fund the system.

There is another option: the government could ration health care access and usage through some mechanism other than price. The most obvious way is through wait time. The government could just keep people waiting longer for tests, operations, and medicines to hold costs down and avoid tax hikes.

This is exactly what appears to happen. While countries with single-payer systems typically pay a smaller share out of their economy for health care, wait times for receiving health care are longer than in the United States's multipayment system. Since when patients receive health care is important along with what care they receive, longer wait times reduce the quality of care.

So once again, economics forces us to consider trade-offs. We can have a health care system that imposes no direct monetary cost on the patient, keeps a lid on overall health care spending, but forces patients to wait longer for care, or we can have a system that might cost more but that delivers care on a timelier basis. Citizens have to decide.

become more prosperous, their desire to live longer and better increases. Something that will help accomplish this goal is better health care.

From 1980 to 2005, income per person (in constant purchasing power dollars to control the effect of inflation) rose 54 percent, and from 1950 to 2005, it jumped 194 percent. Hence it should not be surprising that spending on health care—a luxury good—has risen faster than spending on other products and services.

WHO PAYS MATTERS

So far, it has been argued that there are several good reasons why spending on health care in the United States has increased rapidly in recent decades. However, this does not mean that there are not some issues with health care spending. There are, and one of them revolves around who pays the health care bill.

In the typical buying situation, a person evaluates the benefits a product or service will give him and then judges whether those benefits are greater than the price the person must pay to obtain the product or service. So if hamburgers cost $1 each, you will buy hamburgers up to the point where the last one bought gives you a benefit (satisfying your hunger or the enjoyment of eating) of $1. Since you are paying for the hamburgers, you have a big motivation to compare the costs and benefits of buying them. Usually, the initial units of a product or service give higher benefits than the later ones. So when the price of hamburgers is lower, you will buy more burgers.

What if someone else pays, or partially pays, for the burgers? Say the government subsidizes the cost of hamburgers at the rate of 50 cents per burger. This means that for every burger with a price of $1, the government pays 50 cents, and you pay 50 cents.

What will this do to the number of hamburgers you buy? It will certainly increase it. Now you will purchase burgers up to the point where the last one bought provides a benefit of only 50 cents. Maybe you will not eat all of them at once but take some home and save them for later. But the two important points to realize are that (1) you will buy more burgers and (2) the benefit of the burgers to you does not have to be as great as when you paid the entire bill.

What does this have to do with health care costs? Plenty. Health care costs faced by consumers are heavily subsidized in two ways. First, the government—primarily through Medicare and Medicaid—pays for almost half (44%) of all health care expenditures. Second, private insurance pays a little more than one-third (37%). This means that the consumer of health care only pays directly less than 20 cents on the dollar (19%) of its cost.

Now, of course, the consumer pays for the government subsidy through taxes and for the insurance subsidy via insurance premiums. But there is no direct relationship between the amount of health care a person uses and the taxes he pays. Also, insurance premiums are first paid, and then health care is used later. So if there is any correspondence between the use of health care and insurance premiums, it certainly is not one to one.

What this means is that the heavy subsidization of health care has motivated people to use more health care. In fact, that is likely the purpose of the subsidization. Indeed, as the subsidization of health care has increased, so has spending on health care. As recently as 1960, consumers directly paid for 60 percent of health care expenditures, and in 1980, their share was 30 percent. As the consumer's direct share has dropped, spending on health care has climbed—just as economists would predict.

Yet is it not a good thing that these subsidies encourage people to use more health care than they would have if they directly paid all the costs? Most people

THE UNINSURED AND WHAT TO DO ABOUT THEM

People without insurance—the uninsured—are an issue in the United States. In 2005, about 47 million people, accounting for 16 percent of the population, were recorded as being without health insurance.

Yet there may be some factors making the number of uninsured not quite the problem as it appears at first glance. A substantial portion of the uninsured is without insurance for only a short period of time. For example, studies show over 40 percent of lower-income households who are uninsured are in this situation for less than four months.

Also, about one-third of the uninsured are in households with annual incomes above $50,000. So not all the uninsured are low-income persons. Furthermore, millions of persons who are poor and do not have insurance (perhaps as many as 14 million) are eligible for various kinds of government insurance programs, and for whatever reason, they have not taken advantage of the programs.

So what can be done to reduce the number of persons without health insurance and expand coverage to more Americans? Several things can be done. For low-income persons who are eligible for assistance but have not used it, maybe automatically enrolling them in programs when they file income tax returns is an option. Another option could be to send them health insurance vouchers that must be spent by buying private market health insurance policies.

For higher-income persons with no coverage, the solution may be to make private insurance coverage more affordable. Governments could promote this by allowing stripped-down, plain vanilla health insurance policies to be marketed that only cover large, catastrophic expenses. The policies would be free of the mandates and other requirements for coverage that governments have legislated in recent years, and which, quite naturally, have increased the costs of health insurance policies.

States could also reconsider their restrictions on the expansion of health care facilities and equipment. Most states regulate the supply of health care by forcing providers (hospitals, clinics, doctors, etc.) to receive state approval before new facilities are built or new equipment ordered. Many economists worry that this approval process is time consuming and bureaucratically top-heavy, and as a result, the supply of health care does not keep pace with the demand, and costs and prices rise.

would answer yes, yet economists point out that there is an issue. When a person pays for all the health care she uses, this guarantees that every dollar spent on health care is perceived as at least being worth a dollar of benefits to her. When health care spending is subsidized, this is not the case—every dollar spent on health care is not necessarily worth a dollar of benefits to the person receiving the care.

This implies that health care may be overutilized. Tests, procedures, and medicines are being used that are valued at less than their cost to the consumer.

Consumers and society would be better off if some of that spending was re-directed to other things, including preventive care, proper diet, exercise, and sleep.

FIXES

One way—commonly recommended by economists—to address any finan-cial issues in health care is to put the consumer in charge. When the consumer is king, companies will cater to their needs and desires, and prices will be kept in check by consumers' ability to play off one company against the other.

The way to do this for health care is to force consumers to directly face, and pay for, more of the health care costs they create. Yet how can this be done with-out bankrupting consumers or making them forego using health care?

A promising way is to change the way health care is subsidized, both through private insurance and government programs. A health insurance policy struc-tured in the following way would accomplish this. Each year, a person would be responsible for an initial amount of health care expenses out of his own pocket. Tax advantages tied to saving and investing any money unspent from this fund would motivate people to carefully consider these expenses, search for the best health care deals (e.g., generic rather than brand name drugs), and consider ac-tions that would make them less likely to need health care, like exercise, diet, and sleep. In short, it would give people a financial incentive to be more responsible for their own health. For health care expenses beyond the specified initial amount, insurance would pay, but here the insurance would be for large (catastrophic) health care expenditures. Such polices tend to be relatively inexpensive.

What would happen to people and households who do not earn enough to pay for the initial health care expenses for which they now must be responsible? Here the government would provide a cash voucher to cover those initial ex-penses. Importantly, the same financial incentives would be attached to unspent funds in this voucher, so low-income persons would have the same motivation to carefully use these monies as people who are putting up the initial money themselves. The government could also help low-income people purchase the catastrophic health insurance policy.

The whole idea of this alternative way of paying for health care is to give con-sumers an incentive to be involved with the financial aspects of health care. Since consumers would, for initial expenditures, be using money they could devote to other uses, consumers would want to take personal action to lead a healthier lifestyle, carefully examine health care costs, demand information from health care providers, and shop for the best deals on health care, just like they shop for car deals, the best deals on audiovisual equipment, and deals on just about any consumer product.

LIMITED RESOURCES ARE WITH US

Many people like to think that health care is different because it directly deals with life and death, and what could be more important than life and death?

Furthermore, they reason, economic and financial concerns should not apply to health care because of its preeminent importance.

Although this is a nice sentiment, it flies in the face of reality. The laws of economics—the essential one being that our collective resources are limited at any point in time, thereby necessitating choices—cannot be repealed. The more we spend on health care, the less we have to spend on other things that make us happy.

This reality makes it all the more important that spending on health care is done efficiently, creating the maximum benefits compared to costs for each individual. Including consumers in the financial decision making, while providing them with as much information as possible for their choices, is the route to this goal.

See also: Universal Health Care

Further Reading: Cannon, Michael F., and Michael D. Tanner. 2005. *Healthy Competition: What's Holding Back Health Care and How to Free It.* Washington, DC: Cato Institute; Cogan, John F., R. Glenn Hubbard, and Daniel P. Kessler. 2005. *Healthy, Wealthy, and Wise: Five Steps to a Better Health Care System.* Washington, DC: AEI Press; Congressional Budget Office. 2003. *How Many People Lack Health Insurance and for How Long?* Washington, DC: U.S. Government Accounting Office; Cutler, David M. 2004. *Your Money or Your Life: Strong Medicine for America's Healthcare System.* New York: Oxford University Press; Denavas-Walt, Carmen, Bernadette D. Proctor, and Cheryl Hill Lee. 2006. *Income, Poverty, and Health Insurance Coverage in the United States: 2005.* Washington, DC: U.S. Census Bureau; Fuchs, Victor R. 1993. *The Future of Health Policy.* Cambridge, MA: Harvard University Press; Gratzer, David. 2006. *The Cure: How Capitalism Can Save American Health Care.* New York: Encounter Books; National Center for Policy Analysis. 2006. *Health Care Spending: What the Future Will Look Like.* Study 286. Dallas, TX: National Center for Policy Analysis.

Michael L. Walden

IMMIGRANT WORKERS IN THE UNITED STATES

Immigration policy in the United States has become a highly contentious issue, one that is likely to play an increasingly important role in affecting electoral outcomes at the local, state, and national levels. Currently, members of the U.S. Congress as well as elected public officials in locales across America are embroiled in an emotionally charged debate over the immigration issue. There are a host of concerns that the country will eventually have to grapple with, but some of the key policy areas of contention include how to control unauthorized (illegal) immigration into the United States, how to resolve the status of the illegal aliens who are already working in America, whether we should establish a so-called guest worker program that will allow foreigners to work in the United States temporarily, and whether, on balance, immigrant workers have a positive or negative economic effect on native U.S. workers.

Many Americans believe that as a nation, we should continue to uphold the principle of openness so eloquently captured by the words at the Statue of Liberty: "Give me your tired, your poor, your huddled masses, yearning to breathe free." These individuals also contend that immigrants contribute positively to the economic, political, and social vitality of the country. Many other Americans, on the other hand, believe that uncontrolled immigration, especially of the illegal kind, will create significant adverse economic consequences for the nation that may spill over into the political and social arenas.

It is interesting to note that some of the elements in the current debate are not new. In the 1980s, for example, U.S. officials also faced increasing political pressure to do something about the growing number of unauthorized workers from Mexico and to counteract the widespread perception that U.S. employers who hired illegal aliens were seldom prosecuted. In response, Congress passed the Immigration Reform and Control Act (IRCA) of 1986. Although the IRCA was intended to strengthen enforcement by imposing penalties on U.S. employers who knowingly hired undocumented workers, it did not succeed in significantly reducing illegal immigration, partly due to underfunding of the enforcement efforts and the widespread use of fraudulent documents by unauthorized workers (Martin and Midgley 2003). IRCA also addressed the question of how to treat illegal immigrants who were already in the country, another issue that is looming large in the current debate, essentially by granting legal status to 2.7 million unauthorized foreigners in the United States. While many facets of the current immigration debate have historical antecedents, it remains to be seen how the United States will address this important issue as the first decade of the twenty-first century comes to a close.

ARGUMENTS FOR AND AGAINST IMMIGRATION

Advocates on both sides of the immigration issue have at one time or another put forth arguments based on history, philosophy, politics, culture, or religion in support of their cause. For example, one of the more common arguments put forth by advocates of an open immigration policy is that since its founding, the United States has always been a nation of immigrants, and we should therefore maintain our immigrant heritage by continuing to welcome foreigners to our shores. Other advocates of unrestricted immigration maintain that by introducing greater diversity, immigration strengthens and enriches America's political, social, and cultural institutions. Religious organizations, such as the Roman Catholic Church, are generally in favor of unrestricted immigration because of humanitarian reasons and sometimes issue official pronouncements opposing barriers to human migration.

Those in favor of restricting immigration have argued that the changing ethnic composition of the U.S. immigrant population (which, as will be documented subsequently, is becoming increasingly Hispanic and Asian) will pose difficult political challenges such as deciding whether to offer bilingual education in public schools. A related argument is that unless assimilation into the society on the part of immigrants occurs quickly and smoothly, the increased ethnic diversity associated with a rapidly changing immigrant population may weaken the social and cultural fabric that unites America. It is interesting to note that even Benjamin Franklin expressed concern about the rate of assimilation by German immigrants into U.S. society in the late eighteenth century by asking, "Why should Pennsylvania, founded by the English, become a colony of aliens, who will shortly become so numerous as to Germanize us, instead of our Anglifying them?" (Degler 1970, 50). Proponents of immigration restrictions also point to the additional political challenge of having to deal with increasingly severe strains placed on the environment as a result of the population growth from high levels of immigration. Of course, superimposed on all these arguments for restricting immigration are the concerns for national security that arose after the terrorist attacks on America on September 11, 2001.

But perhaps the most controversial, and hence most scrutinized, arguments put forth by advocates on both sides of the debate are the ones concerning the economic impact of immigration. Those who advocate open borders argue that immigration is economically beneficial both to the immigrants and to the native U.S. population. For example, when immigrants come to the United States from other comparably developed countries, mutual benefits come in the form of new ideas generated from human interaction that ultimately lead to economic growth and higher standards of living for all. According to the proponents of unrestricted immigration, even immigrants who come to the United States from poorer countries benefit from the higher U.S. standard of living at the same time that they contribute to the output, or gross domestic product (GDP), of the U.S. economy.

In contrast, those who argue for restrictions on immigration contend that immigrant workers create significant negative effects for the U.S. economy. For example, in those labor markets where immigrants compete for the same jobs with native-born workers, the earnings and employment opportunities of native-born workers will both be reduced. Additionally, immigrants may create net fiscal burdens for governments at the national, state, and local levels if they contribute less in tax revenues compared to their drain on government resources.

EVIDENCE ON THE ECONOMIC EFFECTS OF IMMIGRATION

Since such a big part of the debate centers around the economic impact of immigration, it is not surprising that economists have conducted extensive research into this very question. So what does the empirical evidence tell us (see Borjas 1994)?

Studies in the late 1970s seemed to suggest a rather optimistic outcome for immigrant workers in the United States. Specifically, researchers reported that immigrants were able to achieve earnings comparable to those of native-born workers with similar socioeconomic characteristics within a relatively short time span. Indeed, the rapid rise of their earnings implied that many immigrant workers appeared to earn more than comparable native-born U.S. workers within only one or two decades after entering the United States. Furthermore, these earlier studies did not provide any strong evidence that immigrant workers reduced the employment opportunities of native-born workers. Consequently, the empirical findings up until the mid-1980s were consistent with the view that immigration was mutually beneficial to immigrant workers (because of their very steep earnings profiles) as well as to the U.S. economy (because of the additional output and income generated).

Starting in the mid-1980s, however, a somewhat different picture emerged as economists conducted new research studies as well as reassessed earlier ones. Partly as a result of discovering methodological weaknesses in some of the earlier studies and applying more elaborate statistical techniques to new data sets, economists began to revise their views on the economic impact of immigration.

For example, especially in light of the fact that the skill levels of immigrants into the United States were shown to have been declining during the postwar years, the new view was that recent immigrants were unlikely to achieve the same earnings levels as native-born workers, even over the entire course of their working years. Moreover, many of the new research studies concluded that immigration may in fact have lowered the earnings of unskilled native-born U.S. workers during the 1980s, although the magnitude of the effect appears to be small. The consensus at present seems to be that immigration has reduced the wages of low-skilled U.S. workers, especially those without a high school degree, by about 1–3 percent (Orrenius 2006).

In addition to these labor market effects, immigration may also create fiscal impacts on government budgets. For instance, highly skilled immigrants in the technology, science, and health fields have a significant positive effect on the U.S. economy not only through their contributions to the nation's GDP, but also through their contributions to tax revenues. Since so much attention is focused on illegal or low-skilled immigrant workers, it may be surprising to many that about 40 percent of the doctoral scientists and engineers in the U.S. are foreign-born immigrants (Orrenius 2006). These foreign-born workers are likely to create a net fiscal benefit for the U.S. economy.

The net fiscal impact of low-skilled immigrant workers is less certain, however. While these immigrants still contribute to the nation's output, they may have a negative fiscal impact if they draw on more public services, such as education and health care, compared to their tax contributions. Furthermore, the distribution of the fiscal burden of these immigrants may become an important policy issue since most of the fiscal benefits (in the form of employment taxes) go to the federal government, while much of the cost (such as health care and educational expenses) must be borne by state and local governments. Recent studies suggest that overall, legal immigrants and their descendants actually end up paying more in taxes compared to what they receive in government benefits, with the difference (measured over the course of the immigrants' lifetimes) estimated at about $80,000 per immigrant (Smith and Edmonston 1997; Lee and Miller 2000).

What about the economic effects of *illegal* immigration? In the current debate, there is much concern that illegal immigration has unambiguous negative fiscal effects in the U.S. economy. But there are several reasons why this may not be the case. For example, illegal immigrants may contribute less to government tax revenues (although they may still have to pay payroll and sales taxes, which are hard to avoid). But illegal immigrants are also ineligible for many government programs such as Social Security and unemployment insurance. Therefore illegal immigrants do not necessarily create a net fiscal burden. Indeed, since illegal immigrants enter the United States primarily to work, lured by the prospects of a higher standard of living, they contribute to the output and economic growth of the country. All these considerations lead some analysts to argue that illegal immigrants may very well make a net positive contribution to the U.S. economy (Ehrenberg and Smith 2006).

BRIEF HISTORY OF U.S. IMMIGRATION POLICY

1776–1880s: Period of Openness

For almost 100 years after achieving independence, the United States adhered to a policy of virtually unrestricted immigration. As a result, immigration increased steadily, especially after 1840, due to industrial and political transformations that started to occur in the United States and Europe.

1880s–1920s: Period of Restrictiveness

Beginning in 1880s, the United States began to restrict immigration by certain types of foreigners. These early restrictions reduced the flow of immigrants briefly, but immigration picked up again and reached a peak in the first decade of the twentieth century. In 1921, Congress passed the Quota Law, which set annual quotas for immigration on the basis of national origin. Partly driven by fears that the influx of unskilled immigrants from eastern and southern Europe would negatively affect native-born U.S. workers, the quota system favored immigrants from northern and western Europe instead.

1960s–1990s: Period of Reform

In 1965, Congress passed the McCarran-Walter Immigration and Nationality Act (INA), which eliminated the quota system based on national origin. Instead, the INA, which was amended in 1990, set immigration quotas based on the following purposes: (1) family reunification, (2) the need for professional and high-skilled workers from abroad, and (3) increasing so-called diversity immigrants from historically underrepresented countries. No limits were placed on political refugees who faced the risk of persecution in their home countries.

In 1986, Congress passed the Immigration Reform and Control Act (IRCA), which granted legal status to 2.7 million illegal immigrants who were already working in the country. IRCA was also intended to discourage future illegal immigration by imposing sanctions on employers who knowingly hired illegal aliens.

The rapid growth of technology led Congress to pass the Immigration Act of 1990, which authorized the Immigration and Naturalization Service to issue 60,000 H-1B visas each year to applicants with higher education in an effort to attract high-skilled workers to the United States. The number of H-1B visas was increased to 115,000 for 2000.

1996 to present: Period of Safeguarding National Security

In 1996, Congress passed three laws relating to immigration: the Antiterrorism and Effective Death Penalty Act, the Personal Responsibility and Work Opportunity Reconciliation Act, and the Illegal Immigration Reform and Immigrant Responsibility Act. These laws were intended to prevent terrorist acts as well as to address the issue of welfare eligibility for legal immigrants.

In 2001, in response to the September 11 terrorist attacks, Congress passed the Uniting and Strengthening America by Providing Appropriate Tools Required to Intercept and Obstruct Terrorism (USA PATRIOT) Act, which provided funds for additional border security and gave the U.S. attorney general the authority to detain foreigners who were deemed to pose potential risks to national security.

POSITIONS OF U.S. POLICY MAKERS WITH RESPECT TO IMMIGRATION

President George W. Bush has repeatedly stated that he is in favor of so-called comprehensive immigration reform. He has called for stricter enforcement to stem the tide of illegal immigrants coming into the country as well as the creation of a guest worker program to address the issue of unauthorized foreigners who are already working here. Under the envisioned guest worker program, unauthorized foreign-born individuals in the United States with jobs would have the opportunity to apply for legal immigrant status after working in the country for 6 years and to apply for U.S. citizenship after 11 years.

In December 2005, the U.S. House of Representatives passed the Border Protection, Antiterrorism, and Illegal Immigration Control Act (H.R. 4437), which mandates employer verification of their immigrant workers' legal status. Among other things, this bill would require all employers to submit the Social Security and immigration numbers of their new workers to the relevant government agencies within three days of hiring them. Employers who do not follow these procedures or who otherwise violate immigration laws would be subject to substantial fines, ranging up to $25,000. Unauthorized presence in the United States would become a felony, jeopardizing the chances of those who are currently illegal immigrants in the United States to become guest workers or legal residents in the future. One provision of the bill also stipulates penalties of up to five years in prison for those who shield illegal immigrants from apprehension or prosecution by authorities. Perhaps the strongest symbolic measure embodied in the House bill (to show the House's determination to reduce the flow of illegal immigrants from Mexico) is a provision authorizing the construction of a 698-mile high-tech fence along the Mexican border that would cost $2.2 billion.

In addition to the House bill, the U.S. Senate passed legislation in May 2006 that focused on creating a guest worker program. The House and Senate will try to settle on a compromise bill in the upcoming months. Like the House bill, the Senate bill also calls for stricter enforcement and border control measures such as hiring more U.S. Border Patrol agents and expanding the verification system to weed out illegal immigrants. However, the Senate bill also explicitly introduces a guest worker program that would allow 200,000 foreign workers to be admitted each year. Under the Senate legislation, illegal immigrants who have lived in the United States for five years or more (about seven million people) would have an opportunity to apply for citizenship if they continued to maintain a job, adequately passed background checks, paid up all past fines and back taxes, and enrolled in English classes. Illegal immigrants who have lived in the country for two to five years (about three million people) would be required to leave the country briefly and apply for a temporary work visa before returning to the United States as a guest worker. They would eventually be given the opportunity to apply for permanent residency and then U.S. citizenship. Illegal immigrants who have lived in the country for less than two years (about one million people) would be required to leave the United States completely. They would be allowed to apply for the guest worker program, but there is no guarantee that their application would be approved (Swarns 2006).

The guest worker program is one of the main stumbling blocks to resolving the House and Senate bills since many representatives in the House are strongly opposed to such a program because they argue that it amounts to amnesty for people who have entered the country illegally.

SOME BASIC STATISTICS ON THE U.S. IMMIGRANT POPULATION

As noted previously, a big part of the debate centers around the impact of immigration on native U.S. workers as well as on how to stem the tide of illegal immigration. So just what are the facts concerning the extent of immigration, both legal and illegal?

The total number of foreign-born residents in the United States in 2005 was estimated to be in the range of 36–37 million, making up approximately 12 percent of the country's overall population. This total figure includes 11.5 million individuals who were naturalized U.S. citizens, 10.5 million who were legal immigrants, and between 11 and 12 million who were unauthorized immigrants (Martin 2006). Of course, the current number of foreign-born residents in the

Table I.1 Immigration to the United States, 1821–2005.

Time period	Number	Annual rate (per 1,000 U.S. population)
1821–1830	143,439	1.2
1831–1840	599,125	3.9
1841–1850	1,713,251	8.4
1851–1860	2,598,214	9.3
1861–1870	2,314,824	6.4
1871–1880	2,812,191	6.2
1881–1890	5,246,613	9.2
1891–1900	3,687,564	5.3
1901–1910	8,795,386	10.4
1911–1920	5,735,811	5.7
1921–1930	4,107,209	3.5
1931–1940	528,431	0.4
1941–1950	1,035,039	0.7
1951–1960	2,515,479	1.5
1961–1970	3,321,677	1.7
1971–1980	4,493,314	2.0
1981–1990	7,338,062	3.1
1991–2000	9,095,417	3.4
2001–2005	4,902,056	

Source: Figures for 1821–2000 from U.S. Department of Homeland Security, *Yearbook of Immigration Statistics* (Washington, DC: U.S. Department of Homeland Security, 2003), Table 1. Figures for 2001–2005 from U.S. Department of Homeland Security, *Yearbook of Immigration Statistics* (Washington, DC: U.S. Department of Homeland Security, 2005), Table 1.

United States is the result of annual immigrant flows that have entered the country over the course of many years. Table I.1 shows the number of immigrants that have (legally) entered the United States in each decade since 1821. As Table I.1 indicates, immigrant flows into the United States rose steadily throughout the nineteenth and early twentieth centuries, reflecting the nation's essentially open door immigration policy during its first 100 years of independence. (During this period, the only groups who were subject to significant immigration restrictions were convicted criminals and individuals from Asia; see Ehrenberg and Smith (2006).) While the absolute number of immigrants grew, especially after 1840, the annual rate of immigrant entry for any decade never exceeded 10 per 1,000 U.S. population until the beginning of the twentieth century. The U.S. immigration rate reached a peak of 10.4 per 1,000 U.S. population (an annual rate of more than 1 percent of the population) during the first decade of the twentieth century, after which it has been declining. Thus, although many who are involved in the current debate often refer to the so-called unprecedented surge in immigration, it is important to remember that the percent of the U.S. population that is foreign born was actually higher in 1910 (at 15 percent) than it is today (at 12 percent) (Martin and Midgley 2003).

One important feature of immigration into the United States is the gradual change over time in the countries of origin of the immigrants. Between the 1960s and the 1990s, the percentage of legal immigrants who were from Europe fell to 13 percent from 40 percent (see Figure I.1). During the same period, the percentage of immigrants from Latin America increased to 51 percent from 38 percent, while the percentage from Asia increased to 30 percent from 11 percent.

Since a large part of the current debate on immigration centers around the economic impact of immigrants, it is instructive to look at some statistics from the U.S. government's Current Population Survey (CPS) that reveal some interesting demographic and economic characteristics of the foreign-born population in the United States. The average age of foreign-born residents in

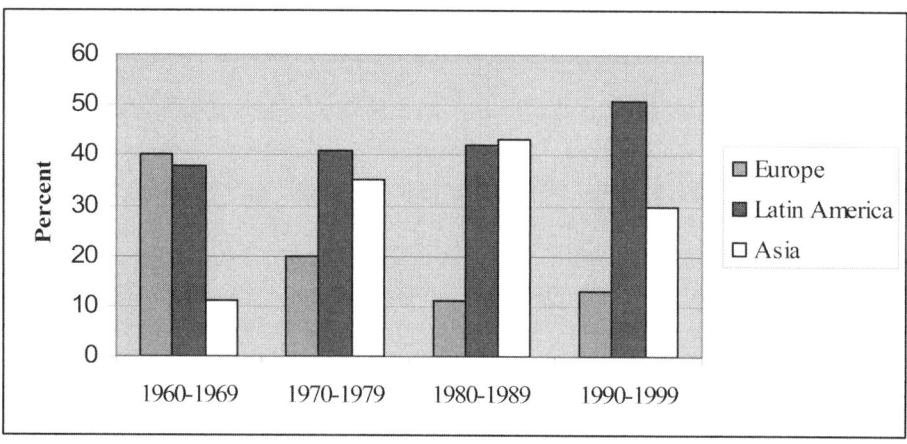

Figure I.1 U.S. immigrants by country of origin, 1960–1999.

Source: Adapted from Philip Martin and Elizabeth Midgley, "Immigration: Shaping and Reshaping America," Population Bulletin 58 (2003): 4, Figure 1.

the United States who worked full-time for at least part of the year in 2001 was 39 years, compared to an average age of 41 years for U.S.-born workers. As a group, foreign-born residents accounted for almost 15 percent of all U.S. workers who were employed full-time for at least part of the year in 2001; however, median (annual) earnings were only $24,000 for foreign-born workers, compared to $31,200 for U.S.-born workers. In addition to the changes in the countries of origin, there have been changes in the demographic and economic profiles of recent U.S. immigrants. The foreign-born residents who came to the United States after 1990 tend, on average, to be younger (average age of 32 years), less educated (34 percent do not have a high school diploma, compared to 16 percent of U.S.-born residents), and have lower median earnings ($20,000). In 2002, about 16 percent of the foreign-born population earned incomes that were below the official poverty line, compared to 11 percent of U.S.-born residents. Almost a quarter (24 percent) of U.S. households that were headed by foreign-born residents received a means-tested federal benefit (i.e., one that uses income level to determine eligibility, such as Medicaid) in 2001, compared to 16 percent of households that were headed by U.S.-born residents (Schmidley 2003; Camarota 2002).

THE EXTENT OF ILLEGAL IMMIGRATION

For purposes of immigration policy, the U.S. government considers foreigners who are in the country without a valid visa and who are therefore violating U.S. immigration laws to be unauthorized immigrants (also called undocumented or illegal immigrants). It is estimated that 850,000 foreigners entered the United States without authorization in 2005, while other illegal immigrants left the country, became legalized residents, or passed away, so that, on balance, the number of unauthorized foreigners in the United States increased by 400,000 during the year (Passel 2006). It is estimated that anywhere between 350,000 and 500,000 illegal immigrants enter and reside in the United States each year, while many others enter to stay temporarily and then leave within the same year. The U.S. Immigration and Naturalization Service (INS) reported 1.4 million apprehensions of illegal aliens in fiscal year 2001 (an individual may be apprehended more than once during the year for trying to enter illegally, and each incident is reported as a separate apprehension) (Martin and Midgley 2003). And in 2005, 1.2 million individuals were apprehended just along the U.S.–Mexico border (Bailey 2006).

A big reason why illegal immigration into the United States has generated so much concern and controversy is that it has grown very dramatically in recent years. In fact, it is estimated that most of the illegal immigrants came to the United States during the last decade: two-thirds have been in the United States for less than 10 years, and 40 percent have been here for less than 5 years. Most of these unauthorized foreigners come from three major regions of the world: over half (56 percent) come from Mexico, while 22 percent come from Latin America, and 13 percent come from Asia. Only 6 percent of illegal immigrants in the United States come from Europe, and only 3 percent come from Africa and elsewhere in the world (Passel 2006; Bailey 2006).

Table I.2 shows the estimated size of the unauthorized resident population in the United States as well as the 10 states with the largest number of unauthorized foreigners in 1990 and 2000. As Table I.2 indicates, the total number of unauthorized foreigners in the United States doubled in the decade from 1990 to 2000, from 3.5 million to an estimated 7 million individuals. Since it is estimated that 11–12 million unauthorized immigrants were residing in the United States in 2005, this means that the number of illegal immigrants increased by another 55–70 percent in the five-year period from 2000 to 2005 alone.

Unauthorized foreigners are not distributed evenly across the country, however. For instance, the top 10 states with the largest number of unauthorized residents accounted for almost 80 percent of the total unauthorized population in the United States in 2000 (Table I.2). While California and Texas experienced the largest increase in the absolute number of unauthorized foreigners, the states that showed the largest percentage increase over the last decade were North Carolina, Georgia, and Colorado.

Of the 11–12 million unauthorized immigrants in the United States in 2005, it is estimated that about 7.2 million were in the labor force, accounting for almost 5 percent of all U.S. workers. Unauthorized foreign-born workers make up at least one-fifth of the total work force in each of the following labor categories: agricultural workers (29%), grounds maintenance (25%), construction laborers (25%), maids (22%), painters (22%), cooks (20%), and hand packers (20%) (Passel 2006). Additionally, and perhaps somewhat contrary to popular perception, it is estimated that 20 percent of computer hardware engineers in the United States are illegal immigrants (Bailey 2006).

Table I.2 Estimated Unauthorized Resident Population, Top 10 States, 1990 and 2000.

State of residence	Estimated unauthorized resident population			Percent of total unauthorized population		U.S. population, 2000 census	
	1990	2000	Percent change, 1990–2000	1990	2000	Total population in 2000	Percent unauthorized
All States	3,500	7,000	100.0	100.0	100.0	281,422	2.5
California	1,476	2,209	49.7	42.2	31.6	33,872	6.5
Texas	438	1,041	137.7	12.5	14.9	20,852	5.0
New York	357	489	37.0	10.2	7.0	18,976	2.6
Illinois	194	432	122.7	5.5	6.2	12,419	3.5
Florida	239	337	41.0	6.8	4.8	15,982	2.1
Arizona	88	283	221.6	2.5	4.0	5,131	5.5
Georgia	34	228	570.6	1.0	3.3	8,186	2.8
New Jersey	95	221	132.6	2.7	3.2	8,414	2.6
North Carolina	26	206	692.3	0.7	2.9	8,049	2.6
Colorado	31	144	364.5	0.9	2.1	4,301	3.3
Total, top 10 states	2,978	5,590	87.7	85.1	79.9	136,182	4.1
All other states	522	1,410	170.1	14.9	20.1	145,240	1.0

SUMMARY

Immigration is an important national issue worthy of serious and objective discussion. Given the many controversial aspects surrounding the nation's immigration policy, it is inevitable that there will be disagreement and highly unlikely that any single comprehensive reform measure will satisfy the preferences of all who are engaged in the debate. Indeed, the debate over immigration policy has gone on for a long time and will likely continue with every change in domestic or international circumstances. The important thing to keep in mind is that any immigration policy should carefully balance the interests of all those who will be affected by the policy since the livelihood and standard of living of millions of individuals, both native and foreign-born, will be affected.

See also: Labor Shortages

References

Bailey, Holly. 2006. "A Border War." *Newsweek* (April 3): 22–25.

Borjas, George J. 1994. "The Economics of Immigration." *Journal of Economic Literature* 32: 1667–1717.

Camarota, Steven A. 2002. "Immigrants in the United States—2002." *Backgrounder* (November). Available at: www.cis.org.

Degler, Carl N. 1970. *Out of Our Past: The Forces That Shaped Modern America.* 2nd ed. New York: Harper and Row.

Ehrenberg, Ronald G., and Robert S. Smith. 2006. *Modern Labor Economics: Theory and Public Policy.* Boston: Pearson Addison-Wesley.

Lee, Ronald, and Timothy Miller. 2000. "Immigration, Social Security, and Broader Fiscal Impacts." *American Economic Review* 90: 350–54.

Martin, Philip. 2006. *The Battle over Unauthorized Immigration to the United States.* Available at: http://www.prb.org/Articles/2006/TheBattleOverUnauthorizedImmigrationto theUnitedStates.aspx.

Martin, Philip, and Elizabeth Midgley. 2003. "Immigration: Shaping and Reshaping America." *Population Bulletin* 58: 30–31.

Orrenius, Pia. 2006. "On the Record: The Economics of Immigration." *Southwest Economy* (March/April).

Passel, Jeffrey. 2006. *The Size and Characteristics of the Unauthorized Migrant Population in the United States.* Research Report 61. Washington, DC: Pew Hispanic Center.

Schmidley, Dianne. 2003. "The Foreign-Born Population in the United States: March 2003." *Current Population Reports* XX: P20–539.

Smith, James P., and Barry Edmonston, eds. 1997. *The New Americans: Economic, Demographic, and Fiscal Effects of Immigration.* Washington, DC: National Academy Press.

Swarns, Rachel L. 2006. "Senate, in Bipartisan Act, Passes an Immigration Bill." *New York Times* (May 26). Available at: www.nytimes.com.

Further Reading: Abowd, John M., and Richard B. Freeman, eds. 1991. *Immigration, Trade, and the Labor Market.* Chicago: University of Chicago Press; Borjas, George J. 1990. *Friends or Strangers: The Impact of Immigrants on the U.S. Economy.* New York: Basic Books; Borjas, George J. 1994. "The Economics of Immigration." *Journal of Economic Literature* 32: 1667–1717; Borjas, George J. 1999. *Heaven's Door: Immigration Policy and the American Economy.* Princeton, NJ: Princeton University Press; Borjas, George J., ed. 2000. *Issues in the Economics of Immigration.* Chicago: University of Chicago

Press; Borjas, George J., and Richard B. Freeman, eds. 1992. *Immigrants and the Work Force.* Chicago: University of Chicago Press; Chiswick, Barry R. 1978. "The Effect of Americanization on the Earnings of Foreign-Born Men." *Journal of Political Economy* 86: 897–921; Chiswick, Barry R. 1988. *Illegal Aliens: Their Employment and Employers.* Kalamazoo, MI: W. E. Upjohn Institute for Employment Research; Pozo, Susan, ed. 1986. *Essays on Legal and Illegal Immigration.* Kalamazoo. MI: W. E. Upjohn Institute for Employment Research.

Kenneth Louie

INCOME TAX, PERSONAL

All Americans are very familiar with the April 15 deadline for filing personal income tax returns. Taxes on personal income accounted for 44 percent of total revenue raised by the federal government in the United States in 2006. All but seven state governments also tax personal income, which now accounts for 30 percent of state revenue. Many view income as a good measure of ability to pay taxes, and the income tax enjoys broad political support in the United States. However, it is also reviled as having become incredibly complex, and there are continual calls to reform the income tax to make it fairer and simpler and to reduce the distortions it causes in economic decision making.

To understand the impact of the income tax on our decisions and the way its burden is distributed among taxpayers, it is first necessary to define the concept of income.

WHAT IS INCOME?

Income is a flow of purchasing power from earnings of labor, capital, land, and other sources that a person receives over a period of one year. The most comprehensive definition of income views it as an annual acquisition of rights to command resources. Income can be used to consume goods and services during the year it is received, or it can be stored up for future use in subsequent years. Income stored up for future use is saving, which increases a person's net worth (a measure of the value of assets less debts). The most comprehensive measure of income views it as the sum of annual consumption plus savings, where savings is any increase in net worth that can result from not spending earnings and other forms of income or from increases in the market value of such assets as stocks, bonds, or housing that a person might own. The annual increase in the value of a person's existing assets are capital gains, which can either be realized (converted to cash) by selling an asset or unrealized (not turned into cash in the current year).

A comprehensive income tax would be levied on the sum of a person's annual consumption plus savings. Consumption plus savings in a given year would represent the uses of the taxpayer's earnings and other sources of income.

TAX EXPENDITURES

Every adjustment, exemption, exclusion, or deduction from the gross income of taxpayers reduces the amount of income that is actually taxed. The many special provisions of the personal income tax code that make taxable income less than actual income therefore reduce the revenue collected by the U.S. Treasury. Indirectly, the reduction in revenue ends up increasing the after-tax income of taxpayers who engage in those transactions for which the tax code affords preferential treatment. This loss in income tax collected can be thought of as subsidizing the activities that people engage in to reduce their income tax burdens.

The federal government is required by law to estimate this loss in income tax revenue and report them as tax expenditures, which are indirect subsidies provided through the income tax. In effect, tax expenditures are a form of federal government spending financed by loss in tax revenue. The table below shows selected tax expenditures resulting from provisions of the federal income tax code reported by the Office of Management and Budget (OMB) in fiscal year 2007:

Selected tax expenditure resulting from preferential treatment of income, fiscal year 2007

Provision	Revenue loss (billions of dollars)
Exclusion of employer contributions	146.8
Medical insurance premiums and care capital gains exclusion on home sales	43.9
Deductibility of mortgage interest on owner-occupied homes	79.9
Deductibility of property taxes on owner-occupied homes	12.8
Exclusion of interest on public purpose state and local bonds	29.6
Deductibility of nonbusiness state and local taxes (other than taxes on owner-occupied homes)	27.2

Source: Office of Management and Budget, Budget of the United States, Fiscal Year 2007, http://www.whitehouse.gov/omb/budget/fy2007.

This is just a small selection of the more than $800 billion of tax expenditures from special provisions of the federal income tax reported each year by OMB. The exclusion of employer-provided medical insurance from the taxable income of employees subsidizes health expenditures. The exclusion of capital gains on home sales subsidizes home ownership in the United States, as does the deductibility of mortgage interest and property taxes. These three tax expenditures together subsidized homeowners in the United States by nearly $140 billion in 2007. Indirectly, the deductibility of property taxes also subsidizes local government by making it easier to get tax increases approved because those taxes mean that part of their burden is shifted to the federal government through reduced federal tax collection.

Similarly, OMB views deductibility of all other nonbusiness state and local taxes as indirect aid to state and local government. Exclusion of interest on state and local debt from federal taxable income makes it possible for these governments to borrow at lower rates than otherwise would be the case. The nearly $30 billion in revenue that the federal government did not collect because of this special provision is also aid to state and local governments.

Tax expenditures make it clear that the personal income tax is used as a mechanism to promote social outcomes, such as home ownership, subsidized health care, and aid to state and local governments, to name a few, in addition to raising revenue to finance federal expenditures. The use of the personal income tax in this way is, in part, responsible for its complexity. As proposals to reform the tax code are considered, those who benefit from these tax expenditures often resist their abolition.

A FLAT RATE INCOME TAX

The simplest form of an income tax would be a flat rate tax. Individuals would report their income based on the comprehensive definition discussed previously, and a flat rate would be levied to collect the tax. For example, if through the political process, it was decided to raise all revenue from the income tax and that a 15 percent rate on income would raise enough revenue, then every citizen earning income would have to pay 15 percent tax on that income to the government to finance public services. All income, irrespective of its source or use, would be subject to the tax. Tax forms would be very simple, with only three lines: one to report income, one to indicate the tax rate, and the other to show the product of the tax rate when multiplied with income. If your income were $30,000 this year, you would multiply that income by 0.15 if the tax rate were 15 percent, and your tax bill would be $4,500.

Under a flat rate comprehensive income tax, those with higher income would pay proportionately higher taxes. For example, a person with only $10,000 annual income would have a tax bill of only $1,500. A person with an annual income of $100,000 would pay $15,000 in taxes, while a person with $1 million in income would pay $150,000 in taxes. So under a flat rate income tax, the rich would pay more than the poor, even though the tax rate is the same for all taxpayers.

Under a comprehensive income tax, there would be no need for a separate tax on corporation income. Corporations are owned by their stockholders. A corporation's net income would simply be allocated to shareholders in proportion to their share of ownership. For example, suppose the XYZ Corporation has 100,000 shares of its corporate stock outstanding and earned $1 million in profit this year. If you own 10,000 shares of the outstanding stock, amounting to a 10 percent share in the ownership of the corporation, then 10 percent of the $1 million profit, or $100,000, would be allocated to you, and you would have to include this amount in your personal income. Under a 15 percent flat rate tax, your tax liability on your share of the corporation's profit would be $15,000 this year.

The flat rate income tax would be easy to administer. Time spent figuring taxes and keeping records would be minimal, and there would be no need for an army of tax accountants and lawyers to help people wade through complex tax laws.

However, even a flat rate income tax can cause distortions in behavior that could impair the efficiency of operation of the economy. The tax would reduce the net return to work and to saving and investment. This is easiest to see if taxes are withheld from earnings as those earnings are received during the year. If you earn $3,000 per month from your job, and the 15 percent income tax is withheld from your paycheck, then your net earnings from work after tax would be $3,000 minus $450, to give you net pay of only $2,550. When deciding how many hours to work, you will base your choice on your net pay rather than the gross amount actually paid by your employer. The reduction in the net wage or salary due to the income tax could impair incentives to work.

The flat rate tax would also reduce the net return to saving and investment. All interest earned on savings, all corporate profits, capital gains, and any other income from use of capital would be taxable. The net return to saving and investment would fall below the actual gross return earned. Because saving and investment decisions are made on the basis of the net, after tax, return, there is the potential for a decline in saving and investment below the amounts that would prevail without taxation.

For example, if you have a savings account in a bank and earn 5 percent interest, then you will have to pay tax on the interest you earn during the year. With a 15 percent flat rate tax, your net interest would amount to only 4.25 percent, calculated by subtracting 15 percent of the 5 percent from the gross interest earned:

$$\text{net interest} = \text{gross interest} (1 - \text{tax rate})$$

So in this case, your net interest earned is only 85 percent of the 5 percent interest rate.

If the lower net interest rate decreases the incentive to save, then total saving in the nation will decline. As saving declines, funds financing for investment will become scarcer, and market interest rates could rise, discouraging investment. Investment could also directly decline because the tax will be levied on all capital income, including corporate profits, rents, and capital gains, decreasing the net return to investment after taxes. A decline in investment could slow the rate of growth of the economy and decrease future living standards by contributing to a decline in the rate of growth of wages and salaries as worker productivity growth slows because of the slowdown in the supply of new capital equipment and technology that investment makes possible.

In short, a flat rate income tax could reduce the size of the economy by contributing to a decrease in work effort. Over the longer term, the tax could also slow economic growth if it adversely affects saving and investment.

HOW IS THE BURDEN OF PAYING THE FEDERAL PERSONAL INCOME TAX DISTRIBUTED?

The federal personal income tax has a progressive tax rate structure but is also riddled with special provisions that allow taxpayers to avoid paying taxes by taking advantage of the various adjustments, exclusions, exemptions, and deductions as well as tax credits. Do the effects of special provisions cancel out the impact of the progressive tax rates on the distribution of the payments of taxes? In other words, does the progressive income tax really result in the rich paying higher tax rates than the poor?

To find out, the Congressional Budget Office (CBO) conducted an analysis of the distribution of the tax burden of the federal personal income tax for 2003, a year when major tax rate cuts and other changes in the tax code became effective. The study began with a comprehensive measure of income and ranked taxpayers according to the amount of income they earned. Taxpayers were grouped into quintiles, starting with the fifth with the lowest income. The CBO then estimated effective (actual) income taxes paid under the provisions of the income tax code and divided total taxes paid in each quintile of households (adjusted for size) ranked according to their incomes by total income earned in that quintile. A household consists of people who share housing, regardless of their relationship (see Congressional Budget Office (2005) for details of adjustments and comprehensive measurement of income).

The following table shows the results of the CBO study.

Effective federal personal income tax rates, 2003

Income category	Effective tax rate (%)
Lowest quintile	−5.9
Second quintile	−1.1
Middle quintile	2.7
Fourth quintile	5.9
Highest quintile	13.9

Source: Congressional Budget Office, U.S. Congress, Historical Effective Federal Tax Rates: 1979 to 2003, December 2005, http://www.cbo.gov/ftpdocs/70xx/doc7000/12-29-FedTaxRates.pdf.

Notice that the two lowest quintiles actually have negative effective tax rates because the earned income tax credit for low-income taxpayers results in net payments to these households from the U.S. Treasury instead of collection of income taxes.

The results of the study show that the distribution of the burden of paying federal personal income taxes is such that upper-income groups do indeed pay higher average tax rates than lower-income groups in the United States. The estimated average effective rate for all households in 2003 was 8.5 percent. The top 1 percent of households ranked according to income were estimated to pay an average effective tax rate of 20.6 percent in 2003. Effective tax rates are progressive.

THE PERSONAL INCOME TAX IN PRACTICE

The personal income tax in the United States does not comprehensively tax all income. Instead, because tax law allows a host of adjustments, exemptions, deductions, and exclusions from income, taxable income falls far short of total income. For tax purposes, gross income includes wages and salaries, taxable interest, dividends, realized capital gains (although long-term gains on many assets are taxed at preferentially low rates), rents, royalties, most pension income, and business income from proprietorships and partnerships. Taxpayers can to some extent control their income tax bills by adjusting the sources and uses of their income. This leads to distortions in behavior as people make decisions based, in part, on the tax advantages of engaging in particular economic transactions, such as buying homes, providing employees with compensation in the form of nontaxable fringe benefits instead of cash, or buying municipal bonds, for which interest payments are exempt from federal taxation.

The federal personal income tax also uses a progressive tax rate structure. Instead of one flat rate, there are several rates. The tax rate applied to additional income after a certain amount is received is called the taxpayer's marginal tax rate. Low marginal tax rates apply to lower ranges of income. Each range of income is called a tax bracket, and as income increases, the amounts falling into higher tax brackets are taxed at higher marginal tax rates. Many citizens believe that a progressive tax rate structure is fairer than a flat rate tax because it subjects those with higher incomes to higher tax rates.

As of 2006, the federal income tax had six tax brackets subject to positive tax rates, with income falling in the highest bracket subject to a 35 percent tax rate. The lowest positive tax rate was 10 percent. Intermediate brackets were 15, 25, 28, and 33 percent. These tax rates are levied on taxable income. Under a progressive income tax system, marginal tax rates exceed average tax rates. Average tax rates can be calculated by simply dividing taxes due by taxable income. For example, a single taxpayer with a taxable income of $74,200 in 2006 would pay $15,107.50 in federal income tax. This taxpayer's average tax rate would be $15,107.50/$74,200 = .2036 = 20.36 percent. However, the taxpayer would be at the beginning of the 28 percent tax bracket with that amount of income, and each extra dollar of taxable income would be subject to a 28 percent marginal tax rate. Marginal tax rates are important for determining the impact of taxes on economic decisions because they influence the net return to going to the effort of earning additional income.

Most taxpayers are entitled to personal exemptions and a standard deduction or can itemize deductions. Tax credits for such expenses as child care can be directly subtracted from tax bills. The standard deduction varies with filing status (single, married filing jointly or separately, or head of household). Adjustments for contributions to retirement accounts and other expenses can also reduce the portion of gross income that is subject to tax.

The personal exemption, the standard deduction, and the beginning points for each tax bracket are adjusted for inflation each year. In 2006, a taxpayer could claim a personal exemption of $3,300 if not claimed as a dependent on some other tax return. Taxpayers can also claim personal exemptions for dependents. A single taxpayer could claim a standard deduction of $5,150 in 2006 or itemize deductions for such expenses as state and local income taxes, property taxes, charitable contributions, interest paid on mortgages, and a host of other expenses eligible to be itemized under the income tax code. If the single taxpayer chooses to take the standard deduction and is eligible for a personal exemption, then $8,450 of gross income would not be taxable. (Under the tax law prevailing in 2006, taxpayers with relatively high incomes have their personal exemptions and itemized deductions reduced, and eventually eliminated, as income increases.)

Finally, there are provisions of the U.S. tax code that result in some low-income taxpayers, particularly those with dependent children, paying negative tax rates. The provision is called the earned income tax credit (EITC) and allowed as much as $4,400 per year to be paid to a low-income taxpayer with dependent children by the U.S. Treasury in 2005. The EITC is a way of using the tax system to increase the incomes and living standards of low-income workers through a tax credit that is payable to the worker by the U.S. Treasury.

The actual personal income tax in the United States can affect incentives to work, save, and invest, just like the flat rate income tax. However, because of complex provisions allowing taxpayers to influence their taxable income tax bills by adjusting the sources and uses of their income, the income tax in the United States effectively subsidizes some activities over others. Provisions in the tax code allowing homeowners to deduct interest on mortgages and property taxes on homes as well as those exempting up to $500,000 in capital gains from the sale of a principal residence from taxation encourage investments in housing. Reduced taxation of long-term capital gains benefit upper-income taxpayers with assets and could encourage them to invest. Exemption of some fringe benefits, such as employer-provided health insurance, encourages compensation of workers in that form instead of in taxable wages. In addition, the complexity of the tax code imposes a burden on taxpayers to keep up with the tax law, keep records, and pay professional tax consultants to help them in filing their tax returns.

ISSUES AND PROBLEMS IN INCOME TAXATION AND PROSPECTS FOR REFORM OF THE TAX CODE

The federal personal income tax has been reformed many times. Each time, it seems to get more complex. Reforming the income tax code is very difficult because there will be both gainers and losers in the process, and the losers use political action to prevent changes that will make them worse off. The most extreme reform would be to move to a flat rate income tax. If this were done, all exemptions and deductions from income would be eliminated, and the average tax rate could be reduced because a much larger portion of actual income received would be subject to taxation. Under a flat rate tax, the average tax rate is equal to the marginal tax rate. A single lower marginal tax rate could reduce the distortions in decision making that result from the impact of taxes on net returns to work and saving. However, many object to a shift to a flat rate tax because it would lower the tax rate for upper-income individuals, while raising the tax rate for many lower-income taxpayers.

A less extreme approach to tax reform would eliminate some exemptions, deductions, and exclusions from taxable income to allow lower marginal and tax rates while retaining a progressive tax rate structure. For example, the report of the President's Advisory Panel on Federal Tax Reform in 2005 recommended limiting deductions for interest on home mortgages and eliminating deductions for state and local income and property taxes. Elimination of deductions generates tax revenue and allows tax rates across the board to decrease without tax revenue collected falling. However, such changes could have adverse affects on homeowners. As the tax advantages to homeownership are reduced, the demand for homes could decline, and this would decrease home prices, reducing the net worth of many households. The President's Advisory Panel on Federal Tax Reform recommended that the mortgage interest deduction be replaced with a tax credit for such interest that would be available to all taxpayers whether or not they itemize deductions. The panel also recommended a cap on the amount of interest that could be claimed as a credit so that the benefit to upper-income households with expensive homes and mortgages in excess of $300,000 would be reduced. This could sharply reduce demand for luxury homes but could increase demand and prices for modest homes.

Similarly, the current deduction for state and local taxes cushions those tax bills for those who itemize deductions by, in effect, allowing them to pay some of those bills through a reduction in federal tax liability. If the deduction were eliminated, it would be more difficult for state and local governments, particularly those whose tax rates are already high, to raise tax rates in the future and could result in political action to decrease tax rates.

The personal income tax system has been used as a means of encouraging individuals to favor one activity over another through its extensive use of adjustments, exemptions, deductions, and credits. This, too, has contributed to the complexity of the code. Congress often enacts tax deductions or credits for such activities as child care or education but limits availability to upper-income households. As a result, the amount of the benefits are often reduced as a taxpayers' adjusted gross income increases, and the tax forms necessary to calculate the reduction in credits or deductions are often quite complex.

Another reform often suggested is to change the tax system to encourage saving and investment. Because of concern about the impact of the current system of income taxation on incentives to save and invest, some economists advocate allowing taxpayers to deduct all of their saving from taxable income and exempting interest from taxation unless it is withdrawn. In effect, such a scheme would tax only consumption because income less saving is equal to consumption.

The tax reform process is inevitably tied to politics because it always results in some people gaining, while others lose. The prospects for a radical reform of the tax code, such as a shift to a flat rate tax, are remote. Instead, small, incremental changes in tax deductions and credits, and simplification of complex provisions of the tax code are more likely. Elimination of these special provisions that reduce revenue can allow across the board decreases in average and marginal tax rates and reductions in the distortions in decision making from the income tax.

See also: Government Subsidies; Saving; Strategic Planning

Reference

Congressional Budget Office, U.S. Congress. 2005. *Historical Effective Federal Tax Rates: 1979 to 2003.* Available at: http://www.cbo.gov/ftpdocs/70xx/doc7000/12-29-FedTaxRates.pdf

Further Reading: Cordes, Joseph, Robert D. Ebel, and Jane G. Gravelle, eds. 2005. *The Encyclopedia of Taxation and Tax Policy.* 2nd ed. Washington, DC: Urban Institute Press; Hyman, David N. 2005. *Public Finance: A Contemporary Application of Theory to Policy.* Mason, OH: South-Western (Thomson Learning).

David N. Hyman

INFLATION

In 2005, a loaf of white bread cost more than six times the price of the same loaf in 1965. You might think that this tells us something special about bread, but on average, all prices were more than six times higher in 2005 than they had been in 1965. Economists call the process of rising average prices inflation. From 1965 to 1985, average prices, as measured by the consumer price index (CPI), in the United States rose at an average rate of 6.1 percent per year, and prices more than tripled in the process. This episode in our economic history is sometimes referred to as the Great Inflation. While the Great Inflation was not as calamitous as the Great Depression, the name calls attention to this period as a significant departure from normal conditions.

Inflation is not a benign process. Periods of inflation are generally accompanied by economic and, sometimes, political unrest. During an inflationary period, inflation is often identified as the most important issue worrying people. In a speech before Congress on October 8, 1974, President Gerald Ford declared inflation "public enemy number one." President Ford even had a brief campaign encouraging people to wear WIN ("whip inflation now") buttons. Repeatedly, in the 1960s and 1970s, attacks were launched against inflation, but only late in 1979 did the tide turn against the surge in prices. Only since the early 1990s has the inflation rate been stable at a (mostly) acceptable level.

Why does inflation matter? Why is it so difficult to control? Has the battle been won, or is inflation still a threat to our national economy?

INFLATION: WHAT IS IT AND WHY DOES IT MATTER?

As noted previously, inflation is a process of sustained increases in the average level of prices of the goods and services we buy. One common measure of the average level of prices is the CPI. If the CPI is rising continuously, we say that the economy is experiencing inflation. Equivalently, inflation is a process that

INFLATION OVER FOUR DECADES

Figure I.2 shows the annual rate of inflation, as measured using the consumer price index (CPI), for the four decades from 1960 to 2000; that is, for each year, the figure shows the percentage change in the CPI from the end of the previous year to the end of the current year. If we think of low inflation as any inflation rate between 0 and 3 percent per year, we can see that the period begins and ends with low inflation. In between, we see the following:

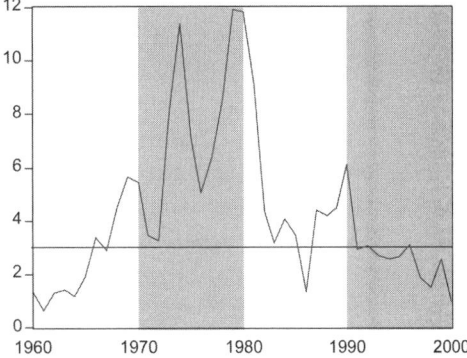

- rising inflation in the second half of the 1960s, repeated (and losing) skirmishes with inflation in the 1970s
- a clearly victorious effort in the early 1980s
- a brief counterattack by inflation in the late 1980s
- an apparent end to the battle in the 1990s

Figure I.2 Inflation rate.

depreciates the value of money over time. If average prices rise by 10 percent in a year, at the end of the year, a dollar will only buy as much as 90 cents would have purchased at the beginning of the year. Over time, this loss of purchasing power accumulates, and this will impose significant hardship on people whose income or wealth is fixed in terms of dollars.

To see the significance of this, consider Emily, who retired in 1970. Suppose Emily expected to finance her retirement with U.S. Treasury bonds that she had purchased through careful saving during the 1960s. Those bonds would have had an average interest rate of about 4 percent. But during each year of the 1970s, except 1972, the inflation rate exceeded 4 percent. This means that each year, Emily's bonds lost more purchasing power (due to rising prices since bonds are a claim on a fixed number of dollars) than she earned in interest payments on her bonds. By the end of the 1970s, Emily's bonds had lost half their purchasing power, that is, half their ability to buy the goods and services that Emily needed during her retirement.

Or consider Dennis, whose union signed a labor contract promising wage increases of 6 percent per year during the early 1970s. This should have provided Dennis and his family with a comfortably rising standard of living. However, from 1973 to 1976, prices rose by more than 8 percent per year, and Dennis had to cut back on his standard of living, despite rising wages.

Naturally, people try to avoid these hardships, and those efforts can lead to inefficiency and costs to the economy. Much of this inefficiency stems from the negative effect of inflation on the future value of money or the value of future monetary payments. One obvious effect is that if people expect prices to rise rapidly, they will not want to hold money (including checking deposit balances) because money will lose value as prices rise. This is especially important for business firms, who will streamline their cash management processes to avoid these costs. The problem, of course, is that advanced money management techniques are not free, and resources devoted to money management are not available for other purposes.

A possibly more important aspect of this problem is that inflation affects the markets for loans. Inflation decreases the value of fixed payments made on loans, which means that the prospect of inflation increases the supply of loans but decreases the demand for them. As a result, for loans to be made, the interest rate charged must be higher. And the higher the expected future rate of inflation, the higher interest rates will be. In fact, the loan market can adjust perfectly for expected inflation, with interest rates rising enough to protect lenders from any loss in value due to expected inflation. However, people are rarely able to predict inflation perfectly, and the possibility that inflation will be higher, or lower, than expected poses serious risks.

When inflation turns out to be worse than people expected, lenders suffer because interest rates are not high enough to compensate for the loss in purchasing power due to rising prices. This was Emily's experience in the previous example because inflation in the 1970s was much higher than anyone expected during the 1960s. But the opposite is also a problem. When inflation declined in the 1980s, actual inflation was lower than had been previously expected. In this case, interest rates were higher than necessary to compensate lenders for the inflation that actually occurred. Payments on loans were worth more than expected. The upshot of this is that if inflation is higher than expected, lenders lose and borrowers gain, but if inflation is lower than expected, borrowers lose and lenders gain.

Thus inflation poses important risks for the financial markets. This risk makes us worse off for two reasons. First, most people do not like risk; in fact, people go to significant lengths to limit their risk exposure. Second, if inflation makes financial markets more risky, people will not use those markets. Greater inflation risk makes both borrowers and lenders avoid financial markets, which means that they lose an important way to save for the future, and businesses lose an important way to finance expansion and growth.

In the Dennis example, we noted that inflation erodes the purchasing power of wages. Naturally, wage earners will try to protect themselves against this risk by negotiating wage rates that increase enough to compensate for rising prices. But suppose workers expect inflation to be higher than employers expect. The wage negotiations are likely to become protracted, and the process may result in strikes, lockouts, or other work interruptions, all of which are costly to both workers and firms. Alternatively, as in Dennis's case, workers may have expectations about inflation that are too low and suffer a loss of income.

These problems that inflation causes in the financial and labor markets are related to the behavior of the average level of prices. However, inflation creates problems at the level of individual prices as well. Inflation does not affect individual prices at the same time. Inevitably, some prices are rising faster than others and will catch up later. Over time, this means that some goods become temporarily more expensive relative to goods whose prices have lagged behind. This disparity increases with the rate of inflation, so as inflation is greater, the variation in the relative prices of different goods increases.

This matters because the relative prices of goods signal the economy how to allocate its resources. As some goods become cheaper, consumers demand more of them, and this extra demand induces firms to produce more. Normally, this process works to create an efficient system—we consume and produce more of the products that are relatively cheaper and conserve resources that are relatively more expensive. But inflation undermines this process by creating confusing signals. Random variations in the adjustment of individual prices to the inflation process create misleading signals that cause us to allocate our resources inefficiently.

All of these aspects of inflation interfere with the ability of our economy to function efficiently. One result of this is that high-inflation economies grow more slowly than do economies with greater price stability. Additionally, some researchers find evidence that higher rates of inflation increase income inequality. So inflation is not just a benign adjustment of the size of a dollar; it imposes significant economic costs.

HOW IS INFLATION CONTROLLED?

When the amount of any good or service people desire to buy exceeds the amount that producers want to produce, the price in that market increases until the two amounts come into balance. This is simply one aspect of the economist's law of supply and demand. Moreover, whether we are considering an individual price or the average of all prices, if market conditions continue to increase the amount people want to buy, the price, or prices, will continue to rise.

Inflation results when the amount spent on goods and services rises more rapidly than the volume of goods and services produced in the economy. To see this, start with the idea that spending in the economy is the price of each item multiplied by the number of that item bought, and then summed over all the items in the economy. If spending—the number of dollars paid to purchase goods and services—rises, either the number of units of each item or the price of each item, or both, must rise. However, the economy's ability to produce goods and services grows pretty slowly—a bit over 3 percent per year on average. If spending grows more rapidly than that for very long, prices, on average, must rise. Therefore, as spending rises more rapidly, prices rise more rapidly; that is, the inflation rate rises.

SPENDING GROWTH AND INFLATION

We can easily illustrate the connection between spending growth and inflation by looking at data on spending growth and inflation over the last four decades. For each of these decades, the accompanying table gives the average annual rate of growth in spending during the decade and the average annual inflation rate.

Decade	Rate of growth of spending (%)	Inflation rate (%)
1960s	6.72	2.43
1970s	9.74	7.07
1980s	7.41	5.05
1990s	5.33	2.91

In the 1960s and 1990s, when spending growth was relatively modest, the economy enjoyed much slower inflation than in the 1970s and 1980s. The worst of the inflation was in the 1970s, which is precisely when spending was growing most rapidly.

The 1980s was a transition period between the inflationary 1970s and the more stable 1990s. In the first half of the 1980s, spending grew at 8.34 percent per year on average, while in the second half, the spending rate decreased to 6.49 percent. This slowdown in spending growth is reflected in the inflation rate, which decreased from an annual average of 6.51 percent in the first half to 3.58 percent in the second half.

The lesson here is clear: the rate of inflation is governed by how rapidly spending on goods and services is allowed to grow.

Controlling the rate of inflation is the responsibility of the Federal Reserve System. The Federal Reserve System, or Fed, influences interest rates in financial markets to affect the growth of spending. If the Fed causes interest rates to rise, spending will grow more slowly, assuming that all other factors in the economy are constant. If the Fed causes interest rates to fall, spending will grow more rapidly, assuming that all other factors in the economy are constant. Therefore, in principle, the Fed can control inflation by raising or lowering interest rates through the effect of interest rates on the growth of spending and the effects of spending on prices.

WHY IS INFLATION SO HARD TO CONTROL?

There are only two problems with this strategy to control inflation. First, all other economic factors are rarely constant, and second, it is very hard to know how fast spending should grow. Many factors other than the level of interest rates affect the rate of spending growth. An interest rate that causes spending to grow at 5 percent one year may cause it to grow at only 2 percent, or 10 percent, in another year, depending on the other factors that influence spending. Additionally, the rate of spending growth that is consistent with price stability is not a constant. If the economy is in a recession or if productive capacity is growing more rapidly than normal, spending can grow more rapidly than usual without triggering inflation. On the other hand, if the economy has been temporarily producing beyond its normal capacity or if cost pressures from oil prices, for example, are raising prices, spending must grow more slowly to contain inflation. In the late 1990s, spending grew uncommonly fast without important inflationary consequences because growing productivity (what workers can produce in a given period of time) raised the economy's ability to produce goods and services more rapidly than usual. In the 1970s, rising oil prices combined with the Fed's failure to decrease the growth rate of spending to create a decade of excessive inflation.

These disconnects between the Fed's policies and inflation would not be a problem if changes in interest rates had an immediate effect on the growth of spending and inflation. The Fed could just watch the price data, and if the inflation rate was too high (or low), it could raise (or lower) interest rates. However, life is not that easy for the Fed. It takes some time for a change in the level of interest rates to affect spending and additional time for a change in spending growth to affect the inflation rate. A rule of thumb is that it takes between one and two years for the Fed to have an appreciable effect on the inflation rate.

THE COSTS OF REDUCING INFLATION

We can easily see the difficulties inherent in trying to reduce a stubborn inflation rate by looking at the experience of the 1970s. Figure I.3 shows the consequences of reducing the

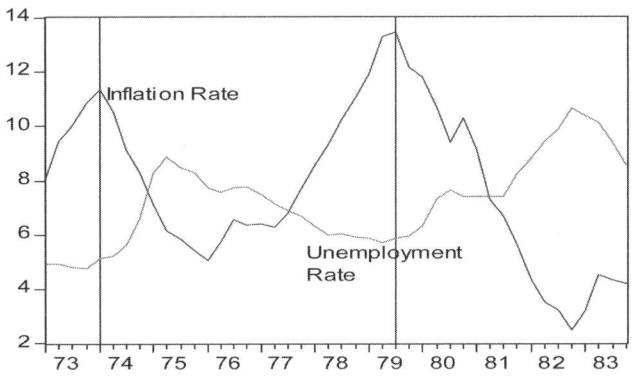

Figure I.3 Inflation and unemployment rates.

inflation rate on two occasions. The first line (labeled "Inflation Rate") shows the quarterly variation in the inflation rate from 1973 through the end of 1983, while the second line shows the same thing for the unemployment rate. The inflation line has been shifted to the left by two quarters to account for the delay in the effect of monetary policy on inflation relative to its effect on economic activity (represented by the unemployment rate here). Increased interest rates and reduced spending growth in the early 1970s succeeded in reducing the inflation rate from about 11 percent to around 5 percent. However, decreasing inflation (starting with the leftmost vertical line) was accompanied by rising unemployment that persisted for several years. We see the same pattern in the more aggressive reduction in inflation at the end of the decade (see the rightmost vertical line).

There is a clear implication of this history: unacceptably high inflation should be avoided because getting rid of it is expensive in terms of the waste of higher unemployment and the reduced production that occur as the inflation rate is decreased.

Unfortunately, the difficulty of controlling inflation only increases if the inflation rate is already too high and the Fed wants to reduce it. As already noted, changes in the rate of growth of spending do not immediately translate into changes in the inflation rate. Spending is just the price per item multiplied by the number of units per item and added over all the items purchased in the economy. The rate of growth of spending is the rate of increase in average prices (the inflation rate) plus the rate of growth in the items purchased (the rate of growth of economic activity). If higher interest rates depress the rate of growth of spending, but have little immediate effect on the inflation rate, the rate of growth of economic activity must decline. In effect, firms see the volume of goods they can sell decline and reduce production in response. In the extreme case, economic activity falls, firms reduce their production of goods and services, profits fall, employees are laid off, the unemployment rate rises—all the characteristics of a business recession. It is important to recognize that this effect on economic activity is temporary. Eventually, slower spending growth results in slower inflation, and economic activity resumes its normal course.

FIGHTING THE GREAT INFLATION

If you look at Figure I.3, it is apparent that inflation was not always with us and that once it began, it did not give up easily. Several times (1967, 1971, 1975), inflation was moderated in response to policy initiatives to constrain aggregate spending. However, in each case, these gains were quickly reversed, and the inflation rate rose even further. We know from the earlier discussion that the resurgent inflation resulted from excessive growth in aggregate spending, but why was excessive spending growth tolerated?

There are several possible answers to this question, but a compelling one comes from J. Bradford DeLong (1998). DeLong argued that the Fed was so sensitive to the memory of the Great Depression that it lowered interest rates and stimulated spending growth in response to the rising unemployment rates that accompanied decreases in the inflation rate. We argued previously that slower spending growth initially affects economic activity and only later affects inflation. If you look once again at Figure I.3, you will see that the drop in inflation in the mid-1970s was accompanied by high and persistent unemployment. It is not surprising that the Fed, afraid of a return to the Great Depression, overreacted and inadvertently launched a new round of inflation.

It was only with a change of leadership at the Fed in 1979, when Paul Volcker was appointed as chairman of the board of governors of the Federal Reserve System, that policy became tenacious enough to drive inflation down and keep it there. As Figure I.3 makes clear, this was accompanied by very high unemployment that only returned to reasonable levels in the mid-1980s. However, unlike the experience of the 1970s, Federal Reserve monetary policy in the 1980s did not respond to elevated unemployment rates by raising spending growth; rather, it was committed to maintaining low inflation because experience, and economic theory, had demonstrated that the Fed cannot maintain an artificially low unemployment rate. On the other hand, monetary policy can maintain low inflation rates. It is true that inflation reemerged briefly in the late 1980s, but this was quickly reversed, and inflation has been less than 3 percent almost continuously since.

IS THE BATTLE OVER?

Our experience since 1979 has demonstrated that the Fed is capable of reducing the rate of inflation to acceptable levels and maintaining reasonable inflation rates. To be sure, since many factors in addition to monetary policy affect the inflation rate over short periods of time, there will be episodes in which it is too high or too low. However, as a purely technical matter, the Fed can maintain an average inflation rate in the range of 2–3 percent. In this sense, the battle is over.

However, this technical capability does not ensure that the policy makers at the Federal Reserve will always choose to maintain low inflation rates. These policy makers are subject to political influences. The leadership, and indeed, the mission, of the Federal Reserve System are dictated by political decisions. In this sense, the battle against inflation is ongoing. The current political resolve that empowers the Fed to restrain inflation could, in principle, erode over time. In some other countries, Canada and the United Kingdom, for example, the central banks have been legislatively charged to achieve a specific inflation rate or an inflation rate within a specific, narrow range. The United States has not adopted inflation targeting, as this practice is called, but some economists have recommended that we do to make the victory over inflation more permanent.

See also: Federal Reserve System

References

DeLong, J. Bradford. 1998. *The Shadow of the Great Depression and the Inflation of the 1970s.* Available at: http://www.sf.frb.org/econrsrch/wklyltr/wklyltr98/el98-14.html.

Further Reading: DeLong, J. Bradford. 1998. *The Shadow of the Great Depression and the Inflation of the 1970s.* Available at: http://www.sf.frb.org/econrsrch/wklyltr/wklyltr98/el98-14.html; Federal Reserve Bank, San Francisco. 2004. *U.S. Monetary Policy: An Introduction.* Available at: http://www.sf.frb.org/publications/federalreserve/monetary/MonetaryPolicy.pdf; Judd, John, and Glenn Rudebusch. 1999. *The Goals of U.S. Monetary Policy.* Available at: http://www.sf.frb.org/econrsrch/wklyltr/wklyltr99/el99-04.html; Rudebusch, Glenn, and Carl Walsh. 1998. *U.S. Inflation Targeting: Pro and Con.* Available at: http://www.sf.frb.org/econrsrch/wklyltr/wklyltr98/el98-18.html.

John S. Lapp

INTELLECTUAL PROPERTY RIGHTS

Historically, ideas have changed the world. They impact cultures, governments, and religions. Ideas also shape businesses on many different levels, influencing marketing, management, and operations decisions on a daily basis. Today, businesses operate in an ever-changing global market, requiring access to information via high-speed communications. The explosion of technological innovation has increased competition and forced businesses to find alternate means to generate profits.

For example, in 1999, Research in Motion Ltd. (RIM), an Ontario-based firm that designs and manufactures wireless mobile devices, introduced the BlackBerry wireless platform (commonly called a BlackBerry). The BlackBerry is a handheld palm computer that uses a radio frequency technology to allow millions of users to instantly access their e-mail, phone messages, Internet, and business data. The introduction of the BlackBerry revolutionized communication capabilities for corporate executives, small businesses, elected officials, and law enforcement agencies. In 2001, NTP Inc., a small patent holding company, filed a patent infringement lawsuit against RIM. NTP claimed that it held the patents to the radio frequency technology used for the BlackBerry and feared that RIM misappropriated the patents without paying royalties. In 2002, a federal jury agreed that RIM had infringed on NTP's patents. In 2003, the court entered a final judgment in favor of NTP and imposed a permanent injunction against RIM for the further manufacture or sale of BlackBerry products. The injunction was stayed pending RIM's appeal. In January 2006, the U.S. Supreme Court declined to hear RIM's appeal (Locy 2006; Spencer and Vascellero 2006).

In March 2006, with an impending shutdown of all BlackBerry products, NTP and RIM settled out of court for $612 million before the trial judge issued a final opinion regarding the form of injunctive relief. The settlement saved approximately four million users from life without their so-called CrackBerries. In May 2006, Visto Inc. filed a patent infringement lawsuit against RIM, alleging that it held the patents to the e-mail technology used in BlackBerry products (Wong 2006; "BlackBerry Maker" n.d.). Since the settlement with NTP, BlackBerry's subscription has increased to 5.5 million customers (Gohring 2006).

The lawsuits against BlackBerry manufacturer RIM provide insight on two important concepts: (1) the importance of innovation in technology, usually in the form of intellectual property, and (2) the importance of protecting those innovations from piracy.

THE IMPORTANCE OF INTELLECTUAL PROPERTY

The idea of protecting intellectual property dates back to ancient times. In Greek mythology, Prometheus arguably committed an infringement when he stole fire from the Olympian gods to give to mankind. Zeus punished Prometheus by chaining him to a mountainside, where an eagle devoured his rejuvenated liver each day. As a consequence of Prometheus's actions, mankind still has fire to the present day.

TOP 30 CORPORATIONS RECEIVING U.S. PATENTS IN 2004

Corporation	No. of patents
1. International Business Machines Corp.	3,248
2. Matsushita Electric Industrial Co. Ltd.	1,934
3. Canon Kabushiki Kaisha	1,805
4. Hewlett-Packard Development Co. L.P.	1,775
5. Micron Technology Inc.	1,760
6. Samsung Electronics Co. Ltd.	1,604
7. Intel Corp.	1,601
8. Hitachi Ltd.	1,514
9. Toshiba Corp.	1,311
10. Sony Corp.	1,305
11. Fujitsu Ltd.	1,296
12. Koninklijke Philips Electronics N.V.	1,217
13. Fuji Photo Film Co. Ltd.	1,025
14. General Electric Co.	976
15. Renesas Technology Corp.	913
16. Robert Bosch GMBH	903
17. Texas Instruments Inc.	898
18. Seiko Epson Corp.	839
19. Nec Corp.	813
20. Advanced Micro Devices Inc.	802
21. Infineon Technologies Ag	785
22. Mitsubishi Denki Kabushiki Kaisha	781
23. Honda Motor Co. Ltd.	736
24. Siemens Aktiengesellschaft	732
25. Eastman Kodak Co.	712
26. Sun Microsystems Inc.	678
27. Denso Corp.	647
28. Agilent Technologies Inc.	645
29. Microsoft Corp.	629
30. Motorola Inc.	563

During the Middle Ages, protection for intellectual property was granted from the crown or a sovereign. Publishing patents were granted to printers of books like the Bible or legal treatises (factors include relative expense and/or politics). Additionally, the Stationers' Company in England maintained a monopoly of registered books, where the government allowed a printer or bookseller, but not the author, copyright protection on a written work. Publishers paid large sums of money to authors not to sell their works (e.g., John Milton's contract for the sale for Paradise Lost in 1667) (Posner 2002).

Modern protections of intellectual property formed with the spread of the Industrial Revolution. In 1710, England instituted the first modern copyright law (Posner 2002). At the Constitutional Convention in 1788, the Founding Fathers recognized the importance of intellectual property when they granted Congress the power to "promote the Progress of Science and useful Arts, by securing for limited times to Authors and Inventors, the exclusive Right to their respective Writings and Discoveries" (Friedman 2002, 426). In comparison with imperial China, "Chinese culture placed continuity with the past, and its suspicion of novelty, both of which encouraged copying" (Posner 2002, 393).

Congress established the Patent and Trademark Office under the auspices of the Department of Commerce. One of the deputy undersecretaries of commerce is the deputy undersecretary of commerce for intellectual property. The Patent and Trademark Office "examines patent and trademark applications, issues patents, registers trademarks, and furnishes patent and trademark information and services to the public" (Garner 1999, 1149). In 1879, Eaton S. Drone published A Treatise on the Law of Property in Intellectual Productions, one of the earliest hornbooks on intellectual property law.

Intellectual property is divided into four categories: (1) patents (ideas), (2) copyrights (expressions), (3) trademarks (source indicators), and (4) trade secrets (business processes).

A patent is defined as the "exclusive right to make, use, or sell an invention for a specified period . . . granted by the federal government to the inventor if the device or process is novel, useful, and non-obvious" (Garner 1999, 1147). In essence, a patent is monopoly granted by the government for a finite amount of time, despite the general premise that monopolies are disfavored in law or public policy.

Most patents cover functional discoveries (known as utility patents, which last 20 years) and original nonfunctional ornamental designs (known as design patents, which last 14 years), but the Plant Patent Act of 1930 expanded patent protection to newly "discovered and asexually reproduced any distinct and new variety of plant" as long as the plant is a product of "human ingenuity and research" (Friedman 2002, 428). Patents cannot be renewed. Frequently, patent owners will improve a product and receive a new patent (e.g., if the patent on automobile brakes expired but the patent holder improved the brakes with an ABS) (Emerson 2004). A common example of a utility patent is computer software or a process like pasteurization. Design patents are ornamental or distinctive in nature but do not improve the functionality of the product. Examples of a design patent are the shape of the Coca-Cola bottle or the Volkswagen Beetle. Design patents are similar to trade dress (Stim 2006).

A copyright is defined as a "property right in an original work of authorship (such as literary, musical, artistic, photographic, or film work) fixed in any tangible medium of expression, giving the holder the exclusive right to reproduce, adapt, distribute, perform, and display the work" and must be creative (an exercise of human intellect) (Garner 1999). Although not required, owners of the copyright can enhance their legal rights by placing a copyright symbol (©) on the work and registering it with the U.S. Copyright Office (Stim 2006).

The rights attributable to a copyright expanded greatly in 1903 after the U.S. Supreme Court ruled that advertisements were protected under the Copyright Act. Thereafter the rights applied to movies, piano rolls and phonograph records, radio and television, photocopying machines, music downloaded from the Internet, and computer software (Friedman 2002). In the late 1990s, Congress extended copyright protection to the life of the author plus 70 or 95 years (formally 50 or 75 years) after heavy lobbying by the Walt Disney Company. In 1998, the Digital Millennium Copyright Act (DMCA) was enacted to protect the burgeoning software businesses and to comply with the treaties signed at the World Intellectual Property Organization (WIPO) Geneva Conference in 1996. Specifically, the DMCA criminalized unauthorized pilfering of computer software, manufacture of code-cracking devices, and subterfuge around antipiracy measures and required Internet companies that performed services like music downloading (e.g., Kazaa, Napster, Apple iTunes) to pay licensing fees to record companies (Duboff 2002; Emerson 2004).

A trademark is defined as a "word, phrase, logo, or other graphic symbol used by a manufacturer or seller to distinguish its product or products from those of others. The main purpose of a trademark is to guarantee a product's genuineness. In effect, the trademark is the commercial substitute for one's signature. To receive federal protection, a trademark must be (1) distinctive rather than merely descriptive, (2) affixed to a product that is actually sold in the marketplace, and (3) registered with the U.S. Patent and Trademark Office" (Garner 1999, 1500). Once a trademark is registered, it is valid for the life of the use of the trademark, as long as it is renewed every 10 years. Trademarks are classified into five categories regarding their inherent distinctiveness: (1) unique logos or symbols (such as the marks used by furniture makers and silversmiths), (2) created or fanciful marks (such as Exxon or Kodak), (3) common or arbitrary marks (such as Olympic for paints and stains or Target for retail sales), (4) suggestive or descriptive marks (such as Chicken of the Sea tuna or Oatnut bread), and (5) generic or common marks that have lost distinctiveness (such as aspirin or elevator). Generic or common marks do not receive trademark protection. Products of distinctive shape may be protected under a concept called trade dress (such as the packaging of a product or the motif used by national chain stores) (Stim 2006).

In 1905, Congress passed legislation to regulate trademarks based on their power to monitor interstate and foreign commerce. In 1946, Congress approved the Lanham Act to codify existing trademark law and afford further protection to businesses from infringement (Friedman 2002).

A trade secret is defined as confidential business information that is designed to maintain an advantage over competitors. The information can appear as a formula, pattern, process, compilation, method, or program. As a trade secret, the information derives value because it grants a distinct advantage to the business owner, and the business owner implements reasonable tactics to maintain its secrecy. This is accomplished by restricting access to the information (to documents and/or areas where documents are stored), implementing confidentiality and nondisclosure agreements with employees, and preparing appropriate form agreements (Garner 1999; Duboff 2002; Emerson 2004).

THE CONSEQUENCES OF PIRACY TO BUSINESS

The United States is the largest exporter of intellectual property in the world, including movies and music (Friedman 2002). Piracy of intellectual property costs businesses and consumers $250 billion and 750,000 jobs each year (U.S. Patent and Trademark Office 2006). Nonmonetary losses to piracy are "fame, prestige, the hope of immortality, therapy and inner satisfaction" (Posner 2002, 390). Piracy or infringement is the illegal reproduction or distribution of intellectual property (not by the exclusive or registered owners) protected by copyright, patent, or trademark law (Garner 1999). Piracy has been especially rampant in the communications, music, pharmaceuticals, and software industries. The important question determined by courts in most infringement actions is who (such as an independent inventor or corporate employee) or what (such as a corporation or organization) has ownership of intellectual property, whether it is an idea, expression, source indicator, or business process. Therefore it is imperative for businesses to protect intellectual property and develop appropriate business and legal strategies to implement that protection.

PROTECTION OF INTELLECTUAL PROPERTY RIGHTS INTERNATIONALLY

Despite the protections afforded by the Constitution and legislation by Congress, infringement is on the rise, especially outside the United States. U.S. companies have filed infringement cases against China-based companies and seek protection from pirates in Latin America, Russia, and other parts of Asia. Once a patent, copyright, or trademark is registered in the United States, the registrar, in essence, becomes the owner and is granted exclusive rights to use that patent, copyright, or trademark within the United States. The registrar may grant a license or sell its interest to another party, domestic or foreign. With the advent of the global economy, industrialized nations and worldwide organizations have pushed for standardized intellectual property protection applicable to every participating country. The most common method to standardize that protection is through the use of treaties and agreements.

For example, agreements with other nations, such as the North American Free Trade Agreement (NAFTA), passed in 1994, strengthened patent and copyright protection in Mexico. Mexico agreed to strengthen its intellectual property laws and honor pharmaceutical patents for 20 years. Treaties like the Patent Cooperation Treaty and the Paris Convention allow U.S. inventors to file for patent protection in selected industrial nations if the inventor files the proper paperwork and fees within a certain time frame. The standards differ from country to country (Stim 2006). In most countries, intellectual property protection begins when it is registered, not on the date it was created or invented (which is true in the United States). In 2005, Congress considered legislation that would change the date of protection to the date of registration, just like in most international markets.

Many patent holders focus on protecting their rights in the United States and file international patents in the European Union and/or Japan, although the benefit of filing patent applications in China, India, and Russia will outweigh the cost in the near future. If infringed goods enter the United States, the owner can contact customs officials to confiscate and destroy the contraband. Likewise, once registered in a foreign country, U.S. registrars can be sued by the host country for alleged infringements, as a China-based corporation did in February 2006 (Parloff 2006). The hope by business analysts is that this type of litigation will force and encourage host countries to seriously police patent infringement.

Copyright protection is stronger internationally than patents because of various treaties like the Uruguay Round Agreement Act of 1994, the WIPO Geneva Convention of 1996 (which extended the Berne Convention), and the DMCA of 1998 (Emerson 2004). But copyright protection is not international because a country signs one of the treaties or agreements. Experts recommend that companies file for trademark protection as well as patent protection (e.g., Reebok in Uruguay) (Bhatnagar 2006).

An additional fear of U.S.-based companies doing business overseas is fighting so-called third-shift products, products produced by an authorized manufacturer but produced in excess of the number agreed in the contract. Often, the excess product is sold on the black market. Courts have a difficult time declaring those products counterfeit because it is nearly impossible to tell the difference or whether that particular product was within the contract or not (Parloff 2006).

LEGAL RELIEF: INFRINGEMENT CAUSES OF ACTION, INJUNCTIONS, AND CONTRACTS

Today, litigants file two different types of lawsuits: (1) an infringement cause of action, which seeks monetary damages and a form of injunctive relief, and (2) a breach of contract action. If someone files an infringement lawsuit, the litigant usually requests the court to issue a restraining order or injunction and the awarding of monetary damages, fines, lost royalties, and/or attorney's fees (Stim 2006).

An injunction is a "court order commanding or preventing an action. To get an injunction, the complainant must show that there is no plain, adequate, and complete remedy at law and that an irreparable injury will result unless the relief if granted" (Garner 1999, 788).

A contract is an "agreement between two or more parties creating obligations that are enforceable or otherwise recognizable at law (a binding contract)" (Garner 1999, 318).

Today, courts interpret contracts narrowly by considering the contractual text and limit most types of extrinsic evidence like the contracting parties'

EXAMPLES OF LAWSUITS DEALING WITH INTELLECTUAL PROPERTY RIGHTS

1. One of the first intellectual property cases heard by the U.S. Supreme Court dealt with copyright infringement of the publishing rights to its own cases: Henry Wheaton and Robert Donaldson v. Richard Peters and John Grigg (1834). Henry Wheaton and Robert Donaldson (plaintiffs), located in Philadelphia, Pennsylvania, were under contract to publish the cases decided by the U.S. Supreme Court, a right that they purchased from a prior publisher. One of the plaintiff's responsibilities was to provide a volume to the secretary of state, located in New York City. Richard Peters and John Grigg (defendants) were sued under the premise that they sold condensed versions of the U.S. Supreme Court reporters in New York City. The plaintiffs sought injunctive relief, but the U.S. Supreme Court ruled that "no reporter of the Supreme Court has, nor can he have, any copyright in the written opinions delivered by the court: and the judges of the court cannot confer on any reporter any such right."

2. Fred Waring, owner and conductor of an orchestra (plaintiff), produced phonograph records of its compositions. WDAS Broadcasting Station Inc. (defendant) broadcasted the records on the radio without a license from the plaintiff. In Waring v. WDAS Broadcasting Station, Inc. (1937), the plaintiff sought an injunction from the court to prevent the defendant from playing the records. The trial court granted the injunction because recording of the plaintiff's music was a "product of novel and artistic creation as to invest him with a property right." The appellate courts affirmed the trial court.

3. Kevin E. George (defendant) was convicted of distributing unauthorized copies of recorded devices and distributing items bearing counterfeit marks, third-degree felonies in Pennsylvania, after two investigators for the Motion Picture Association of America (MPAA) spotted the defendant selling counterfeit videotapes from a vending table on a public sidewalk in Philadelphia. The investigators received training to identify fraudulent packaging, especially "blurry printing on their cases, low-quality cardboard boxes, bogus trademarked studio logos and titles of motion pictures that were currently playing in theaters." The investigators went to the police and reported the defendant, who was subsequently arrested and convicted of the above charges (Commonwealth v. George, 2005).

4. Illinois Tool Works Inc. and Trident Inc., a subsidiary of Illinois Tool Works Inc. (defendants), "manufacture and market printing systems with three relevant components: (1) a patented piezoelectric impulse ink jet printhead; (2) a patented ink container, consisting of a bottle and valved cap, which attaches to the printhead; and (3) specially designed, but unpatented ink." The defendants sell their products to specific manufacturers who have licenses and agree to purchase the defendants' ink exclusively. Independent Ink Inc. (plaintiff) developed an ink with the same chemical composition as the defendants'.

   The defendants' infringement action against the plaintiff was dismissed, but the plaintiff countersued the defendants, seeking a judgment of noninfringement and invalidity of the defendants' patents. The plaintiff also alleged several antitrust claims because of the tying arrangement between the defendants and their licensees. After the discovery phase, the district court granted the defendants' motion to dismiss the plaintiff's antitrust claims. The plaintiff had argued that tying arrangements were per se violations of antitrust laws but failed to present any extrinsic evidence. The plaintiff appealed to the Court of Appeals for the Federal Circuit, which affirmed the district court's ruling, except for one antitrust claim.

The plaintiff appealed to the U.S. Supreme Court, which ruled that the district court should allow the plaintiff to present evidence regarding all antitrust allegations that relate to the tying arrangements (Illinois Tool Works, Inc., et al. v. Independent Ink, Inc., 2006).

5. MercExchange LLC (plaintiff) owned a business method patent for an "electronic market designed to facilitate the sale of goods between private individuals by establishing a central authority to promote trust among participants." Previously, the plaintiff licensed its patent to other companies but was unable to complete an agreement with eBay Inc. or Half.com, an eBay subsidiary (defendants). In its patent infringement action, the plaintiff alleged that the defendants used the patent without permission. A jury found that the plaintiff's patent was valid and that the defendants had infringed that patent. The jury awarded monetary damages, but the trial court refused to grant the plaintiff's request for injunctive relief (Ebay, Inc. et al. v. MercExchange, LLC, 2006).

---

intentions, special meaning of words, and/or trade usage of the industry. The court will regard extrinsic evidence only if the contract is vague or ambiguous (Posner 2002). If a plaintiff proves a breach of contract action, the usual remedy is monetary damages to make the plaintiff whole (returning the plaintiff to his precontract status). Specific performance is an unusual remedy in such situations.

If criminal behavior is suspected, it should be reported to the proper prosecution bodies, namely, the federal government or local authorities. The types of criminal charges available to a prosecuting agency include "mail fraud, interstate transportation of stolen property, voracious state common law charges, and violation of the federal Economic Espionage Act" (Emerson 2004, 558).

The statutory criminal offense for criminal infringement involves "either (1) willfully infringing a copyright to obtain a commercial advantage or financial gain . . . or (2) trafficking in goods or services that bear a counterfeit mark. . . . Under the second category, the statute imposes criminal penalties if the counterfeit mark is (1) identical with, or substantially indistinguishable from, a mark registered on the Principal Register of the U.S. Patent and Trademark Office, and (2) likely to confuse or deceive the public" (Garner 1999, 785).

Although a patent may be registered, companies can still challenge the patent, as Ranbaxy Laboratories Ltd. did to Pfizer's patent on Lipitor. One of Pfizer's two patents was invalidated during the litigation, cutting back Pfizer's protection from June 2011 to March 2010 (Smith 2006a). One strategy to elucidate the status of broad patents is for a registrar to file a declaratory judgment with the court to legally define the status of the patent (Smith 2006b).

CONTROVERSIAL ASPECTS OF INTELLECTUAL PROPERTY

Public opinion indicates that many people believe that America is too litigious and question whether an individual or company can own an idea. This leads to controversy regarding intellectual property laws. In the early part of the twentieth century, large corporations who subsisted on their employees' sweat and brains controlled patents (Friedman 2002).

In many cases, the courts favored defendants, until 1982, when a law abolished the Court of Customs and Patent Appeals and gave the new Court of Appeals for the Federal Circuit the exclusive right to hear patent appeals. Today, plaintiff patent owners benefit from greater legal securities as the image of a patent shifted from "a tool of big business; now it was a legal shield to protect the entrepreneur, the risk taker, the start-up company" (Friedman 2002, 427–28). Additionally, patent lawsuits in federal court doubled between 1998 and 2001, while patent applications increased from 200,000 in 1994 to 380,000 in 2004. Currently, the Patent and Trademark Office is attempting to reform the system to quicken the review of 600,000 backlogged patents (Werner 2005).

Many fear a frivolous lawsuit that will cost a defendant time, money, stress, and years of frustration. Today, some corporations' sole purpose for existence consists of buying patents and litigating possible infringements (Slagle 2006). For instance, the Rock n' Roll Hall of Fame sued a photographer for infringement because he sold a poster depicting the Rock n' Roll Hall of Fame before a "colorful sunset" and labeled "Rock n' Roll Hall of Fame in Cleveland." The court dismissed the case, despite a trademark registration and wide public recognition of the photograph (Duboff 2002).

Although protection of intellectual property is vital to businesses large and small, registration of patents, copyrights, and trademarks places limitations on individual creativity. In ancient times, plagiarism was the sincerest form of flattery; now plagiarism and/or infringement are synonymous with criminal activity. Realistically, intellectual property protections are necessary to protect hardworking inventors against those who seek to subvert the system while chasing ill-gotten gains.

SUMMARY

In a global economy, patents, copyrights, and trademarks have an increased importance for businesses of all sizes. Advances in intellectual property and piracy affect every type of industry; therefore it is imperative that intellectual property be registered in the places where a business conducts business or that businesses are prepared to deal with the consequences. Only the businesses that adapt and enhance their intellectual property protection will be the most competitive and, in the long run, the strongest.

See also: Media Coverage of Business

References

Bhatnagar, Parija. 2006. *China: Your Company Name May Not Be Yours.* Available at: www. CNNMoney.com.

"BlackBerry Maker Put on Patent Defensive Again." Available at: CNNMoney.com.

Commonwealth v. George. 2005. 878 A.2d 881 (Pa.Super.).

Duboff, Leonard D. 2002. *The Law (in Plain English) for Photographers.* New York: Allsworth Press, at 28–29.

Ebay, Inc. et al. v. MercExchange, LLC. 2006. 126 S.Ct. 1837.

Emerson, Robert W. 2004. *Business Law.* 4th ed. Hauppauge, NY: Barron's, at 550–51.

Friedman, Lawrence M. 2002. *American Law in the 20th Century.* New Haven, CT: Yale University Press, at 426.

Garner, Bryan A. 1999. *Black's Law Dictionary.* 7th ed. St. Paul, MN: West Group, at 1149.

Gohring, Nancy. 2006. "BlackBerry Numbers Rising." June 30, IDG News Service.

Henry Wheaton and Robert Donaldson v. Richard Peters and John Grigg. 1834. 33 U.S. 591, 8 L.Ed. 1055.

Illinois Tool Works, Inc., et al. v. Independent Ink, Inc. 2006. 126 S.Ct. 1281, 164 L.Ed.2d 26.

Locy, Toni. 2006. "High Court Rejects BlackBerry Patent Appeal." (January 23). Available at: www.law.com.

Parloff, Roger. 2006. "China Goes A-Courtin'." *Fortune Magazine* (March 7). Available at: http://money.cnn.com/magazines.Fortune.

Parloff, Roger. 2006. "Not Exactly Counterfeit." *Fortune Magazine* (April 26). Available at: http:// money.cnn.com/magazines.Fortune.

Posner, Richard A. 2002. *Law and Literature: Revised and Enlarged Edition.* Cambridge, MA: Harvard University Press, at 391–92.

Slagle, Matt. 2006. "Forgent's Business Model Takes Litigious Path." March 22, The Associated Press.

Smith, Aaron. 2006a. *Pfizer May Lose Billions in Lipitor Sales.* Available at: www.CNNMoney.com.

Smith, Aaron. 2006b. *Eli Lilly Hit with $65M Damages.* Available at: www.CNNMoney.com.

Spencer, Jane, and Jessica E. Vascellaro. 2006. "Imagining a Day without BlackBerrys." *Wall Street Journal* (January 25). Available at: www.wsj.com.

Stim, Richard. 2006. *Patent, Copyright and Trademark: An Intellectual Property Desk Reference.* 8th ed. Berkeley, CA: Nolo, at 14–15.

U.S. Patent and Trademark Office. 2006. "Global Anti-Counterfeiting and Piracy Initiative." Available at: http://www.uspto.gov.

Waring v. WDAS Broadcasting Station, Inc. 1937. 194 A. 631 (Pa.).

Werner, Erica. 2005. "Small-time Inventors Take on Congress, High-Tech Industry over Proposed Patent Law Changes." October 25, The Associated Press.

Wong, Grace. 2006. *Judge: No BlackBerry Shutdown Yet.* Available at: www.CNNMoney.com. Accessed May 1, 2006.

Further Reading: Emerson, Robert W. 2004. *Business Law.* 4th ed. Hauppauge, NY: Barron's; LaRoche, Kevin, Christine Collord, and Walter DiCesare. 2003. *The Business of Innovation: Intellectual Property Transactions in Canada.* Montreal: Borden Ladner Gervais; Leonard, Gregory K., and Lauren J. Stiroh, eds. 2005. *Economic Approaches to Intellectual Property Policy, Litigation, and Management.* White Plains, NY: National Economic Research Associates; Mertha, Andrew. 2005. *The Politics of Piracy: Intellectual Property in Contemporary China.* Ithaca, NY: Cornell University Press; Poltorak, Alexander I., and Paul J. Lerner. 2002. *Essentials of Intellectual Property.* Essentials Series. New York: John Wiley; Schechter, Roger E., and John R. Thomas. 2003. *Intellectual Property: The*

Law of Copyrights, Patents and Trademarks. Hornbooks Series, student ed. St. Paul, MN: West Group; Sell, Susan K. 2003. *Private Power, Public Law: The Globalization of Intellectual Property Rights.* Cambridge Studies in International Relations. New York: Cambridge University Press; Slbanese, Jay S., ed. 2006. *Combating Piracy: Intellectual Property Theft and Fraud.* Piscataway, NJ: Transaction; Smith, Gordon V., and Russell L. Parr. 2005. *Intellectual Property: Valuation, Exploration, and Infringement Damages.* 4th ed. Hoboken, NJ: John Wiley; Stim, Richard. 2006. *Patent, Copyright and Trademark: An Intellectual Property Desk Reference.* 8th ed. Berkeley, CA: Nolo; Yang, Deli. 2003. *Intellectual Property and Doing Business in China.* International Business and Management. New York: Elsevier.

Jason A. Checque

INTEREST RATES

Most people encounter interest several times during their lives. If you want to buy a house, a car, furniture, or appliances, you will likely use an interest rate. If you use a credit card, the interest rate is important. Or if you invest money in the stock market, in mutual funds, or in certificates of deposit at banks, you will come into contact with an interest rate.

Interest rates have two faces. One is a smiling face because interest rates can make money for you. Interest rates measure the rate of return, or earnings, on investments like stocks, bonds, mutual funds, and bank accounts that make savings grow. The other is a frowning face because at the same time, interest rates measure the cost of all those loans that allow us to have things now, rather than waiting.

TIME AND INTEREST

Interest rates exist because of time. An interest rate is the price attached to moving resources through time. To understand this concept, consider these examples. First, say you want to buy a $200,000 house, but you do not have $200,000 in cash. You have a good job that pays well with a good chance for promotion. Therefore you are able to borrow $200,000 against your future income. However, because there is a risk that you will not pay all the money back, and because the owner of the $200,000 has given up use of it for now, you pay a price for the loan in the form of an interest rate. The interest rate on the loan means that you will actually repay more than $200,000 in the future.

As a second example, assume you have $5,000 to save for retirement. You could put the money in a mattress, or better, in a safety deposit box, but it would not be worth $5,000 when you took it out. This is because higher prices in the future will make the $5,000 worth much less, in terms of what it can purchase, than it is today. The good news is that the financial system will usually recognize this fact by rewarding you for giving up use of the $5,000. The reward comes in the form of an interest rate paid on the money. If the interest rate at least covers inflation (more on this later), then you can move the $5,000 to your retirement years without losing any of its purchasing power.

The movement of financial resources through time using interest rates follows a typical pattern for most people called the life cycle of borrowing and saving. For young adults just starting a career, perhaps with financial dependents like children, the value of having more material things now, like a house, car, and furniture, is high. So these individuals are willing to borrow money and pay an interest rate. However, as people age and they begin to worry more about their future, they are more likely to shift money into later years by saving and investing and being paid an interest rate.

Of course, no two people will follow the exact same pattern of borrowing and saving. Some people are always more present oriented, meaning they are unwilling to wait, while others may get more enjoyment from delayed gratification until they have a larger sum of resources and can buy and enjoy something that much more impressive. These people are just wired to be more future oriented. In each case, the interest rate plays a role. It is the cost of being more present oriented and the reward for being more future oriented.

HOW COMPOUND INTEREST CAN WORK FOR YOU

Want interest rates to really work for you? Then take advantage of compounding when you invest. Compounding just means that you earn interest on interest, in addition to earning interest on your initial investment.

Here is a simple example: you invest $1,000 in something that earns 10 percent interest, compounded each year. At the end of year 1, you have $1,000 plus ($1,000 × 0.1), or a total of $1,100. With simple interest, which means you only earn interest on the initial investment, you would earn another $100 in year 2 (for a total of $1,200), a third $100 in year 3 (giving a total of $1,300), and so forth for every year you keep the investment. So at the end of 20 years, you would have $1,000 plus (20 × $100), or $3,000.

With compound interest, you start out the same by earning $100 on the initial investment of $1,000 in year 1. But in year 2, you earn another $100 on the $1,000, but you also earn 10 percent on the first year's earnings of $100, and so your grand total is $1,000 plus $100 plus $100 plus $10, or $1,210. This may not seem like a big deal since it is only $10 more than the $1,200 you would have with simple interest in year 2. But appearances can be deceiving. Compounding is like getting rich slowly because the tiny amounts add up over time. In fact, at the end of 20 years, you would have more than double ($6,727.50) the amount as with simple interest.

To drive this point home, look at the differences in investment amounts using simple and compound interest in the following table. At the end of 20 years, the compounded amount is more than twice as much as the simple interest amount, and after 30 years, the compounded amount is more than four times greater.

Value of investment after number of years from investing an initial $1,000

Years	Simple interest	Compound interest (annual)
5	$1,500	$1,610.51
10	$2,000	$2,593.74
20	$3,000	$6,727.50
30	$4,000	$17,449.40

The differences are even more extraordinary if $1,000 is invested each year, as below. While simple interest would put your nest egg at over $76,000 after 30 years, annually compounding puts it at almost $181,000.

Value of investment after number of years from investing $1,000 each year

Years	Simple interest	Compound interest (annual)
5	$6,500	$6,716
10	$15,500	$17,533
20	$41,000	$63,003
30	$76,500	$180,943

Compounding can get even better than shown. The faster the compounding, the better the results for the investor. There is monthly, weekly, and even daily compounding. Also, the sooner you invest, the more compounding will work for you. Saving $1,000 today for your retirement is better than waiting five years to save the same $1,000.

So put compounding to work for you. Time and compounding are your best allies for growing future financial security.

WILL THE REAL INTEREST RATE STAND UP?

Is an 8 percent interest rate higher than a 5 percent interest rate? The answer is, not necessarily. If the interest rates being compared are in the same year, then it is safe to say that 8 percent is higher than 5 percent. But if the interest rates are in different years, then this is a different story.

Part of what determines an interest rate is how much inflation lenders think will occur in the future. Inflation simply means a general increase in prices, and as already pointed out, higher prices reduce what dollars can buy. So a lender providing a loan when inflation is expected to be 5 percent a year will require a higher interest rate than when inflation is expected to be 3 percent annually. Notice that adding this inflation component to an interest rate does not really make any money for the lender. It actually just keeps the lender from losing money due to the reduced value of future dollars.

So what matters in judging how high or low an interest rate is the difference between the interest rate and the inflation rate. Economists think this difference (interest rate minus inflation rate) is so important that it has been given a special name: the real interest rate. Since that part of the interest rate that covers inflation is a wash, it is the real interest rate that lets us compare interest rates, especially in different years. Thus an interest rate of 8 percent in a year when inflation is 6 percent, giving a real interest rate of 2 percent, is actually lower than an interest rate of 5 percent in a year when inflation is 2 percent, meaning that the real interest rate is 3 percent. Appearances can be deceiving, especially where interest rates are concerned.

THE SHORT AND LONG OF INTEREST RATES

Interest rates also come in different lengths based on the time period of their associated loan or investment. We will call them short-term and long-term interest rates. Each can be advantageous or disadvantageous in certain situations, and although these situations are not easy to predict, it is important to realize when to hold or fold on interest rates.

The difference between short-term and long-term interest rates can best be illustrated with an example, and here I will use a mortgage. A mortgage is a simply a large loan used to purchase a home. Mortgage borrowers face a choice

---

WHY YOU WILL PAY BACK MORE THAN YOU BORROW

Borrowers are often dismayed to learn that they will repay several times the amount of dollars they have borrowed. For example, a home buyer borrowing $100,000 will repay $7,200 each year over 30 years, for a total of $216,000, when the interest rate is 6 percent. Is this fair? Is this not just another example of the little guy being taken to the cleaner's by large financial institutions?

Actually not. In fact, the $216,000 repaid over 30 years for a $100,000 loan is exactly worth $100,000. How can this be?

As you have already learned, time is an important element in economics and business. Dollars in the future are worth less than dollars today for two reasons: first, because prices will likely be higher in the future, the purchasing power of future dollars is less than the purchasing power of today's dollars, so it takes more future dollars to equal the value of a dollar today; second, lenders give up the use of dollars today when they loan money. To compensate them, lenders must be promised more future dollars.

Both these effects are taken into account in the interest rate. The interest rate really shows how the financial marketplace translates dollars between years. For example, with an annual interest rate of 6 percent, the marketplace is saying that it takes $1.06 one year from now to equal $1.00 today, it takes $1.12 two years from now to equal $1.00 today, and it takes $1.18 three years from now to equal $1.00 today.

With this in mind, it is easy to see how $216,000 paid over 30 years can be the same as $100,000 today. It is because the individual dollars in the $216,000 sum are each not worth $1.00 today—they are worth less. In fact, using 6 percent as the translator for dollars between years, each of the dollars paid 30 years in the future is worth only 17 cents today. The following table shows that when the lower value of future dollars is recognized, the $216,000 total payment is worth $100,000 today.

Year	Payment	Value of each dollar today	Value of payment today
1	$7,200	$0.943	$6,789.60
2	$7,200	$0.890	$6,408.00
3	$7,200	$0.840	$6,048.00
4	$7,200	$0.792	$5,702.40
5	$7,200	$0.747	$5,378.40
6	$7,200	$0.705	$5,076.00
7	$7,200	$0.665	$4,788.00
8	$7,200	$0.627	$4,514.40
9	$7,200	$0.592	$4,262.40
10	$7,200	$0.558	$4,017.60
11	$7,200	$0.527	$3,794.40
12	$7,200	$0.497	$3,578.40
13	$7,200	$0.469	$3,376.80
14	$7,200	$0.442	$3,182.40
15	$7,200	$0.417	$3,002.40
16	$7,200	$0.394	$2,836.80
17	$7,200	$0.371	$2,671.20
18	$7,200	$0.350	$2,520.00
19	$7,200	$0.331	$2,383.20
20	$7,200	$0.312	$2,246.40
21	$7,200	$0.294	$2,116.80
22	$7,200	$0.278	$2,001.60
23	$7,200	$0.262	$1,886.40
24	$7,200	$0.247	$1,778.40
25	$7,200	$0.233	$1,677.60
26	$7,200	$0.220	$1,584.00
27	$7,200	$0.207	$1,490.40
28	$7,200	$0.196	$1,411.20
29	$7,200	$0.185	$1,332.00
30	$7,200	$0.174	$1,252.80
Total	$216,000		$99,108.00[a]

[a]Sum is not exactly $100,000 because annual, rather than monthly, payments are used.

in interest rates between a long-term interest rate, often called a fixed rate, and a short-term interest rate, referred to as an adjustable (or variable) rate. With a fixed rate, the interest rate is locked in, or unchanging, for as long as 30 years. On the other hand, adjustable rates can change, maybe as often as twice a year.

Which is better? Well, what if you thought future interest rates were going to rise? Then the fixed rate would likely be better because as future interest rates rose, your rate would stay where it was, and so your monthly loan payment would not rise. Conversely, if you thought future interest rates were set to fall, you would be better off with an adjustable rate, where you could ride the rate and your payment down.

The reverse logic is true with interest rates paid on investments. Here you would like to lock in a fixed interest rate if the betting was that future interest rates would be lower, but the smart move would be an adjustable rate when future interest rates were expected to be higher.

How in the world can anyone tell where interest rates are going down the road? The next section answers this question.

THE CYCLE OF INTEREST RATES

Interest rates go through cycles of ups and downs. This can clearly be seen in Figure I.4. Two sample interest rates are shown, a short-term rate (three-month Treasury bill) and a long-term rate (10-year Treasury note). Notice that the two rates trend up for a while, then move down, then go up again, and so on. Also notice that long-term interest rates are usually higher than short-term interest rates. This is due to the greater risk with loans having a fixed, long-term interest rate. There is a longer time for something to go wrong with the loan, like the borrower not being able to pay. There is also more chance that the lender has guessed wrong about future inflation, in particular, that the lender has forecasted inflation to be too low.

What determines this pattern? The answer can also be seen in Figure I.4. When the economy is growing and businesses and households are borrowing money, interest rates rise. These years are in the unshaded areas in Figure I.4. Then, when the economy stumbles and goes into an economic tailspin (known as a recession), loans to borrowers drop, and interest rates fall. Recessions are indicated by shaded areas in Figure I.4.

Another observation from Figure I.4 is that interest rates are not at the same levels during all growth periods or during all recessionary years. The reason is differing inflation rates. Compare the much higher interest rates during the

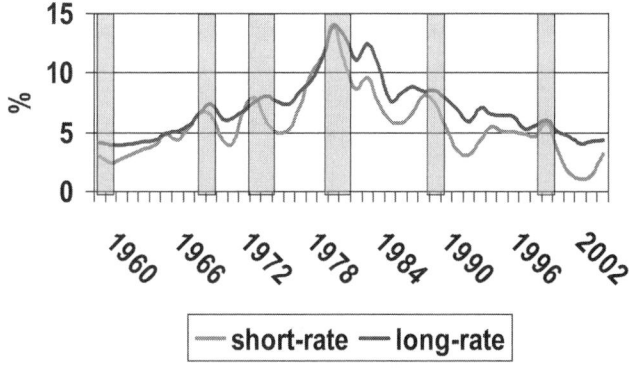

Figure I.4 Cycle of interest rates.

1970s to the lower interest rates in the 1990s. The average inflation rate during the 1970s was 7 percent, compared to 3 percent in the 1990s. The greater expected decline in the purchasing power of the dollar during the 1970s made all interest rates in that decade, in both growth years and recession years, higher than when less inflation was expected in the 1990s.

The practical advice from the cycle of interest is this: if you are borrowing money, it is best to borrow at the bottom of a recession because this is when interest rates are typically at their lowest. Lock in your loan to a nice, low, long-term interest rate, and then laugh as interest rates rise in coming years. Of course, this advice assumes that you are able to borrow in the depths of a recession, when the economic clouds are darkest, meaning you have not lost your job or had your income reduced significantly.

Conversely, do the opposite when investing. Invest in a long-term interest rate at the top of the growth period and just before the economy moves into a recession. Again, this will put you at the high point of interest rates, which is the goal when investing. When investing during a growth period when interest rates are rising, do so with a short-term interest rate.

I do not want to leave the impression that predicting the cycle of interest rates is easy. It is not. Unfortunately, many try, but few succeed. Nevertheless, it is important to know what you would do if you had a perfect crystal ball. Even this realization can help mistakes be avoided.

A FINAL WORD

Over your lifetime, you will both curse and praise interest rates. You will curse them when you have to pay three, four, or five times more for a loan compared to the amount you borrowed. But you will praise interest rates when they are working for you to increase your nest egg. So you will always have a love/hate relationship with interest rates.

Always remember that many, many factors determine the level of interest rates, including the current and expected inflation rate, whether the rate is fixed or variable, and if the economy is doing well or in a recession. Properly used, interest rates can be used to your advantage. However, to do so takes discipline, foresight, and a large amount of luck.

See also: Booms and Busts; The Dollar; Inflation

Further Reading: Lee, Dwight R., and Richard B. McKenzie. 1999. *Getting Rich in America.* New York: HarperCollins.

Michael L. Walden

LABOR, ORGANIZED

Many questions arise when one considers organized labor and collective bargaining. Among them are the following:

Why do people join unions?

What can unions, in fact, do for their members?
What are the economic and social effects of organized labor?
How have those effects changed over time?
What is the future of U.S. organized labor in the new world economy?

One approach to answering these (and similar) questions is, first, to define what unions are and what they are not, and, second, to trace out the history of the American unions through good times and bad up to the present.

TYPES OF UNIONS

Although unions are an economic entity, they are or can be much more than that. Indeed, organized labor (or unionism) represents a broad socioeconomic movement, a movement that has taken many forms in many different countries. Among these are the following:

Uplift unions. Associations of workers that seek to raise the incomes and/or alter the living conditions of their members (and others) by raising the skills and cultural levels of members and by providing aid to members who have experienced economic reverses. Leadership of these unions is often external (priests, rabbis, ministers, philanthropic volunteers), as distinguished from rank and file.

Political unions. Associations of workers that seek to achieve similar objectives primarily through political action, often in alliance with a political party or parties. Unions in democratic socialist nations often fall into this category.

Revolutionary unions. Associations that seek the same objectives by overthrowing the system, that is, by forcibly altering the property right and/or economic-political system.

Business unions. Associations that seek to raise the incomes of their members and alter the conditions of employment primarily through collective bargaining. Business unionists generally accept and seek to work within the existing political and economic system.

Although all four types of unions have existed in the United States, business unions have been the predominant form.

THE RISE AND DECLINE OF UNIONS IN THE UNITED STATES

While union membership was relatively low prior to the First World War, it grew sharply during that conflict, peaking at five to six million—including Canadian members of U.S. international unions. Throughout the decade of the 1920s and the early 1930s, union membership declined to about three million workers, representing 11–12 percent of nonagricultural employment in the early 1930s. Figure L.1 shows the changing pattern of unionism in the United States since 1930, both in total membership and as a percentage of nonagricultural employment. Although the available data involve differences in definitions and contain some gaps over the years, the general trends are clear. Union membership grew very rapidly during the late 1930s and the World War II period, both in membership and as a percentage of employment. In 1945, unions represented over 14 million workers—about 35 percent of nonagricultural employment. Hence one-third of American wage and salary workers were unionized. Unions were heavily concentrated in mining, manufacturing, and construction and were located particularly in the northern and western industrial states. Beginning in

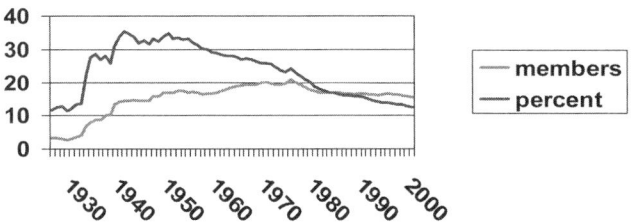

Figure L.1 Union membership (in millions) and percent of total employment.

Source: U.S. Bureau of Labor Statistics, Handbook of Labor Statistics (Washington, DC: U.S. Government Printing Office, 1978), Table 150, and Eva E. Jacobs, ed., Handbook of Labor Statistics, 9th ed. (Lanham, MD: Bernam Press, 2006), 464.

THINGS MAY NOT BE WHAT THEY SEEM

Seeking to limit union monopoly power via the Taft-Hartley Act of 1947, Congress outlawed the closed shop. Closed shops involve practices or contractual arrangements whereby employees are obtained exclusively through a union hiring hall or a union business agent. Hence only persons who are union members (or approved by the union) are eligible for employment.

Despite the legislative ban, de facto closed shops still exist. Is that fact evidence that employers are intimidated by union (or union mob) muscle, as some people contend? Does it mean also that the legal authorities are refusing to enforce the law? While the answer to both questions could be yes, there is an alternative explanation.

Note, first, that unions in such instances generally guarantee some acceptable level of skill or experience among those referred for employment. Note also that de facto closed shops seem to exist primarily (if not exclusively) in activities involving intermittent employment. Construction, entertainment, and longshoring are good examples. While there may be alternative ways for employers to staff those positions (say, by conducting a new search each time workers are needed or by hiring temps through various agencies), the union hiring hall may be the least expensive way of obtaining qualified workers whenever and wherever needed. Hence the closed shop may still exist because it serves the interests of the unionists *and* the employers.

the late 1940s and the 1950s, union membership grew more slowly, and membership began a slow decline as a proportion of employment (or labor force). Total membership peaked in 1979 at 21 million workers (about 24 percent of nonagricultural employment). Thereafter, membership gradually fell. In 2004–2005, unions represented only 15 million workers, or about 12 percent of wage and salary workers. Moreover, the largest unions in 2004 were not in manufacturing or mining, but in construction and in the service industries: education, protective services, utilities, telecommunications, and maintenance and/or repair work. In these sectors, 20–40 percent of workers were covered by collective bargaining contracts, in contrast to only 12–14 percent in the old stronghold of manufacturing. While these changes in unionism have been substantial, the forces behind both the rise and the decline are quite clear. Moreover, these forces are closely interrelated.

WORKER ATTITUDES

One powerful influence in the growth of unions was the attitudinal set of many workers toward collective action, both in the workplace and in other aspects of their lives. Many immigrant groups saw collective action as necessary in the struggle for dignity and higher incomes. German, Scandinavian, and Midland English immigrants brought with them a strong pride of craftsmanship and/or allegiance to the working class. While, to some degree, these attitudes were foreign imports, they also resulted from and/or were strengthened by social and economic pressures created by the rapid industrialization of America in the late 1800s, the growing social divide of the times, and serious concern about the distribution of income among the population. Clearly, pride of craftsmanship was a strong component in the earliest unions, unions that were usually organized along craft lines: printers, carpenters and joiners, plumbers, machinists, railroad engineers, and so on. Other immigrants, like the Irish and the Jews, were alienated from their new environment and saw a need for group solidarity and protection against the so-called bosses. No doubt, those attitudes reflected previous experiences with foreign overlords as well as ethnic and religious discrimination. Somewhat later, African Americans and Mexican Americans mirrored those attitudes and joined unions in large numbers.

THE DESIRE FOR MORE

"More" was his answer when Samuel Gompers, president of the (craft-oriented) American Federation of Labor, was asked what organized labor wanted. Clearly, with national income rising, with vast fortunes being earned by the bosses, and with periodic depressions and recessions, labor wanted both a larger share of the economic pie and greater security. Moreover, unions were prepared to use collective bargaining, strikes, and boycotts to achieve what they believed to be a more equitable distribution of income. However, it was not until the 1930s that there was any widespread unionization beyond the traditional craft unions. At that time, the Congress of Industrial Organizations (CIO) spearheaded union organization by industry rather than by crafts and organized large numbers of semiskilled and low-skilled workers into unions. The success of unions in achieving "more" is discussed subsequently.

LABOR MARKET MONOPSONY AND FEELINGS OF IMPOTENCE

Closely related to workers' attitudes and desires (and some political initiatives) were (1) feelings of economic impotence among workers and (2) the existence of labor market monopsony (where one or a few firms provide most of the employment in the area). In such so-called company towns, there was often considerable tension between workers and management. Coal and other mining communities are good examples. Moreover, under such conditions, workers might risk their jobs by complaining. Obviously, workers could use what Freeman (1976) calls exit voice to relieve their workplace grievances, but union voice (including grievance procedures established in the collective bargaining contract) was an alternative approach, one that provided workplace dignity without the need to search for a new job.

As automobile transport became cheaper, as roads improved, as labor markets became more competitive, as information concerning alternative employment opportunities increased, and as immigrant and other workers became less alienated and part of the burgeoning middle class, the demand for unionism to address labor market problems diminished, but it did not disappear. Workers in large firms continued to support union efforts to standardize wages and process workers' grievances. In response, many firms established open door policies, ombudsmen, and employee relations offices to encourage communication between the firm and the workers, to provide a better human relations climate, and to maintain a regular check on the fairness (and limit the arbitrariness) of first-line and other supervisors.

THE LEGAL FRAMEWORK

Despite company towns, strong feelings of alienation and inequity, and the desire for "more," unionization and union activities for many years were sharply limited by law. From the early 1800s, unions and union activities were often treated by the courts under the common law as criminal conspiracies, that is, actions or associations in restraint of trade. After Commonwealth v. Hunt (1842), unions per se were no longer illegal, but most of their economic actions were. Indeed, under the Sherman Anti-Trust Act of 1890, treble damages were a possibility on conviction. It is not surprising, therefore, that unionism did not grow rapidly until the legal strictures were temporarily relaxed during World War I and later in the 1930s, when the Wagner Act (The National Labor Relations Act of 1935) somewhat belatedly encouraged unionization as an offset to the power of businesses in labor markets.

The legal climate changed again after World War II with the passage of the Labor-Management Relations (or Taft-Hartley) Act of 1947 and subsequent rulings by the National Labor Relations Board. The 1950s saw the passage of the Labor-Management Racketeering (or Hobbs) Act of 1951 and major congressional hearings. The latter resulted in the prosecution and/or disgrace of several top labor leaders. While the growth and decline of unionism were affected by changes in the legislative and regulatory climate, those changes cannot account fully for what occurred during the latter half of the twentieth century.

UNION SUCCESSES AND CHANGING LABOR MARKETS

As an economic entity, unions can be more successful in raising wage levels when the wage increases do not lead to major reductions in the employment of their members. When it is difficult or expensive to substitute machinery or other inputs for labor (as, say, in the case of airline pilots), the ability of unions to raise wages above what might otherwise exist is strengthened. The ability to substitute other inputs for labor, however, varies substantially from industry to industry, and it changes over time with new products and new technology. So does the profitability of the firm(s) and the ability to substitute nonunion and/or foreign labor for U.S. union labor. Hence the ability of unions to raise wages declines when changes in technology, skill levels, and/or import/export restrictions make substitutions easier or when firms become less profitable.

It is not surprising, therefore, that Lewis (1963) (and his colleagues and students at the University of Chicago and elsewhere) found very sizeable differences in union wage effects across industries and across time periods. Their studies show effects ranging from 100 percent in 1921–1922 for bituminous coal mining to a zero effect in 1945. Only a few studies, however, showed changes in relative wages greater than 25 percent. Indeed, the average wage effect shown by these studies was approximately 10–15 percent. Many seemingly strong unions had little or no effect on wage levels but were apparently able to provide workers with grievance and other workplace protections. As suggested, these protections may be highly valued by workers. Indeed, according to Lewis, less than

6 percent of the labor force showed union wage effects of 20 percent or more. As suggested, these effects varied among and within industries and over time.

Most of these estimates were made in or prior to the 1960s. During the entire post–World War II period, however, there were massive changes in industrial composition and the U.S. labor market. In particular, manufacturing was affected by (1) a substantial rise in productivity (similar to that experienced earlier in U.S. agriculture), (2) the movement of population and some industry to the less unionized southern states, and (3) the increased ability of Japanese and European firms to export their products to the United States.

Indeed, as a result of these and other factors, manufacturing employment in the United States fell by about five million workers during the last three decades, reducing the workforce in manufacturing from about 20 percent of total employment in 1979 to about 11 percent in 2005. In addition to the factors noted previously, the U.S. economy and unions in the United States have been affected by globalization and the emergence of world market conditions that increased further the availability of foreign products. Globalization, of course, affected more than the unionized sector. Indeed, many of the low-skill intensive and often nonunion industries (particularly in the South) were heavily impacted by free trade and the formation of new truly global corporations in both manufacturing and commerce. Included among these were textile, garment, and sewing firms. Mergers created numerous new international corporations with plants around the world. In addition, some American firms simply closed their plants in the United States and even overseas, choosing to become wholesalers who contract with foreign-owned firms to meet the product specifications established by the American firm(s). In addition, the massive transformation of the economy in the late 1980s and 1990s known as the Dot.com boom sharply altered job skills, communications, business procedures, and industrial composition.

All of these factors sharply affected the ability of unions to raise or even maintain wage levels in the industries and areas where unions had previously exhibited clout, lowering the extent of unionization and altering the composition of the labor movement. As noted, the largest U.S. unions are now concentrated in construction and in the various service industries, industries where the possibilities for foreign labor substitution are smaller than in, say, manufacturing.

According to Deitz and Orr (2006), job losses in manufacturing "are almost certain to continue." Nonetheless, Deitz and Orr found that in recent years, high-skilled employment in manufacturing has risen substantially in almost all manufacturing industries and in all parts of the country. That finding is consistent with the comparative advantage of the United States over many other countries in highly skilled activities. It also reflects the fact that it is often more difficult to substitute other inputs for skilled labor. In a previous age, that was one of the strengths of the craft-oriented unions.

UNION LEADERSHIP

No listing of the factors influencing U.S. unionism would be complete without some mention of the many charismatic and often controversial leaders of the movement. Samuel Gompers of the American Federation of Labor (AFL) was cited previously. John L. Lewis, initially with the Coal Miner's Union, championed the rise of industrial unionism and led in the formation of the CIO. The Reuther brothers, Walter and Victor, developed the sitdown strike into a formidable weapon and directed the once powerful United Auto Workers Union. George Meany, the longtime president of the combined AFL-CIO, also deserves mention. So does Jimmy Hoffa of the Teamsters Union, who was regularly accused of racketeering and connections to the Mob. That circumstance, among other concerns, led to the passage of the Labor-Management Racketeering Act of 1951. In 2005, Andrew Stern, president of the Service Employees International Union, led his large union out of the unified AFL-CIO in a dispute over how to reorganize the labor movement to meet the challenges of globalization and changing technology. Each of these individuals contributed to the nature and/or success of unions in the United States, as did a raft of other leaders.

THE FUTURE OF ORGANIZED LABOR IN THE UNITED STATES

The ups and downs of unionism combined with the uncertainties of the future make any predictions extremely difficult. All one can reasonably do is outline the major factors that could affect unions and union membership now that membership as a proportion of employment is only about 12 percent and falling.

Several factors weigh heavily in what may occur in the near future. These factors include (1) globalization, (2) the change in the composition of the labor movement from the manufacturing/mining to the service industries, (3) the growing skill levels of American workers within manufacturing and beyond, and (4) the growth of social discord in both the United States and the newly industrializing nations. Moreover, as in the past, legal-legislative changes could have major impacts.

Clearly, the old feelings of alienation, impotency in the workplace, and even class struggle have risen recently with industrial relocation and new technology. Barring a major war, depression, or inflation, however, it is likely that these concerns will be addressed among skilled and professional workers largely by exit voice, rather than by union voice. That certainly was the pattern in the 1990s and the early 2000s. Indeed, exit voice among such workers may even entail migration across national boundaries, going where the jobs are. Among lower-skilled and semiskilled workers, however, the emerging world labor market may limit the opportunities for exit voice both within and outside the United States, and that may encourage unionization. Many displaced workers have already found their way into the service industries, now the most heavily unionized sector of the economy. Some of these workers, of course, have left the labor force, have relocated into nonunion jobs, and/or have been retrained for higher-skilled occupations. Union leaders like Andrew Stern argue that recent events require both the reorganization of existing unions and an emphasis on industry-wide (rather than firm-level) bargaining. Whether such changes could or would reinvigorate unions or increase membership, however, is problematical. It is also problematical whether the new immigrants to America, legal or illegal, will be as supportive of unions as were the immigrants of the middle to late 1800s and early 1900s.

Alternative approaches to strengthen unions may be tried, particularly the formation of truly international unions to match the new international corporations or the insistence on international labor standards via the courts, the United Nations, and various treaties. These approaches face many obstacles. The first is somewhat daunting since political (rather than business) unionism has been the norm in many other developed nations. Moreover, there are innumerable differences in labor laws and regulatory climates among the nations. Also, there are important questions of national sovereignty. Finally, some nations are rejecting globalization and even capitalism, nationalizing industries and hence limiting the opportunities for collective bargaining on either a firm-wide or industry-wide basis. Nevertheless, there is some agitation overseas (say, in China) for independent business unionism now that there are private employers throughout that nation. Of course, American unions would welcome and support such a development in China and elsewhere.

Finally, to the degree that perceived income differences grow among Americans, there will be stronger demands for government regulation of the labor market via living wage and minimum wage laws, governmentally regulated pension arrangements, and the like. As in the past, organized labor in the United States is likely to support both collective bargaining and governmental initiatives to address the overall distribution of income.

See also: Blue-Collar and White-Collar Jobs; Employee Loyalty and Engagement; Labor Shortages; Outsourcing and Offshoring

References

Deitz, Richard, and James Orr. 2006. "A Leaner, More Skilled U.S. Manufacturing Workforce." *Current Issues in Economics and Finance* 12: 1–7.

Freeman, Richard. 1976. "Individual Mobility and Union Voice in the Labor Market." *American Economic Review* 66: 361–68.

Lewis, H. Gregg. 1963. *Unionism and Relative Wages in the United States.* Chicago: University of Chicago Press.

Further Reading: Fearn, Robert M. 1981. *Labor Economics: The Emerging Synthesis.* Cambridge, MA: Winthrop; Jacobs, Eva E., ed. 2006. *Handbook of Labor Statistics, 2006.* 9th ed. Lanham, MD: Bernam Press; Martinez, Rick. 2005. "Can Unions Fly High Once More?" *The News and Observer* (August 25): 13A; Troy, Leo. 1965. *Trade Union Membership, 1897–1962.* Occasional Paper 92. New York: National Bureau of Economic Research; U.S. Bureau of Labor Statistics. 1978. *Handbook of Labor Statistics, 1978.* Bulletin 2000. Washington, DC: U.S. Government Printing Office.

Robert M. Fearn

LABOR SHORTAGES

Whether or not there is a labor shortage depends on where you live. In many Rust Belt cities in the midwestern and northeastern United States, unemployment is above the national average, and it appears to many people that there are too many workers and not enough jobs. However, in other regions where economic growth is high, there are shortages of workers qualified to do many jobs, including menial labor requiring minimal levels of education. This phenomenon is true all over the world. So there is a labor shortage, and there is not a labor shortage.

If you asked executives in many organizations, they would tell you that there is always a shortage of employees who are conscientious and work hard. That might make an interesting topic for another entry in this reference work. However, for purposes of this entry, I will assume that all workers are motivated to do their jobs and that the exceptions fall within an accepted margin of error.

It is also important to note that some labor shortages found across the nation have to do with changing gender roles. Historically, women who attended college were more likely to major in education and nursing than other fields, either because those careers were more socially acceptable or because they were not admitted to others. Today, more women are majoring in business, science, and engineering than ever before. This has created labor shortages in fields that women used to subsidize. By subsidizing a field, I mean that women were willing to work for less pay than men for a variety of reasons, thereby creating a subsidy for schools and hospitals. Those subsidies and their accompanying labor source are now gone. Shortages of nurses and teachers are due in large part to these shifting expectations.

LABOR SURPLUSES IN THE RUST BELT REGIONS OF THE UNITED STATES

In the U.S. Rust Belt, many large manufacturing industries have closed. For example, in Pittsburgh, Youngstown, and Cleveland, the steel industry has all but disappeared during the past 20–30 years. Low-cost steel made in other countries replaced the higher-cost steel made in the United States with high-quality metal. Many other products, like clothing, shoes, appliances, textiles, and other consumer goods, are now predominantly made in other countries. One industry that has been hurt, but not completely decimated, by foreign manufacturers is the automobile industry. Many Americans who swore that they would never drive the tiny boxes on wheels that the first Hondas on the U.S. market appeared to be now buy Japanese autos exclusively. The quality, price, and acceptance of non-U.S.-made cars has hurt the U.S. automobile industry.

Before foreign cars gained acceptance, they were exclusively manufactured in their countries of origin. More recently, however, many Japanese cars are manufactured in the United States. In Japan, employees and labor unions are considered useful partners in manufacturing, but in the United States, labor and management are often enemies, working against each other. The Japanese very carefully chose to locate their new plants in towns and cities where they were more likely to have productive relationships with workers. As Sullivan (1992) noted, the Japanese learned a great deal about how to and how not to manage automobile companies by watching Ford and General Motors (GM). The bottom line is that the Japanese did not build their new automobile plants in the old

Rust Belt areas of the United States where the United Auto Workers (UAW) was strong, opposed to foreign competition, and likely to make exorbitant salary and benefit demands. Honda of America now employs thousands of Americans in the United States.

In addition to the job losses in the Rust Belt region due to foreign competition, U.S. automakers began to manufacture their own products outside of the United States. This may have been only a part or two of an automobile initially, but now many Fords sold in the United States are assembled in Canada. This strategy was used to reduce the influence and cost of the UAW.

Nonetheless, owing to declining sales, General Motors and Ford are cutting workers and closing plants all over the United States at this time. General Motors is currently in the process of a large downsizing. An initial goal of 30,000 early retirements has been well received by GM workers. These job reductions will be implemented over the next few years.

A shift in attitudes regarding employment also occurred during the same period. Historically, if a man worked in a particular factory, the sons of that man would also work in that factory. This is not surprising since men and women typically followed the example of their fathers in choosing a career, usually owing to opportunity, rather than habit. Something different began to happen in the 1960s and 1970s, however. Fathers began to work harder to send their children (males initially, but later, females) to college. Instead of talking about wanting their sons to follow them into well-paying jobs at the local plant, fathers wanted to give their children the opportunity to do what they never could: work in professional (maybe even management) positions. As the number of well-paying factory jobs began to decline in the Rust Belt regions, the percentage of people attending college increased. When they graduated, many left the Rust Belt to find work. This is referred to as the brain drain, and many people believe that the exodus of educated young people from the Rust Belt has further hurt these areas. Fewer nonmanufacturing companies exist in the Rust Belt regions than in developing regions.

As examples, take Erie, Pennsylvania, and Columbus, Ohio. Erie was a classic industrial city that had a large General Electric (GE) plant making refrigerators and locomotives. In addition, the city thrived with many GE suppliers and other large industrial companies like Hammermill Paper Company. GE has phased out the appliance business in Erie, along with over 10,000 jobs. The paper company was sold to International Paper, which recently closed the local plant. Thousands of other jobs and many companies have also been lost. The young people fortunate to graduate from college must go to other cities to find work if they cannot get a job at one of the handful of good employers left. Erie, like much of western Pennsylvania, is a demographically old region of the second oldest state in the United States.

Job shortages are a problem in Erie. The unemployment rate is above the national average. There have been layoffs of firefighters, police officers, and school-teachers—professions in short supply in other regions of the country. The city and county where it is located are now looking to the gaming and recreation industries to create jobs, although both types of businesses have historically low pay. Another growing business is health care, in part due to the aging population.

A large percentage of older citizens is a large problem for any region. Older citizens pay lower taxes, utilize more entitlement programs and community services than younger citizens, and vote. The Rust Belt regions are seeing some labor shortages in the health care field. Erie, for example, has a shortage of dermatologists. Like the rest of the country, nurses are in short supply and are being courted by hospitals in other parts of the country. If we can still assume that nurses are typically female, married, and view their husbands' work as primary (it sounds sexist but is still generally true), we can also assume that as their husbands seek employment out of the region, the shortage of nurses in the Rust Belt will get worse.

Columbus, on the other hand, is the state capital of Ohio and the location of The Ohio State University, one of the original land grant universities in the United States. The organizations that evolved were related to government, education, and agriculture. Eventually, the insurance industry, banking, and small manufacturing companies began to grow as well. The city has a steady influx of ambitious and well-educated young people from all over the world. The economy and population of Columbus have grown, while Erie is dealing with financial problems and the population is shrinking and aging. Although the recent recession had a negative effect on employment, as it did all over the United States, the job prospects in Columbus are substantially better than in Erie.

It is important to note that although the so-called Rust Belt is found in the Midwest and Northeast, there are cities (even some with historically bad weather) in these regions that are thriving. Minneapolis/St. Paul, Minnesota, and Madison, Wisconsin, are developing cities in the Midwest.

LABOR SHORTAGES IN DEVELOPING REGIONS OF THE UNITED STATES

There are many developing regions of the United States where we are seeing tremendous job growth and accompanying labor shortages. The Southwest, the Pacific Northwest, the Rocky Mountain region, and the Southeast are the areas of the country that are rapidly developing at this time.

Keep in mind that growth can also bring problems. For example, in many cities in developing regions, pollution is growing, serious water shortages are developing, the cost of living (especially housing) is becoming prohibitive in many cities, taxes are rising as there is more demand for community services, the school systems are overcrowded and unable to keep up with the growing population, and the labor shortages make it difficult to hire qualified employees. If these regions become less desirable over time, organizations and people will leave, and the labor situation will change. Given these caveats, there are labor shortages in the developing regions of the United States currently.

Some of the many industries where there are labor shortages are construction, health care, education, personal service, recreation, agriculture, and small manufacturing. In addition, there are many professional positions available. There are severe shortages of firefighters, police officers, nurses, and schoolteachers. These labor shortages cut across educational and professional levels. The West has traditionally relied on migrant workers for agriculture, but construction is now offering better-paying options for immigrants, both legal and illegal.

Communities in rapidly developing regions are creating new approaches to fill positions with the most severe shortages. A number of cities are aggressively recruiting firefighters and police officers. For example, Houston is budgeted for 5,300 officers but has only 4,600 currently (Hahn 2006). Houston, like many other cities in the Southwest, is recruiting officers who have been laid off in Rust Belt cities. Some hospitals in the Southwest have implemented programs that allow them to hire nurses from other parts of the country for short periods, perhaps four to six weeks, provide transportation and housing, and pay an extraordinary wage during that period. Although a costly approach, it has allowed hospitals to deal with peak need periods.

Twenty years ago, new teachers would be lucky to find jobs. They often did substitute teaching to prove themselves until a full-time position became available. Now, school districts are making recruiting visits to every college of education and offering signing bonuses, relocation packages, and starting salaries in the middle to high 30s. Some school districts are offering retired teachers the option of continuing to draw their retirement while returning to the classrooms at the top of the pay scale. In some districts, the top of the pay scale with a master's degree is $80,000 or more. We can expect to see these kinds of strategies in the future.

With new regions and laws come different types of businesses and organizations. I mentioned the gambling industry earlier. Gambling, which was illegal in the United States everywhere until recently, employs different types of workers who need different types of skill sets. For example, our schools do not teach blackjack dealing as part of the curriculum. As gambling becomes an important industry nationwide, will skills that help our children learn to count cards, psych out opponents, and catch customers trying to beat the house be added to the curriculum? You may cringe at the thought, but we now teach sex education and require boys to take home economics in almost every school. Jobs change, and the skills required do, too.

The United States is in a better place now than many other industrialized countries from a labor standpoint, according to Wattenberg (2004). He suggested that despite a U.S. fertility rate slightly below replacement level, that rate is better than found today in most other developed countries. In addition, he believed that the United States does immigration better. This may come as a shock to many who believe that our immigration policies are a mess. Unlike our European counterparts, America really does have a melting pot. Although we initially resist changing and force everyone to speak English, we do allow immigrants to become citizens, and we do allow them to bring their ideas and customs to the United States. This makes the United States a better place for immigrants to live than other countries where culture, customs, and religion are forced. Wattenberg believes that the United States will weather the decline in the world's population better if we continue our immigration practices, however flawed they may seem. This takes us to the next section of this entry: the declining population.

WHY BUSINESSES ARE LEAVING THE RUST BELT

1. The weather is better in the South.
2. Many of these regions are seen as having a higher quality of life.
3. These regions are where we find the so-called right-to-work states. This is a term that refers to the passage of a state law which says that workers employed in a unionized organization cannot be forced to join the union. Although technically, this does not eliminate unions (that would be against federal law), it has had the effect of making labor unions less powerful. This, in turn, makes it cheaper to employ workers in these states.
4. Other regions have more available land and less crowded cities. This all changes, of course, as people migrate to these regions. The price of housing in Denver and Phoenix is an example of what can happen to property costs (or values, as citizens would prefer to call it) as cities grow.
5. State and city taxes may be lower, and there may be fewer or different state and city laws affecting business. For example, look at the impact of legalized gambling and prostitution in Nevada.
6. The development and availability of air-conditioning may be more common.
7. The developing regions offered incentives to businesses to relocate, usually in the form of lower taxes, and these incentives in some cases include a contractual commitment to an area for 20 years or longer.

DECLINING POPULATION AND THE IMPACT ON LABOR MARKETS AROUND THE WORLD

The world's population is growing due to past fertility rates. However, a substantial change has occurred during the past 10 years that is affecting the entire world: total fertility rates are rapidly declining. The population of every country that has not already done so will peak by 2050 and begin to decline. Many countries have already peaked and are in decline now.

During the 1960s, the birth control pill was introduced and began to be widely used. A new form of birth control was important, but this one has had an impact that few expected. It put birth control into the hands of women. As long as men and women have known what causes pregnancy, birth control has existed. Yes, abstinence. Abstinence, of course, is easier said than done. However, a woman who has given birth 1–10 times before and is currently caring for children is probably more inclined to sacrifice the moment for the consequence nine months later. The male, who does not get pregnant, give birth, or necessarily care for the children may not be as motivated. At best, women of childbearing age wanted and/or were influenced to do it anyway, and at worst, they were forced even when they did not want more children. The pill, as it is simply known, let women control their fertility. It did not interfere with pleasure, and it could be used secretly if need be. In addition to the pill, women now have patches and other methods that allow them to use one treatment to provide protection for months.

New fertility data suggest that Coontz (1992) was right when she reported that women will use birth control when they have the power to do so. Many other reasons are also given for the declining fertility rates worldwide, including urbanization, women's rights and career options, and women having children later due to increased educational opportunities. The bottom line is that women all over the world now have lower fertility rates than they did even 10 years ago.

The total fertility rate (TFR) is defined as the average number of children that a woman in a particular country or region will have during her childbearing life. If the average woman in a country has three children, the fertility rate is 3.0. The replacement level is 2.1. That means that every woman, on average, must have 2.1 children to maintain the same population of the country. The United States is slightly below the replacement level, at around 2.01 children per woman.

Owing to lower fertility rates and improving health care, which is increasing life expectancy, the world is seeing an increasingly older population, living off the resources of the country but no longer adding value through work and taxes. This is primarily true in the United States, Europe, and parts of Asia. In the United States, 10,000 people turn 55 every day (Jamrog 2005). The baby boomers are retiring to longer lives and increased needs for health care. In the United States, the elderly are the only Americans with a national health plan: Medicare.

Declining fertility rates have affected western Europe and Japan before the rest of the world. The fertility rate in both these regions is currently around 1.3, which is a 38 percent decline in just 10 years. According to Jamrog (2005) with the Human Resource Institute, the population of western Europe and Japan is currently declining 1 percent per year. In Europe, this amounts to about 700,000 fewer people per year. In approximately 10 years, this decline will grow to 1.5 percent per year.

Surprisingly, religion does not seem to affect fertility rates. We are seeing this in Italy, with one of the lowest fertility rates in Europe; Mexico, which currently has a fertility rate around the replacement level (think about all the work done by Mexican immigrants in the United States); South America; and the Middle East. Africa has gone from fertility rates of 8.0 children per woman to 3.8 currently. Given the high death rates in Africa, especially due to AIDS, this may actually be a replacement level. In less developed countries in general, the fertility rate is now 2.9 children per woman, compared to 6.0 children in the 1960s (Wattenberg 2004).

In China, fertility rates are also low due in part to the aggressive population control policies of the government. We have heard rumors about how newborn daughters are treated in China. Although these rumors have been somewhat exaggerated, we know that today, there about 118 boys born for every 100 girls. This mismatch will probably further reduce the fertility rate. However, fertility rates are rapidly declining all over Asia, even in countries with no population control laws or practices. This includes the most populous country, India, where very aggressive population control policies have been in effect and gender selection strategies are widely used; that is, pregnant women are tested and female fetuses are aborted before birth.

So how have the declining fertility rates affected labor markets around the world? In most less developed countries, there are still high unemployment rates due to their high current populations. After all, current mothers are the daughters of women who had anywhere from six to eight children. However, the end is in sight. It will be around 2050, according to Wattenberg (2004), before the world's population will peak and begin the decline. The United Nations has projected a world population of 12 billion people by 2050, but Wattenberg is predicting that it will actually peak at 8–10 billion. No one predicted the very sharp declines in fertility rates.

We are already seeing the effects of a declining population. European nations need immigrant workers, but the riots in France and the recent violence in the Netherlands are indicative of problems that Europeans have with immigrant workers. The immigrants want the rights of citizenship, including the right to practice their own beliefs. Europeans tend to be ethnocentric and want to maintain their unique cultural identities. The conflicts occur when immigrants do not accept the culture of the host country. For example, in the Netherlands, the government has begun a program to expose potential immigrants to the liberal nature of the Dutch culture prior to immigration. Prospective immigrants are forced to watch a film that shows scenes from nude clubs and hashish bars. Many immigrants find the film and some liberal practices of the Dutch to be very offensive. Although workers are needed, the Dutch are unwilling to adjust their culture to a changing population. In addition, the worker permits used in many European countries do not allow citizenship and force immigrants into low social status with few rights and into living in ghettos of large cities.

The population decline in Russia is so bad that women are given 250,000 rubles (about $9,200) to have a second child. In Portugal, pensions are being tied to the number of children a woman has (i.e., more children provides more pension). Other European countries have offered incentives with little success. It appears that the declining fertility rates cannot be easily changed. The cost (both financial and emotional) of childbearing and rearing is very high.

In China, labor shortages are intense. How could that be in one of the most populous countries in the world? It is because the factories are located in regions where the population is fully employed. Many Chinese are poor farmers in central China. In addition, a populous country can hardly afford to interfere with food production. China is beginning to use immigrant workers from other countries to work in the burgeoning industries and growing cities.

SUMMARY

Yes, there are few labor shortages in Rust Belt regions of the United States, which is probably true in comparable communities around the world. However, there are labor shortages in many developing areas of the United States and the world. The populations of Europe and Japan are already in decline, and the fertility rates of every country in the rest of the world are in a dramatic decline. Although very populous countries like China, India, and the United States will not see the decline for a few decades, less developed countries in Africa and South

America will see population declines in the near future. Labor shortages are sure to develop as aging populations become the norm. The puzzle is how to encourage fertility rates within each country to replacement levels, effectively and fairly use immigrant workers, and maintain the valuable aspects of our culture. The countries that solve this puzzle will survive. Others will not.

See also: Dual Earners; Immigrant Workers in the United States; The Middle Class

References

Coontz, Stephanie. 1992. *The Way We Never Were: American Families and the Nostalgia Trap.* New York: Basic Books.

Hahn, Tim. 2006. "Houston: Police Department Looks to Hire from Erie." *Erie Times News* (July 2). Available at: www.goerie.com.

Jamrog, Jay J. 2005. "The perfect storm." Paper presented at the AACSB Meeting, Tampa, FL.

Sullivan, Jerry. 1992. *The Invasion of the Salarymen: The Japanese Business Presence in America.* Westport, CT: Praeger.

Wattenberg, Ben J. 2004. *Fewer: How the New Demography of Depopulation Will Shape Our Future.* Chicago: Ivan R. Dee.

Further Reading: Gordon, Edward E. 2005. *The 2010 Meltdown: Solving the Impending Jobs Crisis.* Westport, CT: Praeger; Hedge, Jerry W., Walter C. Borman, and Steven E. Lammlein. 2005. *The Aging Workforce: Realities, Myths, and Implications for Organizations.* Washington, DC: American Psychological Association; Longman, Philip. 2004. *Empty Cradle: How Falling Birthrates Threaten World Prosperity and What to Do about It.* Cambridge, MA; Wattenber, Ben J. 2004. *Fewer: How the New Demography of Depopulation Will Shape Our Future.* Chicago: Ivan R. Dee.

Peg Thoms

LOTTERIES

Every day, millions of Americans stop by a local store or visit a Web site, plunk down a few dollars, and hope for a miracle. Very few who play state lotteries will ever win any significant sums, and everyone except a handful of jackpot winners is guaranteed to lose more money buying tickets than they will gain in (mostly small) prizes over a lifetime. Yet these millions of Americans seem happy to continue playing—happy that some of the proceeds go to fund popular state programs such as schools and parks, and happy for the chance, however remote, of striking it rich.

The regeneration of a state lottery industry in the United States—the term regeneration is apt, as discussed later—has been one of the most striking developments in state government in the past 40 years. The trend began in 1964, when New Hampshire created the first modern state lottery. New York and New Jersey soon followed. By the mid-1970s, there were a dozen state lotteries, mostly in the Northeast. After a 1975 federal law allowed more lottery advertising, other states began to enter the gambling business. As of 2006, 42 states and the District of Columbia featured some form of state-sponsored lottery game. Many of these states also participated in multistate games with jackpots in the hundreds of millions of dollars. Players bought nearly $53 billion in lottery tickets in fiscal year 2005, with net proceeds of $16.5 billion flowing into state coffers to fund a variety of governmental expenditures (North American

LOTTERIES ARE ANCIENT HISTORY, LITERALLY

In some form, games in which players draw lots to determine the winner have been around as long as humans have recorded their history. Passages in the Hebrew and Christian Bible describe the casting of lots to settle public disputes and distribute common lands to individual owners, as the prophet Moses was said to have done with regard to lands found west of the Jordan River in Canaan. Across the Mediterranean Sea, in ancient Greece, several city-states used some version of a lottery as a means of selecting public officials. In Athens, for example, male citizens over the age of 30 drew lots to determine who would sit for a year on the city's governing council. Because these citizen-lawmakers, 400 at a time, drew a small public income for their service, one might say that this was the first known instance of lotteries being used in public finance, albeit on a small scale. Lotteries were also evident in Roman history from the late republic through the imperial centuries. Prominent Roman hosts used lotteries to distribute valuable gifts to their guests, much as many people today have door prize drawings.

As far as governments using lotteries to raise significant revenue for public purposes, the innovator appears to be Han China. Tradition has it that Cheung Leung, who ruled a besieged Chinese city around 200 B.C., invented the game of keno to help finance fortifications and army provisions. The story provides interesting parallels to the creation of modern lotteries in America: Cheung's people believed that they were overtaxed, and he feared that further exactions to finance his defenses against barbarian incursions might result in revolt. Instead, his keno game, using written characters from a popular children's poem, seemed to make paying for defense not only voluntary, but also fun. Peasants waited eagerly for messenger birds to bring news of lottery drawings from the city; for this reason, the lottery become known as the White Dove game. It may also have financed significant portions of the Great Wall, built by a series of subsequent emperors as a line of defense and to demarcate the line between China and the barbarian lands to the northwest.

In the West, government-sponsored lotteries may date back as early as the rule of the first Roman emperor, Caesar Augustus, who was said to have used a lottery to finance city repairs. But firmer evidence is available for government lotteries in Europe starting in the fifteenth and sixteenth centuries. In 1530, for example, the Italian city of Florence ran a lottery to fund civic improvements. French cities adopted the practice a few years later, and in 1539, the king of France held a lottery to replenish his depleted national treasury. By 1567, the government of Elizabeth I was operating the first English lottery games to raise money for the crown. Her cousin, King James I, staged a royal lottery in 1612 to help sponsor the founding of the first British colony in North America: Jamestown.

Association of State and Provincial Lotteries n.d.). Still, it is important to keep these figures in proper perspective. Lotteries represent about one-fourth of the commercial gambling industry in the United States, as measured by gross revenue. They generate less than 3 percent of total state revenues, and in no state does a lottery contribute more than about 7 percent of revenue (Hansen 2004).

State lotteries may not dominate the gambling business or pay for a significant swath of state government, but they have nevertheless accounted for some of the most spirited and passionate public policy debates held in state capitals over the past quarter century. Proponents and opponents have made a series of arguments, touching on a range of concerns and issues: education, elder care, land preservation, fraudulent advertising, tax equity, the initiative and referendum process, organized crime, economic development, family values, and the proper role of morality in lawmaking. The nature and persuasiveness of the arguments made during state-by-state battles to create lotteries reveal much about how public policy is made and understood by public officials and average citizens alike.

AMERICAN LOTTERIES: BOOM AND BUST

When arguing for the creation of state lotteries in the 1970s, 1980s, and 1990s, proponents frequently emphasized the extensive use of lotteries during America's Founding Period to finance major infrastructure, military assets, and public buildings. They were right to do so. Many of the country's most famous leaders, institutions, and monuments have some connection to lotteries. For starters, George Washington helped to set up several lotteries for purposes that included building a road over the Blue Ridge Mountains (1768) and paying the Continental Army during the American Revolution (1776 and 1777). Benjamin Franklin sponsored a lottery to purchase cannons to bolster the defenses of Philadelphia against an approaching British army. Several buildings at universities ranging from Harvard and Yale to the University of North Carolina, the first government-created college in America, were constructed with lottery proceeds (Clotfelter and Cook 1989). And a large number of roads, bridges, courthouses, lighthouses, and other buildings were financed by the more than 160 lotteries in operation within the colonies prior to the Revolution and by the many more lotteries held during and immediately after the war (Hansen 2004).

However, it is important to distinguish between these early American lotteries and the state-run games that would be created in the late twentieth century. The line between public and private sponsorship of colonial lotteries was blurry. Because colonial governments were much smaller institutions than modern states and had few regular sources of tax revenue (or local banks from which to borrow funds), prominent citizens stepped forward to organize and operate lotteries, passing along a relatively modest share of the proceeds to government treasuries. For example, while it is typical today for prizes to consume a little more than half of state lottery proceeds, with about one-third flowing into government coffers as net revenue (and the remainder covering operating and marketing costs), lotteries during the colonial era paid out roughly 85 percent of revenue as prizes to participants, leaving recipient governments or private in-stitutions to share the remaining 15 percent with those citizens actually running the games. But the latter group apparently got very little of that 15 percent, given that their costs were extremely low—they did not pay commissioners, compen-sate vendors, or employ large staffs. "These public works lotteries had far more in common with church and school charity raffles than with today's state lotter-ies," wrote The New Republic's Robyn Gearey (1997, 22).

After the United States won its independence, the new and rapidly grow-ing states faced tremendous infrastructure needs. Lacking as yet other effective

---

IS A STATE LOTTERY A TAX?

In most of the states that have created lotteries during the past 40 years, supporters have argued that even if some lawmakers or citizens have reservations about getting the govern-ment into the gambling business, it is still better than the alternative of raising taxes to pay for state programs benefiting schools, colleges, senior citizens, the environment, and other causes. But is a state lottery an alternative to state taxation, or a form of state taxation?

The celebrated English poet Henry Fielding expressed a clear answer to this question in his 1732 farce The Lottery: "A Lottery is a Taxation / Upon all the Fools in Creation / And Heav'n be prais'd, It is easily rais'd / Credulity's always in Fashion." A modern version of this calumny is to allege that lotteries are a tax on stupidity or a tax on the statistically illiterate.

At first glance, it would seem odd to argue that a state lottery, which relies on proceeds from citizens voluntarily deciding whether to play a game, could ever be defined as a form of taxation. Indeed, public opinion surveys show that most Americans distinguish between lotteries and taxes and decisively prefer the former to the latter as a means of paying gov-ernment's bills. Further reflection about the idea that a government exaction on a voluntary purchase is not a tax, however, will show that this definition does not really work. No one doubts that excise taxes on cigarettes and alcohol, for example, are taxes. But citizens only pay these taxes if they choose to buy the products. The same is true for goods and services taxed by a general sales tax. The purchase may be voluntary, but if one chooses to buy, then having a share of one's money taken for governmental purposes is completely mandatory, just as other taxes are. In the lottery case, one could think of the government's share of the take as either the equivalent of a sales tax embedded in the ticket price or as an income tax imposed on a state lottery commission or agency.

Of course, logic is one thing. The law is another. After North Carolina's legislature created a state lottery in 2005, the North Carolina Institute for Constitutional Law sued in state court to overturn the law. Its attorneys argued that the state constitution required any bill impos-ing a tax to be subjected to separate votes on separate days, which the legislature did not do. The state's attorneys responded that the provision did not apply to a lottery bill, and in dismissing the lawsuit, the court agreed. "No person is forced to purchase a lottery ticket," the judge wrote. "The lottery act does not impose a tax on the purchaser of a lottery ticket" (Weigl 2006).

means of taxation, they turned to the lottery technique and began expanding its size, scope, and frequency. No longer one-time affairs staged by prominent political leaders or civic-minded citizens to fund particular projects, lotteries became professionalized. In the early nineteenth century, private firms began to specialize in running lotteries on behalf of state governments. They innovatively created ticket designs, machines, marketing strategies, and broker compensation schemes to increase the ease and speed of play. These firms were sometimes connected to early financial service companies in major cities, some of which parlayed their lottery experience into the banking or bond businesses. In several states, they introduced the idea of private shops devoted to the sale of lottery tickets. For example, by 1831, there were 177 of these lottery-only shops in operation just in the city in Philadelphia (Clotfelter and Cook 1989).

While these lotteries continued to attract significant patronage—amounting to as much as 3 percent of total national expenditures on all goods and services in 1832, several times the modern-day lotteries' share of gross domestic product (Hansen 2004)—and remained popular among politicians as a means of financing public services without generating taxpayer ire, they also generated problems. In ancient Rome, the so-called tax farmers, or publicans, became notorious for fraud and corruption. These were private interests who received permission from the senate to wring a specific amount of taxes out of a province. Whatever additional so-called tax they imposed on the provincials, the tax farmers could keep—and they did, aggressively (Adams 1993). In the case of nineteenth-century lotteries, of course, Americans were never required to play. But those who wanted to gamble in this way had to patronize the officially sanctioned lottery vendors, who began to abuse their captive audiences with exaggerated claims and out-and-out fraud. Governments, too, became the victim of financial chicanery by the lottery operators, who failed to provide accurate reports of ticket sales, subtracted huge amounts from the gross to cover so-called expenses, and often passed through only a tiny fraction to states. In a notable 1811 case, a lottery set up to fund a government-chartered canal in Pennsylvania routed less than one-half of 1 percent of the proceeds to the canal company (Hansen 2004).

These scandals provoked public backlash and state attempts to rein in abuses. At the same time, social reformers began to agitate for a number of changes in American public life, on issues ranging from slavery and temperance to poverty and mental illness. Many of them shared a religious or moral animus toward gambling and viewed state-sponsored lotteries as a source of public corruption and a means of taking advantage of the poor and gullible. Beginning with Pennsylvania, New York, and Massachusetts, state governments began to move from increased lottery regulation to outright prohibition. Except for a brief period after the Civil War—during which a few states used lotteries to fund reconstruction efforts and, once again, saw fraud and corruption flourish—the state lottery industry remained a historical footnote, and an occasional cause célèbre among tax-averse politicians, until the 1960s.

However, just because government-sanctioned lotteries did not exist, one should not draw the erroneous conclusion that Americans did not play lottery-type games during the late nineteenth and early twentieth centuries. Numbers rackets were common in major U.S. cities. At a smaller scale, raffles and sweepstakes run by churches and charities remained ubiquitous in urban and small-town America alike. Unlike a lottery, which requires someone to buy a ticket to win a prize, a sweepstakes game typically does not require a purchase to play. Associations and companies used sweepstakes as a marketing device to sell insurance, subscriptions, and other goods and services, a practice that continues to this day (Hills 2003).

THE NEW CASE FOR STATE LOTTERIES

The modern lottery industry began, in part, as a response to this proliferation of private, often illegal games of chance. In 1964, when New Hampshire became the first state to renew the practice of state-sponsored lotteries, advocates argued that legalizing some forms of gambling would create an attractive alternative to the numbers rackets infested by crime syndicates. Still, there was enough of a lingering presumption against the old-style lotteries that New Hampshire officials called their game a sweepstakes and associated it with horseracing to give it at least the sheen of having a component of skill and athleticism. Following the Granite State's lead were New York in 1967 and New Jersey in 1970. As proponents began making the case for state lotteries, they found several arguments to be the most persuasive in debating legislative foes:

- *Legal gambling is the antidote to organized crime.* Citing the experience of alcohol prohibition and its repeal, lottery supporters argued that state efforts to protect their residents from unscrupulous games and gambling addictions were a cure worse than the disease. Since a large segment of the public wants to play lottery-type games anyway, why not have state government or its contractor operate a clean, honest lottery, much as many states operated liquor store monopolies to control the sale of legal alcoholic beverages? That way, they argued, organized crime would lose its hold, and state coffers would benefit from enterprises that, previously underground and illegal, had not been paying their fair share of taxes (Gearey 1997).
- *Lotteries are a better revenue source than generally applied taxes.* Relying on the widespread perception that lotteries were not taxes, proponents played up the voluntary nature of the game. If you do not play, you do not have to pay. Because lotteries generate revenues through sales rather than by taxing property or income, some argued, they were also better for local economies by shifting some of the fiscal burden for financing public services to visitors, tourists, the underground economy, and workers who live in neighboring states. Finally, some politicians explicitly argued that lotteries were simply less unpopular than other forms of taxation, thus making it possible to increase government spending—for education and other services they believed to be drastically underfunded—without getting themselves defeated in the next election.

- *States cannot afford not to have lotteries.* Eventually, as state-sponsored lotteries became more common, the remaining states without them began to see another argument emphasized: that cross-border sales of lottery tickets represented a significant lost opportunity for nonlottery states. To the extent that residents of these nonlottery states drove to neighboring jurisdictions to play the game, they were contributing tax dollars to those governments' coffers, while also buying gasoline and sundries there. Using an economic argument about the multiple effects of consumer spending, proponents argued that nonlottery states were not only losing the opportunity to fund public schools, park systems, or elder care programs, but were also losing jobs and income growth (Lamme 1999).
- *The popular will on gambling should prevail through a public vote.* Despite the attractiveness of political, fiscal, and economic arguments to many state politicians, there was still a strong core of opposition in state legislatures across the country. To overcome it, lottery supporters cited public opinion polls showing widespread support for state lotteries, particularly when respondents were asked to choose between lotteries and generally applied tax increases to pay for schools and other government programs. The supporters then either put state lottery initiatives directly on the ballot or, in states where initiatives were not allowed, successfully convinced reluctant lawmakers to at least authorize a referendum to decide the issue. Of the 42 states that created lotteries through 2004, 31 used either initiatives or referendums to accomplish the task (Hansen 2004).

THE MODERN CASE AGAINST STATE LOTTERIES

These arguments, while often persuasive in state lottery debates, did not automatically prevail. For one thing, the New Hampshire and New York lotteries of the 1960s were not financially successful. Their drawings were too infrequent and marketing too limited. Only with the success of New Jersey's lottery in the 1970s did the prospect of lottery financing of government programs become attractive to many states previously opposed to the idea. Eleven additional states created lotteries in the 1970s—northeastern states along with Ohio, Illinois, and Michigan. During the 1980s, the movement spread across the Great Plains and to the West Coast, encompassing 18 additional states. In the more traditional South, only atypical Florida yet had a state lottery. During the 1990s, Texas, Georgia, and four other states enacted lotteries, often after spirited legislative debates and hotly contested political campaigns in which the lottery was a key issue. In Alabama, a successful effort to authorize a lottery referendum in 1999 did not yield the expected outcome, as a majority of voters defeated the idea in a special election (Kantrow 1999). Since then, however, other longtime holdouts such as Tennessee, South Carolina, North Dakota, and North Carolina have yielded to the pressure and become lottery states.

Lottery foes also developed a range of fiscal, political, economic, and moral arguments that proved effective, at least in blocking passage for many years. They included the following:

- *Lotteries are an uncertain and costly way to raise funds.* Because state lotteries are a form of gaming that competes with other entertainment options, both legal and illegal, they require significant and ever-escalating expenditures for marketing, advertising, and introducing exciting new games, lottery opponents argue. They further suggest that even with costly marketing efforts, lotteries do not provide the solid, predictable revenue stream that more generalized taxes generate, in part because prizes must grow at the expense of revenue payouts to make lottery play more attractive. "It's a self-destructive cycle," an industry consultant explained to *Business Week* (Berner 2001, 40).

- *Lotteries do not truly boost spending on education.* Most state lotteries devote a share of net proceeds, sometimes an overwhelming share, to public education. The result appears to be billions of additional dollars a year to fund class size reductions, new buildings, and other popular expenditures. However, lottery opponents argue that these lottery revenues do not necessarily increase education spending above the level it would be in the absence of the lottery, but instead *supplant* tax revenues that would otherwise flow to schools. With lottery revenues earmarked for public education, politicians can then use their tax money to fund lower-priority items in state budgets, while still appearing to place education first on the list (Trussell 1998).

- *Lotteries are an inequitable way to pay for public services.* Some opponents explicitly call lotteries a regressive tax, while others argue that any revenue source, tax or not, that draws from an unrepresentative, self-selected share of the general public is an unfair way to pay for services that benefit that general public. Supporters of the lottery contest the allegation that it is unfair or inequitable, pointing to surveys that show that the propensity to play the lottery is present all the way up the income ladder, not just among the poor (North American Association of State and Provincial Lotteries n.d.). But this response is insufficient if the term *regressive* is correctly defined: it does not refer to whether everyone in a society, regardless of income, generates *any* government revenue, but rather whether that revenue is *proportional* to income, wealth, or living standards. There is no serious dispute that lotteries are regressive by this definition, with the average share of income or consumption devoted to lottery purchases much higher among poorer, disproportionately nonwhite households than among wealthier ones (Gerlach 1999). Only if millionaires spent many thousands of dollars a month playing the lottery would this not be true.

- *Government should not endorse or promote gambling.* Many Americans have strong religious or moral convictions about gambling that lead them to oppose giving legal status to virtually all large-scale gambling enterprises, whether operated by governments, private firms, or Indian tribes. They also cite statistics on the dangers of gambling addictions (Daniels 2000). Obviously, antigambling citizens strongly oppose state-run lotteries, but they are not the only ones who do so on moral grounds. Other politicians, organizations, and voters who do not oppose legalized gambling per se remain against the idea that their state government should own, operate, endorse, or promote gambling. Their reasons vary. Some argue that in a free society respectful of diverse viewpoints, it should be wrong to force their fellow antigambling citizens to be associated with lotteries or have their public officials promoting the sale of lottery tickets. Others believe that there is something particularly exploitative or damaging about state lotteries, citing the fact that lotteries can afford to offer poor odds and relatively meager prizes because state law prohibits direct competition from private lotteries and that, unlike other forms of gambling, state lotteries are not subject to laws requiring truthful advertising claims. Statistics reveal that private casinos and sports betting do offer far better odds to players than state lotteries (Walsh 1996).

- *Legislatures, not direct democracy, should fashion public policy on gambling.* In states where lottery supporters pressed for public votes rather than legislative approval alone, opponents argued that representative government is a superior means of evaluating complex policy issues, while serving as a restraint on public passions that, if acted on, are not in the public's best long-term interest.

CONCLUSION

The policy debates about state-run gambling in America have been energetic, complicated, and lengthy. While almost all the 50 states now have some kind of state lottery, these policy debates promise to continue. Not only will lottery proponents continue their push to create lotteries in the remaining states, but even within lottery states, there are frequent pressures to authorize new drawings and multistate options, change the mix of payouts and revenue earmarks, and expand state-sponsored gambling to encompass sports betting and other games. Competition from Internet-based gambling operations, some operating outside the bounds of current state and federal law, may also have a significant effect on the operations and politics of state lotteries in the early twenty-first century.

See also: The Middle Class

References

Adams, Charles. 1993. *For Good and Evil: The Impact of Taxes on the Course of Civilization.* New York: Madison Books.

Berner, Robert. 2001. "State Lotteries Are Coming Up Snake Eyes." *Business Week* (May 7): 40.

Clotfelter, Charles T., and Philip J. Cook. 1989. *Selling Hope: State Lotteries in America.* Cambridge, MA: Harvard University Press.

Daniels, Stephen. 2000. "Gambling in America." *Findings,* 1–4.

Gearey, Robyn. 1997. "The Numbers Game." *The New Republic* (May 19): 22.

Gerlach, Dan. 1999. "The Lottery Tax: Still a Bad Idea for North Carolina." *BTC Reports* (February): 1–3.

Hansen, Alicia. 2004. *Lotteries and State Fiscal Policy.* Background Paper 46. Washington, DC: Tax Foundation.

Hills, Chad. 2003. "A History of the Lottery." *Citizen Link* (June 20). Available at: http://www.family.org/cforum/fosi/gambling/lottery/a0026528.cfm.

Kantrow, Buster. 1999. "Supporters Shocked, Dismayed As Siegelman's Crusade Fails." *Mobile Register* (October 13): 1A.

Lamme, Robert. 1999. "Lottery Debate Has Begun." *Greensboro News & Record* (January 17): B1.

North American Association of State and Provincial Lotteries. n.d. Available at: http://www.naspl.org/sales&profits05.html.

North American Association of State and Provincial Lotteries. n.d. Available at: http://www.naspl.org/faq.html#whoplays.

Trussell, Tait. 1998. "The Florida Lottery: A Critical Examination." *Journal of the James Madison Institute* (July/August): 5–9.

Walsh, James. 1996. "Why Do People Play the Lottery?" *Consumers' Research* (March): 25.

Weigl, Andrea. 2006. "Judge Rules Lottery Law Method Legal." *Raleigh News & Observer* (March 21). Available at: http://www.newsobserver.com/114/story/420422.html.

John M. Hood

M

MARKETING OF ALCOHOL AND TOBACCO

Alcohol and tobacco have served a variety of functions and played a significant role in the marketplace throughout history. Alcohol has long been used as part of religious customs, as medicine, and as a form of sustenance. Tobacco was used as collateral for loans from France during the American Revolutionary War, as a cure-all, and as a diet aid. However, for the last 200 years or so, alcohol and tobacco have been consumed in a fashion consistent with present-day usage, primarily for pleasure. Regardless of the reason for their use, both substances have been popular for most of human history. And both substances and their marketing have become controversial.

THE HISTORY OF THE MARKETING OF ALCOHOL AND TOBACCO

As early as the Civil War (1861–1865), American organizations were formed to protest alcohol consumption. Although alcohol remained popular among portions of the population, independent movements calling for voluntary abstinence and eventually the prohibition of alcohol by law emerged.

Eventually, as living conditions improved and humans began to live longer, the hazards of alcohol surfaced. The public took notice and actions were taken. Prohibition, a result of the temperance movement and made the sale and consumption of alcohol illegal, began on January 16, 1919. It was abolished in May 10, 1924.

To date, the marketing of alcohol remains largely self-regulated, and legal limitations on marketing and sales have been more lenient than those on tobacco. Nonetheless, the knowledge that alcohol can contribute to health problems and beliefs that it is responsible for corrupting the family unit have lead to the establishment of dry counties in various states. In existence to this day, a dry county is one that prohibits the sale of alcohol.

It was not until the surgeon general released a report called "Smoking and Health" in 1964 that the hazards of smoking were officially and publicly recognized. Negative press surrounding tobacco surfaced due to the health concerns associated with the product. This caused many of the major tobacco producers of the 1960s to consider changing the names of their companies and diversifying their range of products. In marketing, names are important because they convey information about the company to the consumer. The information communicated to the consumer influences how the company is perceived, and how it is positioned in regards to purchasing habits. Tobacco companies acknowledged the importance of brand names and a trend started that saw tobacco companies actively change their names and even products to avoid negative perceptions.

In America in the 1960s, a company that produced only tobacco products or had the word "tobacco" in its name was looked upon unfavorably. As a result, American Tobacco Company became American Brands, and Philip Morris bought part of Miller Brewing Company. RJ Reynolds Tobacco Company changed its name to RJ Reynolds Industries and ventured into the aluminum industry. Reynolds Wrap aluminum foil is now the most popular product in the RJ Reynolds line of products. The government has regulated the sales and advertising of cigarettes and since 1966 has even forced the industry to place health-risk warnings on all packaging. Sales of both alcohol and tobacco to minors are limited; these age limitations vary according to state laws.

ADVANTAGES OF POINT-OF-PURCHASE ADVERTISING

According to the Point-of-Purchase Advertising Institute, sales of point-of-purchase materials bring in nearly $13 billion annually; this makes the sales of point-of-purchase advertising materials third highest of all media in dollar expenditures. Point-of-purchase advertising consists of:

a. Displays, which can range from countertop to refrigerated dispensers
b. Signs, which serve notice of special pricing or other important information about a product
c. Shelf media, which attach to the front of retail shelving and tell the customer about special offers without taking up valuable retail space
d. New media, which can include video displays, coupon dispensers, interactive displays, and audio devices

THE COSTS OF MARKETING ALCOHOL AND TOBACCO

In the United States alone, $4 billion is spent each year to promote alcoholic beverages (Corporate Accountability International n.d.). The alcohol industry claims that advertising only affects brand choice and that the marketing of products is done to establish brand differentiation, or anything that positively distinguishes the identity of a company and its products and/or services to consumers from other companies' products. Popular examples of brand differentiation in the alcohol industry include promotions for Samuel Adams reminding consumers that the company uses more hops for flavor in its beer, and Coors Brewing Company's description of its beer as shipped cold and made with Rocky Mountain spring water.

While alcohol producers claim that advertising only promotes distinguishing characteristics to consumers, alcohol researchers, the U.S. surgeon general, and the National Institute on Alcohol Abuse and Alcoholism disagree. They say that heavy episodic drinking, or binge drinking, is at least partially fueled by commercial messages (Center an Alcohol Marketing and Youth n.d.). Binge drinking is regarded as the consumption of five or more consecutive drinks by a male or four or more consecutive drinks by a female. National studies have concluded that 40 percent of college students are binge drinkers.

Alcohol consumption among college students has also been shown to have an elastic demand. This means that as the price of alcohol decreases, consumption increases. Since traditional college students are around the legal drinking age, marketing helps fuel the desire for experimentation. Of course many influences other than marketing (such as parenting and peer pressure) factor into one's decision to consume alcohol. But given alcohol's accessibility, it is believed that marketing initiatives and promotional measures that constantly bombard people with advertising and discounted prices increase consumption by keeping alcohol financially accessible and on consumers' minds (Kuo et al. 2003). Unfortunately, increased drinking by college students leads to a greater number of accidents. The National Council of Drug and Alcohol Dependency estimates that drinking by college students results in 1,400 alcohol-related deaths each year (National Center for Chronic Disease Prevention 2006).

It is projected that more than $243 million was spent in 1999 alone to sponsor public service activities that combat alcohol abuse and related problems. Nearly $11 million is spent annually to educate the public about the harm of tobacco (Corporate Accountability International n.d.). (Note that the industry itself has a daily marketing budget of about the same amount; Educational Forum on Adolescent Health 2006.) While both the alcohol and tobacco industries have marketing programs that are intended to educate the public about potential risks, the difference is that tobacco education has federal funding, whereas alcohol does not. Alcohol education programs are funded by institutions such as Century Council, the Beer Institute, the National Beer Wholesalers Association, Brewers' Association of America, and the alcohol companies themselves.

AGGRESSIVE MARKETING OF ALCOHOL AND TOBACCO

Some organizations and activists believe that the products' aggressive marketing practices have an adverse impact on the long-term behavior of the population. Thus certain marketing approaches may have a variety of opponents. It is logical to ask why companies in these industries would continue practices that lead to such unfavorable attacks on their businesses.

The answer lies in the nearly 5,000 customers that the tobacco industry loses in the United States alone on a daily basis (approximately 3,500 quit and 1,200 die), and the estimated 105,000 Americans dying annually from alcohol-related causes (Corporate Accountability International n.d.). In fact, it is projected by the U.S. Office on Smoking and Health that smoking results in more than 5.5 million years of potential life lost nationally each year (National Center for Chronic Disease Prevention 2006). Simply put, in order to replace the revenue from those customers that the industries are losing, new customers must be acquired. This is accomplished through multimillion-dollar marketing campaigns. Campaigns of this magnitude are widespread, encompassing many media outlets. This means that marketing messages about alcohol and tobacco will reach the eyes and ears of youths, regardless of the demographic groups that the messages are geared toward.

Consequently, rules surrounding the marketing of tobacco and alcohol are evolving, and marketing campaigns in nearly all parts of the world are aimed at preventing children from developing these habits. The theory is that preventative measures will translate into an absence of alcohol- and tobacco-related problems and health risks in the future.

MARKETING TACTICS

When marketing abroad, the alcohol and tobacco industries often attach American themes to their brands. This practice is particularly common in tobacco advertisements; for example, in one ad circulated in the Czech Republic, a pack of Philip Morris cigarettes is seen merging with the New York City skyline in the Czech Republic, and a Polish Winchester Cigarette advertisement features the Statue of Liberty holding an oversized pack of cigarettes. Others showcase prominent American cities; red, white, and blue color schemes; and scenes that depict an American lifestyle (Essential Action 2006).

Goldberg and Baumgartner found that the use of American imagery in smoking advertisements works because smoking is seen as an attractive part of the American lifestyle in many countries. Those attracted to the United States and regard it as a place they would like to live are more likely to smoke. Having decided to smoke because they see it as an important part of the American lifestyle, they are more likely to smoke an American brand of cigarette (Goldberg and Baumgartner n.d.).

RJR Reynolds found in a 1983 study that marketing using American themes is not successful in the United States. Statements made by study respondents included: "It is too nationalistic," "America is not that great," and "It is not appropriate to sell America when selling cigarettes, or at least not in such a directly nationalistic way" (Essential Action 2006).

Nonetheless, the promotion of the perceived customs and norms of a product's place of origin has surfaced in the domestic advertising of alcoholic beverages. Smirnoff Ice, an alcoholic beverage, employs actors with Russian accents and wearing Russian garb for its current television advertising campaign. Beer companies such as Heineken and Becks also proudly promote the heritage of the beer's national origin.

Another method that has been effective among American consumers is what author Edward Abbey calls "industrial recreation" (The Maria Institute n.d.). Often referred to today as "wreckreation" or "ecotainment," the term refers to the utilization of landscape to promote a product. It is argued that such use of terrain in advertising may change the way that the community uses and even experiences public space.

Some new marketing campaigns are prompting questions as to whether or not they are bending the rules of marketing. The prevailing rules of marketing rely primarily on codes that are geared toward traditional media. New technologies that utilize both traditional and untraditional marketing techniques are complicating efforts to restrict and monitor marketing aimed at susceptible groups. These new technologies allow questionable marketing practices, such as cloaking, to go undetected by policy.

Cloaking, or stealth, is an ethically questionable technique employed online by Web sites to index Web pages within search engines in a fashion that is different from the way the page is indexed to other sources. Basically, the technique of cloaking can be used to trick a search engine. Successful cloaking results in higher rankings of inappropriate matches—for example, a search for a word unrelated to alcohol might bring up the sites of alcohol companies, which may lead the user to browse those sites. The logic here is that the more visitors a Web site receives, the more valuable it becomes. Some Web sites that employ cloaking have considerably different content from what the user intended to find and are often of pornographic nature. As such, some feel that the rules that govern marketing need to be revamped to ensure consistency among standards in relation to newly emerging marketing tactics.

SHOULD THE MARKETING OF ALCOHOL AND TOBACCO BE LIMITED?

Yes

Ninety percent of all smokers begin before age 21, and 60 percent of current smokers picked up the habit before age 14 (U.S. Department of Health and Human Services 1989). The U.S. Office on Smoking and Health states that every day "an estimated 3,900 young people under the age of 18 try their first cigarette" (National Center for Chronic Disease Prevention 2006). Clearly, children are the growth opportunity for the tobacco industry. If people do not start as children, they are significantly less likely ever to use the products. Cartoon characters were banned from tobacco advertising in 1991 after Camel Joe, the famous cartoon representative of the Camel cigarette brand, was shown to be more appealing to children than adults (National Center for Chronic Disease Prevention 2006). Marketing stipulations such as these are an attempt to prevent the marketing of tobacco to children, which the tobacco industry has long been accused of doing.

Possibly the most disturbing of such accusations is the charge that the marketing and advertising firms working for the tobacco industry employed psychologists to better understand children and how to more effectively target them. Oe of the revelations of the recent tobacco-related court cases was that tobacco companies asked retail outlets to place tobacco products in proximity to external doors in unlocked cabinets. They told the store owners that they would be reimbursed for stolen products. A few stolen cigarettes today can lead to hundreds of cartons of cigarettes sold 20, 30, and 40 years later. Health departments have been quick to encourage stores to discontinue this practice.

The alcohol industry has not seen the same level of concern that the advertising of alcoholic beverages has attracted. For instance, the introduction of spirits advertising on cable television was not opposed in 1996, even though, according to the "1986 Nielsen Report on Television," children watch an average of 28 hours of television per week. Ironically, permission to advertise alcohol on television was granted five years after the banishment of cartoon characters from cigarette advertisements.

Currently, 70 percent of the American population is 21 years of age or older. In accordance with industry codes for beer and distilled spirits, the placement of alcohol-related advertisements is permissible in nearly any piece of media that is not specifically geared toward young children (National Center for Chronic Disease Prevention 2006). The concern is that the messages of alcohol companies are reaching a vast number of youths through the television programs they watched and the magazines they read in their homes. Some argue that seeing an advertisement for alcohol or tobacco next to an advertisement for a prestigious or widely desirable product may still be harmful because of an unconscious association that may be drawn by the reader (The Maria Institute n.d.).

The Federal Trade Commission and the National Academies Press agree that there should be a reduction in the exposure of youth to alcohol advertising (National Center for Chronic Disease Prevention 2006). Research shows that limitations placed on marketing initiatives in the tobacco industry, in addition to federally funded tobacco education programs, have decreased the amount of tobacco usage. This suggests that similar actions regarding alcohol would decrease sales and consumption, as well as the occurrence of the third-leading cause of preventable death in alcohol-related fatalities in the United States (Centers for Disease Control and Prevention 2003). Though exposure of alcohol advertising to youths has been shown to have decreased 31 percent between 2001 and 2004, children are still more exposed, per capita, than adults ("Diosoned Out" 2006).

Organizations such as Mothers Against Drunk Driving and the Center on Alcohol Marketing and Youth feel that the alcohol industry should not be the only supplier of education concerning alcohol consumption. They advocate federal funding for alcohol education and suggest that the alcohol industry no longer be permitted to practice self-regulation, as was done with the tobacco industry. Self-regulation of alcohol marketing means that the industry itself helps set the standards of regulation in regards to advertising.

Opponents of alcohol self-regulation were recently disappointed when the viability of Australia's self-regulation policy, which mirrors that of the United States, was questioned in a series of allegations. Some marketing tactics that were examined were deemed to be sexually explicit or specifically geared toward children. One of the alcohol advertisements that was often singled out featured the phrase "Come out to play" written in ink on the palm of a woman's hand. It was argued that this advertisement was aimed at children.

The criticism did not bring about a substantial change in self-regulation policy, and this lack of action was felt by many alcohol activists to be a slap on the wrist for a major violation against alcohol advertising regulations and a reminder of the alcohol industry's power. The alcohol companies themselves claim no wrongdoing.

No

Alcohol and tobacco companies already face advertising restrictions that are unheard of in other industries. The International Code of Advertising, issued by the International Chamber of Commerce, asserts that "advertising should be legal, decent, honest, truthful, and prepared with a sense of social responsibility to the consumer and society and with proper respect for the rules of fair competition" (National Center for Chronic Disease Prevention 2006). Yet tobacco and alcohol must adhere to additional stipulations. Tobacco has been the target of a national campaign called "We Card" that requires cashiers to ask for identification from anyone who appears to be younger than 30 years old, and limitations are placed on point-of-purchase, or on-site, marketing initiatives for alcoholic products.

Many products in the marketplace have associated risks, but alcohol and tobacco are among the few that face marketing regulations because of the detrimental effects on their comsumers' health. For example, an estimated 17 percent of children and adolescents in America are overweight (Centers for Disease Control and Prevention 2006). Being overweight can lead to numerous health problems, such as type 2 diabetes, hypertension, stroke, heart attack, heart failure, gout, gallstones, and osteoporosis. However, there are no laws limiting fast-food commercials that target youths. A Burger King Whopper with a large fries and a Coke has 1,375 calories, yet there is no surgeon general's warning on fast-food wrappers (Healthy Weight Forum n.d.). Considering the marketing efforts, availability, and low cost of such restaurants, one would think they would require additional marketing rules, just like alcohol and tobacco. Yet even as obesity is being proclaimed a national epidemic, the post-meal cigarette is still getting all the attention.

The self-regulation policy of the alcohol industry receives much criticism, yet it has many positive attributes. For example, an extensive amount of marketing issues can be attended to without involving constitutional issues of government regulation (Federal Trade Commission 2003). The lack of costly deliberation in high courts concerning alcohol marketing issues saves considerable amounts of tax-payer dollars. A 1999 report to Congress noted that most companies in the alcohol industry complied with the codes of self-regulation and that the culture of some companies causes their practices to supersede industry standards (Federal Trade Commission 2003).

Sports Illustrated is a magazine devoted to sports that is enjoyed by both adolescents and adults. Figure M.1 shows the results of an examination of the alcohol and tobacco advertisements in the last issue for July and the first issue for August from 1986, 1996, and 2006. The following was found:

- In 1986 there were nine alcohol advertisements and five tobacco advertisements (Sports Illustrated July 28 and August 4, 1986).
- In 1996 there were five alcohol advertisements and three tobacco advertisements (Sports Illustrated July 22 and August 5, 1996).
- In 2006 there were four alcohol advertisements, one tobacco advertisement, and one advertisement for Nicorette gum, a nicotine replacement therapy designed to reduce nicotine cravings (Sports Illustrated July 31 and August 7, 2006).

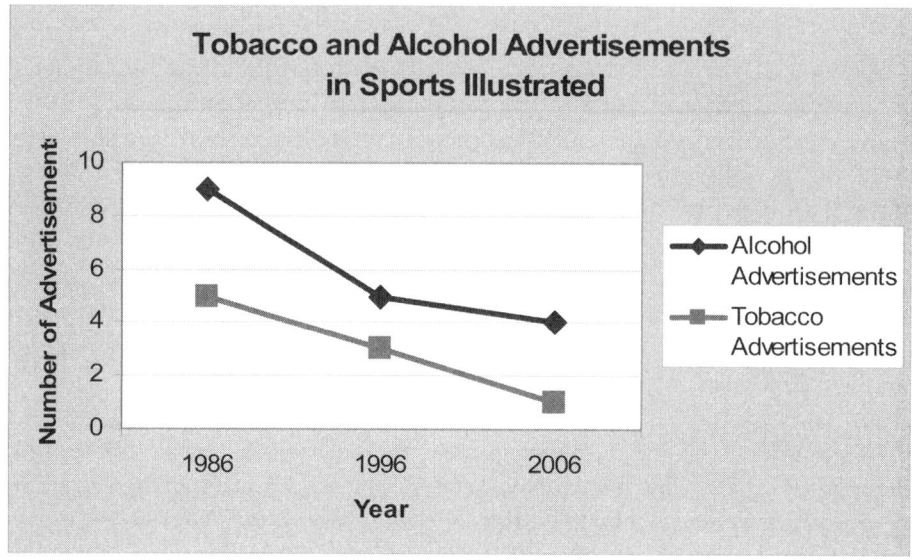

Figure M.1 Tobacco and Alcohol Advertisements in Sports Illustrated.

This example shows a decrease in the marketing of alcohol and tobacco over the 20-year period. Also note that the 2006 issues included an advertisement for Nicorette, a product used to assist in breaking the smoking addiction. This is just one illustration of the change that has already taken place. Additional changes are superfluous.

CONCLUSION

Ultimately the burden of counteracting the adverse impact of marketing alcohol and tobacco lies with each of us, as does the decision whether or not to use such substances. Most organizational and legislative movements do not seek to revoke the right of adults to use these legal substances. The provision of all the facts that will allow individuals to make their own informed decisions seems to be the desire of most groups, regardless of their stance on the product.

The marketing issues surrounding alcohol and tobacco focus on who is really making your decisions, you or marketers? Marketers are trained so well in the art of manipulation that most people fall victim to their messages without realizing it. The most prevalent question about the marketing of alcohol and tobacco is whether or not such advertising leads the average person (or child) to make poor lifestyle choices.

Should restrictions regarding the marketing of harmful products be implemented in order to save us from ourselves, and, if so, what should be deemed harmful? For example, is eating fast food on a regular basis harmful? The answer is probably dependent on the individual.

Marketing works. It convinces us to buy products that we do not need, cannot afford, and, in some cases, shouldn't use for a variety of reasons. The goal in regards to the marketing of potentially harmful products is to present both the good and bad features and then allow people to decide for themselves.

See also: Marketing to Children

References

The Center on Alcohol Marketing and Youth. (n.d.). *Fact Sheets*. Available at http://camy.org/factsheets/index.php?FactsheetID = 16. Accessed June 2006.

Centers for Disease Control and Prevention. 2003. "Point-of-Purchase Alcohol Marketing and Promotion by Store Type—United States, 2000 –2001." *Morbidity and Mortality Weekly Report* 52 (14): 310–13. Available at http://www.cdc.gov/mmwr/preview/mmwrhtml/mm5214a4.htm. Accessed May 2006.

Centers for Disease Control and Prevention, National Center for Health Statistics. *Prevelance of Overweight Among Children and Adolescents, United States, 2003–2004.* Available at http://www.cdc.gov/nchs/products/pubs/pubd/hestats/obese03_04/overwght_child_03.htm. Accessed June 2006.

Corporate Accountability International. (n.d.). Available at http://www.stopcorporateabuse-now.org. Accessed June 2006.

"Drowned Out: Alcohol Indusry 'Responsibility' Advertising on Television, 2001–2005." Available at www.camy.org. Accessed June 2006.

Educational Forum on Adolescent Health Youth Drinking Patterns and Alcohol Advertising Available at www.ama-assn.org. Accessed June 2006.

Essential Action, Global Partnerships for Tobacco Control. (n.d.). *Marketing Tobacco and the USA*. Available at http://www.essentialaction.org/tobacco/photos/usa.html. Accessed May 2006.

Federal Trade Commission. (2003, September). *Alcohol Marketing and Advertising: A Report to Congress*. Available at http://www.ftc.gov/os/2003/09/alcohol08report.pdf. Accessed June 2006.

Goldberg, Marvin E., and Hans Baumgartner. (n.d.). *Cross-Country Attraction as a Motivation for Product Consumption*. Available at http://marketing.byu.edu/htmlpages/ccrs/proceedings99/goldberg.htm. Accessed May 2006.

Healthy Weight Forum. (n.d.). *Calorie Counter: Burger King*. Available at http://www.healthyweightforum.org/eng/calorie-counter/burger_king_calories. Accessed July 2006.

Kuo Meichun, Henry Wechsler, Patty Greenberg, and Hang Lee. 2003. "The Marketing of Alcohol to College Students, The Role of Low Prices and Special Promotions." *American Journal of Preventive Medicine* 25 (3): 204–11.

The Marin Institute. (n.d.). *Alcohol Facts: Marketing to Youth*. Available at http://www.marininstitute.org/alcohol_industry/marketing_to_youth.htm. Accessed June 2006.

National Center for Chronic Disease Prevention and Health Promotion. Available at http://www.cdc.gov/tobacco/issue.htm. Accessed June 2006.

U.S. Department of Health and Human Services. 1989. *Reducing the Health Consequences of Smoking:25 Years of Progress. A Report of the Surgeon General.* Atlanta: Center for Chronic Disease Prevention and Health Promotion, Office on Smoking and Health.

Further Reading: Cronin, Anne M. 2004. *Advertising Myths*. London: Routledge; Tells, Gerard J. 2003. *Effective Advertising*. Thousand Oaks, CA: Sage; Pennock, Pamela E. 2007. *Advertising Sin and Sickness: The Politics of Alcohol and Tobacco Marketing, 1950–1990.* Dekalb, IL: Northern Illinois University Press.

Paul W. Schneider

MARKETING TO BABY BOOMERS

The television is tuned to the ABC evening news broadcast while I am preparing a summer evening's meal. As a 20-something young professional, I am not often home in time to catch the 6:30 p.m. broadcast. The program begins with the usual national news, including commentary from journalists across the globe. We come to a commercial break. First a common over-the-counter painkiller helps a 30-something sign language translator with the pain in her hands; next a car company flaunts its recent awards; finally we see a concerned woman who appears to be in her fifties. Her father has recently been diagnosed with Alzheimer's disease. His doctor has given her information about a new prescription drug that could keep him out of a nursing home. We return to the evening news. This evening's broadcast includes a segment on American baby boomers featuring an assisted living community for viewers with elderly parents. Residents are equipped with badges that can be monitored in real time by their relatives via a Web connection. "For these seniors it's not about a place to live until the end of their lives; it is about the freedom to live life until the end," closes the journalist, while shots of seniors exercising in their wheelchairs and watering the plants bring the segment to an end. In the two commercial breaks during the remainder of the show's broadcast, a theme becomes evident. Six of the next seven commercials center on boomers—four of those six pitch prescription drugs, the fifth describes the benefits of aspirin, and the sixth promotes a retirement investment option from a well-known financial company. What grabbed my attention in those 30 minutes has had the attention of marketers for over 30 years. The generation that took a nation by storm, leaving its mark on everything that it came in contact with—from the way we do business to how we raise a family, and even how we look at the future. This generation has kept marketers on their toes. They are called baby boomers.

Who exactly are the baby boomers? To put it simply, they are the 78 million people born in the United States between 1946 and 1964 directly following World War II. To put it in perspective, consider that the previous generation, those born between 1909 and 1945, totaled 68 million, and even more of a gap existed between the boomers and the generation that followed it (Generation X), which totaled a mere 49 million.

There are few individuals as familiar with this generation as Dan Yankelovich. In 1958, he formed Yankelovich Partners, a consumer research organization. The firm has maintained its position as an industry leader and has published an annual report on consumer behavior since 1971. It was with his company that the concept of generational marketing began, and it was the baby boomers who set the stage. This generation would prove that understanding the four P's (a well-known marketing concept covering product, price, position, and place) was no longer enough. Yankelovich's firm was willing to listen.

In his 1997 book, Yankelovich suggests, "Understanding generation values and motivations has become essential because each generation is driven by unique ideas about the lifestyle to which it aspire's" (Smith and Clurman 1997). He goes on to say that while knowing your customer remains the first rule of marketing, that's not the hard part. "The most difficult part is getting a handle on exactly what it is about your customer that is most important to know."

What is important to the boomers? Here is what we know today:

- Don't call them old. This generation has an obsession with aging, more specifically, the prevention of it.
- They have money. It is estimated that the boomers' annual spending power totals approximately $2.1 trillion.
- They are not homogenous. And they won't accept being marketed to as such. Today's boomers are socially outgoing, independent, physically active, financially secure, and family-focused people. However, they are these traits to varying degrees. The combination of these traits and the degree to which each trait applies to them creates a range of different consumers with different needs and desires.
- They refuse to be like their parents. Boomers are ready to experience every aspect of life with a youthful vitality all the way through retirement until death. To them, their parents' values of hard work, conformity, and social conservatism resulted in a stagnant and lonely life.
- They are marketing savvy. This is the first generation that grew up with television. Marketing media has surrounded them since childhood.
- They are outside of most advertisers' target group. The "golden group" for most advertisers is those consumers ages 18 to 49. It's no coincidence that the average age of advertising agents also falls in this range. Marketers tend to look at advertising from their own generation's perspective rather that of the one they are studying.

The September/October 2006 issue of AARP: The Magazine asked its readers who were born in 1946 (some of the 2.9 million Americans celebrating their 60th birthday this year), "If you could have anything you would want for your birthday, what would it be?" The answers given supported almost every statement made above, yet they were quite diverse in nature.

Those companies that have prepared for the baby boomer market have fine-tuned everything from convenience items to medication to real estate. Even AARP gave itself a makeover starting in 1998, when those four letters became its official name. Soon after, the organization began a five-year rebranding plan aimed at positioning AARP as the association of choice for the baby boomer generation of members. So, exactly how much has this generation affected marketers? So much in fact, that BusinessWeek's 100 top-growth companies of 2006 included several that attributed their success to the boomers (Weintraub 2006). Boomers have certainly proved themselves to be a worthy force; they have had an impact on almost every product market.

Boomers have experienced unbridled economic growth for the majority of their lives as consumers. Their upbringing was in an environment of surplus and excess. If you wanted it, it existed for you, and you should have it. It was frame of mind that Yankelovich says drove boomers to develop a sense of entitlement and expectation—the confidence that the prosperity would forever continue (Weintraub 2006).

WHAT WILL YOU BE WISHING FOR?

Title: Happy 60th Birthday!
From: AARPNews, Jul-25, 2006
To: ALL

In the related article from AARP The Magazine, editor Karen Reyes celebrates her 60th birthday—and those of many other boomer cohorts this year—with a peek at the results of a special AARP survey that sought boomers' birthday wishes and dreams. Tell us, what will you be wishing for when you blow out the candles on your 60th—birthday cake?

Title: Happy 60th Birthday!
From Anne Lucy, Jul-29, 2006

Well, it's my 60th too this years. . . . On my way to 60 I have reinvented myself. I am taking yoga classes to help with balance and strengthen back and groin muscles I never knew I had!

. . . It all started with an alumni reunion in 2004: I knew all the women would look great, and the men would be confrontationally competitive. It was that kind of school. So I dropped 30 lbs in 6 months[and] . . . went a little blonder, a little more oomph. Quit smoking finally and forever. You could say that the tipping point was the book of the same name. Learned to use an ATM/Debit card—must have been one of the last people for that. Tried Match.com, eHarmony and Silver Singles—and decided to go my own way. . . .

Bought a new scanner, went to the artsy movies by myself. Just decided that all work and no play made Jill a dull girl. . . .

As to my birthday wish: A visit to the facelift doc in Bangkok with the visit to a spa, as profiled in MORE Magazine so I don't take after the Brit side of the family with a vague resemblance to a bulldog. A singles column/group truly for the 60+ group—we're not dead yet. . . .

Still, I am determined to have some fun: A jazz concert, Carmina Burana, an antiques show, an Excel class, maybe Tai Chi, foreign films, a hiking club maybe, a theater group, a car rally.

It's still important to have some goals, not earth shattering/far reaching, but some goals for the mind and the body.

Title: Happy 60th Birthday!
From: Vev, Aug-02, 2006

Like many women at 60, I still feel young and hopefully and expectant of good things still to come. Still active, employed full-time and grateful for all my blessings, there is still one wish I would make for myself. I would dearly love to find my soulmate, someone to join me in getting the best from the years we have left; someone to share stories of the sixties and share awe at the marvelous things we have witnesses since 1946. What a birthday present!

Title: Happy 60th Birthday!
From: Gerrie, August 12, 2006

I turn 60 on October 29, 2006. My husband passed away two years ago. . . . It's been hard accenting the single life, but now I want to learn to enjoy being single. I hope to simplify my life by moving into a smaller home . . . [and] do[ing] volunteer work and having diner parties and cookouts with family and friends. Also I hope to travel with my sister. . . . Last spring we went to Spain and had a terrific time. I let my sister plan the trips we take and we always have a great time exploring many locals and dining on great food and wine. . . .

Turning 60 to me means getting better not old. Not old in the since of sitting in a rocking chair waiting for my end. I look forward to many happy and healthy years ahead of me.

Title: Happy 60th Birthday!
From: fwburch, Aug-12, 2006

Guess What!! I'm past the significant 60. I've experienced the experience so to speak. So I can tell you what it WILL be like. In one word, Glorious. I turned 75 this past month. I'm healthy but my friends are falling like flies. This is my advice: Enjoy your sixties. Sixties aren't too old, nor too young. Life glides along, floats like a cranes most of the time. . . .

Title: Happy 60th Birthday!
From: madmac, Aug-15, 2006

Yes, I turned 60 this year while my dad turned 87 and his father . . . turned 106. Just passed my 40th wedding anniversary and am looking forward to my 50th. My wish is to share it with my wife and have many more years with my 9 grandchildren. Retirement is great and golf keeps me fit walking about 5 miles a day. I play with 80 year olds so it's a game I can enjoy for a long time and keep fit doing it. It's fun beating the 30 somethings, just staying competitive keeps me sharp.

As marketers try to reach this very large segment of the population, instances of predatory marketing are on the rise. Controversy arises from two marketing trends—first, preying on the fears of the consumer, and secondly, old-fashioned scams.

Baby boomers have two distinctive traits as consumers. First, boomers—sometimes referred to as the sandwich generation—are in a unique position, as they often carry the double duty of caring for their parents as well as supporting their own children. We all recognize the home alert system that can bring help in the event that a senior falls and is unable to reach a phone. As consumers boomers serve a dual purpose: products appeal to them not only to potentially meet their own needs, but also the needs of their parents and their own kids. Marketers recognize this, and some exploit it.

The second lucrative trait that makes this generation attractive to marketers is the boomers' obsession with aging. They live during an era that celebrates youth. They do not want to do things the way their parents did; they do not feel their physical age. These ideals manifest themselves in the marketplace. Boomers fear vulnerability and helplessness. They refuse to accept aging and hold their independence very dear. This appeals to marketing companies because they are able to capitalize on these fears and exploit niche markets for their own self-maximization. What makes this work is the fact that boomers are hard wired by their formative years of prosperity. Regardless of whether a product is necessary, or they can even afford it, boomers will buy it. Consider the recent onslaught of advertisements for a little blue pill claiming to help men who are suffering from the effects of erectile dysfunction. Is this company benefiting from the boomers' obsession with youth? Is this a medication that they may not need?

Or consider credit card companies' countless advertisements concerning identity theft protection. Is there some type of extra protection these credit card companies offer that others do not? Is identity theft such a threat that consumers need additional protection? Or have these companies done their best to create products to fulfill legitimate market needs? Due diligence or not, these companies are making profits.

A second area of controversy concerning marketing to boomers is scams. A 2006 Pennsylvania State Department of Aging report stated that 18.3 percent of all elder abuse cases reported statewide for the 2004–2005 fiscal year were related to financial exploitation (Morgan-Besecker 2006). Today, scam artists are getting crafty, and their trickery comes from almost every angle. Recently, newsworthy scams have been reported in the areas of health care, real estate, lottery winnings, financial investment, jury duty, credit cards, home improvement, pay in advance, the sale of prayer rugs, and identity theft—just to name a few. There are differing opinions on boomers' susceptibility to such scams. Some think that the boomers' media-rich upbringing has given them the market sophistication they need to be aware of scams and protect themselves. Still others believe that older consumers are more vulnerable and need assistance in scam protection. In either case, people have an interest in protecting consumers, and this is a subject of great interest to many. On the "Money" section of AARP's Web site, the top article listed addresses identity theft and ways that it can be stopped. On the same site, a worksheet is provided to assist the user in avoiding becoming a victim of telephone scams. Even the SEC has tips for older investors to protect themselves. It is in the best interests of businesses to keep the boomers from being cheated. Working together with the boomers and providing helpful information empowers them to make knowledgeable decisions about how to spend their money. In return, these businesses can hope that the discretionary income that they have helped the boomers keep in their pockets will be passed along to their products and services.

Baby boomers offer marketers several unique opportunities. The first and most significant advantage is that there is money to be made. Their estimated annual spending power of $2.1 trillion is hard to ignore. Next, the boomers who have retired are likely to be watching television outside of primetime hours. This means that markets targeting boomers can take advantage of cheaper advertising costs. Additionally, by targeting boomers, marketers have a chance to capture many generations. This is a benefit brought about by the "sandwich" characteristic of boomers who are taking care of their parents and their own kids. Furthermore, boomers by nature are very active people. Retirement is no longer a termination, but a transition; this is something many financial companies have recognized and exploited. Even the onslaught of pharmaceutical advertisements has a added benefits. Not only are they generating profit for the parent companies, but they are also communicating options to keep boomers and their parents healthy and active. Finally, the fears of losing their independence and youthful vitality that consume the boomer are not going away. Marketers have a wide-open window of opportunity to benefit from this generation for many years to come.

Marketing to boomers does have its disadvantages. The greatest disadvantage is that boomers are not brand loyal. They want an experience when they buy a product. They are adventurous in the marketplace. They do not practice conformity. Additionally, they are not a homogenous market which can be a nightmare for some marketers. Even though there are 78 million boomers, there is no one way to reach them. They are also outside of what many marketers identify as their key demographic of consumers between the ages of 18 and 49. This could be a direct result of the fact that most advertising agents themselves fall into that age bracket. Those marketers who do make boomers their target demographic also are trying to overcome a lot of competition. Finding a niche, or a specific section of the boomers to target, can be costly. Finally, it may be disadvantageous to other consumers because marketing to boomers can negatively affect them in terms of costs. Advertising expenditures by firms can drive up the costs of the products that they offer. Even scams and fraud drive costs up.

In summary, the baby boomers have kept marketers on their toes for over 30 years. They are the first generation to have spent their entire lives surrounded by television. They experienced unbridled economic prosperity in their formative years as consumers, and they approach life with an enthusiasm that distinguishes them from their parents. They are individualists, and they value youthfulness, activity, and family to varying degrees. Their size and characteristics are lucrative to marketers. As William Novelli, executive director and CEO of AARP, has said, "People turning 50 today have half of their adult lives ahead of them. That's a lot of time to buy products, use services, eat in restaurants, go to movies, stay in hotels, work out, build new homes and renovate existing ones, rent cars, go back to school, and experience other new adventures" (Novelli 2002).

References

Morgan-Besecker, Terrie. 2006."Elderly a Frequent Target for Financial Exploitation: Attorney Says Pittston Case Is Different in that Alleged Abuser, Victim Not Related." *Knight Ridder Tribune Business News,* June 23.

Novelli, William D. 2002. "How Aging Boomers Will Impact American Business." Paper presented at the meeting of the Wisemen, the Harvard Club, New York. Available at http://www.aarp.org/about_aarp/aarp_leadership/on_issues/baby_boomers/how_aging_boomers_will_impact_american_business.html. Accessed June 22, 2006.

Smith, J. Walker, and Ann Clurman. 1997. *Rocking the Ages: The Yankelovich Report on Generational Marketing.* New York: HarperCollins.

Weintraub, Arlene. 2006. "Hot Growth Companies." *BusinessWeek,* May 25.

Further Reading: Dchtwald, Maddy. 2003. *Cycles: How We Will Live, Work, and Buy.* New York: Free Press; Morgan, Carol M., and Doran J. Levy. 1996. *Segmenting the Mature Market.* Ithaca, NY: American Demographics Books; Steinhorn, Leonard. 2006. *The Greater Generation: In Defense of the Baby Boom Legacy.* New York: St. Martin's Press.

Rebecca A. Smith

MARKETING TO CHILDREN

Purple ketchup, blue squeeze butter, and French fries that are flavored with cinnamon or chocolate—these were all products that were developed specifically to be marketed to children. But products marketed directly to children are nothing new. In the 1950s, the products were toys like Silly Putty, Monopoly, and Barbie. Today, those toys still exist, although the new Christmas wish list includes items like iPods and cell phones.

Even the use of celebrity characters as advertising spokespeople is not a recent phenomenon. Today we have SpongeBob SquarePants, Dora the Explorer, and Blue from Blues' Clues; in the 1950s there were Tony the Tiger, Cinderella, and Mickey Mouse.

Every one of us at one time or another has probably nagged a parent until a favorite toy was purchased. However, in today's society there is growing concern over the increased consumption and spending by children. Some critics believe that companies are too aggressive in targeting children. Marketers respond that they are only providing the product; it is the parent's job to monitor how much the child spends.

But are our children really different from children of past generations? Are marketers today taking unfair advantage of children, or is the growth in children's consumption just a trickle-down effect of a larger consumer culture?

CHILDREN AS CONSUMERS

Children are becoming consumers at an increasingly younger age. Just a few decades ago, children were considered to be consumers, or brand aware, by the age of 7; now it's more like 3. Not only are they becoming more brand aware at an earlier age, but they are also spending their own money and influencing family spending in a significant way. In the United States, children ages 4 to 12 spend over $50 billion directly and are estimated to influence over $500 billion each year in family purchases, from furniture to the family minivan (Dotson and Hyatt 2005). In fact, kids influence about 62 percent of minivan and SUV purchases, which may be why one prominent manufacturer ran a recent ad campaign with children inspecting the vehicle and approving its features (Nickelodeon 2005).

THE BUYING POWER OF KIDS

Every day in the United States:

$14,000,000 in adult purchases is influenced by children ages 4 to 12.

20 percent of all sales at McDonald's are Happy Meals.

$42,000,000 is spent on advertising directed at children.

172,800 Barbie dolls are sold around the world.

3,000 children ages eleven to eighteen start smoking.

565 elective plastic surgeries are performed on children under the age of 18.[13]

CHILDREN LEARN TO SPEND

Older children are turning to making their own money in order to support their spending habits. Over 55 percent of American high school seniors work more than three hours each day, compared to 27 percent of their foreign counterparts. While many parents may feel that teen employment instills a work ethic early in life, it has been shown that grades and participation in school activities suffer when teens work during the school year (Quart 2003). It is difficult to determine which comes first, however: the positive work ethic a child develops as a productive member of society, or the consuming culture that tells the teen he or she has to have the latest and coolest brand.

Similar logic has been used by parents to justify their children's use of debit and credit cards. Marketers promote the cards as ways to teach the children how to spend money. However, they may also encourage them to spend money they don't have. Children as young as 8 years old have been targeted by marketers with their own credit card. Hello Kitty, a popular children's brand, has licensed its brand name to MasterCard, which markets the service directly to the parents. The card can be used at stores like a regular credit card, or at an ATM to withdraw cash. Kids love it because it makes them look cooler than if they were just using cash (Bodnar 2005). Even the youngest consumers are taught to use plastic in their play. One toy company has a toddler's "first purse" play set that comes complete with a debit card and case. And the Hasbro company recently announced a British version of Monopoly that will use a debit card—no cash play money.

Marketers may tell parents that giving a child plastic helps them learn how to spend, but sociology experts tell parents that direct teaching episodes are a better way to teach children how to become good consumers. Some of the TV networks that target kids and teens have turned to a new old-fashioned way to offer these teaching episodes by promoting "co-viewing," where the child and the parent watch TV together. Marketers actually promote their products—brands and products whose purchase children significantly influence—to both the parent and the child at once. Cartoon Network now shows commercials for automobiles, vacation destinations, and sit-down restaurants alongside those for McDonald's, Cheerios, and Mattel. To better understand this interchange of information, Disney ABC Kids Networks Group commissioned a research study of children's influence on purchases in which mothers and children between the ages of 6 and 14 were interviewed about their purchasing behavior. Some of the results are shown in Table M.1 (Downey 2006).

Table M.1

Percent of mothers who said:	Percentage
Kids are influential on purchases made in discount stores.	92
Kids are influential in deciding on vacations.	38
Kids are influential in deciding on computers.	33
Kids are influential in deciding on cell phones.	32
Kids are influential in deciding on family car.	28
They have asked kids to go online and research purchases for themselves.	77
They have asked kids to go online and research family purchases.	25

CRITICISM OF CHILDREN'S MARKETING

The growth in the spending power and influence of children has prompted criticism of marketers, parents, and legislators. Juliet Schor, an expert in consumerism and family studies, is one of those critics. In Born to Buy she describes how children as consumers are changing: "Kids can recognize logos by eighteen months, and before reaching their second birthday, they're asking for products by brand name" (Schor 2004).

The increase in brand recognition by young children is at least partially due to the impact of television. In the 1950s families typically had one television per household, and the programs directed at children were mostly Saturday morning cartoons and a few daily morning shows. Today, there is a proliferation of children's programming, some educational, some not so, and most accompanied by commercials. The typical commercial during a children's program is 15 seconds, half the length of a commercial targeted at older consumers. Children's attention spans are shorter, requiring only a brief ad message. The commercials are also more colorful and action oriented.

In addition to the increased number of ads directed at the children's market, there has also been an increase in the number of hours that children spend watching television and a decrease in the amount of parental control over what is viewed. Schor says that approximately 25 percent of preschool-age children have a TV in their own bedroom, and they watch that TV for a little over two hours each day. It is estimated that American children watch a total of 40,000 television commercials annually.

One research study by doctors at Stanford University found that children's demands for specific toys and foods increased with the time they spent in front of the television. The third-grade children who were interviewed averaged 11 hours of TV time each week, and another 12 spent on video games or computers. The children were even able to identify where the ideas for their requests for toys or food items came from—whether it was from the television or their peers (Murphy 2006).

The quest for brand loyalty is moving to increasingly younger television audiences. Marketers once targeted 7- to 12-year-olds. However, companies realized that they need to attract consumers to their brands at an even earlier age. The new target segment is the preschooler—children ages two to five. In fact, the preschooler market has become increasingly competitive, and television has become a primary medium for advertising messages. "It is estimated that a successful preschool TV show generates more than $1 billion in retail sales in any given year across all related categories, including recorded media, in the U.S.," says Simon Waters, vice president of Disney Consumer Products, Disney's global franchise management branch (Facenda 2006).

SOCIAL ISSUES

While parents are accountable for the consumer behavior of their children, there is still the question of corporate and social responsibility. The number of advertisements for children's products embedded in television programs and the increase of product placements and movie tie-ins have made the parent's job increasingly more difficult. SpongeBob SquarePants has his own toothpaste and toothbrush product line; Dora the Explorer has a lunchbox, and every time a children's movie is released it is now paired with some type of premium at a fast-food restaurant.

But parents have had to contend with spokes-characters like SpongeBob SquarePants for decades (i.e., the Donald Duck lunch boxes of the 1950s). What is it about today's environment that makes it different from that of previous generations? Two factors that have an impact on the consumer behavior of children are time and money. Parents spend less time with their children today than they did in previous decades. Many children living in single-parent or two-income households obtain a large portion of their skills from their peers at day care or at school. And even schools, once a sanctuary from pervasive marketing tactics, have become the new frontier for commercialism. Faced with declining budgets, schools are turning to subsidies from corporations, which are allowed to come into the school with a program, albeit it educational, that is sponsored by their firm. These sponsorships are considered by some to be subtle forms of advertising.

Children are also more active in sports and other extracurricular activities than they were in previous decades. Many parents find themselves shuttling their children from one event to another after school, their children's calendars booked almost as tightly as those of their parents. Parents are also feeling pressure from longer working hours, which leave them leaving less time and energy to spend with their children. Add to that the fact that the square footage of the average home in the United States has increased significantly, which requires more upkeep and maintenance, and parents have more to do during their off-hours. We are working more and spending more, yet relaxing less. In fact, the U.S. worker spends more hours at work each week and has less vacation time than workers in any other industrialized nation in the world.

Marketers know that parents who spend less time with their children are willing to spend more *on* them, a relationship that has been substantiated by researchers. It is probably no surprise that children are moving from reasonably priced toys to more expensive electronic products at an ever-decreasing age. Younger children are requesting expensive products like Xboxes, cell phones, iPods, and laptops—the type of products that used to be reserved for teenagers and adults. Marketers say that the market for electronic products aimed at tweens grew 46 percent in 2004 (Kang 2005).

WHEN MARKETING TACTICS ARE QUESTIONABLE

Marketers can use subtle messages to get to young consumers that parents may find difficult to overrule. When the tobacco companies were required to remove from cigarette ads from media and even withdraw their sponsorship of the Winston Cup NASCAR race, they were forced to look for other ways to promote and increase the sales of their products. One such way is through the product itself. R. J. Reynolds, the company that first used Joe Camel in questionable advertising campaigns, is now marketing its products to younger smokers in a different way. R. J. Reynolds has introduced a new line of candy-flavored cigarettes. They come packaged in a shiny tin box and have names like Beach Breezer (watermelon), Bayou Blast (berry), and Kauai Kolada (pineapple and

---

SMOKIN' JOE

R. J. Reynolds, the second-largest cigarette manufacturer in the United States, brought its Joe Camel cartoon character over from France for use in the United States in 1988. Joe Camel was portrayed as suave and sophisticated in different social settings like pool halls and bars. Joe Camel instantly became a household name, as kids recognized the cool cartoon character and parents recognized its association with smoking.[12] The Journal of the American Medical Association published two reports on Joe Camel and his relationship to kids. The first report found that 91 percent of 6-year-olds recognized Joe Camel, similar to the percent of children who recognized Mickey Mouse (Cheap-Cigarettes com.

The Joe Camel character and complementary advertising campaigns like "Camel Cash" clearly appealed to adolescents. R. J. Reynolds had masterminded a campaign that was legal but was also directly targeting youths, who would become its lifelong consumers. Tobacco companies had a strong financial incentive to recruit children and young teens to smoke since a new smoker can be expected to generate a daily revenue stream for the ensuing 20 or more years (Glantz 1993). The second study published in the Journal of the American Medical Association found that four years after the introduction of the Joe Camel campaign in 1988, Camel cigarettes' share of the under-18 market had risen from 0.5 percent to 32.8 percent, worth more than $400 million per year in sales (Bynum 1998).

After critics, including the American Medical Association and President Bill Clinton, said that the Joe Camel character and advertising campaigns were a blatant example of cigarette marketing aimed at children, R. J. Reynolds agreed to cease using the Joe Camel character entirely in July of 1997 (Deutsch 1999).

coconut). The cigarettes are flavored with a tiny pellet that is slipped into the filter (Califano and Sullivan 2006). R. J. Reynolds was criticized for marketing their product to children, who are more likely to begin to smoke if the product tastes better. They maintained that they were only marketing the product to the adult who already was a smoker but wanted a change of flavor. It is common knowledge that most adult smokers begin prior to their eighteenth birthday. Currently, the average age at which young people begin to smoke is 11 (Mansfield, Thoms, and Nixon 2005).

The flavored cigarettes were once advertised heavily in magazines read by young boys and girls; however, pressure from federal legislators made them retract the ads. The cigarettes are still selling, and new flavors have been added.

WHEN MARKETING TACTICS ARE USED FOR GOOD

Not all marketing is necessarily evil, however, even when it is directed toward children. Marketing programs throughout the years have helped children to learn basic skills. Think of McGruff taking "a bite out of crime." Today one area of concern in the United States is the growing epidemic of childhood obesity. In response to this epidemic, several corporations have developed new marketing campaigns to offset the negative effects of their products. Both Coca-Cola and McDonald's launched fitness programs that are presented in schools and encourage healthy food choices and exercise. Fast-food restaurants like Wendy's and McDonald's have added selections like apple slices and mandarin oranges to their children's menus as an alternative to French fries. General Mills now produces its cereals with whole grains. Other companies are reducing the trans-fats in their cookies, crackers, and other baked goods. While the trend toward more healthful eating is at least for now being directed at children, it will be interesting to see how many of the products that are typically sold to this target audience will actually change.

THE MARKETER'S POSITION

The KidPower Conference meets annually to discuss the latest techniques, successes, and failures of marketing to children and teens. Marketers come to learn the latest on how to maximize the appeal of their brand—more specifically, to target certain age groups and create ads that appeal to different ethnic targets. Additionally, there are sessions on how to do social marketing. Social marketing is using traditional advertising and other marketing techniques to change a child's behavior on issues like refusing drugs, exercising more, and becoming more tolerant of others. While the social marketing conference sessions are definitely targeted at improving society, the overwhelming majority of the conference is on how to market products and brands to kids.

Marketers feel that they are just offering a product that is for sale and that ultimately consumer education needs to start at home. Some consumer advocates agree that parents have a significant portion of the responsibility. Jeff Dess, a prevention specialist for schools in Cobb County, Georgia, says, "We need to talk with our kids about these issues and consider changing our own habits" (McAulay 2006). Some ad agency executives are in agreement with Dess's statement and assert that it is parents and other relatives who are working in ad agencies and in corporations who are advertising the products, so they are also concerned about what the children in their lives are exposed to. Ultimately it is the parent's job to determine what food his or her children eat and what they buy (McAulay 2006).

See also: Marketing of Alcohol and Tobacco; Marketing to Women and Girls

References

Bodnar, Janet. 2005. "Give Kids Credit? Not So Fast." *Kiplinger's Personal Finance,* March. Available at www.kiplinger.com.

Bynum, Russ. 1998. "CDC: Joe Camel Years Saw Jump in Teen Smoking." *Marketing News* 32 (23): 16.

Calfee, John E. 2000. "The Historical Significance of Joe Camel." *Journal of Public Policy & Marketing* 19 (2): 168–82.

Califano, Joseph, and Louis Sullivan. 2006. "The Flavor of Marketing to Kids." *Washington Post,* June 29.

Cheap-Cigarettes.com. (n.d.). *Camel Cigarettes.* Available at www.cheap-cigarettes.com/camel-cigarettes.asp. Accessed June 14, 2006.

Deutsch, Robert D. 1999. "A Eulogy for Joe Camel." *Brandweek,* May 3, p. 29.

Dotson, Michael J., and Eva M. Hyatt. 2005. "Major Influence Factors in Children's Consumer Socialization." *Journal of Consumer Marketing* 22 (1): 35–42.

Downey, Kevin. 2006. "What Children Teach Their Parents." *Broadcasting & Cable,* March. Available at www.broadcastingcable.com.

Facenda, Vanessa. 2006. "Targeting Tots." *Retail Merchandiser,* June.

Glantz, Stanton A. 1993. "Removing the Incentive to Sell Kids Tobacco." *Journal of the American Medical Association* 269 (6): 793–94.

Kang, Stephanie. 2005. "Babes in iPodland; Chidren Go from $30 toys to $300 Electronic Gadgets at Alarmingly Early Ages." *Wall Street Journal,* November 28.

Mansfield, Phylis, Peg Thoms, and Charisse Nixon. 2005. "An Exploratory Analysis of the Relationship between Consumer Socialization Agents and Children's Consumption of Tobacco." *Journal of College Teaching and Learning.*

McAulay, Jean. 2006. "Buy-Buy, Childhood Pervasive Marketing Aimed at Kids Worries Parents and Experts." *Atlanta Journal-Constitution,* February 19.

Murphy, Dave. 2006. "Children's Demands for Toys and Food Increase with TV Time, Researchers Say." *San Francisco Chronicle,* April 5.

Quart, Alissa. 2003. *Branded: The Buying and Selling of Teenagers.* Cambridge, MA: Perseus.

Schor, Juliet. 2004. *Born to Buy.* New York: Scribner.

Further Reading: Carlsson-Paige, Nancy, and Diane Levin. 1998. *Before Push Comes to Shove: Building Conflict Resolution Skills with Children.* St. Paul, MN: Redleaf Press; McNeal, James U. 1999. *The Kids' Market: Myths and Realities.* Ithaca, NY: Paramount Market Publishing; Walsh, David. 1995. *Selling Out America's Children: How America Puts Profits Before Values and What Parents Can Do.* Minneapolis, MN: Fairview Press.

Phylis M. Mansfield

MARKETING TO WOMEN AND GIRLS

Cosmetics, age-defying cream, weight-loss products, and revealing clothing—these are all products almost exclusively marketed to women. The marketing of beauty products to women is not a new practice. Several decades ago products were marketed to women with the assumption that they were housewives or were looking for a husband. The product being marketed was designed to assist them in either of these endeavors. Betty Crocker made your life easier if you were struggling to do the laundry, feed the children, and put a decent dinner on the table by 5:30 P.M. when your husband came home from work. Other products addressed the woman who was either trying to stay youthful or trying to be attractive in order to get a husband. Even cigarette companies employed tactics targeted toward this group of women. During the mid-1920s it was unacceptable for women to smoke in public; however, the tobacco companies saw women as a large target segment of the population that was virtually untouched. The American Tobacco Company began a campaign for its brand, Lucky Strike, targeted at women with the slogan, "Reach for a Lucky Instead of a Sweet." It was the first cigarette campaign that featured a picture of a woman in the ad and that began to associate the idea of smoking with having a slim body (*Albert Lasker* 2006).

THE IMPACT OF SOCIAL CHANGE

In the 1970s and 1980s social convention began to change with regard to the role of women, possibly due to the rise in women's participation in the work force. Advertising changed and began portraying women as confident individuals who could effectively balance their personal and private endeavors. One such ad campaign was that for the perfume Enjoli, by Revlon. Debuting during the late 1970s, its jingle began, "I can bring home the bacon, fry it up in a pan, and make you never forget you're a man. Cause I'm a W-O-M-A-N" (Varnica 2003). In recent years advertising strategy has reflected the success of women as breadwinners, CEOs, and business owners. Many products that were traditionally marketed to men, or the household as a whole, are now marketed to women. Sellers of automobiles and homes and investment banking advertise to women specifically, acknowledging their status in the marketplace. However, despite the movement toward affirming women as self-confident and successful, there is also another trend that appears to discredit their accomplishments and demean them as sexual objects. Marketers present the idea that women must be physically perfect in order to be truly accomplished. This quest for the perfect body has made it now socially acceptable to openly discuss one's latest cosmetic surgery. The negative impact that this pressure from the media has on women may be filtering down to their daughters, even those of a very young age.

WHAT IS THE AD SELLING?

Those who have browsed the pages of Cosmopolitan, Vogue, or GQ have most likely perused page after page of half-naked females advertising various beauty products. In some, just a silk scarf is strategically placed across the woman, who

WHAT'S IN A SIZE?

For some time the clothing industry has not been held to any standardized measurements in the design and creation of women's apparel. It's not a secret between women that finding waist sizes that fit is as much of a gamble as picking a horse based on its name. One of the main reasons for the large discrepancy between designers' sizes is their original consumer segment. All clothing is designed with a specific consumer in mind. In women's fashion, consumers at higher-end stores usually prefer high fashion that typically conforms to the prescribed industry image for body size—which is tall and thin. For example, the women auditioning for the popular television program America's Next Top Model need to be at least five foot seven inches tall—and contestants who happen to be six feet tall need to weigh around 135 lbs.

This creates a bit of a discrepancy since in 2006 the average American woman weighed 142 pounds and was five feet four inches tall, therefore not the targets of high-end retailers. Moderate retailers offer the average American woman a wide range of sizes to fit the variations of women's bodies. Recently the sizes of high-end and moderately priced designers have been growing further apart. High-end retailers have stringent measurements based on industry standards while those at moderately priced retailers have more flexibility because they target a wider audience and their clothes are not necessarily connected with status. A trend of stores providing so-called vanity sizing has developed. For example, over the past 20 years the average size 8 dress has increased two inches in waist size. By increasing the actual waist measurement while keeping the pants size the same, corporations can be more profitable. Women want to feel like the models they see in advertisements and are more likely to shop at a store where size 6 pants fit like a size 10.

"Problem areas" women have listed when looking for clothing include:

Hips (35%)
Bust (32%)
Waist (32%)
Rear (23%)
Length (20%)
Thighs (17%)
Back (13%)

Note: The percentage besides each "problem area" indicated the percentage of women who found this area to be problematic.

is selling a product such as moisturizing lotion, shampoo, or even men's cologne. Airbrushing and other technologies provide the magazine glossies with perfect-looking models, devoid of any blemish or cellulite. There's no doubt that sexy photos of women can help sell products to men, but how do women and girls respond to this marketing technique? Clearly the photos used in many ads have no connection to the actual use or purpose of the product. For example, diet products and exercise machines should be used only for health-related reasons and should only be used under the direct supervision of a doctor. The ads rarely present this aspect of the product's use and instead focus on the physical attractiveness of the user.

There is a growing concern about the effect this type of advertisement has on women's and girls' self-images. One doesn't have to look far to see the impact that this type of body consciousness has on young women in the movie industry. Tabloids contain story after story discussing how a young star is looking extremely thin after losing weight, some to the point of anorexia. Even a 2006 television advertising campaign for a health insurance company stresses the physical appeal rather than the health-related benefits of physical exercise programs for young girls. HealthMark, a BlueCross BlueShield affiliate, has a young girl playing soccer while talking about how she used to hate to shop for clothes because she was "big." Now she doesn't mind shopping and loves her team picture because she doesn't look "big" anymore (Health Market 2006). In an effort to diminish the obesity epidemic in the United States among children, the ads promoting increased activity should be applauded. It is questionable, however, whether they should focus more on a child's appearance than the health benefits that result from exercise.

THE FINANCIAL SIDE OF COSMETIC SURGERY

Considering plastic surgery? Don't have the funds to get it? Cosmetic—or elective—plastic surgery is a booming business. Americans spent $9.4 billion on cosmetic procedures in 2006. Now a number of financial institutions now offering financing options for individuals who would like to go under the knife but don't have the funds. According to Dr. Helen Colen, "It's exploding; everyone is jumping in." Currently the cosmetic lending market is worth about $500 million, but experts expect it to be an $8 billion market within the next five years.

The application process is very simple. Patients can have doctors offices make a phone call to a lending institution and can be approved within an hour. However, not all is as rosy as it seems. Critics have suggested that people are borrowing money they don't have—to get a procedure they don't need. The majority of cosmetic procedures in 2005 were performed on individuals who earned between $30,000 and $60,000. People who opt for financial assistance are most likely those who don't have access to the funds.

Here are the average costs for some cosmetic procedures:

Botox injection: under $1,000
Liposuction: $5,000 to $10,000
Nose job: $8,000 to $10,000
Face lift: $8,000 to $12,000
Eyelid tuck: $5,000 to $8,000
Breast enhancement: $6,000 to $8,000

Source: Furman, Phyllis. 2006. "Financing Nips & Tucks." New York Daily News, May 24. Available at www.nydailynews.com.

A CAUSE FOR ALARM?

Advertisements reflect and shape cultural norms, selling values and concepts that are important to daily living. The trend of using objectified images of the female body in the media is not a new area of research, nor a new area of concern. Consumer activists and some researchers believe that marketers have gone too far in their advertising strategies to women by presenting an unattainable or unhealthy image. One voice of criticism back in 1963 was that of Betty Friedan, who railed against the "feminine mystique." Friedan reported that by the end of the 1950s, women who had once wanted careers were now making careers out of having babies. Manufacturers sold bras with false bosoms made of foam rubber for girls as young as 10. Thirty percent of women dyed their hair blonde and dieted so they could shrink to the size of the super-thin models. According to department stores at that time, women had become three to four sizes smaller than they had been in the late 1930s in order to fit into the clothes that were marketed to them (Friedan 2001). Freidan believed that women were being manipulated into becoming the ideal housewife—a Stepford-type housewife—and were feeling a great sense of emptiness in their lives.

The fashion industry may be turning a corner, however. In 2006, the organizers of Madrid's fashion week in Spain banned models who were deemed to be too skinny. After a model died during a fashion show in South America in August of 2006, the subject of extreme dieting became a topic of discussion, resulting in the ban. The typical runway model in the industry is reported to be five feet nine inches tall and weighs 110 pounds, with a BMI (height-to-weight ratio) of 16. She wears a size 2 or 4. The organizers of the Madrid show required the models to have a BMI above 18, which is closer to 5 feet 9 inches tall and a weight of 123. In contrast, the average American woman is five feet four inches tall, weighs 142 pounds, and wears a size 14 (Klonick 2006).

THE EMPHASIS ON BEAUTY

Critics of advertising suggest that the use of nonfunctional aspects in advertising creates an artificial need for many products that don't fulfill a basic physiological need. They believe that the use of perfectly airbrushed models and those with extremely thin bodies suggests to women that they should be just as attractive as the models. This quest for perfect beauty has contributed to the explosive growth of the plastic surgery industry in the United States, where women account for almost 90 percent of all surgeries. In 2005, surgeons performed over 10.2 million cosmetic procedures, up 11 percent from the previous year. The trend is very profitable, as Americans spent $15 billion on these cosmetic procedures (American Academy of Facial Plastic 2006). Cosmetic surgery is becoming so commonplace that plastic surgeons are seeing increased numbers of men giving it to their girlfriends and wives as Valentine's Day gifts. Dr. John W. Jacobs, a Manhattan psychiatrist, believes that the gift can be romantic if the recipient longs for it (Kerr 2006).

WHAT IS THE EFFECT ON YOUNG GIRLS?

This focus on the emotional and sexual enhancement that products or services offer only feeds into the problem of distorted body image and the low-self esteem of many young women. The fascination with the feminine ideal can develop early and can be seen as early as age six, according to a recently televised program of The Oprah Winfrey Show. "Children are becoming obsessed with external beauty at a much younger age," Winfrey says, "and the consequences are going to be shattering." One story was about a young toddler, only three years old, who was obsessed with her looks. The young girl demanded lipstick, makeup, and hairspray in order to look beautiful. When refused these items, she looks into the mirror, cries, and says that she doesn't look pretty. The young girl's mother fears what the youngster will be like in another 10 years and worries that her own insecurities have added to the problem (Oprah Winfrey Show 2006).

A study by the Dove Campaign for Real Beauty found that 57 percent of young girls are currently dieting, fasting, or smoking to lose weight. And almost two-thirds of teens ages 15 to 17 avoid activities because they feel badly about their looks (Etcoff et al. 2006). Girls at younger ages are also feeling the need to diet. One four-year-old girl studied skips breakfast and eats only fruit for lunch because it will make her skinny. While her mother thinks that other children's comments about her daughter being fat are to blame for the young girl's behavior, interviews uncovered other possible reasons. The girl's mother reported that she measures out exact portions of her own food at mealtimes and exercises at least once each day, sometimes twice (Oprah Winfrey Show 2006). Dr. Robin Smith, a psychiatrist, says that mothers unconsciously hand down their insecurities to their children. Parents, as well as peers and the media, shape children's self-image and must work to break the curse that is handed down from generation to generation (Etcoff et al. 2006).

During adolescence a girl's obsession with her body becomes even more apparent. This is accompanied by increased attention to what her peers think and increased attention to the media and advertising. Not only are younger girls and adolescents using cosmetics and dieting, but they are also turning to plastic surgery at younger ages than ever before. Like their mothers, they are in search of the perfect body, and it shows in the numbers of surgeries done on young girls under the age of 18. In 2003, the number of plastic surgeries on children under 18 was almost 75,000 in the United States, a 14 percent increase over those performed in 2000. According to the American Society of Plastic Surgeons, the number of breast augmentation surgeries done on girls under 18 tripled in just one year (Kreimer 2004).

This focus on the perfect and slimmest of bodies may also be the root of the increase in cigarette smoking by young females. The number of teenage girls who smoke and abuse prescription drugs has now surpassed that of boys. In 2005, more girls began smoking than did boys (Connolly 2006). One reason for this increase may be body image. While these young women haven't seen the advertisement for the Lucky Strike cigarettes that urged consumers to "Reach for a Lucky Instead of a Sweet," they are getting the message that cigarettes can help you stay slim. Girls as young as 9 years old have been reported to take up smoking in attempts to lose weight (Greene 1999).

ON THE OTHER HAND—THE BENEFITS OF ADVERTISING

In today's fast-paced society, marketers play an important role in educating consumers about new products and processes available to them. The average consumer has a plethora of choices available to him or her in an infinite marketplace. If each person had to personally evaluate each product, no one would ever be able to make an informed or timely decision concerning the functionality of a product for a certain purpose.

This is particularly apparent in the cosmetic and beauty industry. Technology is constantly evolving so that new products providing better health rewards without potentially damaging consequences can be created. The marketing of these types of products allows consumers to quickly evaluate the products in a company's product line. This type of marketing strategy only shows the consumer what is available in the marketplace. It does not make consumers purchase the product or buy into the idea of the marketing message; it is purely informative. Marketers assert that they cannot make someone buy a product; they can only influence people.

The companies that market beauty and fashion products suggest that the healthy-looking models in beauty advertisements provide good role models for females to aspire to. The products they are advertising provide women the means to achieve whatever level of beauty and healthiness they desire. Therefore, they say, marketers are actually providing a public service to today's busy woman.

The dynamic nature of marketing allows the consumer to make the decision to listen to the message or to move on. Advertisements on television and in magazines clearly give the consumer the right to change the channel or flip the page if he or she does not approve of the message. Ultimately it is the consumer who chooses to listen to or ignore the message that is presented.

References

Albert Lasker Promoted Lucky Strike. Available at www.wclynx.com/burntofferings/adslasker.html. Accessed September 18, 2006.

American Academy of Facial Plastic and Reconstructive Surgery. Available at http://aafprs.org. Accessed June 12, 2006.

Connolly, Ceci. 2006. "Teen Girls Using Pills, Smoking More Than Boys." *Washington Post,* February 9.

Etcoff, Nancy, Susie Orbach, Jennifer Scott, and Heidi D'Agostino. 2006. *The Real Truth About Beauty.* Available at http://www.campaignforrealbeauty.com. Accessed September 28, 2006.

Friedan, Betty. [1964]. 2001. *The Feminine Mystique.* New York: Norton.

Greene, Alan. 1999. "Preteens Start Smoking to Control Weight." *Pediatrics,* (October): 918–24.

HealthMark advertisement. 2006. Broadcast on NBC, May–September.

Kerr, Kathleen. 2006. "Plastic Surgery Becomes Hot New Gift for Valentines." *Knight Ridder Tribune Business News,* p. 1.

Klonick, Kate. 2006. "New Message to Models: Eat!" *ABC News Internet Ventures,* September 15. Available at http://abcnews.go.com/Entertainment/print?id=2450069. Accessed June 17, 2006.

Kreimer, Susan. 2004. "Teens Getting Breast Implants for Graduation." *Women's eNews.* Available at http://www.womensenews.org. Accessed August 28, 2006.

The Oprah Winfrey Show. 2006. *Healing Mothers, Healing Daughters,* April 28.

Vranica, Suzanne. 2003. "Marketing and Media Advertising: Stereotypes of Women Persist in Ads; Bikinis Still Sell the Suds, as Masculine Views Reign; Agency Gender Gap Blamed." *Wall Street Journal,* October 17.

Further Reading: Grogan, Sarah. 2007. *Body Image.* New York: Routledge Press; Kilbourne, Jean. 1999. *Deadly Persuasion: Why Women and Girls Must Fight the Addictive Power of Advertising.* New York: Free Press; Kilbourne, Jean. 2000. *Can't Buy My Love: How Advertising Changes the Way We Think and Feel.* New York: Simon & Schuster; Wykes, Maggie, and Barry Gunter. 2005. *The Media and Body Image.* Thousand Oaks, CA: Sage.

Phylis M. Mansfield and John D. Crane

MEDIA COVERAGE OF BUSINESS

Many Americans today are convinced that chemical companies regularly dump their toxic wastes into streams and rivers with impunity, that greedy firms deliberately sell unsafe and defective products to unsuspecting customers, that defense contractors gouge taxpayers by selling the government $400 hammers and $600 toilet seats, and that Big Oil manipulates the market to gain obscene profits for themselves. Many intelligent individuals are led to believe by what gets reported in the press that business leaders act in selfish, greedy ways to the detriment of their employees, their customers, and society at large. In addition, there are many watchdog organizations and politicians, each pursuing separate social or political agendas, who are tireless in their efforts to oppose businesses at every turn. But there are also others who believe that free enterprise and those who are leading it have achieved a solid record of creating opportunity and abundance. These people are quick to point out all the good things that business leaders have accomplished. And they believe that the anti-business sentiments held by others are an outgrowth of slanted and biased reporting. To be sure, there are examples aplenty that one can hold up to buttress either claim—that business leaders act reprehensibly and irresponsibly, and that business leaders are the victims of inaccurate reporting by some in the media who are biased and who are further encouraged and applauded by a cynical anti-business minority. The question is, Are those who are commonly regarded as the bad boys of business really villains or are they the victims of sloppy, inaccurate, or biased reporting?

DOES BUSINESS PRODUCE THE WORST SORTS OF SCOUNDRELS?

Arguing that the words that come out of a person's mouth are an accurate reflection of what's inside that person, critics are quick to draw attention to the most shocking and outrageous utterances of well-known business leaders. It is asserted that their own words reveal business leaders to be corrupt and uncaring and that they are willing to do anything to survive and profit. A good illustration of one such statement is that of investment banker Ivan Boesky—who was later convicted of illegal insider trading—as he addressed the graduating class of the business school at the University of California at Berkeley in 1986. In his commencement speech, Boesky proclaimed "Greed is all right. Greed is healthy. . . . You can be greedy and still feel good about yourself." The graduating class of MBAs cheered and roared with laughter to show their approval (Horton 1987). Later this statement found its way into the motion picture Wall Street, staring Michael Douglas. Who can doubt that this had an impact on the perceptions of the average moviegoer as to what those on Wall Street are really like?

Other often-repeated statements made by business giants that critics point to are often inaccurate portrayals of reality. Among these is the statement of John D. Rockefeller, who said at the University of Chicago, "God gave me my money." Taken out of context, his remark created an image of this philanthropist as sanctimonious and arrogant. Actually, Rockefeller uttered this remark in complete humility. True to his strict Baptist upbringing, he devoutly believed that Providence had made him a trustee for his hundreds of millions of dollars, which were not to be kept but disbursed widely to do the utmost good. What he actually said was this: "God gave me my money. I believe the power to make money is a gift from God to be developed and used to the best of our ability for the good of mankind. Having been endowed with the gift I possess, I believe it is my duty to make money and still more money and to use the money I make for the good of my fellow man according to the dictates of my conscience" (Diamond 1995).

The remark "History is bunk," attributed to Henry Ford, paints a picture of him as an anti-intellectual, an ignoramus single-mindedly consumed by the pursuit of wealth and indifferent to the world and its problems. However, Ford's remark was this: "History as sometimes written is mostly bunk. But history that you can see is of great value." While the automobile stirred Henry Ford's mind, it was his love of the past that consumed him. He accumulated an incredible amount of Americana, which he assembled into one of the world's great historical restorations, his Greenfield Village (Diamond 1995).

During his confirmation hearings, a former president of General Motors, Charles E. Wilson, was being grilled by U.S. senators on the question of whether he, as a businessman, could be loyal to the interests of the United States if he were confirmed as secretary of defense. Practically everyone is familiar with the infamous line "What's good for General Motors is good for the country," the implication being that Wilson believed the public interest ought to be subordinate to the interests of giant corporations. This was a deliberate misquotation. The transcripts made that day reveal what Wilson really said: "For years I thought that what was good for our country was good for General Motors, and vice versa" ("Businessmen Go to Washington" 1953). The essential idea he wanted to convey was that a strong and healthy United States was good for business and that putting the interests of the country first benefits us all, including the nation's corporations. However, what stuck was the sentiment of the "and vice versa." It was recast into the misquotation to serve as fodder for those who had an axe to grind with business.

Perhaps the supreme example of an anti-public statement was that uttered by William Henry Vanderbilt, son of "the Commodore," Cornelius Vanderbilt. On October 8, 1882, while riding in his private car, William Henry Vanderbilt was explaining to reporters that his New York Central Railroad could not make a profit on a $15 fare between New York and Chicago, but that it was maintaining the route because of a fare war it was battling with its rival, the Pennsylvania Railroad. Clarence Dresser, a freelance writer, pressed Vanderbilt with a baiting question: "Don't you run the train for the public benefit?" In a momentary outburst, Vanderbilt shot back, "The public be damned! I'm working for my stockholders. If the public wants the train why don't they pay for it?" (Holbrook 1953). This remark provided critics of capitalism with what they wanted: proof that business moguls of the day were greedy and anti-public. While it would be accurate to say that William Henry Vanderbilt and his father, Cornelius, were neither always high minded or altruistic, it would be equally untrue to say that their business actions did not benefit the public. Cornelius Vanderbilt, formed the base of his fortune on a fleet of steamships operating on the Hudson River by cutting fares and offering unheard-of luxury to passengers, thereby driving competitors out of business. Later, these competitors paid him to leave the business. "Serve the public, and ye make money" were the Commodore's words (Smith 1927).

SORTING DISTORTIONS FROM REALITIES

Most thoughtful people agree that the news media does society a great service when it exposes incidences of illegal, hurtful, and downright dishonest actions in business. Indeed, many would argue that the light of day is one of the best antidotes to unwanted behavior. Most people would not do the things they might do in private and under the cover of darkness if others were looking. It would be naive and unfair, however, to conclude that the despicable actions reported in the press represent the normal, everyday, and acceptable actions of everyone in business. The point is that what makes these stories of unethical and illegal actions news is the simple fact that they are unusual events and, therefore, worthy of reporting. At the same time, one would be wise to question the abilities and motives of those who do the reporting. Are the reports found in the press always accurate, and are they reported in an unbiased way? When stories are inaccurate and deliberately distorted against business, as some stories have been shown to be, innocent individuals are unfairly harmed, and the public's confidence in decent businesspeople, who constitute the majority, is diminished.

Greed

Clearly, there is no shortage of examples of greedy, self-serving individuals running some of America's best-known companies. Dennis Kozlowski, former CEO of Tyco, is a prime example. During "his ten-year rein of greed," as Fortune magazine put it, Kozlowski "spared no expense in using company funds to adorn his corporate offices and his numerous personal residences" (Warner 2003). There was, among other extravagances, the $20 million birthday party he gave for his wife (he reportedly charged $10 million of this to his company because many of the guests were Tyco employees), a $6,000 shower curtain, and $15,000 apiece for umbrella stands for his home. Charged with pilfering $400 million from company coffers, Kozlowski and his CFO, Mark Swartz, left the conglomerate's reputation in tatters, and its financial condition precarious.

Another area in which the press has gone after greed and excess is in its reports of the huge compensation packages for CEOs—some of these run into the hundreds of millions of dollars, and many more in the tens of millions. Even as their companies' share prices have fallen, a fair number of CEOs have accepted pay packages in the tens of millions. In 2002, for example, when the total return of the S&P 500 fell by 22.1 percent, the median pay for CEOs rose 14 percent (Useem 2003).

In one regard the news media gets it right when they report the compensation packages of senior businesspeople—at least the dollar amounts are reported correctly. While these news stories steer clear of whether these pay packages are justified, the implication in the fact that they are being reported is that they are not. That's an opinion at which people are free to arrive themselves. It is far from true to say that all people in business and those closely connected with business feel that compensation for CEOs in the hundreds of millions of dollars is a good idea. Indeed, the late Peter F. Drucker—the philosopher, consultant, and author—was highly critical of these high levels of executive compensation. He argued that CEO pay had rocketed out of control and urged boards to hold CEO pay to no more than 20 times that of what the rank and file made (Byrne 2005).

Where the press gets it wrong in reporting compensation packages is that most of the hundreds of millions earned are not cash payments. The CEO pay is made up of cash payments (salary, an expense deducted from revenues) and the value of stock options (the increased value of shares of stock the executive has the option of purchasing at a set value). The average person reads a headline stating, "CEO Jones Earns $350 Million," and is led to believe that CEO Jones received $350 million in cash (salary) that year. This impression might make the average person inclined to think that were CEO Jones not paid so extravagantly, then customers, like the average person, would be able to purchase products sold by Jones's firm at prices substantially lower than what they are. This simply isn't so. This is because Jones's huge pay package is not entirely a charge against yearly company earnings.

Deception and Fraud

The names of Ken Lay and Jeff Skilling, who were recently found guilty of securities and bank fraud, will forever be linked with the largest business failure in history: the collapse of Enron, which rendered its stock worthless, resulting in a loss of over $60 billion in market value for investors, not to mention the loss of $2.5 billion of employee pensions. The exact actions of those at the highest levels at Enron may never be fully known or understood. The methods they employed to obscure the truth about their firm's profitability, its flows of cash, and the levels of risk to which they exposed their firm were complicated, convoluted, and nearly impossible to follow. Their legality or illegality can be debated by the experts. Yet in the end, a jury judged these men guilty. The 12 who sat in the jury box saw enough of what Lay and Skilling did to conclude that their actions were misleading and deserving of punishment. What seemed to prove most damaging to these defendants was the fact that while they encouraged the public and their employees to buy Enron stock, they and other top executives sold tens of millions of dollars of their stock—much of it secretly—and in the end, employees and outside investors were left with nothing (McClean and Elkind 2006).

In 2005, a jury found Bernard J. Ebbers, former CEO of WorldCom, guilty of conspiracy, securities fraud, and false regulatory filings. This was a case of massive accounting fraud that led to the downfall of the nation's second-largest telecommunications firm and cost investors billions (Masters 2005). The court found that Ebbers was responsible for filings that boosted WorldCom's reported earnings and hid the fact that its business had been deteriorating for nearly two years.

Disposal of Toxic Wastes

The manner in which the news media handled the Love Canal incident provides an illustration of how inaccurate reports and the repeating of misinformation can create a picture of guilt in the mind of the public. The commonly told story is that the Hooker Chemicals and Plastics Corporation irresponsibly dumped toxic waste, which later seeped into the ground and basements of neighborhood homes, thereby endangering humans and leading to a flood of government and private lawsuits. Hooker did dispose of toxic wastes between 1942 and 1952 at an approved 15-acre site located in an old canal. The dump site was excellent; it was large and the walls were lined with thick impermeable clay. In 1941, Hooker began studies of the suitability of using the site and by the next year, after finding that the site was suitable for the disposal of toxic wastes, completed the legal transactions to commence dumping. Ultimately approximately 21,800 tons of the company's wastes went into the dump, as did other wastes disposed there (according to New York State officials and federal agencies) by the army and the city of Niagara Falls. When the site was nearly full, it was capped with clay. The design, which was meant to keep water out and prevent harmful seepage, was working; grass and weeds grew on the surface. Even under current Environmental Protection Agency standards the design would be considered state of the art today. The only thing that would be different according to current standards would be that the wells around the perimeter would need to be monitored to find out if some water was getting inside. On April 28, 1953, Hooker donated the land to the city of Niagara Falls for one dollar, with the understanding that if the company did not willingly deed the land over to the Niagara Falls Board of Education, the property would be seized under eminent domain for the construction of a school. The postwar baby boom produced a need for more schools and every piece of real estate of a suitable size was being eyed for the construction of new school buildings.

The deed of transfer contains very clear specific language clarifying that the land had been used as a dumpsite for the disposal of certain chemicals. Company officials warned, in no uncertain terms, that the site should never be disturbed. The school board, which took possession of the land, had no intention of using the land for a playground, as Hooker recommended, but instead planned to use the site to build a school. When the board announced its intention to do this, Hooker officials went to the city and stated publicly why it should not be done. Despite Hooker's warnings and the misgivings voiced publicly by the construction firm that did the work, the school board ordered construction to begin, which disturbed the integrity of the dump site. In August 1953, the board voted unanimously to remove 4,000 cubic yards of "fill from the Love Canal to complete the top grading" at another school on 93rd Street. In January 1954, the board approved the removal of 3,000 more cubic yards. On the same day, the school's architect wrote to the chairman of the building committee and reported that the general contractor had hit a soft spot in the ground that gave off a strong chemical odor. This should not have been a surprise to the board, as some of its members had been present when test holes were bored into the clay cover over the site to check for chemical leakage. Construction continued; roads were built across the property. Next they dug a drainage system connecting groundwater to the storm sewer system, which dumped into the Niagara River. These actions disturbed the cap that Hooker had put over the site to keep water out (Zuesse 1981).

Some 20 years later the drainage of toxic wastes poisoned the water and the land surrounding the site. The same newspaper that had carried stories of Hooker's warnings not to disturb the site and had accurately reported the provisions in the deed of transfer attacked Hooker Chemical. The same reporter from the local paper who had covered the 1953 hearings chose not to report the facts concerning Hooker's stance (Zuesse 1981). Residents of the area maintained that Hooker used fly ash, not clay, to cap the fill. Although the presence of fly ash in the Niagara Falls area is documented and it was used to fill in the canal, there is no evidence to show that Hooker used fly ash to cap the dump site. Notes from maps made at the time support Hooker's contention that it laid four feet of clay over the fill. A private engineering firm hired by the city in 1957 concluded that Hooker's practices could not be faulted (Zuesse 1981).

Overcharging Taxpayers

In the case of the government purchase of a $435 hammer, reporters again either failed to get their facts straight or intentionally wrote things that were not true for reasons only they know. When the details finally came out about the "overpriced" hammer, it turned out that the charge for the hammer was really $22. But there was another charge of $413 on the same invoice for engineering services unrelated to the hammer, a detail that never showed up in newspapers (Anderson 1987).

The purchase of $7,500 coffee pots by the air force for its C-5 aircrafts built by Lockheed deserves an explanation beyond the naive conclusion that the contractor greedily gouged American taxpayers. In the early 1970s Lockheed won a contract from the air force to build 80 C-5 aircrafts. In reviewing the specifications, Lockheed told the air force that they believed the cost of design specifications for the coffee-maker units were unnecessarily high, that what was used on commercial airlines would be a smarter choice. These units are big and have shock-resistant features and lock mechanisms to prevent the actual coffee pots (the metal pots you see flight attendants use to serve passengers, which cost around $10) from flying out in the event of a jolt. These could be obtained from a subcontractor who made them for commercial aircrafts at a price between $1,200 and $1,500. But the air force insisted that they wanted exactly what their specifications called for. A few years later, the air force placed an order for another 50 C-5s. Again, Lockheed suggested using commercial airline coffee-maker units as a way of cutting costs. In the meantime, when the air force wanted to reorder small quantities (one to three units at a time) of these coffee-maker units with more detailed specifications, the air force received quotations from the subcontractor at $7,500 apiece, a price that reflected the true cost of manufacturing them in small batches (Anderson 1987).

The toilet seats Lockheed made for the P-3 aircraft were not toilet seats at all. They are specially molded plastic shrouds that encompass what is referred to as a honey bucket. A common toilet seat, which Lockheed bought for around $10, fits on top. However, the entire unit—the specially molded shroud made to fit the airplane and the cover and the $10 seat itself—was priced around $600 (Anderson 1987).

Disregard for Human Life

The Ford Pinto stands out as the classic example of deliberate neglect of public safety. In the late 1960s, Ford saw the need to build and market a subcompact to compete with the popular Volkswagen. Lee Iacoccoa set clear and unambiguous specifications: the car would weigh no more than 2,000 pounds and cost no more than $2,000, and it would be in American dealer showrooms with the 1971 models. Normally, it took Ford 43 months to take a car from concept to production. Iacocca's schedule for the Pinto shrank this time line to just 25 months.

In pre-production crash tests, Ford engineers discovered that rear-end collisions ruptured the Pinto's fuel system. In an article on the Pinto for Mother Jones, Mark Dowie claimed to have secured internal Ford documents that showed their engineers crash tested the Pinto more than 40 times and that every test made at over 25 mph without special structural alterations to the car resulted in a ruptured fuel tank. A car driving at 30 mph that rear-ended a stopped Pinto would buckle like an accordion, right up to the backseat. The tube leading to the gas tank would be ripped away, and gas would spill out onto the road and the car. At 40 mph, chances were that the doors would jam and the person or people inside would be trapped, unable to escape. Did they bring this bit of bad news to the attention of Iacocca? "Hell no," one engineer was reported to have answered. "That person would have been fired." Besides, by then assembly-line machinery was already tooled and it would require several more months to retool, resulting in delays and extra costs that would price the Pinto above the targeted amount. Engineers tried several fixes to prevent fire. The cheapest was the placement of a rubber bladder inside the tank that would have cost $5.08 for purchase and installation. Tests done with the bladder showed that the tank still ruptured, but no fuel leaked. In the end, cost concerns and weight constraints trumped safety concerns and the bladder, as well as two other less costly fixes that worked for rear-end crashes below 31 mph were scuttled. None of these protective measures was used in the mass-produced Pinto. It wasn't until 1977 that Ford, after arguing and lobbying against the imposition of safety standards, was forced to change the fire-prone Pinto gas tank (Dowie 1977).

Ford's consideration of the problem came down to simple cost-benefit analysis. They figured it would cost them $11 per car or truck to make the safety changes. With sales of 11 million cars and 1.5 million light trucks, this would total $137 million. They weighed this against what it would cost them to pay victims of Pinto-related deaths and injuries. According to Ford's estimates, unsafe tanks would result in 180 burn deaths, 180 burn injuries, and 2,100 burned vehicles each year. They estimated they would have to pay $200,000 per death, $67,000 per injury, and $700 per vehicle. The total cost of not fixing the gas tank problem would amount to 180 × $200,000 + 180 × $67,000 + 2,100 × $700 = $49.53 million. Ford's conclusion was that it would be most profitable not to fix the gas tank problem.

In 1972 a woman drove her new pinto onto a Minneapolis highway. Riding with her was a 13-year-old boy. Suddenly her car stalled as she tried to merge into a stream of traffic. Another car rear-ended hers at 28 mph, rupturing its gas tank. Vapors mixed with the air inside the passenger compartment. A spark ignited the mixture and the car bust into flames. The woman died in agony several hours later in the hospital. The boy was severely scarred. By conservative estimates, Pinto crashes caused 500 burn deaths between 1971 and 1977 (which is in line with Ford's estimates) and this figure could be as high as 900. But what Ford did not count on was the huge settlements juries awarded victims of fires caused by rear-end collisions. In February 1978, for example, a California jury awarded $128 million in a lawsuit stemming from an accident. The damages awarded in this one lawsuit cost three times what Ford executives and engineers had estimated their final cost would be.

Obscene Profits

Whenever gasoline prices in the United States spike (as they did in the late 1970s and again recently in 2005 and 2006), critics are quick to charge Big Oil with price gouging. Politicians and commentators proclaim that energy giants are reaping obscene profits. Part of their argument hinges on the belief that we need gasoline, and we must have it. Presumably, these critics believe that whatever the public needs ought to be sold at prices that do not allow a profit level for those companies providing the product or that permits a profit level that is substantially less than what they have might have achieved. The list below shows the profit margins earned by well-known companies in 2005 ("Fortune 500" 2006).

Anheuser-Busch	12.2%
Chevron	7.1%
Duke Energy	10.8%
ExxonMobil	9.7%
Harley-Davidson	16.9%
Kraft Foods	7.7%
New York Times	7.7%
Verizon	9.8%

CONCLUSION

Are there bad guys in the world of American business? The answer is obvious—yes. And it is also true that those who do get caught make the news. But the interesting thing to note is that these miscreants are newsworthy precisely because their misdeeds are out of the ordinary. Those in business who are honest and decent go about their work lives day after day unnoticed. Occasionally, however, special interest groups catch the attention of reporters, who are constantly on the lookout for controversy. That's how people in the media define what constitutes news—it is controversy. Controversy elicits interest. It sells newspapers and boosts ratings. And there are plenty of special interest groups that have an axe to grind with business and those who run large publicly held corporations. As we've seen from the examples above, some of the stories about bad business behaviors have been reported accurately, while others have not. In an age of 10-second sound bites and vicious politics, citizens would be wise to be suspicious of what they read and hear. A wise person is one who is extremely skeptical of what he or she reads and hears and who investigates the facts thoroughly before arriving at conclusions.

See also: Price Gouging

References

Anderson, Roy. 1987. Personal communication.

"Businessmen Go to Washington: It Costs Them Plenty to Serve in Government." 1953. *U.S. News & World Report,* February 6, p. 86.

Byrne, John A. 2005. "The Man Who Invented Management." *Business Week,* November 28, pp. 96–100, 102, 104, 106.

Diamond, Sigmund. 1995. *The Reputation of the American Businessman.* Cambridge, MA: Harvard University Press..

Dowie, Mark. 1977. "Pinto Madness." *Mother Jones,* September/October. Available at www.motherjones.com.

"Fortune 500." *Fortune,* April 17, 2006. Available at www.money.cnn.com/magazines/fortune.

Holbrook, Stewart H. 1953. *The Age of the Moguls.* New York: Doubleday.

Horton, Thomas R. 1987. "Villainy and Heroism in the Executive Suite." *Management Review,* September, p. 5.

Masters, Brooke A. 2005. "WorldCom's Ebbers Convicted." *Washington Post,* March 16.

McClean, Bethany, and Peter Elkind. 2006. "The Guiltiest Guys in the Room." *Fortune,* June 12, pp. 26–28.

Smith, Arthur D. Howden. 1927. *Commodore Vanderbilt: An Epic of American Achievement,* New York: McBride.

Useem, Jerry. 2003. "Have They No Shame?" *Fortune,* April 28, pp. 56–60, 64.

Warner, Melanie. 2003. "Exorcism at Tyco." *Fortune,* April 28, pp. 106–8, 110.

Zuesse, Eric. 1981. "Love Canal: The Truth Seeps Out." *Reason,* February. Available at www.reason.com.

Further Reading: Johnson, Larry, and Bob Phillips. 2003. *Absolute Honesty: Building a Corporate Culture That Values Straight Talk and Rewards Integrity.* New York: AMACOM; Watson, Charles E. 1990. *Managing with Integrity: Lessons from America's CEOs.* Westport, CT: Praeger; Watson, Charles E. 2005. *How Honesty Pays: Restoring Integrity to the Workplace.* Westport, CT: Praeger.

Charles E. Watson

THE MIDDLE CLASS

America has long been known as a middle class-country. We are a country without kings and queens and feudal lords, and we're a nation where a poor person can work hard and move up the income ladder. America has been called the land of opportunity, and we were different in this respect from many other countries.

But there's a feeling among many that this may have changed—that America as a country of shopkeepers, factory workers, farmers, and salespeople earning a middle-class income is disappearing. There's a sense that the rich have gotten richer, the poor have increased in numbers, and the middle class has been squeezed smaller.

So what's happened to the middle class in America? Is it disappearing, and with it the dreams of many poor households of a better life? Or is it shrinking, but for a better reason—because households are moving up the income ladder faster than ever before?

WHAT IS "MIDDLE CLASS"?

What do we mean by "middle class"? Certainly we know that households with incomes in the middle range of all incomes are middle class, but where do we start and where do we end? Is $40,000 middle class? What about $60,000, or even $100,000?

There are many factors that make defining what it means to be middle class difficult. The number of people in a household who work, their educational levels, and the number of years they have been working all influence household income. So should incomes be adjusted for these factors before a household is defined as middle class or any other income class? Age is also related to income. Typically, income rises as earners in the household age, then income falls at retirement. Does this mean some measure of lifetime income, rather than simply the household income at a snapshot of time, needs to be used in classifying the income class of a household?

A related issue is the fact that an individual household's income can change dramatically over time. This is called income mobility. Income mobility means that while a household may be classified as middle class one year, that same household may move up or down the income ladder in future years.

INCOME MOBILITY

Journalists and others often speak of the poor, the middle class, and the rich as if they are set groups that don't change over time. That is, if you're poor this year, you'll be poor next year, in five years, and in a decade, and the same is true for the other income groups. It's as if your income classification is permanent.

While this may be the case in some societies, it's not true in the United States. Look at Table M.2. It divides households in 1974 into five income categories: the lowest 20 percent, the second 20 percent, the third 20 percent, the fourth 20 percent, and the highest 20 percent. Next it shows whether households in each category were in a lower income category, the same income category, or a higher income category in 1991.

Only between one-third and one-half of households were in the same income category in 1991 as they were in 1974. This means that between one-half and two-thirds were in a higher income group in 1991. Also, the chances of moving to a higher income category are greater for households in lower income groups.

Table M.2

Income category in 1974	Income category in 1991		
	Lower	Same	Higher
Lowest 20%	NA	42.1%	57.9%
Second 20%	28.7%	36.5%	34.8%
Third 20%	35.3%	32.1%	32.6%
Fourth 20%	45.9%	32.4%	21.7%
Highest 20%	46.1%	53.9%	NA

Source: Calculations made from data in Gottshalk, Peter. 1997. "Inequality, Income Growth, and Mobility: The Basic Facts." Journal of Economic Perspectives 11 (2): 21–40.

Although the above points are all very valid and important, the fact is that most analyses of the middle class define it according to some range of household income at a point in time. Unfortunately, even using this simple approach, there's no agreement over what the appropriate income range is. Even the federal government has no official definition. Economists and others outside government have defined the middle-class income range in several different categories, such as $25,000 to $100,000, $18,000 to $88,000, and $40,000 to $95,000.

WHAT'S HAPPENED

Rather than picking a specific income range for the definition of middle class, an alternative approach is to look at what's happened to all income categories in recent decades. Then people can apply their own definitions of middle class and draw conclusions.

Figure M.2 shows the percentages of households in various income categories in two different years, 1967 and 2005. The income amounts in the two years have been adjusted to have the same purchasing power, so they are directly comparable. This means, for example, that income in the range of $25,000 to $34,000 in 1967 could purchase the same quantities of goods and services as incomes in the $25,000 to $34,000 range in 2005, and the same is true for all companion income ranges.

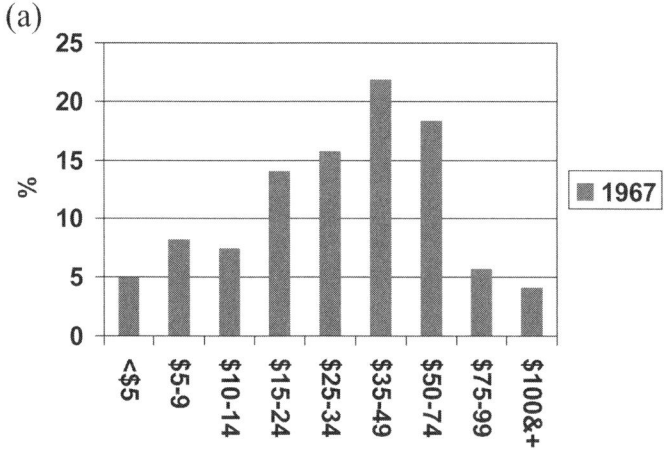

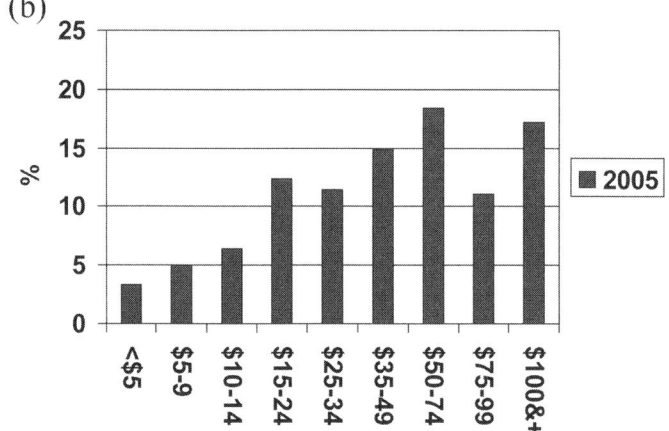

Figure M.2

Source: Denavas-Watt, Carmen, Bernadette Proctor, and Cheryl Lee Hill. 2006. Income, Poverty, and Health Insurance Coverage in the U.S. Current Population Reports P60-231. Washington, DC: Bureau of the Census.

In comparing the income distributions in the two years, it appears as if some households in the lower and middle income ranges in 1967 were pushed into higher income categories in 2005. There was a lower percentage of households in each of the six lowest income categories (<$5,000, $5,000–9,000, $10,000–14,000, $15,000–24,000, $25,000–35,000, $35,000–49,000) in 2005 than in 1967. In contrast, there was a higher percentage of households in the three highest income categories ($50,000–74,000, $75,000–99,000, $100,000+) in 2005 than in 1967. In particular, the percentage of households in the second-highest income category ($75,000–99,000) almost doubled (5.7% to 11.1%), and the percentage of households in the top income category ($100,000+) increased an amazing four times (4.1% to 17.2%).

So what do these statistics imply about the middle class? Once again, it depends on the definition of middle class. If the definition is the middle three income categories, from $15,000 to $49,000, then the percentage of middle-class households dropped from 52 percent in 1967 to 39 percent in 2005. If a narrower definition that includes households with incomes between $25,000 and $49,000 is used, then the percentage fell from 38 percent in 1967 to 26 percent in 2005. Or if a broader definition using households with incomes from $25,000 to $100,000 is used, then the percentage still fell, but slightly, from 62 percent to 56 percent.

Is this decline in the middle class bad? It would be if the lost middle-class households were pushed into lower income categories. However, it appears the movement occurred in the opposite direction. Losses in middle-class households became gains in upper-income households.

DOWNSIDES

Even though the reduction in the middle class has occurred because more households are earning more income, the change has produced one major effect that many see as a big downside—an increase in income inequality. Income inequality measures the distribution in incomes. If all households had the same income, there would be no income inequality. Income inequality increases as the spread between incomes of different households increases. (There is a comparable issue of wealth inequality.)

It should be easy to see why income inequality has increased in almost the last 50 years. Look again at Figure M.2. In 1967, there was a range of low-, middle-, and high-income households, but the greatest percentage of households were in the middle-income ranges. In other words, there was a lot of "glue" of middle-income households between the lower-income and higher-income categories.

The lower panel of Figure M.2 for 2005, with the shift upward in income of many middle-class households, shows there is less "glue" in the middle. Since there are relatively more upper-income households than lower-income households, income inequality has increased.

Multiple changes in the economy have been responsible for this increased income inequality. Technological advances have increased the value of education, and consequently workers with higher levels of education have been rewarded with large increases in income, relative to other workers. At the same

WEALTH VERSUS INCOME

Income and wealth are often confused, but they are different measures. Income is the annual amount of wages and salaries earned by a household. Wealth is the net worth of a household, defined as the value of assets (investments) owned by the household minus the value of debts owed by the household. So if the Smiths have $100,000 in various kinds of investments and they have debts of $75,000, then they have wealth of $25,000.

Income and wealth usually move together. Households with more income have the ability to save and invest more and build up their assets. With more income, they also have less need to borrow. Of course, there are exceptions. There are many stories of people with limited income who pinched pennies and lived very frugal lifestyles so they could save large amounts of income and amass big fortunes. Likewise, there are families with six-figure incomes who live beyond their means and are thousands of dollars in debt.

Has wealth become more concentrated in the hands of higher-income households in recent years? Government data suggest it has. The following table shows the percentage increases in wealth between 1995 and 2004 for households in different income categories. The biggest gains were for high-income households, and small gains or even losses occurred for low-income households.

But a longer-run look at wealth concentration reveals a different trend. Wealth was much less concentrated in the latter part of the twentieth century than in the early part. The top 1 percent of U.S. households owned 40 percent of the nation's wealth in the early 1900s, compared to 20 percent in the late 1900s.

Income Category	Percentage Change in Average* Wealth (1995–2004)
Lowest 20%	1.4%
Second 20%	−17.0%
Third 20%	25.4%
Fourth 20%	70.9%
Highest 20%	104.4%

* Average is the median. Dollar values are in constant purchasing power values in both years.

Source: Calculations made from data in Bucks, Brian, Arthur Kennickell, and Kevin Moore. 2006. "Recent Changes in U.S. Family Finances: Evidence from the 2001 and 2004 Survey of Consumer Finances." Federal Reserve Bulletin 92, A1–A38. Saez, Emmanuel. 2004. "Income and Wealth Concentration in a Historical and International Perspective." Working paper, Department of Economics, University of California at Berkeley, February 21.

time, globalization has dramatically increased the availability of low-skilled, lower-paid workers worldwide to both manufacture products and provide some services. This situation has caused the incomes of low-income workers to grow more slowly. There's also some evidence that the increased turnover of businesses in today's economy has contributed to greater income inequality.

IS THE AMERICAN DREAM STILL ALIVE?

The American dream, the belief that a person can work hard and achieve a decent standard of living, is still alive. In fact, statistics indicate the dream is being achieved by a greater percentage of households than in the past. The percentage of households in the three lowest income categories dropped from 21 percent to 15 percent between 1967 and 2005, while the percentage in the upper three income groups jumped from 28 percent to 47 percent. Average incomes, in constant purchasing power dollars, increased for every income category between 1967 and 2005.

While these trends are positive, two factors have made some—especially those households in lower income categories—question the viability of the American dream. One is the aforementioned reduction in the percentage of households in the middle income categories—the middle class. Lower-income households may interpret this as a sign that moving up the income ladder is too challenging, and maybe even impossible. The other is that income gains for higher-income households have exceeded those for lower- and middle-income households during the last four decades.

A major force behind all these changes is education. At no point in our nation's history have wages and salaries been as strongly related to education as today. If the American dream needs to be amended, it should read thus: if you acquire an education beyond high school, keep your skills current, and work hard, you can achieve an outstanding standard of living.

Further Reading: Comin, Diego, Erica Groshen, and Bess Rabin. 2006. *Turbulent Firms, Turbulent Wages?* Staff Report #238. New York: Federal Reserve Bank of New York; Denavas-Watt, Carmen, Bernadette Proctor, and Cheryl Lee Hill. 2006. *Income, Poverty, and Health Insurance Coverage in the U.S.* Current Population Reports P60–231. Washington, DC: Bureau of the Census; Sullivan, Teresa A., Elizabeth Warren, and Jay Westbrook. 2001. *The Fragile Middle Class.* New Haven, CT: Yale University Press; U.S. Bureau of Labor Statistics. 2006. *100 Years of U.S. Consumer Spending.* Report 991. Washington, DC: U.S. Department of Labor.

Michael L. Walden

MINIMUM WAGE

Minimum wage laws set the minimum hourly wage a worker can be paid. A minimum wage of $5.15, for example, means a worker cannot contract with an employer to work for below $5.15 an hour.

The federal minimum wage sets the wage for the whole nation. In 2006 the minimum wage was $5.15. The federal minimum wage for tipped workers is lower than the standard minimum wage (in 2006, it was $2.13 if the worker got enough in tips to earn $5.15 an hour or more). On the other hand, many states have a minimum wage that is higher than that mandated at the federal level. Information on the current minimum wage, both federal and state, and who is covered by the law is available at www.bls.gov.

Approximately half of those earning the minimum wage (or less) are young workers (below age 25). Most are adults living alone (23%) or teenagers living with their parents (41%). Only about 15 percent are adults raising a family. Another way to look at the statistics is to consider that about 10 percent of teenagers earn the minimum wage (or less) while only 2 percent of those above age 25 earn the minimum wage or less. Most studies show that increasing the minimum wage has little impact on the poor. One study, for example, found that if the minimum wage were raised from $5.15 to $6.65, less than 2 percent of those living in poverty would have their wages directly increased.

Many economists oppose the minimum wage for two reasons. First, the minimum wage law, in effect, prohibits anyone who can not produce enough value in their work to cover the minimum wage from working. A minimum wage of $7 an hour does not help the person who can only produce a value of $5 an hour. In addition, it does not seem worthwhile to help 10 workers to earn $1 more an hour, for example, if still another worker is forced out of a job paying $5 an hour. While there is controversy about whether a small increase in the minimum wage will reduce jobs, there is no doubt that a very high minimum wage will cause substantial job losses. It may be argued that a very high minimum wage is necessary to give workers a living wage, but this would be counterproductive if the worker can't get hired at all. To a worker put out of a job, a hiring wage is better than a living wage.

The second reason many economists oppose the minimum wage is that there is a more efficient method of helping the working poor without jeopardizing their jobs—the earned income tax credit. If a person is poor, the earned income tax credit supplements his or her wage earnings. For example, a poor person earning $5 an hour might get another $3 an hour from the government. While the current earned income tax credit program it not that generous, it could be changed to be so and to significantly increase the incomes of the poor.

An earned income tax credit has several key advantages over the minimum wage. First, it only goes to the poor, while the minimum wage favors those whom employers want to retain (who are often the better-educated teenagers whose parents who are well off). Second, the minimum wage does impose a cost on society in the form of higher prices and lower profits. Because the poor are a small fraction of minimum-wage workers, and because the earned income tax credit only goes to the poor, for the same social cost, the earned income tax credit can give the poor a much higher wage than a minimum wage having the same social cost. Third, there is a social justice argument. The earned income credit is paid for by taxpayers, not employers. It can be argued that society (mainly taxpayers) benefits from making the poor better off, so it is just that society—not employers—should pay the cost of making the poor better off. The earned income tax credit is more just than the minimum wage because it is paid for by society. There are some who feel that employers should do more for workers. But employers are doing something for workers—they are giving them a job. Blaming employers for not doing more is as unjust as saying the Salvation Army is responsible for poverty because it could do more.

THE MINIMUM WAGE AND EMPLOYMENT

Does economic theory say that the minimum wage reduces employment? It does say that a large increase in the minimum wage would reduce employment. But what about a small increase similar in magnitude to past increases in the minimum wage? When labor markets are competitive, wages are bid up to the value of what workers produce. Thus, an increase in the minimum wage would push the wages of some workers above the value of what they are producing and these workers would lose their jobs. On the other hand, when labor markets are not competitive, it is possible that a higher minimum wage would not reduce employment and in some cases would actually increase employment.

A minimum wage can increase employment if an employer is a monopsony. A monopsony is a situation where there is only one employer in a labor market. More generally, any employer who has to pay increasingly higher wages as he or she hires more workers (for example, paying $4 to hire the first worker and $5 for the second, and having to raise their wage to $6 to get a third) is a monopsony. Because a monopsony faces rising wage costs, the cost of each added worker includes the worker's wage plus the dollar amount the employer has to pay in order to raise the wages of the other workers to the new wage. For example, suppose an employer employs nine workers at $10 and must pay $11 to hire the tenth worker. The tenth worker costs $11 plus the $9 needed to raise the pay of the first nine workers from $10 to $11. Thus, the tenth worker costs $20. If the worker produces a value of $15, the monopsony would not hire him or her. However, if there were a minimum wage of $11, the tenth worker would only cost $11 (since the wages of the first nine workers do not have to be increased, as they are already at $11). In this case, the worker would be hired. A sufficiently high minimum wage (for example, $16) will cause this worker not to be hired and, if even higher, may cause others to lose their jobs. Over some range, a minimum wage causes a monopsony to hire more workers, but at some point, an even higher wage will cause jobs to be lost.

Research has found that restaurants have monopsony power over tipped workers. In the absence of a minimum wage, a restaurant hiring more tipped servers would find, at some point, that each tipped server earns less in tips per hour (as each will serve fewer patrons in an hour when more waiters are hired). As a result, the restaurant will have to raise the hourly cash wage to remain competitive with other employers. Therefore, a restaurant has monopsony power, and a minimum wage has the potential to increase employment of tipped servers. However, it was also found that when the minimum wage for tipped workers was increased too much, employment fell.

What do the data say about the effect of minimum wages on employment? Most studies of teenagers suggest that the minimum wage does reduce employment: every 10 percent increase in the minimum wage reduces teenage employment by 1 to 2 percent. The reason that most research on minimum wages involves teenagers is that they are the only group sizably affected by the minimum wage, which makes its effects more discernable. David Card and Alan Krueger have conducted considerable research that shows that minimum wages do not reduce employment. For example, they concluded that when the minimum wage was increased in 1990 and 1991, states with a larger fraction of low-wage workers did not suffer a greater loss in jobs. However, a study of the 1996–1997 increase in the federal minimum wage did show a greater job loss in jobs in states with larger fractions of low-wage workers. Thus, using their methodology, it appears that the minimum wage did reduce employment.

Another Card and Krueger study compared employment at fast-food restaurants in two adjoining towns, one in New Jersey, where the minimum wage was increased, and the other in Pennsylvania, where the minimum wage was not increased. They found no difference in before-after employment trends between the two towns and concluded the minimum wage had no effect.

Yet for the study's results to be valid, both towns must have basically the same business conditions before and after the minimum wage increase. Otherwise, it is possible that the town with the minimum wage increase also had an improvement in business conditions (while the other town did not) that offset the negative effect of the minimum wage on employment. This is why nationwide studies usually are better sources of evidence—the year-to-year variations in local business conditions usually net out when averaged across the nation. The drawback

THE LIVING WAGE

Many cities and counties have living wages. The living wage is a minimum wage set above the federal minimum wage level and usually applies only to employers who have a contract with the city or county. It is called a living wage because it is usually set at a level that allows a full-time worker to support a family of four at the poverty line.

Because the institution of a living wage is relatively recent, it is hard to judge whether it decreases employment. The current evidence suggests that the living wage may reduce employment, but this is open to argument. There are three main reasons why one would expect living wage laws to not reduce employment. First, the very passage of these laws has shown that the cities and counties passing them are willing to absorb added cost increases. Second, the type of services cities contract for cannot be supplied by low-wage foreign or out-of-area firms. Thus, there is less competitive pressure on these firms to keep prices and, therefore, costs down. Finally, the third reason is that the living wage laws may not significantly affect the costs of doing business for many of the affected firms. For example, suppose 10 percent of a firm's cost are increased 30 percent by the living wage law: this will increase its total cost by only 3 percent.

If the living wage laws result in affected jobs paying sizably more, then it might be expected that employers over time would fill vacated jobs with better workers (more experienced and better educated) than they currently are hiring. Employers may not explicitly set out to hire better workers, but the higher wage will attract better workers to apply and it will be the better workers whom firms will hire. Thus, while current low-skilled workers may benefit from the law, over time, new low-skilled applicants will not. Instead, they will find fewer jobs open to them.

to using nationwide studies is that the business cycle can be a potentially confounding factor. For example, the increase in the federal minimum wage in 1990 occurred during a recession, and it is possible that the negative effects of the minimum wage found then could have actually been caused by the business downturn. However, the minimum wage has been found to reduce employment in many business conditions.

OTHER EFFECTS OF THE MINIMUM WAGE

Minimum wages also have other effects. One major effect is that they raise the wages not only of minimum-wage workers but also of those earning more than the minimum wage. Studies have shown that a 10 percent increase in the minimum wage increases the average wage of all teenagers around 2 percent. This estimate is probably too low; most other studies have found a larger effect.

Another effect of the minimum wage is that it makes employers cut back on other amenities (by cutting fringe benefits, tightening work rules, and reducing on-the-job training). In this way, employers partially offset the effect of higher wages on their cost. The net effect for workers is that the minimum wage may not make them as well off as the increase in wages might indicate. One piece of evidence suggesting that this is the case is the fact that the past increases in the minimum wage have reduced (or had no effect) on the fraction of teenagers who want to work (as measured by their labor force participation rate). If the minimum wage increases the expected value of seeking and finding work, then it should increase the size of the labor force—but it does not.

A common error concerning the minimum wage is the belief that an increase in the minimum wage will be offset by workers becoming more productive and that, as a result, this will keep employment from decreasing. Various reasons have been given for the minimum wage increasing productivity, including the speculation that workers value their higher-paid jobs more, or alternatively, that employers try to offset the higher wage costs. If this were true, the minimum wage would reduce employment far more than it does. For example, suppose a minimum wage increases wages 10 percent and workers become 10 percent more productive. This will offset the effect of minimum wages on cost and leave the price of products unchanged. As goods cost the same amount, employers will produce and sell the same number of goods as before. But workers are 10 percent more productive so employers would need 10 percent fewer workers to produce the same numbers of goods as before (indeed, that is what being more productive means). In this case, a 10 percent increase in the minimum wage would lead to a 10 percent decrease in employment. This is a far greater cut in employment than most studies find.

FINAL COMMENT

The poor would be far better off if the political energy that goes into increasing the minimum wage were used instead to develop programs that truly help the poor (including the earned income tax credit). The minimum wage reduces employment, but not sizably. More troubling, it does not increase the number of people who want to work, which suggests that it creates some offset such that workers on net are not better off. Economists like to say that there is no such thing as a free lunch. The minimum wage is definitely not a free lunch. It may have benefits, but it also has sizable costs.

Further Reading: Card, David, and Alan Krueger. 1994. "Minimum Wages and Employment: A Case Study of the Fast Food Industry in New Jersey and Pennsylvania." *American Economic Review* 84: 772–93; Card, David, and Alan Krueger. 1995. *Myth and Measurement: The New Economics of the Minimum Wage.* Princeton, NJ: Princeton University Press; Wessels, Walter. 2005. "Does the Minimum Wage Drive Teenagers Out of the Labor Market?" *Journal of Labor Research* 26: 169–76; Wessels, Walter. 2007. "A Reexamination of Card and Krueger's State-Level Study of the Minimum Wage." *Journal of Labor Research* 28 (1): 135–46.

Walter J. Wessels

MISSION STATEMENTS

Organizations have used mission statements for years to answer the questions, Why do we exist? and What do we do? for both their public and their members. Recently, however, some have questioned the value of mission statements. That debate promises to continue as organizations operate in an ever-changing, increasingly complex world.

DEFINITION

A mission statement is a brief summation of an organization's mission, which defines, in broad terms, why the organization exists and what value it provides to its constituents or to society. It is usually one to several sentences in length, often in the form of a very short paragraph that can be printed on letterhead or posted on an organization's Web site. Mission statements are sometimes confused with vision statements, but the two have different purposes. A mission statement reflects an organization's present state, which distinguishes it from a vision statement, which proposes an organization's desired future state in terms of what it aspires to become.

PREVALENCE OF MISSION STATEMENTS

Mission statements are ubiquitous these days. In fact, they are among the most popular management tools used by top executives. Most formal organizations, regardless of their governance or size, have developed and publicized them. If asked, many organization members—especially leaders, executives, and managers—can quickly produce copies of their organization's mission statement or, alternatively, download their mission statement from the organization's Web site. Some are able to paraphrase it verbally, and a few are even able to recite it from memory. The emphasis has recently been on succinct mission statements that sum up what organizations do, or at least what they promise to do, for their stakeholders.

USE OF MISSION STATEMENTS

It has long been assumed that well-conceived mission statements provide a good context for organizational planning and can serve as a reference point for making critical resource allocation decisions, because they state clearly what the organization exists to do and serve as a realistic foundation for planning. Although the reason an organization exists might be fairly evident, there are often aspects of an organization that might not be as obvious. For example, one might consider the case of the Environmental Protection Agency and logically assume that it exists to protect the U.S. environment. However, let's examine the agency's mission statement, which reads:

> To protect and improve the natural environment for present and future generations, taking into account the environmental, social and economic principles of sustainable development.

Now we see that it is not simply the environment that is the concern of the agency, but a balance among the environment, social good, and economic concerns. Accordingly, the agency must consider more than just protecting the environment, in spite of the importance of that responsibility. As a result, planning needs to incorporate a number of factors, some perhaps at odds with others. Without that mission statement to provide broad guidance, the agency's planning efforts would be likely to encounter resistance or disapproval from its funding sources.

CONTENTS OF A TYPICAL MISSION STATEMENT

Although there is no universally accepted recipe for what is contained in a mission statement, its elements often include the following: the scope of products or services it provides, what clients or customers it serves, and what it does differently from other similar organizations that makes it unique. A well-conceived and well-written mission statement defines the purpose of an organization and what sets it apart from all other organizations. Can you guess what organization uses the following mission statement?

> We create happiness by providing the finest in entertainment to people of all ages, everywhere.

SO WHAT IS THE DEBATE?

There is disagreement among researchers who have studied mission statements concerning their importance. Whereas conventional wisdom suggests that a mission statement can be a valuable and simple way to keep an organization focused, research is mixed.

Many studies have reported that mission statements help keep organizations on track by focusing the attention of managers and members on activities fundamental to their organizations' purpose. Others, however, have suggested that mission statements can lock organizations into certain prescribed ways of thinking and doing that might have worked well in the past but than can seriously hamper their ability to seek out opportunities and change direction in response to societal, economic, technological, and industrial changes. Worse, some have suggested that mission statements can be construed by organizational members as attempts to control or manipulate their behavior.

Those mixed findings have been echoed by a number of business leaders who have used mission statements in an effort to shape behavior as well as improve the effectiveness of their organizations. Many report feeling pride in their organizations' missions, how they serve to establish and communicate succinctly their collective sense of purpose, and how they guide their organizations' actions and activities by providing a common general direction for their members. Others argue that mission statements are, at best, little more than carefully arranged window dressing suited for public relations purposes and, at worst, blinders and barriers—blinders in the sense that they constrain their organizations' vision and obscure external changes that are occurring in their operating environments, and barriers in that they impede internal changes that need to be made to ensure their continued success. Wal-Mart is an example of a well-known organization that does not have a formal mission statement but instead relies on a philosophy "to provide everyday low prices with exceptional customer service."

There are two debates concerning mission statements. The first, more fundamental debate involves the question of whether an organization is better served by having a defined mission statement or ignoring the concept of a mission statement altogether. That debate has intensified since the early 1990s with the rapid change that has come about with the information age. The second debate follows logically from the first. It centers on what kind of mission statement is most useful given the dynamic nature of our world in terms of the appropriate level of specificity or detail that should be communicated. We will examine both sides of each of those debates.

THE FIRST DEBATE: WHETHER TO HAVE A MISSION STATEMENT

Some of the advantages and disadvantages of developing an organizational mission statement are shown in Table M.3.

So how do we reconcile that fundamental debate? If we examine the arguments on both sides, we can see how we might synthesize them to find a happy middle ground. An organization can certainly benefit from having an established mission statement, but it must take measures to ensure that mission statement actually works. In short, it is important for organizations to exploit the advantages and limit the disadvantages of mission statements when they create their own. This brings us to the second debate.

Table M.3

Advantages	Disadvantages
Identifies the organization and its unique attributes	Defines the organization either too broadly or too narrowly
Captures the essence of the organization for its members and outsiders	Constricts imagination and creative thinking if too tightly defined
Creates a common purpose among the organization's members	Fosters groupthink, where achieving harmony among members becomes more important than devising effective decisions and actions designed to manage change
Unifies and energizes members to act in the best interests of the organization	Fails to provide any real increase in people's efforts to support the organization
Establishes a general sense of direction to guide the organization to achieving success	Reflects the view of top managers, but not the rank and file who must carry out the organization's objectives
Serves as the foundation for planning and strategic thinking	Oversimplifies complex corporate aims that simply cannot be condensed into a single statement
Guides important decisions	Becomes static, ossified, and ultimately useless as an instrument to guide the organization's decisions
Suggests where resources should be allocated	Wastes resources in terms of the time and energy it takes to generate
Focuses attention on what is really important	Presents unrealistic, empty hyperbole
Provides a rallying point or touchstone in times of turbulent change	Limits the organization's ability or willingness to adapt to changes
Motivates the behavior of the organization's members	Becomes stilted rhetoric that engenders skepticism rather than inspiring commitment
Solidifies the psychological commitment of the people who must work to support it	Broadcasts empty initiatives designed more for public relations than for viable organizational action
Demonstrates some positive effects on various measures of organizational performance	Lacks conclusive empirical evidence of a positive effect on overall organizational performance

THE SECOND DEBATE: WHAT MAKES A MISSION STATEMENT MOST EFFECTIVE?

Some proponents of mission statements suggest that they should be inspirational and lofty in order to stimulate members to have ever-higher ambitions for the greater good. Others prefer that they be terse statements written and distributed to keep everybody focused and on track. The middle ground is that to be most effective, mission statements should combine elements from both schools of thought. Therefore, it is essential that a mission statement be an accurate reflection of the organization's purpose and inspire some excitement while stopping short of being an empty proclamation that fails to capture the true essence of the organization. Effective mission statements are neither painfully obvious nor glaringly incongruent; they should be consistent with people's impressions and expectations of, and experiences with, an organization if they are to be of any value. Overly broad mission statements fail to provide any direction or motivation for people to move ahead; excessively narrow mission statements can limit managerial thinking and constrain them from pursuing potentially profitable endeavors.

A banal or trite mission statement can be worse than having no mission statement at all. Consider, for example, the mission statement of an actual company that shall remain unnamed:

> Our mission, simply stated, is to be the best there is at whatever we do.

Such a mission statement is essentially useless; either the organization is all things to all people or it doesn't know where its next dollar is coming from. If the organization desires to operate in stealth, perhaps such a mission statement is just the ticket. Most organizations, however, desire to communicate their purpose to the world. Generic missions statements that overuse words and phrases such as "excellent," "the best worldwide," and "a leader in our industry" without linking them to substance are not much better; they could describe the goals of just about any organization. Rather, a mission statement should be specifically tailored to the unique features and offerings of each organization so that it reflects that organization's identity. A simple test of whether a mission statement is too vague is to ask outsiders to read it and try to identify the organization. If they have no idea (as in the example above), then the mission statement is probably too broad. Mission statements should help channel organizational action to areas of obvious interest and expertise. Overly specific mission statements, on the other hand, err by providing too much information, which in turn constrains organizations from pursuing opportunities. They also run the risk of revealing important elements of an organization's strategy, which should not be displayed to outsiders. Specific organizational goals are better off left out of the mission statement, because they change more often than the mission does. Stilted mission statements that try to appeal to our emotions often make us groan or, worse, laugh out loud, and they are seldom very effective. The popular comic strip Dilbert offers a clever take on how employees view bombastic mission statements.

Mission statements cannot be allowed to be cast in stone and left for the ages; they must be reviewed periodically and modified as organizations and their situational realities change. At the same time, it is important that they not be changed on a whim or every time some disturbance is felt in an organization's performance or its environment. If that happens, they cannot serve to provide any meaningful sense of direction. Crafting a mission statement for a highly diversified company is exceedingly difficult. Take the example of General Electric, a company involved in so many unrelated businesses that it is impossible to capture the essence of the company in a succinct statement. The company does not have a corporate mission statement; instead, it touts its values—"Imagine, solve, build and lead"—and develops mission statements for each of its many independent operating units.

For a large organization that is less diversified, an effective mission statement can help refocus efforts to expand and prosper. For example, consider the mission statement that Otis Elevator Company adopted some years ago. Chances are everybody has ridden on an Otis elevator at some time. Elisha Graves Otis invented the world's first safety elevator in 1853, which allowed buildings to be constructed beyond the limitations of staircases. It is no exaggeration to say that Otis Elevator was instrumental in shaping the skylines of our modern cities—Otis elevators operate in the Eiffel Tower, the Empire State Building, and in 10 of the world's 20 tallest buildings. The company has earned the industry's highest reputation for quality, reliability, safety, and service. Otis Elevator today boasts more than 1.7 million elevator installations worldwide and annual revenues of nearly $10 billion (almost 80% of which is generated outside the United States). It might not surprise most people to learn that Otis is the world's largest manufacturer of elevators, but far fewer would have any idea that Otis's leadership extends as well to escalators and moving walkways. In fact, the company touts itself as "the world's leading people mover." That leadership is a fairly recent phenomenon. Faced by a flat market for high-rise building construction in the 1980s, the company realized that the growth of its elevator manufacturing and service operations was limited. It therefore re-created itself; no longer just an elevator company, it became a movement system company. The company's mission statement articulates that change in philosophy succinctly:

> To provide any customer a means of moving people and things up, down, and sideways over short distances with higher reliability than any similar enterprise in the world.

By broadening its mission, the company found new sources of revenue growth based on its already outstanding engineering, manufacturing, and service capabilities.

Note that some of the examples of effective mission statements provided here are very short but still capture the essence of the organization. Others are a bit longer, generally to communicate important aspects of the organizations' identities. They all share several common features. First, they are well written, communicating simply and precisely the purpose of each organization. Second, they are brief, lacking any superfluous verbiage. Third, they are believable yet sufficiently aggressive to inspire and sustain organizational action. Fourth, they are recognized both internally and externally as accurately representing each organization. Incidentally, the mission statement cited earlier in this chapter ("We create happiness . . .") is also an example of an effective one. It belongs to Walt Disney Parks and Resorts, a major operating unit of the Walt Disney Company.

EFFECTIVE MISSION STATEMENTS

Cannondale

"Our mission is to create innovative, quality products that inspire cyclists around the world."

Dell Computer

"Dell's mission is to be the most successful computer company in the world at delivering the best customer experience in markets we serve. In doing so, Dell will meet customer expectations of highest quality, leading technology, competitive pricing, individual and company accountability, best-in-class service and support, flexible customization capability, superior corporate citizenship, and financial stability."

Dow Chemical

"To constantly improve what is essential to human progress by mastering science and technology."

eBay

"eBay's mission is to provide a global trading platform where practically anyone can trade practically anything."

Kelly Services

"To serve our customers, employees, shareholders, and society by providing a broad range of staffing services and products."

Microsoft

"At Microsoft, we work to help people and businesses throughout the world realize their full potential."

Salvation Army USA

"The Salvation Army, an international movement, is an evangelical part of the universal Christian Church. Its message is based on the Bible. Its ministry is motivated by the love of God. Its mission is to preach the gospel of Jesus Christ and to meet human needs in His name without discrimination."

Edinboro University of Pennsylvania

"The mission of Edinboro University is to create and share knowledge by providing access to education and learning experiences for the academic, cultural and personal growth of the students and the larger community we serve."

DEVELOPING MISSION STATEMENTS

Developing a mission statement need not be a controversial undertaking, but the process sometimes sparks disagreement among senior managers. If they cannot resolve their differences, it is unlikely that the mission statement will accurately represent what the organization actually does. However, the process of developing mission statements can also free people from limitations and static thinking. Accordingly, it is wise to involve as many of the right people in the process as possible and provide them sufficient time to discuss what the mission should communicate and reflect on the views of others. Eventually, a meeting of the participants might be scheduled so that the pieces can come together and a consensus can be reached. An outside facilitator is often valuable at that time. Experienced facilitators will not strive for consensus early in the process. Instead, they will encourage participants to brainstorm ideas and look for common themes. While some studies suggest that higher-performing organizations have more comprehensive mission statements than lower-performing organizations, that is not always the case. In their efforts to be comprehensive, managers can run the risk of making their mission statements too specific. Explicit strategies and performance goals should not be included in the mission statement.

Some have argued that because mission statements share many similarities, the creative process behind the mission statement might be even more important than the actual content of the mission statement itself. Think about it—although effective missions are short and direct, the process that organizations go through to arrive at them is not. This process perspective is important. In fact, studies have reported that a greater percentage of executives express satisfaction with the process used for developing their organizations' mission statements than with the mission statements themselves. In short, what the mission statement ultimately says is perhaps less important than what is learned in the process of creating it. A significant amount of time and high-level effort often goes into creating mission statements—it has been stated that 90 percent of the work developing mission statements is thinking, discussing, interacting, revising, and eventual consensus, while only 10 percent of the work is the actual drafting, revising, and smoothing out of the written statement. In general, the more people are involved with writing the mission statement, the better, and that means people at levels other than just the executive or leadership. Good ideas can come from all sectors of an organization.

As mentioned earlier, mission statements have a number of potentially valuable purposes, one of the most important of which is their use as a foundation for strategic planning. Developing an effective mission statement is one of the first steps in the process of formulating strategy and is also a critical factor in the establishment of sensible organizational goals. Keeping the mission statement in full view during strategic planning ensures that all the activities of an organization relate directly to and support its mission, thereby enhancing its effectiveness by minimizing wasteful or marginal action.

COMMUNICATING MISSION STATEMENTS

An effective mission statement is a working document that should be communicated and disseminated as widely as possible, both to internal and external stakeholder groups. In that way, it can go a long way toward unifying organization members with a single collective purpose and securing the commitment of outsiders who also have an interest in the organization. After the mission statement is developed, it should be made available to all interested stakeholder groups for their assessment. If people can't identify the organization from its mission statement, it probably needs to be developed further before it can be of any use. Alternatively, the mission statement might be just fine, while the organization itself is already off track.

SUMMARY AND CONCLUSION

In addition to describing an organization's purpose, a good mission statement captures its essential uniqueness and enduring character—in short, an organization's identity. It should be the organization's compass, providing focus and direction. It can serve as a foundation for action—to guide strategic planning, define the scope of an organization's operations and activities, assess major initiatives, allocate resources most effectively, provide a common purpose that transcends individual wants and needs and focuses instead on shared expectations, and inspire members to act in the best interest of the organization. Mission statements should be clear and understandable to all who read them; they should not be filled with jargon or industry-specific terminology. They should be precise and concise to help people remember what types of customers and markets the organization exists to serve. But mission statements cannot simply be slogans, either—if they are allowed to become empty rhetoric, their meaning and seriousness erode and they become just a collection of words that lack true meaning and purpose.

Further Reading: Baetz, Mark C., and Christopher K. Bart. 1996. "Developing Mission Statements which Work." *Long Range Planning* 29 (4): 526–33; Bart, Christopher K., Nick Bontis, and Simon Taggar. 2001. "A Model of the Impact of Mission Statements on Firm Performance." *Management Decision* 39 (1): 19–35; Pearce, John A., II. 1982. "The Company Mission as a Strategic Goal." *Sloan Management Review* 29 (3): 15–24; Pearce, John A., II, and Fred David. 1987. "Corporate Mission Statements: The Bottom Line." *Academy of Management Executive* 1 (2): 109–15.

James F. Fairbank

MOMMY TRACK

In 1989, Felice N. Schwartz wrote an article in the Harvard Business Review that led to tremendous controversy among women in the business world (Schwartz 1989). She asserted that "Two facts matter to business: only women have babies and only men make rules." She suggested that organizations should allow highly qualified women who were on the fast track in their organizations the flexibility to have and raise children by creating a slower career track. This is when the real debate about the so-called mommy track began. The mommy track is an alternate career path that temporarily takes women off the fast track while they are dealing with their "womanly" duties, primarily the care of an infant. The idea was that the woman would go back to her career path when her children were either in child care or school.

Major corporations have found that female managers are likely to leave when they have children. Many executives over the years have been very frustrated to lose well-educated, top-performing women managers to maternity. They often find that the competitive woman they hired, developed, and groomed for the executive ranks seems to have lost her drive and ambition since she had children. Leaving the workforce tends to strengthen stereotypes about women in general and women at the higher levels in organizations, more specifically. Women lose contact with colleagues, clients, and customers during their maternity leaves; have less time for collegial lunches and meetings after regular hours; and have more than work to think and talk about when they do interact with people from work. They begin to place more value on their homes, children, and other personal obligations. They spend a great deal of money on child care in order to work and still have very restrictive time limitations.

Meanwhile, many women have become frustrated when they see less competent men who started after they did get promoted above them. To a woman, it appears she is penalized for deciding to have a family and meeting her social and personal responsibilities. She has to deal with the guilt of leaving a child with a care provider, which may be a decision she makes herself or that is influenced by relatives, neighbors, religious or political leaders, or spouses. She has less money, less free time, and more work. In addition to all that, she may begin to see through the glass ceiling and notice that working mothers are rarely at the top.

The primary controversy concerns the establishment of mother-friendly policies, which may include a mommy track. Is a mommy track, along with other family-friendly policies, a good or bad idea for businesses? Are they good or bad for women?

THE ADVANTAGES OF A MOMMY TRACK AND FAMILY-FRIENDLY POLICIES

The cost of turnover is very high. When employees who leave are managers or hold other professional positions, the cost is even higher. Organizations invest hundreds of hours and thousands of dollars in the recruiting, employment, training, and development of their managerial staff. In addition to the formal practices used to find and develop managers, there is a great deal of informal mentoring, customer relationship building, and networking involved in the creation of an effective manager or professional, who has an incalculable value to an organization. Women are more likely than men to leave organizations when they have children. Although it is politically incorrect to talk openly about this problem with female managers, everyone knows that it exists and most large companies have tracked this exodus.

THE REAL WORLD

Susan held a degree in accounting from a good college and had worked in Chicago for a few years for one of the large public accounting firms. That is where she met an ambitious young man who shared her interests in skiing and mountain biking. They moved to Colorado, where they both got jobs in the ski resort industry. In between their very active sports activities and their jobs, they both decided to return to school. He pursued an MBA, and she went to law school. Susan's professors suggested that she was capable of a more challenging law program, and with their urging, she transferred to one of the top law schools in the United States for her last two years of course work. Susan's parents were pleased with her decision and contributed the extra money, which amounted to tens of thousands of dollars. When Susan and her boyfriend graduated, they married. She briefly worked as a clerk for a judge and eventually landed a job with a large law firm. After about one year, Susan became pregnant. Much to the surprise of her parents, Susan quit her job with the law firm. About one year after the birth of her first child, she began to do some legal work at home, with thoughts of returning part time, but quickly became pregnant again. This time, she had twins, one of whom has a serious medical condition. Within a year after their birth, Susan became pregnant again. Susan had had a previous problem pregnancy, so they have hired a nanny to help with the children. At this point, the family's need for income is greater than ever, but she cannot practice law until the situation with the sick twin is resolved. Meanwhile, close family members mourn the loss of her potential career, complain quietly about the waste of their money, wonder how they could have predicted this, and worry about her and the children. Susan and her husband struggle to maintain the lifestyle they envisioned during their younger days and take more money from relatives. Susan misses the interesting interactions with colleagues and is overwhelmed by the responsibilities of motherhood, especially since her husband travels for work regularly.

A mommy track is designed to save the organization money by encouraging women to return to their jobs in the management ranks when they are able. The theory is that by accommodating the specific needs of working mothers, organizations can hold onto them and preserve the investment they have already made. The mommy track must be tailored to each individual organization and the type of work being done. In general, it can involve allowing more time in rank (e.g., more time to make partner in a law or accounting firm), a flexible work schedule (e.g. starting work earlier in the day in order to leave earlier to spend more time with children in the afternoon), job sharing with other working mothers (e.g., two women who had babies at the same time sharing one actuarial position for a year), allowing employees to use their sick time for children's illnesses, and telecommuting (e.g., working with clients via the Internet and telephone). Meanwhile, the woman would be considered an equal member of the professional staff but coworkers would understand that she is not going to be available for the same number of hours as she was before or attend as many meetings.

The organization keeps the effective employee, she can focus on both her job and her family without penalty, and she can add work responsibilities as her children grow, start school, and require less of her time. Eventually, the working mother can go back to the fast track and continue climbing the corporate ladder to executive positions.

Every October, *Working Mother* magazine publishes a list of the 100 best companies for working mothers ("100 Best Companies" 2004). These are the companies that offer a range of programs designed to make working easier for mothers. Although few, if any, organizations would ever publicize the fact that they have a mommy track, many of these top companies offer features that amount to a slower track. These include flextime, compressed workweeks, job sharing, telecommuting, elder-care and child care referral services, emergency backup care for children, paternity leave, adoption leave, and pay for extended maternity leave. Note that the most important features of companies that are good for working mothers involve policies that give them more time.

Traditionally, corporate managers have scheduled meetings after normal work hours (because it is quiet and nothing else is happening), met early every morning over coffee to discuss problem issues or plan the day, come into their offices on weekends (sometimes specifically to write a memo that will be dated on a weekend), based promotional decisions on the number of hours worked (this might even have necessitated the monitoring of security tapes to see when managers arrived and left), golfed with clients in the afternoons, and scheduled evening meetings with professional associations. It is common for executives to consider participation in these types of sessions, which take hours of time outside of what is considered a normal work schedule, tests of loyalty to the firm and indications of how ambitious one is (i.e., Will you do whatever it takes?).

Organizations that want to keep working mothers with high potential must create new policies that:

1. Place a greater emphasis on the performance and results of managers rather than the number of hours they spend on the clock. This is hard because measuring job performance is difficult, whereas tracking how many hours one spends in the office is easy.
2. Stop scheduling meetings that begin before and after normal work hours. This must include meetings with customers. Some experts have found that workaholism is really escapism for working men (i.e., it eliminates time spent at home interacting with the wife and children and doing housework). Recently, women have been accused of this as well.
3. Cut back on out-of-town travel. (Many companies have already done this to save money anyway.) With the advent of conference calls and video conferencing, much travel is now unnecessary except to build personal professional relationships with customers. Travel for working mothers is difficult and more costly than it is for men. As one woman who was interviewed by the author put it, "When my husband travels on business, I pack his bag and he leaves. When I travel on business, I pack my own bag, arrange child care and rides for them, prepare and store the meals for the time while I will be gone with preparation instructions, list all of the emergency phone numbers, and arrange for the neighbor to let out the dog. I am exhausted

before I leave." Some of the 100 best companies for mothers now pay for child care when an employee must travel out of town for work.

4. Allow flexible work hours
5. Provide for telecommuting, at least part-time
6. Assist employees with maternity leave, which might include extended pay and part-time work
7. Explore job-sharing possibilities. Generally, professional women who share a position put in more hours overall than a single employee working in one position.

THE DISADVANTAGES OF A MOMMY TRACK AND FAMILY-FRIENDLY POLICIES

When an organization creates a mommy track, the assumption is that women can easily shift back to the fast track when their other responsibilities are finished. In reality, taking time to go on a mommy track diminishes a woman's career opportunities in many organizations. (Some members of the National Guard returning from Iraq have found that being away from their jobs for a year hurt their careers too.) The reasons for this have to do with reduced face time (with executives and customers), a perception that she cares less about her job than other employees do, and a concern that she might have another baby, as well as the fact that others have learned more and developed skills during the time the woman was off. This makes others more qualified, literally, than the woman hired at the same time with the same qualifications who left the job (even if she was gone for only six weeks). In other words, she has fallen behind in both others' perceptions of her abilities and, depending on the length of the time off, her actual job skills, compared to others who did not take time off.

Another disadvantage of creating a mommy track is that only women take advantage of reduced hours, flexible work schedules, telecommuting, and other timesaving policies even though they might be available to both mothers and fathers. This is true as well in other countries where generous paid leave policies are national law. Because men (with the help of their wives) choose not to use family-friendly benefits, these programs are feminized. The reasons that men provide as to why they do not use these programs are varied, and not enough research has been conducted yet to provide a complete answer. However, we might speculate that men may not want to stay at home with a new infant because it is so much work, because they lack confidence regarding their ability to care for the baby, because they fear the social stigma attached to being a house husband, because there is a lack of support from their parents and friends and other relatives, or because they are concerned about placing themselves on a daddy track with their own careers.

Being on a mommy track for a year can be a double-edged sword. Because few men take advantage of family-friendly policies, those policies may appear to men and childless women to be an expensive benefit just for one specific type of employee, working mothers, forcing those left behind to work longer and harder. Single men, married men with stay-at-home wives, and single women may even resent two-income families as well. When a promotional opportunity becomes available two years later, is it fair to give the promotion to the working mother? If she gets it, the other candidates resent that fact that they worked harder and didn't take time off. If the working mother does not get the promotion, she may be resentful that she was passed over because she took time to care for her child—a worthwhile reason to be off work, and hardly a vacation.

Since the mommy track is defined as taking time off the traditional career track to care for children, it would be interesting to know how many companies offer these alternate paths. Unfortunately, there is no way to count them. However, the recent issue of *Working Mother* lists the various ways that an alternative can be chosen ("100 Best Companies" 2005). Companies that made the list of the 100 best companies for working mothers in 2005 typically offer alternate career paths involving such options as telecommuting, paid and partially paid leaves for new mothers (including adoptive mothers), and job sharing. It is important to note, however, that even among the 100 best, 23 provide no pay for any of the 12 weeks covered under the Family and Medical Leave Act of 1993 (which does not specify that the time off must be paid.) This means that women must use accumulated vacation and sick leave in order to get any pay for their maternity leaves. Since women of childbearing age are typically young, they are less likely to have the large amounts of accumulated leave necessary to cover 6 weeks, let alone 12 weeks. Only 9 of the 100 on the 2005 list provide 12 weeks of full pay. One of the most common complaints about the Family and Medical Leave Act of 1993 is that most women must take the time off without pay, which means that few can afford to take the full 12 weeks. This falls well short of the full-year leaves with partial to full pay that are required by law in many other industrialized countries.

Recently, a series of articles in major publications has suggested that women are taking off-ramps (Hewlett and Luce 2005) and leaving top corporate and professional jobs to have and care for children. "Off-ramps" is an updated and less threatening name for mommy track. There is some controversy as to the validity of the claim that women are leaving the workforce in large numbers. This debate is occurring in part because much of the reported data and anecdotal evidence comes from the best-educated women. Poor and minority women are significantly less likely to leave the workforce after having children.

Nonetheless, there appears to be a trend toward successful women dropping out either temporarily or permanently to pursue other interests including children. Hewlett and Luce report that approximately 40 percent of highly qualified women say that they have left work voluntarily (Hewlett and Luce 2005). Forty-three percent of women with children report leaving at some point in their careers. The reasons they have for leaving the workforce depend on the age of the woman. Younger women are more likely to leave to have children and women in the 41–55 age group may be caring for their aging parents. Granted, some of these women are also leaving to start their own businesses, to consult, to write, to improve their lifestyles, and to do community service. The bottom line is that businesses are losing qualified and trained female executives and professionals after years of investment into their careers. By comparison, only 24 percent of men, regardless of whether or not they have children, have taken off-ramps. For men, the reasons are less likely to be related to family and more likely to be related to career shifts and to a desire to obtain further education.

Hewlett and Luce identify both "push" and "pull" reasons for women's departures (Hewlett and Luce 2005). Pull reasons include the care of family members, a responsibility that falls to women even today and is the primary reason women leave. Push reasons include a lack of satisfaction with their work. Lack of opportunities and understimulation are big issues for women. Only 6 percent in Hewlett and Luce's study left because the work was too demanding. Many of the women in the study who left good jobs indicated that their spouses' incomes were sufficient for their families. This, however, is a luxury which most women do not have. Other women must go to another job to find more challenges and ways to achieve. As Hewlett and Luce point out, many women have both push and pull reasons for taking an off-ramp.

Most highly qualified women who leave their jobs intend to return to work. In general, they need the income and enjoy their work. Hewlett and Luce found that the women they interviewed feel that work give shape and structure to their lives, increases confidence and self-esteem, and provides status for them. The biggest problem when a woman takes a break from her career, whether it is called a mommy track or an off-ramp, is that it is very difficult to return. Depending on the length of the leave, their old jobs may disappear—the Family and Medical Leave Act of 1993 provides a guarantee of a return to a position after a 12-week leave. Women who take one to three years off must go on the job market again. They have been out of the mainstream and may not know about recent changes in legal and professional standards of practice, do not know the customers and their representatives, may have credibility problems with colleagues, and may appear to be less motivated. There are other potential issues that might make finding another job more difficult. The prime childbearing years also happen to be the prime career-building years.

In many cases, their earning potential will also drop. Hewlett and Luce found that after three years, women average a 37 percent reduction in salary upon their return ("100 Best Companies" 2005). Loss of raises and promotions, even for just a few years, has an exponential effect on overall earnings. If a woman's husband has a sufficient income, perhaps this isn't a problem. However, with a 50 percent divorce rate in the United States, few women currently have guarantees that they will not need their salaries to support themselves and their children in the future.

As more data showing that some women are dropping out became available, a few authors have begun to speculate that women are not ambitious or do not want positions of power. For example, Fels suggests that women do not like to think of themselves as ambitious; they prefer to talk about the work they do rather than about themselves (Fels 2004). Fels has found that women receive fewer rewards, both tangible rewards and recognition, than men at every level of education from preschool through graduate school. She also points to studies that show the same phenomenon in first jobs and careers. More importantly, Fels

WHAT DOES ONE YEAR OFF WORK REALLY COST?

Lisa is making $200,000 per year. She and her husband decide that Lisa will take off one year after the birth of their child. She works for a very progressive company that supports her decision and guarantees her a comparable job when she returns at the same pay.

Lost Income

One year's salary	$200,000
Merit increase (3.5%) after year 1	$7,000
Bonus for year 1	$8,000
401(k) company contribution (50% of employee contribution up to 10% of earnings)	$20,000
Merit increase after year 2 (3.5% based on $200,000 rather than $207,000)*	$245
Bonus for year 2 (4% based on $200,000 rather than $207,000)*	$280
Impact on benefits like pension, life insurance, long-term disability*	$20,700
Lost promotion (8% plus 2% prorated merit increase) in year 3	$256,225

Savings

Child care	$7,800
Clothing, gas mileage, and other work-related incidentals	5000
	$12,800

Conservatively calculated, the net cost to Lisa of one year off would be $243,425 plus all the incremental increases lost to one year without a raise.

*The effects of the lost year's merit increase are exponential. Each year, the lost $7,000 will lead to lower dollar amounts than would have been earned if she had not taken one year off. The percentages used are deliberately conservative. The lost benefit value is also exponential. They are calculated on salary, they are extremely complex, and the cost of the lost merit increase depends on the point at which the benefit is used. For example, if a long-term disability benefit is claimed 20 years later, the lost value will be substantially higher than it will be if it is claimed in two years.

believes that women deliberately push attention away from themselves and give it away to others, usually men. Being ambitious is not feminine and can actually hurt women's chances of getting married. Handicapping one's career would be a good way to appear more of a woman. This is a different take on this issue from what previous authors have used.

Sellers gives numerous examples of women who have turned down promotions, who prefer talking about leadership instead of power, and who have voluntarily dropped out of successful careers (Sellers 2003). Like others, Sellers found that women believe that they cannot have high-powered careers and children, and she reports that one-third of the women on the Fortune 50 list have stay-at-home husbands. Sellers suggests that women will achieve parity with men in terms of the top corporate spots only if they want it, and right now, women appear not to want it.

Other authors find that men want the top jobs more than women do. Tischler reports that men are willing to put in more hours, relocate, put work ahead of family and other personal commitments, and compete harder than women (Tischler 2004).

Many variables have been used to explain the lower incidence of women in the executive suite, including covert bias, but empirical evidence is lacking at this point. Trying to capture the female work experience and then average it for research purposes is impossible. For example, "family reasons" may mean a new baby, an adoption, a child with an illness, a teen with a behavior problem, an elderly parent or sibling, or a spouse with legal problems. There are as many different types of family problems as there are people. Most women work; however, every woman has a different job and a different life with widely varying circumstances. Most of the data that we have on women leaving good jobs comes from highly qualified women who have more options than less educated women in low-paying positions. Economics will continue to play a part in all decisions made by women now and in the future.

See also: Glass Ceiling

References

Fels, Anna. 2004. "Do Women Lack Ambition?" *Harvard Business Review* 82 (4): 50–60.

Hewlett, Sylvia A., & Luce, Carolyn B. 2005. "Off-Ramps and On-Ramps: Keeping Talented Women on the Road to Success." *Harvard Business Review* 83 (3): 43–54.

"100 Best Companies." 2004. *Working Mother,* October, pp. 101–70.

"100 Best Companies." 2005. *Working Mother,* October, pp. 80–83.

Schwartz, Felice N. 1989. "Management Women and the New Facts of Life." *Harvard Business Review* 67 (1): 65–76.

Sellers, Patricia. 2003. "Power: Do Women Really Want It?" *Fortune,* October, p. 80.

Tischler, Linda. 2004. "Where Are the Women?" *Fast Company,* February, p. 52.

Further Reading: Coontz, Stephanie. 2005. *Marriage: A History.* New York: Viking; Hewlett, Sylvia Ann, Carolyn Buck Luce, Peggy Shiller, and Sandra Southwell. 2005. *The Hidden Brain Drain: Off-Ramps and On-Ramps in Women's Careers.* Harvard Business Review Research Report, Product No. 9491; "100 Best Companies." [Annual]. *Working Mother,* October; Schwartz, Felice N. 1989. "Management Women and the New Facts of Life." *Harvard Business Review* 67 (1): 65–76.

Peg Thoms